History of the UNITED STATES OF AMERICA
during the Administrations of Jefferson and Madison

CLASSIC AMERICAN HISTORIANS

Paul M. Angle, GENERAL EDITOR

History of the
UNITED STATES OF AMERICA

during the Administrations of
Jefferson and Madison

Henry Adams

abridged and edited by Ernest Samuels

THE UNIVERSITY OF CHICAGO PRESS   *Chicago & London*

The selections in this book are taken from the nine volumes of the 1921 edition of Henry Adams's *History of the United States of America during the Administrations of Jefferson and Madison,* published by Charles Scribner's Sons. The map on page 7 is reproduced with the permission of Charles Scribner's Sons from *Atlas of American History,* plate 82, by James Truslow Adams. Copyright 1943 by Charles Scribner's Sons.

The University of Chicago Press, Chicago 60637
The University of Chicago Press, Ltd., London

ISBN: 0-226-00512-7
LCN: 78-66081

General Editor's Preface

FEW today read the great American historians. Few can. If a reader limited himself to those chosen for inclusion in this series —Prescott, Parkman, Bancroft, McMaster, Moses Coit Tyler, Henry Adams, Nicolay and Hay, and Rhodes—he would find himself straining his eyes eight hours a day for at least a year. This, in the modern world, is an impossible requirement.

Yet that the works of these men should remain unknown is deplorable. Something is better than nothing. From that conviction this series was born. But what should that "something" be? A series of condensations? How can one condense the sixteen volumes of Parkman, or the nine volumes of Henry Adams, into one volume without doing inexcusable violence to the whole? On the other hand, representative selections, each of substantial length, can convey a good idea of point of view, breadth of treatment, narrative skill, and style. This was the method chosen.

After this choice was made, the general editor came across a relevant pronouncement which John Hay made during the serialization of *Abraham Lincoln: A History*. "The only question," Hay wrote to Richard Watson Gilder, editor of the *Century*, "is whether you want the Life to run three years or four. If the former, you must take heroic measures. Leaving out a chapter here and there, or retrenching an adjective, will do no good. . . . You must cut great chunks of topics out. . . . Neither

Nicolay nor I can write the work over again for the purpose of saving a half chapter here and there." Nor, we submit, can anyone else.

The books in this series were designed for reading, not research. All documentation has, therefore, been eliminated. Editors of individual volumes have used their discretion in retaining expository footnotes. Such footnotes as they have added are identified by their initials. The typographical style, punctuation, and spelling of the original texts have been followed.

PAUL M. ANGLE

Introduction

"THE quarrel between law and history is old," Henry Adams declared in one of the early volumes of his monumental *History*, "and its sources lie deep. Perhaps no good historian was ever a good lawyer; whether any good lawyer could be a good historian might equally be doubted. The lawyer is required to give facts the mould of a theory; the historian need only state facts in their sequence." What Adams meant to stress was a significant difference in the respective attitudes toward the truth.

His comment was provoked by his reflections upon the 1805 decision of the Lords of Appeal in the case of the seizure of the American ship *Essex*. In that decision Sir William Scott, one of England's most distinguished judges, had reversed one of his own previous rulings. When examined in their true sequence, the facts showed, according to Adams, that the new ruling was really a political decision and not a judicial one. It was designed to give legitimacy to Prime Minister William Pitt's wartime plan to cut off neutral American commerce with the West Indies. Adams's good friend Oliver Wendell Holmes, Jr., had recently pointed up the question in the *Common Law* of 1881: "The life of the law has not been logic; it has been experience." For Adams, history imposed a higher standard. Neither "the felt necessities of the time" nor the "institutions of public policy" which Holmes cited should be allowed to distort the truth. Adams's ideal for the historian—complete scientific detachment in the tracing of cause and effect—pointed the way to the new school of historical writing. His remarkable success in meeting this criterion in the *History* caused one reviewer to remark that it "approaches nearer the standard of science than any extended historical work yet written on this side of the Atlantic."

Adams developed this ideal through one of the most expensive educations in the world, as he explained in his famous *Education of Henry Adams*, loading his words as always with double meaning. Part of that education had been provided by the Civil War, whose diplomatic side he studied in London as the young private secretary to his father Charles Francis Adams, the American minister to the Court of St. James. This was but one of the many experiences which sharpened his skepticism concerning the veracity and the intelligence of statesmen. The older he grew the more he became convinced that statesmen habitually lie. In consequence, he developed an instinct for ferreting out the unspoken truth.

It was in England also during the impressionable years from twenty-three to thirty that he was caught up in the excitements of the scientific discoveries that were sweeping away the old ways of looking at nature and human experience. All the mental clichés by which men lived were being scrutinized by scientific investigators. August Comte's positivist sociology, as popularized by John Stuart Mill, one of the frequent visitors at the American Legation, held the center of the stage. Turn where he would, young Henry Adams found science challenging the secure ideas he had absorbed as an undergraduate at Harvard. Most revolutionary of all influences was Charles Darwin's *Origin of Species*, published only two years before Adams landed in England with his parents. The concept of life and even of society as an evolutionary process in a world of matter and mechanical energy captured the imagination. Adams wrote to his elder brother Charles, who was an officer in the Union army, "These are great times. Man has mounted science and is now run away with. . . . Some day science may have the existence of mankind in its power, and the human race commit suicide by blowing up the world." This preoccupation with science was to color all of his subsequent writings.

Adams came to the writing of his *History* by a winding yet inevitable route. He was born into one of the most famous political families in America, the grandson of one President and the great-grandson of another. He had every right to consider himself destined for a career as a patrician statesman rather than a historian. Adamses commonly made history. His family had been a nursery for statesmen ever since John Adams, a country lawyer, was summoned to Boston from Quincy to cope with the Stamp Act crisis. John Adams became one of the great leaders of the new nation, and his writings on constitutional law helped shape its form. As the Federalist second President he carried on the nationalizing task of Washington. His uncompromising conservatism, however, made him unpopular, and after a single term he was replaced by the democratic Republican Thomas Jefferson. Adams did what he could through his so-called midnight appointments of Federalist officials to thwart his successor.

John Adams's son John Quincy Adams, the grandfather of Henry Adams, played an important role in the administrations of Jefferson and Madison as a result of his abandoning the factious views of his own Federalist party. Madison appointed him one of the peace commissioners at Ghent in 1814. He in turn became the sixth President of the United States. Defeated for reelection by Andrew Jackson in a campaign marked by slander and scurrility, John Quincy Adams returned to Washington as a member of congress to oppose the proslavery faction led by Calhoun and Randolph. It was John Randolph of Roanoke who "for thirty years," as Henry Adams commented in his biography of him, "never missed a chance to have his fling at both the Adamses, father and son. 'The cub (said Randolph) is a greater bear than the old one.' "

Henry Adams grew up in a Beacon Hill home in the atmosphere of Massachusetts and national politics, an atmosphere brilliantly described by him in the early chapters of the *Education*. As a boy he knew intimately such New England leaders as Senator Charles Sumner, John Gorham Palfrey, the noted historian of New England, and Richard Henry Dana, the Free Soil leader. His education in public affairs leaped forward when he went to Washington in 1860 as private secretary to his congressman father. In Washington and London he sharpened his pen as a newspaper correspondent and publicist.

The turning point in his career came in 1868 when he returned to Washington as a political journalist and found himself driven by his reformist ideals into opposition to the scandal-ridden administration of President Grant. In addition, he came to feel that with two politically ambitious elder brothers ahead of him, his path was blocked, as he was third in line for "promotion." His elder brother Charles, he once wrote, was "a man of action, with strong love for power. I for that reason, was almost compelled to become a man of contemplation, a critic and a writer." He was rescued from the dead end of Grant's Washington by an appointment in 1870 as assistant professor of history at Harvard College, his magazine articles having shown his remarkable capacity for historical scholarship. Although he had no German Ph.D. behind him, he taught himself all that the German and English masters like Von Ranke and Stubbs had to offer concerning historical method and launched the doctoral study of history at Harvard. He began by teaching medieval history and early English legal institutions. It was only a step to apply institutional analysis and the study of source materials to the teaching of American history. He took that step in the mid-seventies. He had at his disposal the enormous family archives of three generations, including all the official papers of John Adams and John Quincy Adams. One of his first projects was a book, *Documents Relating to New England Federalism, 1800–1815*, in which he presented the crucial documents proving that grandfather John Quincy Adams was not guilty of a "betrayal" of his party in supporting Jefferson's

Embargo, as a recent historian had written. On the contrary, the Massachusetts Federalists had dishonored the party and forfeited support by taking part in the separatist conspiracy of the Essex Junto and the later Hartford Convention.

This research whetted Henry Adams's desire to get at the true hidden history of that faction-ridden period. In little more than a half-century the facts had been distorted by legend, partisan pamphlets, and uncritical eulogies. By getting at the documentary sources a historian might be able to bring American history into the nineteenth-century scientific movement, find the laws of its movement, and perhaps predict its direction. Henry Buckle in England and John Fiske, the popularizer of Herbert Spencer's theory of social evolution, in America raised the hope of a genuine science of history. Adams had himself attempted to measure the progress of American life in the 1876 Centennial issue of the *North American Review* of which he was then editor.

Only one final impetus was needed to launch him on his master work. It came in the form of a commission from the Gallatin family to do a biography of Jefferson's great secretary of the treasury and to edit his papers. Tired of "teaching boys," Adams resigned from Harvard and settled in Washington as a professional historian. He had carte blanche to the priceless State Department archives. A neighbor was his wife's cousin, George Bancroft, the dean of American historians, and another one of the remarkable group of gentleman historians who wrote the classics of American history.

With the *Gallatin* out of the way in 1879 Adams began his assault on the European archives. Nothing was to be taken at second hand. This resolution took him to Madrid, Paris, and London for nearly eighteen months and his name opened archives hitherto closed to all historians. From London he wrote his protégé, Henry Cabot Lodge: "My work is done, at least so far as it ever will be done. I have made a careful study of English politics from 1801 to 1815, and have got my authorities in order. My Spanish papers have mostly arrived. The French documents are, I hope, coming, although I am still nervous about them. My material is enormous, and I now fear that the task of compression will be painful. Burr alone is good for a volume. Canning and Perceval are figures that can't be put in a nutshell, and Napoleon is vast. I have got to contemplate six volumes for the sixteen years as inevitable." His estimate fell three volumes short.

In London he discussed the responsibilities of the historian with men like John Richard Green, the famous author of the *Short History of the English People*, and with William Lecky, whose *History of the Rise and Influence of the Spirit of Rationalism in Europe* pointed the way of the new history. Green, a master of dramatic narrative, "bade fair," as Adams wrote, " to become my most intimate guardian and teacher." He also met scientists like Thomas Huxley and John Tyndall and at one notable dinner encountered the French historian Ernest Renan. All were Darwinists and enthusiasts of the New Science and they helped fix the direction of Adams's thought.

On his return to Washington the study and writing went on under the happiest circumstances. His wife, a witty Boston heiress, presided over a salon that became a center of Washington political and intellectual life. Six hours or so a day at the State Department or in his study would be followed by a canter through the Virginia countryside or by tea or dinner where diplomats and senators and writers like Henry James and Matthew Arnold were made to feel at home.

Not only did Adams ransack archives in Europe and America, he also collected every published record relating to the period—contemporary newspapers, legislative reports, histories, memoirs, biographies, and literary works—until his library shelves overflowed with hundreds of volumes, and he read them usually with a critical pencil in hand, jotting down in the margin his agreement or, more often, his disagreement.

As the larger implications of his history became clearer to him, he tried out some of his ideas on his friends. He disputed with William James the importance of the hero in history.

"With hero-worship like Carlyle's, I have little patience. In history heroes have neutralized each other, and the result is no more than would have been reached without them." In a similar vein he wrote to his friend Samuel J. Tilden, the man whom he had backed for the presidency against Rutherford B. Hayes: "To do justice to Gallatin was a labor of love. . . . That he made mistakes I can see, but even in his blunders he was respectable. I cannot say as much for his friends Jefferson, Madison, and Monroe, about whom I have for years been hard at work. . . . There is no possibility of reconciling their theories with their acts, or their extraordinary foreign policy with dignity. They were carried along on a stream which floated them after a fashion, without much regard to themselves. . . . My own conclusion is that history is simply social development along the lines of weakest resistance, and that in most cases the line of weakest resistance is found as unconsciously by society as by water."

The principle that the individual's power of decision had little influence upon the course of history was a hard one to write by, for it obliged Adams to resist temptation almost every step of the way. Fortunately for the reader the literary artist overcame the handicap, though the shift in perspective and in emphasis gave his prose an Olympian and classic quality, reminiscent, as the French historian Charles Seignobos said, of Thucydides and Polybius. He justified the apparent inconsistency of his method by the simple explanation that his chief object of interest was to define "national character." "For that reason," he explained in his concluding chapter, "in the story of Jefferson and Madison individuals retained their old interest as types of character, if not sources of power." Although Adams recognized that his *History* would be at best only an approach to truly scientific history, one encounters again and again in his pages evidence of his effort to provide objective measurement of the historical movement and of the forces at work. The significance of the *History* lay in the contrasts of power. Statistics of the movement of foreign exchange served well, as did also the figures on the relative firepower of British and American artillery. Years later, when discussing power politics with his brother Brooks, he said: "More than ten years ago I labored to get at the numerical value of the energies, in the last three volumes of the *History*, and I figured it then as about two to one against England, and four to one against Europe." At the same time, the central riddle that defied solution was the movement of thought, the psychic component of the diagram of power. This he left to challenge the hoped-for Newton of history. His own work was "intended only to serve the future historian with a fixed and documented starting point."

Early in the writing his friend John T. Morse persuaded him to interrupt his history long enough to contribute a biography of John Randolph of Roanoke to the American Statesmen series. Stirred by the challenge to set his family's record straight against its greatest traducer, he finished the scintillating study in about two months. In it he displayed all the psychologist's perceptiveness of Randolph's weaknesses and eccentricities and he did not spare his victim. Although the book gave offence to Virginians, it still remains the most satisfactory short biography of that brilliant and erratic statesman.

Progress on the history was also delayed by two anonymous literary ventures. Just as his friends Parkman and Bancroft had relieved the tedium of their historical research with novel-writing, so Adams gave his pen release by writing the novel *Democracy*, a slashing satire on Washington politics which created a sensation in England and America—his "only success" as Adams used to say—and *Esther*, a touching evocation of the life of the Adamses' Washington salon, where controversies over science and religion and the role of the modern woman animated the dinner table. Not until after Adams's death in 1918 at the age of eighty did the fact of his authorship of these novels become generally known, the secret of *Esther* being the better kept of the two. That novel came to have a special sacredness for him because in 1885, the year after its publication, his wife committed suicide during a period of great mental depression. The tragedy broke his life in half and confirmed him in his pose of cynical disillusionment. He was saved from breakdown by the habit of unremitting work. The fabric of the *History* was to show no mark of the terrible strain. But to his confidante, Elizabeth Cameron, he declared, "I care more for one chapter, or any dozen pages of *Esther* than for the whole History, including maps and indexes."

Painstaking to the last degree, Adams decided to make a draft printing of six copies of his manuscript so as to be able to circulate it among a few discriminating readers for their corrections. George Bancroft was one of them. The first two draft volumes, covering the two administrations of Jefferson, were ready in 1884 in two massive quartos with wide margins. He wanted "all the marginal notes, suggestions, corrections and general vituperation you can annotate with," he told Wayne MacVeagh. Only his brother Charles fully accepted the challenge. He saw that in spite of Henry's effort to maintain the detachment of a scientist, the artist and the Puritan moralist kept entering the narrative. One of his many marginal comments rebuked a purple passage with the admonition: "In writing history suppress the patriotic glow." To a considerable degree Henry Adams accepted his brother's suggestions and toned down the narrative. But as the selections reprinted in this volume show, the artist triumphed nonetheless in the panoramic sweep of the opening and closing sections, in the vivid character sketches and dramatic confrontations of the key episodes. His points are made with colorful figures of speech and apt literary comparisons. His pages often vibrate with an eloquence reminiscent of the grand style of Gibbon and Macaulay. Through the whole runs a silver thread of irony.

Beneath the drama and the intrigue of the narrative Adams does not allow one for long to lose sight of his overriding thesis that the Republican, that is to say the democratic, polity did not square with the facts of political life or the limitations of human nature. True, he had once argued in a letter to President

Eliot of Harvard that his young colleague Henry Cabot Lodge should be allowed to teach a course in United States history parallel to his. "His views being Federalist and conservative have as good a right to expression in the College as mine which tend to democracy and radicalism." In reviewing Jefferson's character and the frustrations of his administration he was forced to the conclusion, however, that, ideals aside, the moderate Federalists were more responsive to the realities of economic and political power than the Republicans. Jefferson's mistakes came from his attempting to go against the tide of centralizing forces; his successes came from ignoring party dogmas. But if he is critical of Jefferson's statecraft, he respects his ideals and his patriotism. He has only contempt for the extremists of both parties who would sacrifice the Union to their ambitions. One feels, indeed, that Adams saw mirrored in Jefferson something of his own inability to act decisively and something of his own forlorn hopes for democracy in America. As his brother Brooks said: "In theory you believe, as I do, that men are automatic, that we cannot do otherwise than we do —that there is no advance—and in practice you are always worrying for an American Eutopia." The famous questions at the end of the *History* reflect his doubts and irresolution. Some years later he wrote, "As history stands, it is a sort of Chinese play, without end and without lesson. With these impressions I wrote the last line of my History, asking for a round century before going further."

The draft printing helped tighten the structure of the complicated story. In the original draft each of the large volumes was blocked out symmetrically into five books," if one may judge from the surviving two volumes of the privately printed edition (Volume II, Jefferson's second administration, and Volume III, Madison's first administration). Draft Volume IV remained in manuscript and the printing of the three concluding volumes of the Scribner edition was made directly from it. Adams's desire for symmetrical form extended into the constituent books. Each ran to either seven or eight chapters, collected under such titles as: "The Florida Negotiation and the Carrying Trade" (eight chapters); "Burr's Conspiracy" (seven chapters); "The Embargo (eight chapters); "The Repeal of the Embargo" (eight chapters).

Determined to make his history readable, as he said, he kept his chapters relatively short. They range from twenty to thirty pages and average, as he pointed out to his publisher, just twenty-three and one-half pages. The extensive correspondence carried on by him and his secretary Theodore Dwight with Charles Scribner and his chief editor shows that Adams insisted on methodically supervising every detail of publication including the choice of type, paper, binding, and page layout. By the time the *History* began to go to press late in 1888 Adams became aware that the division into books was a cumbersome device. "If you assent," Adams wrote to Scribner, "I propose to drop the arrangement into books, and run the chapters through the volume. Each volume then serves as a book. Under any circumstances, I cannot retain my old arrangement, as the new volume [i.e., each second volume] would begin in the middle of a Book." (Each of his draft volumes containing five books was to have made two volumes in the trade edition.) The patient cutting and fitting and correcting went on until August, 1890, when Adams set out for Polynesia with the artist John LaFarge. All but the last three volumes were then in print, having been issued two at a time, each pair of volumes covering one administration. The final three volumes were published in January, 1891, the extra volume made necessary by the space devoted to the New Orleans campaign and to the large index.

The importance of Adams's project was recognized from the beginning, and historians followed its progress with keen interest. One catches a sidelight in the diary of John Franklin Jameson, a young assistant professor of history at Johns Hopkins. Jameson, who was then at the beginning of a very distinguished career, called on Adams in 1884. "Had a long and interesting talk with him," Jameson wrote, "and got quite

waked up on some points. He showed one of the privately
printed advance copies of his great book on Jefferson's and
Madison's administrations, vol. 1, and talked much about an
American historical society. His abilities impress me greatly;
I would give a great deal to be under him, as some of those
Harvard fellows were. . . . I should be glad to put my services
at his command, so far as possible, for the benefit of sitting at
his feet, for it seems to me he must be Bancroft's successor."

The American Historical Association was then being organized, and within a few years Adams was elected president.
His presidential address "The Tendency of History," which
was read in 1894, made a classic statement of the case for a
science of history—and the resistance that the vested interests
in society would offer to its findings. Such a science would
"apply Darwin's method to the facts of human history." Privately, he thought another fifty years would do it.

Early reviews of the *History* on both sides of the Atlantic
hailed the work as a definitive achievement. The British were
especially impressed by Adams's impartiality. In the United
States, where family and sectional feelings were still tender,
there was a tendency in a few quarters, as Adams had foreseen,
to regard it as a defense of the Adams family. The *New York
Times* expressed the majority view that it was "a historical
work of great importance," and the *Critic* added that it fulfilled "the expectation of a brilliant narrative." Scribner wrote
to his London agent that "the exceptional success here has led
us to expect some market abroad." In spite of criticism of a
few details the work has withstood the careful scrutiny of modern scholarship. In a poll of the American Historical Association taken at mid-century, it was acknowledged to be one of the
half-dozen classics of American historical writing. Some writers
like the literary critic Yvor Winters and the historian John
Higham regard it as perhaps the most brilliant of them all.

For Adams there must have been a certain wry humor in the
final irony of which he himself was the victim. He had put his
greatest efforts into the *History* and had hoped that his work

might stand alongside that of Gibbon and Macaulay and like theirs reach a wide public. Reading fashions had changed, however. He had an inkling of the change when he heard of the humiliating reception of Francis Parkman's *Montcalm and Wolfe.* A first edition of only fifteen hundred copies had been published. Adams had assumed, as he told Parkman that "ten thousand ought to be a very moderate supply." In negotiating his own contract with Scribner Adams pointed out that he had spent some $20,000 collecting materials and that a conservative estimate of the value of his time for the many years of work would be $60,000. The book therefore cost him $80,000. He conceded that "in truth the historian gives his work to the public and publisher" and did not expect any normal business return on his investment. History had always been "for that reason, the most aristocratic of all literary pursuits, because it obliges the historian to be rich as well as educated." If it became really profitable, "the luxury of its social distinction would vanish." His analysis turned out to be only too accurate. In ten years fewer than three thousand sets were sold, for a total royalty of $5,200. Thereafter, Adams turned his back on the public and printed his later works, including his twin master-pieces, *Mont-Saint-Michel and Chartres* and the *Education of Henry Adams,* at his own expense and gave the few hundred copies to friends and other important persons who he thought deserved them. Later he gave the copyright of the *Chartres* to the American Institute of Architects, which brought out the volume in 1913 to a chorus of praise that has grown with the years. The *Education,* which he gave to the Massachusetts Historical Society, was published immediately after his death by Houghton Mifflin Company and turned out to be one of its greatest publishing triumphs.

Only a few of the high points of the *History* could be represented here, mainly those that significantly relate to Adam's theme and at the same time illustrate his skill in re-creating the moments of drama and bringing onto the stage his principal actors. Others have been selected to exhibit the historian's

artistry in breaking up the complicated narrative into
relatively self-contained sections. The long series of chapters on
Aaron Burr, chapters probably salvaged from his abandoned
biography of the man, has been omitted on Adams's own warrant that Burr, in spite of the popular interest in him, was a
swindler and of little historical importance.

One can admire the skill and persistence with which Adams
threads his way through the rancorous congressional debates of
the period and keeps afloat in the confusing cross currents of
national and sectional politics, but these portions are of interest
chiefly to the specialist. So, too, is much of the exhaustively
detailed military history of the various ill-fated campaigns. The
few chapters given here on land and naval warfare show
Adams's expert grasp of military affairs. If a somewhat undue
emphasis seems to have been put on diplomacy, it is because
Adams had a unique mastery of the field and because it dom-
inated the history of the period.

ERNEST SAMUELS

Contents

Maps

History of the UNITED STATES OF AMERICA
during the Administrations of Jefferson and Madison

Prologue: The United States in 1800

By common consent the first six chapters of the His-
tory, which Adams regarded as a prologue or intro-
duction not only to his period but the whole century to
follow, have become classics of historical generalization.
They show Adams's supple and imaginative style at its
best. They are given here in their entirety.

Physical and Economical Conditions

PHYSICAL CONDITIONS

ACCORDING to the census of 1800, the United States of America contained 5,308,483 persons. In the same year the British
Islands contained upwards of fifteen millions; the French
Republic, more than twenty-seven millions. Nearly one
fifth of the American people were negro slaves; the true political
population consisted of four and a half million free whites, or
less than one million able-bodied males, on whose shoulders fell
the burden of a continent. Even after two centuries of struggle
the land was still untamed; forest covered every portion, except
here and there a strip of cultivated soil; the minerals lay undisturbed in their rocky beds, and more than two thirds of the
people clung to the seaboard within fifty miles of tide-water,
where alone the wants of civilized life could be supplied. The
centre of population rested within eighteen miles of Baltimore,
north and east of Washington. Except in political arrangement,
the interior was little more civilized than in 1750, and was not
much easier to penetrate than when La Salle and Hennepin
found their way to the Mississippi more than a century before.

A great exception broke this rule. Two wagon-roads crossed
the Alleghany Mountains in Pennsylvania—one leading from
Philadelphia to Pittsburg; one from the Potomac to the
Monongahela; while a third passed through Virginia southwest-
ward to the Holston River and Knoxville in Tennessee, with a
branch through the Cumberland Gap into Kentucky. By these
roads and by trails less passable from North and South Caro-

lina, or by water-ways from the lakes, between four and five hundred thousand persons had invaded the country beyond the Alleghanies. At Pittsburg and on the Monongahela existed a society, already old, numbering seventy or eighty thousand persons, while on the Ohio River the settlements had grown to an importance which threatened to force a difficult problem on the union of the older States. One hundred and eighty thousand whites, with forty thousand negro slaves, made Kentucky the largest community west of the mountains; and about ninety thousand whites and fourteen thousand slaves were scattered over Tennessee. In the territory north of the Ohio less progress had been made. A New England colony existed at Marietta; some fifteen thousand people were gathered at Cincinnati; halfway between the two, a small town had grown up at Chillicothe, and other villages or straggling cabins were to be found elsewhere; but the whole Ohio territory contained only forty-five thousand inhabitants. The entire population, both free and slave, west of the mountains, reached not yet half a million; but already they were partly disposed to think themselves, and the old thirteen States were not altogether unwilling to consider them, the germ of an independent empire, which was to find its outlet, not through the Alleghanies to the seaboard, but by the Mississippi River to the Gulf.

Nowhere did eastern settlements touch the western. At least one hundred miles of mountainous country held the two regions everywhere apart. The shore of Lake Erie, where alone contact seemed easy, was still unsettled. The Indians had been pushed back to the Cuyahoga River, and a few cabins were built on the site of Cleveland; but in 1800, as in 1700, this intermediate region was only a portage where emigrants and merchandise were transferred from Lake Erie to the Muskingum and Ohio valleys. Even western New York remained a wilderness: Buffalo was not laid out; Indian titles were not extinguished; Rochester did not exist; and the county of Onondaga numbered a population of less than eight thousand. In 1799 Utica contained fifty houses, mostly small and temporary. Albany was

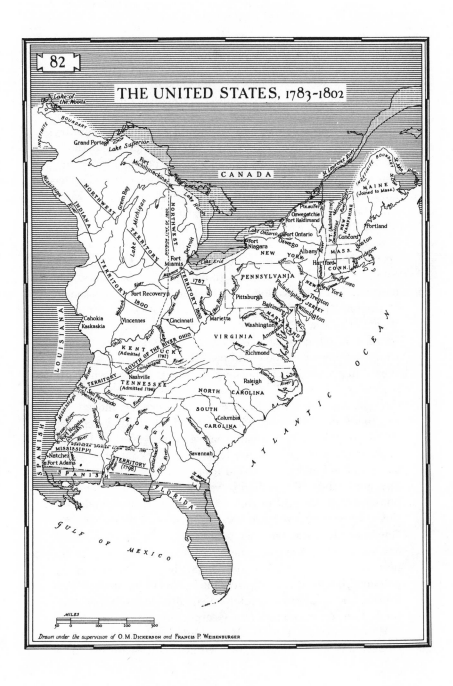

THE UNITED STATES, 1783–1802

82

Lake of the Woods
INDEFINITE BOUNDARY
Grand Portage
Lake Superior
Fort Michilimackinac
NORTHWEST
Green Bay
Lake Michigan
INDIANA
NORTHWEST TERRITORY
NORTHWEST TERRITORY
Lake Huron
CANADA
St Lawrence River
INDEFINITE BOUNDARY
St John River
MAINE
(Joined to Mass.)
Portland
VT. (Admitted 1791)
Montpelier
NEW HAMPSHIRE
Concord
Pte.au Fer
Oswegatchie
Fort Haldimand
Fort Ontario
Lake Ontario
Oswego
Fort Niagara
Detroit
Lake Erie
Fort Miamis
Maumee River
1787
NEW YORK
Albany
Hartford
CONN.
MASS.
Providence
Boston
New Haven
New York
Mississippi River
LOUISIANA
Wisconsin River
Fort Recovery
1800
TERRITORY
TERRITORY 1800
Miami River
Cahokia
Kaskaskia
Vincennes
Cincinnati
Wabash River
Ohio River
Marietta
Scioto River
PENNSYLVANIA
Pittsburgh
NEW JERSEY
Philadelphia
Trenton
Wilmington
Baltimore
Potomac River
MARYLAND
Washington
Annapolis
VIRGINIA
James River
Richmond
KENTUCKY
(Admitted 1792)
SOUTH OF THE RIVER OHIO
Cumberland River
Nashville
TENNESSEE
(Admitted 1796)
Tennessee River
Holston River
Roanoke River
Raleigh
NORTH CAROLINA
SOUTH CAROLINA
Columbia
TERRITORY
Fort San Fernando
(Spanish)
Tennessee River
GEORGIA
Savannah River
Yazoo River
SPANISH
Mississippi River
Walnut Hills
Nogales
MISSISSIPPI
Natchez
Fort Adams
SPANISH
TERRITORY
(1798)
Pearl River
Tombigbee River
Alabama River
Coosa River
FRONTIER SPAIN CLAIMED UNTIL 1795
Chattahoochee River
Flint River
Savannah
St Mary's River
FLORIDA
SPANISH
ATLANTIC OCEAN

GULF OF MEXICO

MILES
50 0   100   200   300

Drawn under the supervision of O. M. Dickerson and Francis P. Weisenburger still a Dutch city, with some five thousand inhabitants; and the tide of immigration flowed slowly through it into the valley of the Mohawk, while another stream from Pennsylvania, following the Susquehanna, spread toward the Genesee country.

The people of the old thirteen States, along the Atlantic seaboard, thus sent westward a wedge-shaped mass of nearly half a million persons, penetrating by the Tennessee, Cumberland, and Ohio rivers toward the western limit of the Union. The Indians offered sharp resistance to this invasion, exacting life for life, and yielding only as their warriors perished. By the close of the century the wedge of white settlements, with its apex at Nashville and its flanks covered by the Ohio and Tennessee rivers, nearly split the Indian country in halves. The northern half—consisting of the later States of Wisconsin, Michigan, Illinois, Indiana, and one third of Ohio—contained Wyandottes and Shawanese, Miamis, Kickapoos, and other tribes, able to send some five thousand warriors to hunt or fight. In the southern half, powerful confederacies of Creeks, Cherokees, Chickasaws, and Choctaws lived and hunted where the States of Mississippi, Alabama, and the western parts of Georgia, Tennessee, and Kentucky were to extend; and so weak was the State of Georgia, which claimed the southwestern territory for its own, that a well-concerted movement of Indians might without much difficulty have swept back its white population of one hundred thousand toward the ocean or across the Savannah River. The Indian power had been broken in halves, but each half was still terrible to the colonists on the edges of their vast domain, and was used as a political weapon by the Governments whose territory bounded the Union on the north and south. The governors-general of Canada intrigued with the northwestern Indians, that they might hold in check any aggression from Washington; while the Spanish governors of West Florida and Louisiana maintained equally close relations with the Indian confederacies of the Georgia territory.

With the exception that half a million people had crossed the Alleghanies and were struggling with difficulties all their own, in an isolation like that of Jutes or Angles in the fifth century, America, so far as concerned physical problems, had changed little in fifty years. The old landmarks remained nearly where they stood before. The same bad roads and difficult rivers, connecting the same small towns, stretched into the same forests in 1800 as when the armies of Braddock and Amherst pierced the western and northern wilderness, except that these roads extended a few miles farther from the seacoast. Nature was rather man's master than his servant, and the five million Americans struggling with the untamed continent seemed hardly more competent to their task than the beavers and buffalo which had for countless generations made bridges and roads of their own.

Even by water, along the seaboard, communication was as slow and almost as irregular as in colonial times. The wars in Europe caused a sudden and great increase in American shipping employed in foreign commerce, without yet leading to general improvement in navigation. The ordinary sea-going vessel carried a freight of about two hundred and fifty tons; the largest merchant ships hardly reached four hundred tons; the largest frigate in the United States navy, the "line-of-battle ship in disguise," had a capacity of fifteen hundred and seventy-six tons. Elaborately rigged as ships or brigs, the small merchant craft required large crews and were slow sailers; but the voyage to Europe was comparatively more comfortable and more regular than the voyage from New York to Albany, or through Long Island Sound to Providence. No regular packet plied between New York and Albany. Passengers waited till a sloop was advertised to sail; they provided their own bedding and supplies; and within the nineteenth century Captain Elias Bunker won much fame by building the sloop "Experiment," of one hundred and ten tons, to start regularly on a fixed day for Albany, for the convenience of passengers only, supplying beds, wine, and provisions for the voyage of one hundred and fifty miles. A week on the North River or on the Sound was an experience not at all unknown to travellers.

While little improvement had been made in water-travel, every increase of distance added to the difficulties of the westward journey. The settler who after buying wagon and horses hauled his family and goods across the mountains, might buy or build a broad flat-bottomed ark, to float with him and his fortunes down the Ohio, in constant peril of upsetting or of being sunk; but only light boats with strong oars could mount the stream, or boats forced against the current by laboriously poling in shallow water. If he carried his tobacco and wheat down the Mississippi to the Spanish port of New Orleans, and sold it, he might return to his home in Kentucky or Ohio by a long and dangerous journey on horseback through the Indian country from Natchez to Nashville, or he might take ship to Philadelphia, if a ship were about to sail, and again cross the Alleghanies. Compared with river travel, the sea was commonly an easy and safe highway. Nearly all the rivers which penetrated the interior were unsure, liable to be made dangerous by freshets, and both dangerous and impassable by drought; yet such as they were, these streams made the main paths of traffic. Through the mountainous gorges of the Susquehanna the produce of western New York first found an outlet; the Cuyahoga and Muskingum were the first highway from the Lakes to the Ohio; the Ohio itself, with its great tributaries the Cumberland and the Tennessee, marked the lines of western migration; and every stream which could at high water float a boat was thought likely to become a path for commerce. As General Washington, not twenty years earlier, hoped that the brawling waters of the Cheat and Youghiogheny might become the channel of trade between Chesapeake Bay and Pittsburg, so the Americans of 1800 were prepared to risk life and property on any streamlet that fell foaming down either flank of the Alleghanies. The experience of mankind proved trade to be dependent on water communications, and as yet Americans did not dream that the experience of mankind was useless to them.

If America was to be developed along the lines of water communication alone, by such means as were known to Europe,

Nature had decided that the experiment of a single republican government must meet extreme difficulties. The valley of the Ohio had no more to do with that of the Hudson, the Susquehanna, the Potomac, the Roanoke, and the Santee, than the valley of the Danube with that of the Rhone, the Po, or the Elbe. Close communication by land could alone hold the great geographical divisions together either in interest or in fear. The union of New England with New York and Pennsylvania was not an easy task even as a problem of geography, and with an ocean highway; but the union of New England with the Carolinas, and of the seacoast with the interior, promised to be a hopeless undertaking. Physical contact alone could make one country of these isolated empires, but to the patriotic American of 1800, struggling for the continued existence of an embryo nation, with machinery so inadequate, the idea of ever bringing the Mississippi River, either by land or water, into close contact with New England, must have seemed wild. By water, an Erie Canal was already foreseen; by land, centuries of labor could alone conquer those obstacles which Nature permitted to be overcome.

In the minds of practical men, the experience of Europe left few doubts on this point. After two thousand years of public labor and private savings, even despotic monarchs, who employed the resources of their subjects as they pleased, could in 1800 pass from one part of their European dominions to another little more quickly than they might have done in the age of the Antonines. A few short canals had been made, a few bridges had been built, an excellent postroad extended from Madrid to St. Petersburg; but the heavy diligence that rumbled from Calais to Paris required three days for its journey of one hundred and fifty miles, and if travellers ventured on a trip to Marseilles they met with rough roads and hardships like those of the Middle Ages. Italy was in 1800 almost as remote from the north of Europe as when carriage-roads were first built. Neither in time nor in thought was Florence or Rome much nearer to London in Wordsworth's youth than in the youth of

Milton or Gray. Indeed, such changes as had occurred were partly for the worse, owing to the violence of revolutionary wars during the last ten years of the eighteenth century. Horace Walpole at his life's close saw about him a world which in many respects was less civilized than when as a boy he made the grand tour of Europe.

While so little had been done on the great highways of European travel, these highways were themselves luxuries which furnished no sure measure of progress. The post-horses toiled as painfully as ever through the sand from Hamburg to Berlin, while the coach between York and London rolled along an excellent road at the rate of ten miles an hour; yet neither in England nor on the Continent was the post-road a great channel of commerce. No matter how good the road, it could not compete with water, nor could heavy freights in great quantities be hauled long distances without extravagant cost. Water communication was as necessary for European commerce in 1800 as it had been for the Phoenicians and Egyptians; the Rhine, the Rhone, the Danube, the Elbe, were still the true commercial highways, and except for government post-roads, Europe was as dependent on these rivers in the eighteenth century as in the thirteenth. No certainty could be offered of more rapid progress in the coming century than in the past; the chief hope seemed to lie in the construction of canals.

While Europe had thus consumed centuries in improving paths of trade, until merchandise could be brought by canal a few score miles from the Rhone to the Loire and Seine, to the Garonne and the Rhine, and while all her wealth and energy had not yet united the Danube with other river systems, America was required to construct, without delay, at least three great roads and canals, each several hundred miles long, across mountain ranges, through a country not yet inhabited, to points where no great markets existed—and this under constant peril of losing her political union, which could not even by such connections be with certainty secured. After this should be accomplished, the Alleghanies must still remain between the eastern and western States, and at any known rate of travel Nashville could not be reached in less than a fortnight or three weeks from Philadelphia. Meanwhile the simpler problem of bringing New England nearer to Virginia and Georgia had not advanced even with the aid of a direct ocean highway. In becoming politically independent of England, the old thirteen provinces developed little more commercial intercourse with each other in proportion to their wealth and population than they had maintained in colonial days. The material ties that united them grew in strength no more rapidly than the ties which bound them to Europe. Each group of States lived a life apart.

Even the lightly equipped traveller found a short journey no slight effort. Between Boston and New York was a tolerable highway, along which, thrice a week, light stage-coaches carried passengers and the mail, in three days. From New York a stage-coach started every week-day for Philadelphia, consuming the greater part of two days in the journey; and the road between Paulus Hook, the modern Jersey City, and Hackensack, was declared by the newspapers in 1802 to be as bad as any other part of the route between Maine and Georgia. South of Philadelphia the road was tolerable as far as Baltimore, but between Baltimore and the new city of Washington it meandered through forests; the driver chose the track which seemed least dangerous, and rejoiced if in wet seasons he reached Washington without miring or upsetting his wagon. In the Northern States, four miles an hour was the average speed for any coach between Bangor and Baltimore. Beyond the Potomac the roads became steadily worse, until south of Petersburg even the mails were carried on horseback. Except for a stage-coach which plied between Charleston and Savannah, no public conveyance of any kind was mentioned in the three southernmost States.

The stage-coach was itself a rude conveyance, of a kind still familiar to experienced travellers. Twelve persons, crowded into one wagon, were jolted over rough roads, their bags and parcels, thrust inside, cramping their legs, while they were protected from the heat and dust of mid-summer and the intense cold and driving snow of winter only by leather flaps buttoned to the roof and sides. In fine, dry weather this mode of travel was not unpleasant, when compared with the heavy vehicles of Europe and the hard English turnpikes; but when spring rains drew the frost from the ground the roads became nearly impassable, and in winter, when the rivers froze, a serious peril was added, for the Susquehanna or the North River at Paulus Hook must be crossed in an open boat—an affair of hours at best, sometime leading to fatal accidents. Smaller annoyances of many kinds were habitual. The public, as a rule, grumbled less than might have been expected, but occasionally newspapers contained bitter complaints. An angry Philadelphian, probably a foreigner, wrote in 1796 that, "with a few exceptions, brutality, negligence, and filching are as naturally expected by people accustomed to travelling in America, as a mouth, a nose, and two eyes are looked for in a man's face." This sweeping charge, probably unjust, and certainly supported by little public evidence, was chiefly founded on the experience of an alleged journey from New York—

At Bordentown we went into a second boat where we met with very sorry accommodation. This was about four o'clock in the afternoon. We had about twenty miles down the Delaware to reach Philadelphia. The captain, who had a most provoking tongue, was a boy about eighteen years of age. He and a few companions despatched a dozen or eighteen bottles of porter. We ran three different times against other vessels that were coming up the stream. The women and children lay all night on the bare boards of the cabin floor. . . . We reached Arch Street wharf about eight o'clock on the Wednesday morning, having been about sixteen hours on a voyage of twenty miles.

In the Southern States the difficulties and perils of travel were so great as to form a barrier almost insuperable. Even Virginia was no exception to this rule. At each interval of a few miles the horseman found himself stopped by a river, liable to sudden freshets, and rarely bridged. Jefferson in his frequent journeys between Monticello and Washington was happy to reach the end of the hundred miles without some vexatious delay. "Of eight rivers between here and Washington," he wrote to his Attorney-General in 1801, "five have neither bridges nor boats."

Expense caused an equally serious obstacle to travel. The usual charge in the Northern States was six cents a mile by stage. In the year 1796, according to Francis Baily, President of the Royal Astronomical Society, three or four stages ran daily from Baltimore to Philadelphia, the fare six dollars, with charges amounting to two dollars and a quarter a day at the inns on the road. Baily was three days in making the journey. From Philadelphia to New York he paid the same fare and charges, arriving in one day and a half. The entire journey of two hundred miles cost him twenty-one dollars. He remarked that travelling on the main lines of road in the settled country was about as expensive as in England, and when the roads were good, about as rapid. Congress allowed its members six dollars for every twenty miles travelled. The actual cost, including hotel expenses, could hardly have fallen below ten cents a mile.

Heavy traffic never used stage routes if it could find cheaper. Commerce between one State and another, or even between the seaboard and the interior of the same State, was scarcely possible on any large scale unless navigable water connected them. Except the great highway to Pittsburg, no road served as a channel of commerce between different regions of the country. In this respect New England east of Connecticut was as independent of New York as both were independent of Virginia, and as Virginia in her turn was independent of Georgia and South Carolina. The chief value of inter-State communication by land rested in the postal system; but the post furnished another illustration of the difficulties which barred progress. In the year 1800 one general mail-route extended from Portland in Maine to Louisville in Georgia, the time required for the trip being twenty days. Between New York and

Petersburg in Virginia was a daily service; between New York
and Boston, and also between Petersburg and Augusta, the mail
was carried thrice a week. Branching from the main line at
New York, a mail went to Canandaigua in ten days; from Philadelphia another branch line went to Lexington in sixteen days,
to Nashville in twenty-two days. Thus more than twenty thousand miles of post-road, with nine hundred post offices, proved
the vastness of the country and the smallness of the result; for
the gross receipts for postage in the year ending Oct. 1, 1801,
were only $320,000.

Throughout the land the eighteenth century ruled supreme.
Only within a few years had the New Englander begun to
abandon his struggle with a barren soil, among granite hills, to
learn the comforts of easier existence in the valleys of the
Mohawk and Ohio; yet the New England man was thought the
shrewdest and most enterprising of Americans. If the Puritans
and the Dutch needed a century or more to reach the Mohawk,
when would they reach the Mississippi? The distance from New
York to the Mississippi was about one thousand miles; from
Washington to the extreme southwestern military post, below
Natchez, was about twelve hundred. Scarcely a portion of western Europe was three hundred miles distant from some sea, but
a width of three hundred miles was hardly more than an out-
skirt of the United States. No civilized country had yet been
required to deal with physical difficulties so serious, nor did
experience warrant conviction that such difficulties could be
overcome.

ECONOMICAL CONDITIONS

If the physical task which lay before the American people
had advanced but a short way toward completion, little more
change could be seen in the economical conditions of American
life. The man who in the year 1800 ventured to hope for a new
era in the coming century, could lay his hand on no statistics
that silenced doubt. The machinery of production showed no

radical difference from that familiar to ages long past. The
Saxon farmer of the eighth century enjoyed most of the comforts known to Saxon farmers of the eighteenth. The eorls and
ceorls of Offa and Ecgbert could not read or write, and did not
receive a weekly newspaper with such information as newspapers in that age could supply; yet neither their houses, their
clothing, their food and drink, their agricultural tools and
methods, their stock, nor their habits were so greatly altered
or improved by time that they would have found much difficulty
in accommodating their lives to that of their descendants in the
eighteenth century. In this respect America was backward.
Fifty or a hundred miles inland more than half the houses were
log-cabins, which might or might not enjoy the luxury of a glass
window. Throughout the South and West houses showed little
attempt at luxury; but even in New England the ordinary farm-
house was hardly so well built, so spacious, or so warm as that
of a well-to-do contemporary of Charlemagne. The cloth which
the farmer's family wore was still homespun. The hats were
manufactured by the village hatter; the clothes were cut and
made at home; the shirts, socks, and nearly every other article
of dress were also homemade. Hence came a marked air of
rusticity which distinguished country from town—awkward
shapes of hat, coat, and trousers, which gave to the Yankee
caricature those typical traits that soon disappeared almost as
completely as coats of mail and steel headpieces. The plough
was rude and clumsy; the sickle as old as Tubal Cain, and even
the cradle not in general use; the flail was unchanged since the
Aryan exodus; in Virginia, grain was still commonly trodden
out by horses. Enterprising gentlemen-farmers introduced
threshing-machines and invented scientific ploughs; but these
were novelties. Stock was as a rule not only unimproved, but ill
cared for. The swine ran loose; the cattle were left to feed on
what pasture they could find, and even in New England were
not housed until the severest frosts, on the excuse that exposure
hardened them. Near half a century afterward a competent
judge asserted that the general treatment of cows in New Eng-

land was fair matter of presentment by a grand jury. Except among the best farmers, drainage, manures, and rotation of crops were uncommon. The ordinary cultivator planted his corn as his father had planted it, sowing as much rye to the acre, using the same number of oxen to plough, and getting in his crops on the same day. He was even known to remove his barn on account of the manure accumulated round it, although the New England soil was never so rich as to warrant neglect to enrich it. The money for which he sold his wheat and chickens was of the Old World; he reckoned in shillings or pistareens, and rarely handled an American coin more valuable than a large copper cent.

At a time when the wealth and science of London and Paris could not supply an article so necessary as a common sulphur-match, the backwardness of remote country districts could hardly be exaggerated. Yet remote districts were not the only sufferers. Of the whole United States New England claimed to be the most civilized province, yet New England was a region in which life had yet gained few charms of sense and few advantages over its rivals. Wilson, the ornithologist, a Pennsylvania Scotchman, a confirmed grumbler, but a shrewd judge, and the most thorough of American travellers, said in 1808: "My journey through almost the whole of New England has rather lowered the Yankees in my esteem. Except a few neat academies, I found their schoolhouses equally ruinous and deserted with ours; fields covered with stones; stone fences; scrubby oaks and pine-trees; wretched orchards; scarcely one grain-field in twenty miles; the taverns along the road dirty, and filled with loungers brawling about lawsuits and politics; the people snappish and extortioners, lazy, and two hundred years behind the Pennsylvanians in agricultural improvements." The description was exaggerated, for Wilson forgot to speak of the districts where fields were not covered with stones, and where wheat could be grown to advantage. Twenty years earlier, Albert Gallatin, who knew Pennsylvania well, having reached Hartford on his way to Boston, wrote: "I have seen nothing in

America equal to the establishments on the Connecticut River."
Yet Wilson's account described the first general effect of districts in the New England States, where agriculture was backward and the country poor. The houses were thin wooden
buildings, not well suited to the climate; the churches were
unwarmed; the clothing was poor; sanitary laws were few, and
a bathroom or a soil-pipe was unknown. Consumption, typhoid,
scarlet fever, diphtheria, and rheumatic fevers were common;
habits of drinking were still a scourge in every family, and
dyspepsia destroyed more victims than were consumed by
drink. Population increased slowly, as though the conditions
of life were more than usually hard. A century earlier, Massachusetts was supposed to contain sixty thousand inhabitants.
Governor Hutchinson complained that while the other colonies
quadrupled their numbers, Massachusetts failed to double its
population in fifty years. In 1790 the State contained 378,000
people, not including the province of Maine; in 1800 the number
rose to 423,000, which showed that a period of more rapid
growth had begun, for the emigration into other States was
also large.

A better measure of the difficulties with which New England
struggled was given by the progress of Boston, which was supposed to have contained about eighteen thousand inhabitants
as early as 1730, and twenty thousand in 1770. For several
years after the Revolution it numbered less than twenty thousand, but in 1800 the census showed twenty-five thousand
inhabitants. In appearance, Boston resembled an English
market-town, of a kind even then old-fashioned. The footways
or sidewalks were paved, like the crooked and narrow streets,
with round cobblestones, and were divided from the carriage
way only by posts and a gutter. The streets were almost un-
lighted at night, a few oil-lamps rendering the darkness more
visible and the rough pavement rougher. Police hardly existed.
The system of taxation was defective. The town was managed
by selectmen, the elected instruments of town-meetings whose
jealousy of granting power was even greater than their objection

to spending money, and whose hostility to city government was
not to be overcome.

Although on all sides increase of ease and comfort was evident, and roads, canals, and new buildings, public and private,
were already in course of construction on a scale before unknown, yet in spite of more than a century and a half of
incessant industry, intelligent labor, and pinching economy
Boston and New England were still poor. A few merchants
enjoyed incomes derived from foreign trade, which allowed
them to imitate in a quiet way the style of the English mercantile class; but the clergy and the lawyers, who stood at the head
of society, lived with much economy. Many a country clergyman, eminent for piety and even for hospitality, brought up a
family and laid aside some savings on a salary of five hundred
dollars a year. President Dwight, who knew well the class to
which he belonged, eulogizing the life of Abijah Weld, pastor
of Attleborough, declared that on a salary of two hundred and
twenty dollars a year Mr. Weld brought up eleven children,
besides keeping a hospitable house and maintaining charity to
the poor.

On the Exchange a few merchants had done most of the
business of Boston since the peace of 1783, but a mail thrice a
week to New York, and an occasional arrival from Europe or
the departure of a ship to China, left ample leisure for correspondence and even for gossip. The habits of the commercial
class had not been greatly affected by recent prosperity. Within
ten or fifteen years before 1800 three Banks had been created to
supply the commercial needs of Boston. One of these was a
branch Bank of the United States, which employed there whatever part of its capital it could profitably use; the two others
were local Banks, with capital of $1,600,000, toward which the
State subscribed $400,000. Altogether the banking capital of
Boston might amount to two millions and a half. A number of
small Banks, representing in all about two and a half millions
more, were scattered through the smaller New England towns.
The extraordinary prosperity caused by the French wars

opened to Boston a new career. Wealth and population were doubling; the exports and imports of New England were surprisingly large, and the shipping was greater than that of New York and Pennsylvania combined; but Boston had already learned, and was to learn again, how fleeting were the riches that depended on foreign commerce, and conservative habits were not easily changed by a few years of accidental gain.

Of manufactures New England had many, but none on a large scale. The people could feed or clothe themselves only by household industry; their whaleoil, salt fish, lumber, and rum were mostly sent abroad; but they freighted coasters with turners' articles, home-made linens and cloths, cheese, butter, shoes, nails, and what were called Yankee Notions of all sorts, which were sent to Norfolk and the Southern ports, and often peddled from the deck, as goods of every sort were peddled on the flat-boats of the Ohio. Two or three small mills spun cotton with doubtful success; but England supplied ordinary manufactures more cheaply and better than Massachusetts could hope to do. A tri-weekly mail and a few coasting sloops provided for the business of New England with domestic ports. One packet sloop plied regularly to New York.

The State of New York was little in advance of Massachusetts and Maine. In 1800 for the first time New York gained the lead in population by the difference between 589,000 and 573,000. The valuation of New York for the direct tax in 1799 was $100,000,000; that of Massachusetts was $84,000,000. New York was still a frontier State, and although the city was European in its age and habits, travellers needed to go few miles from the Hudson in order to find a wilderness like that of Ohio and Tennessee. In most material respects the State was behind New England; outside the city was to be seen less wealth and less appearance of comfort. The first impression commonly received of any new country was from its inns, and on the whole few better tests of material condition then existed. President Dwight, though maintaining that the best old-fashioned inns of New England were in their way perfect, being in fact excellent

private houses, could not wholly approve what he called the
modern inns, even in Connecticut; but when he passed into New
York he asserted that everything suffered an instant change for
the worse. He explained that in Massachusetts the authorities
were strict in refusing licenses to any but respectable and responsible persons, whereas in New York licenses were granted
to any one who would pay for them—which caused a multiplication of dram-shops, bad accommodations, and a gathering of
loafers and tipplers about every tavern porch, whose rude
appearance, clownish manners, drunkenness, swearing, and
obscenity confirmed the chief of Federalist clergymen in his
belief that democracy had an evil influence on morals.

Far more movement was to be seen, and accumulation was
more rapid than in colonial days; but little had yet been done
for improvement, either by Government or by individuals, beyond some provision for extending roads and clearing water-
courses behind the advancing settlers. If Washington Irving
was right, Rip Van Winkle, who woke from his long slumber
about the year 1800, saw little that was new to him, except the
head of President Washington where that of King George had
once hung, and strange faces instead of familiar ones. Except in
numbers, the city was relatively no farther advanced than the
country. Between 1790 and 1800 its population rose from 33,000
to 60,000; and if Boston resembled an old-fashioned English
market-town, New York was like a foreign seaport, badly paved,
undrained, and as foul as a town surrounded by the tides could
be. Although the Manhattan Company was laying wooden
pipes for a water supply, no sanitary regulations were enforced,
and every few years—as in 1798 and 1803—yellow fever swept
away crowds of victims, and drove the rest of the population,
panic stricken, into the highlands. No day-police existed; con-
stables were still officers of the courts; the night-police consisted
of two captains, two deputies, and seventy-two men. The estimate for the city's expenses in 1800 amounted to $130,000. One
marked advantage New York enjoyed over Boston, in the possession of a city government able to introduce reforms. Thus,

although still mediaeval in regard to drainage and cleanliness, the town had taken advantage of recurring fires to rebuild some of the streets with brick sidewalks and curbstones. Travellers dwelt much on this improvement, which only New York and Philadelphia had yet adopted, and Europeans agreed that both had the air of true cities: that while Boston was the Bristol of America, New York was the Liverpool, and Philadelphia the London.

In respect to trade and capital, New York possessed growing advantages, supplying half New Jersey and Connecticut, a part of Massachusetts, and all the rapidly increasing settlements on the branches of the Hudson; but no great amount of wealth, no considerable industry or new creation of power was yet to be seen. Two Banks, besides the branch Bank of the United States, supplied the business wants of the city, and employed about the same amount of capital in loans and discounts as was required for Boston. Besides these city institutions but two other Banks existed in the State—at Hudson and at Albany.

The proportion of capital in private hands seemed to be no larger. The value of exports from New York in 1800 was but $14,000,000; the net revenue on imports for 1799 was $2,373,-000, against $1,607,000 collected in Massachusetts. Such a foreign trade required little capital, yet these values represented a great proportion of all the exchanges. Domestic manufactures could not compete with foreign, and employed little bank credit. Speculation was slow, mostly confined to lands which required patience to exchange or sell. The most important undertakings were turnpikes, bridges such as Boston built across the Charles, or new blocks of houses; and a canal, such as Boston designed to the Merrimac, overstrained the resources of capital. The entire banking means of the United States in 1800 would not have answered the stock-jobbing purposes of one great operator of Wall Street in 1875. The nominal capital of all the Banks, including the Bank of the United States, fell short of $29,000,-000. The limit of credit was quickly reached, for only the richest could borrow more than fifteen or twenty thousand dollars at a time, and the United States Government itself was gravely embarrassed whenever obliged to raise money. In 1798 the Secretary of the Treasury could obtain five million dollars only by paying eight per cent interest for a term of years; and in 1814 the Government was forced to stop payments for the want of twenty millions.

The precise value of American trade was uncertain, but in 1800 the gross exports and imports of the United States may have balanced at about seventy-five million dollars. The actual consumption of foreign merchandise amounted perhaps to the value of forty or fifty million dollars, paid in wheat, cotton, and other staples, and by the profits on the shipping employed in carrying West India produce to Europe. The amount of American capital involved in a trade of fifty millions, with credits of three, six, and nine months, must have been small, and the rates of profit large.

As a rule American capital was absorbed in shipping or agriculture, whence it could not be suddenly withdrawn. No stock-exchange existed, and no broker exclusively engaged in stock-jobbing, for there were few stocks. The national debt, of about eighty millions, was held abroad, or as a permanent investment at home. States and municipalities had not learned to borrow. Except for a few banks and insurance offices, turnpikes, bridges, canals, and land-companies, neither bonds nor stocks were known. The city of New York was so small as to make extravagance difficult; the Battery was a fashionable walk, Broadway a country drive, and Wall Street an uptown residence. Great accumulations of wealth had hardly begun. The Patroon was still the richest man in the State. John Jacob Astor was a fur-merchant living where the Astor House afterward stood, and had not yet begun those purchases of real estate which secured his fortune. Cornelius Vanderbilt was a boy of six years old, playing about his father's ferryboat at Staten Island. New York city itself was what it had been for a hundred years past—a local market.

As a national capital New York made no claim to consideration. If Bostonians for a moment forgot their town-meetings, or if Virginians overcame their dislike for cities and pavements, they visited and admired, not New York, but Philadelphia. "Philadelphia," wrote the Duc de Liancourt, "is not only the finest city in the United States, but may be deemed one of the most beautiful cities in the world." In truth, it surpassed any of its size on either side of the Atlantic for most of the comforts and some of the elegancies of life. While Boston contained twenty-five thousand inhabitants and New York sixty thousand, the census of 1800 showed that Philadelphia was about the size of Liverpool—a city of seventy thousand people. The repeated ravages of yellow fever roused there a regard for sanitary precautions and cleanliness; the city, well paved and partly drained, was supplied with water in wooden pipes, and was the best-lighted town in America; its market was a model, and its jail was intended also for a model—although the first experiment proved unsuccessful, because the prisoners went mad or idiotic in solitary confinement. In and about the city flourished industries considerable for the time. The iron-works were already important; paper and gunpowder, pleasure carriages and many other manufactures, were produced on a larger scale than elsewhere in the Union. Philadelphia held the seat of government until July, 1800, and continued to hold the Bank of the United States, with its capital of ten millions, besides private banking capital to the amount of five millions more. Public spirit was more active in Pennsylvania than in New York. More roads and canals were building; a new turnpike ran from Philadelphia to Lancaster, and the great highway to Pittsburg was a more important artery of national life than was controlled by any other State. The exports of Pennsylvania amounted to $12,000,000, and the custom-house produced $1,350,000. The State contained six hundred thousand inhabitants—a population somewhat larger than that of New York.

Of all parts of the Union, Pennsylvania seemed to have made most use of her national advantages; but her progress was not more rapid than the natural increase of population and wealth demanded, while to deal with the needs of America, man's resources and his power over Nature must be increased in a ratio far more rapid than that which governed his numbers. Nevertheless, Pennsylvania was the most encouraging spectacle in the field of vision. Baltimore, which had suddenly sprung to a population and commerce greater than those of Boston, also offered strong hope of future improvement; but farther South the people showed fewer signs of change.

The city of Washington, rising in a solitude on the banks of the Potomac, was a symbol of American nationality in the Southern States. The contrast between the immensity of the task and the paucity of means seemed to challenge suspicion that the nation itself was a magnificent scheme like the federal city, which could show only a few log-cabins and negro quarters where the plan provided for the traffic of London and the elegance of Versailles. When in the summer of 1800 the government was transferred to what was regarded by most persons as a fever-stricken morass, the half-finished White House stood in a naked field overlooking the Potomac, with two awkward Department buildings near it, a single row of brick houses and a few isolated dwellings within sight, and nothing more; until across a swamp, a mile and a half away, the shapeless, unfinished Capitol was seen, two wings without a body, ambitious enough in design to make more grotesque the nature of its surroundings. The conception proved that the United States understood the vastness of their task, and were willing to stake something on their faith in it. Never did hermit or saint condemn himself to solitude more consciously than Congress and the Executive in removing the government from Philadelphia to Washington: the discontented men clustered together in eight or ten boarding-houses as near as possible to the Capitol, and there lived, like a convent of monks, with no other amusement or occupation than that of going from their lodgings to the Chambers and back again. Even private wealth could do little to improve their situation, for there was nothing which wealth could buy; there were in Washington no shops or markets, skilled labor, commerce, or people. Public efforts and lavish use of public money could alone make the place tolerable; but Congress doled out funds for this national and personal object with so sparing a hand, that their Capitol threatened to crumble in pieces and crush Senate and House under the ruins, long before the building was complete.

A government capable of sketching a magnificent plan, and willing to give only a half-hearted pledge for its fulfilment; a people eager to advertise a vast undertaking beyond their present powers, which when completed would become an object of jealousy and fear—this was the impression made upon the traveller who visited Washington in 1800, and mused among the unraised columns of the Capitol upon the destiny of the United States. As he travelled farther south his doubts were strengthened, for across the Potomac he could detect no sign of a new spirit. Manufactures had no existence. Alexandria owned a bank with half a million of capital, but no other was to be found between Washington and Charleston, except the branch Bank of the United States at Norfolk, nor any industry to which loans and discounts could safely be made. Virginia, the most populous and powerful of all the States, had a white population of 514,000, nearly equal to that of Pennsylvania and New York, besides about 350,000 slaves. Her energies had pierced the mountains and settled the western territory before the slow-moving Northern people had torn themselves from the safer and more comfortable life by the seaboard; but the Virginia ideal was patriarchal, and an American continent on the Virginia type might reproduce the virtues of Cato, and perhaps the eloquence of Cicero, but was little likely to produce anything more practical in the way of modern progress. The Shenandoah Valley rivalled Pennsylvania and Connecticut in richness and skill of husbandry; but even agriculture, the favorite industry in Virginia, had suffered from the competition of Kentucky and Tennessee, and from the emigration which had drawn away fully one hundred thousand people. The land was no longer very productive. Even Jefferson, the most active-minded and sanguine of all Virginians—the inventor of the first scientific plough, the importer of the first threshing-machine known in Virginia, the experimenter with a new drilling-machine, the owner of one hundred and fifty slaves and ten thousand acres of land, whose negroes were trained to carpentry, cabinet-making, house-building, weaving, tailoring, shoe-making—claimed to get from his land no more than six or eight bushels of wheat to an acre, and had been forced to abandon the more profitable cultivation of tobacco. Except in a few favored districts like the Shenandoah Valley, land in Virginia did not average eight bushels of wheat to an acre. The cultivation of tobacco had been almost the sole object of land-owners, and even where the lands were not exhausted, a bad system of agriculture and the force of habit prevented improvement.

The great planters lavished money in vain on experiments to improve their crops and their stock. They devoted themselves to the task with energy and knowledge; but they needed a diversity of interests and local markets, and except at Baltimore these were far from making their appearance. Neither the products, the markets, the relative amount of capital, nor the machinery of production had perceptibly changed. "The Virginians were not generally rich," said the Duc de Liancourt, "especially in net revenue. Thus one often finds a well-served table, covered with silver, in a room where for ten years half the window panes have been missing, and where they will be missed for ten years more. There are few houses in a passable state of repair, and of all parts of the establishment those best cared for are the stables." Wealth reckoned in slaves or land was plenty; but the best Virginians, from President Washington downward, were most outspoken in their warnings against the Virginia system both of slavery and agriculture.

The contrast between Virginia and Pennsylvania was the subject of incessant comment.

In Pennsylvania [said Robert Sutcliffe, an English Friend who published travels made in 1804–1806] we meet great numbers of wagons drawn by four or more fine fat horses, the carriages firm and well made, and covered with stout good linen, bleached almost white; and it is not uncommon to see ten or fifteen together travelling cheerfully along the road, the driver riding on one of his horses. Many of these come more than three hundred miles to Philadelphia from the Ohio, Pittsburg, and other places, and I have been told by a respectable Friend, a native of Philadelphia, that more than one thousand covered carriages frequently come to Philadelphia market. . . . The appearance of things in the Slave States is quite the reverse of this. We sometimes meet a ragged black boy or girl driving a team consisting of a lean cow and a mule; sometimes a lean bull or an ox and a mule; and I have seen a mule, a bull, and a cow each miserable in its appearance, composing one team, with a half-naked black slave or two riding or driving as occasion suited. The carriage or wagon, if it may be called such, appeared in as wretched a condition as the team and its driver. Sometimes a couple of horses, mules, or cows would be dragging a hogshead of tobacco, with a pivot or axle driven into each end of the hogshead, and something like a shaft attached, by which it was drawn or rolled along the road. I have seen two oxen and two slaves pretty fully employed in getting along a single hogshead; and some of these come from a great distance inland.

In the middle of these primitive sights, Sutcliffe was startled by a contrast such as Virginia could always show. Between Richmond and Fredericksburg—

In the afternoon, as our road lay through the woods, I was surprised to meet a family party travelling along in as elegant a coach as is usually met with in the neighborhood of London, and attended by several gayly dressed footmen.

The country south of Virginia seemed unpromising even to Virginians. In the year 1796 President Washington gave to Sir John Sinclair his opinion upon the relative value of American lands. He then thought the valley of Virginia the garden of America; but he would say nothing to induce others to settle in more southern regions.

The uplands of North and South Carolina and Georgia are not dissimilar in soil [he wrote] but as they approach the lower latitudes are less congenial to wheat, and are supposed to be proportionably more unhealthy. Towards the seaboard of all the

Southern States, and farther south more so, the lands are low, sandy, and unhealthy; for which reason I shall say little concerning them, for as I should not choose to be an inhabitant of them myself, I ought not to say anything that would induce others to be so. . . . I understand that from thirty to forty dollars per acre may be denominated the medium price in the vicinity of the Susquehanna in the State of Pennsylvania, from twenty to thirty on the Potomac in what is called the Valley, . . . and less, as I have noticed before, as you proceed southerly.

Whatever was the cause, the State of North Carolina seemed to offer few temptations to immigrants or capital. Even in white population ranking fifth among the sixteen States, her 478,000 inhabitants were unknown to the world. The beautiful upper country attracted travellers neither for pleasure nor for gain, while the country along the sea-coast was avoided except by hardy wanderers. The grumbling Wilson, who knew every nook and corner of the United States, and who found New England so dreary, painted this part of North Carolina in colors compared with which his sketch of New England was gay. "The taverns are the most desolate and beggarly imaginable; bare, bleak, and dirty walls, one or two old broken chairs and a bench form all the furniture. The white females seldom make their appearance. At supper you sit down to a meal the very sight of which is sufficient to deaden the most eager appetite, and you are surrounded by half-a-dozen dirty, half-naked blacks, male and female, whom any man of common scent might smell a quarter of a mile off. The house itself is raised upon props four or five feet, and the space below is left open for the hogs, with whose charming vocal performance the wearied traveller is serenaded the whole night long." The landscape pleased him no better—"immense solitary pine savannahs through which the road winds among stagnant ponds; dark, sluggish creeks of the color of brandy, over which are thrown high wooden bridges without railings," crazy and rotten.

North Carolina was relatively among the poorest States. The exports and imports were of trifling value, less than one tenth of those returned for Massachusetts, which were more than twice as great as those of North Carolina and Virginia together. That under these conditions America should receive any strong impulse from such a quarter seemed unlikely; yet perhaps for the moment more was to be expected from the Carolinas than from Virginia. Backward as these States in some respects were, they possessed one new element of wealth which promised more for them than anything Virginia could hope. The steam-engines of Watt had been applied in England to spinning, weaving, and printing cotton; an immense demand had risen for that staple, and the cotton-gin had been simultaneously invented. A sudden impetus was given to industry; land which had been worthless and estates which had become bankrupt acquired new value, and in 1800 every planter was growing cotton, buying negroes, and breaking fresh soil. North Carolina felt the strong flood of prosperity, but South Carolina, and particularly the town of Charleston, had most to hope. The exports of South Carolina were nearly equal in value to those of Massachusetts or Pennsylvania; the imports were equally large. Charleston might reasonably expect to rival Boston, New York, Philadelphia, and Baltimore. In 1800 these cities still stood, as far as concerned their foreign trade, within some range of comparison; and between Boston, Baltimore, and Charleston, many plausible reasons could be given for thinking that the last might have the most brilliant future. The three towns stood abreast. If Charleston had but about eighteen thousand inhabitants, this was the number reported by Boston only ten years before, and was five thousand more than Baltimore then boasted. Neither Boston nor Baltimore saw about them a vaster region to supply, or so profitable a staple to export. A cotton crop of two hundred thousand pounds sent abroad in 1791 grew to twenty millions in 1801, and was to double again by 1803. An export of fifty thousand bales was enormous, yet was only the beginning. What use might not Charleston, the only considerable town in the entire South, make of this golden flood?

The town promised hopefully to prove equal to its task. Nowhere in the Union was intelligence, wealth, and education greater in proportion to numbers than in the little society of cotton and rice planters who ruled South Carolina; and they were in 1800 not behind—they hoped soon to outstrip—their rivals. If Boston was building a canal to the Merrimac, and Philadelphia one along the Schuylkill to the Susquehanna, Charleston had nearly completed another which brought the Santee River to its harbor, and was planning a road to Tennessee which should draw the whole interior within reach. Nashville was nearer to Charleston than to any other seaport of the Union, and Charleston lay nearest to the rich trade of the West Indies. Not even New York seemed more clearly marked for prosperity than this solitary Southern city, which already possessed banking capital in abundance, intelligence, enterprise, the traditions of high culture and aristocratic ambition, all supported by slave-labor, which could be indefinitely increased by the African slave-trade.

If any portion of the United States might hope for a sudden and magnificent bloom, South Carolina seemed entitled to expect it. Rarely had such a situation, combined with such resources, failed to produce some wonderful result. Yet as Washington warned Sinclair, these advantages were counterbalanced by serious evils. The climate in summer was too relaxing. The sun was too hot. The sea-coast was unhealthy, and at certain seasons even deadly to the whites. Finally, if history was a guide, no permanent success could be prophesied for a society like that of the low country in South Carolina, where some thirty thousand whites were surrounded by a dense mass of nearly one hundred thousand negro slaves. Even Georgia, then only partially settled, contained sixty thousand slaves and but one hundred thousand whites. The cotton States might still argue that if slavery, malaria, or summer heat barred civilization, all the civilization that was ever known must have been blighted in its infancy; but although the future of South Carolina might be brilliant, like that of other oligarchies in which only a few thousand freemen took part, such a development seemed to diverge far from the path likely to be followed by

Northern society, and bade fair to increase and complicate the social and economical difficulties with which Americans had to deal.

A probable valuation of the whole United States in 1800 was eighteen hundred million dollars, equal to $328 for each human being, including slaves; or $418 to each free white. This property was distributed with an approach to equality, except in a few of the Southern States. In New York and Philadelphia a private fortune of one hundred thousand dollars was considered handsome, and three hundred thousand was great wealth. Inequalities were frequent; but they were chiefly those of a landed aristocracy. Equality was so far the rule that every white family of five persons might be supposed to own land, stock, or utensils, a house and furniture, worth about two thousand dollars; and as the only considerable industry was agriculture, their scale of life was easy to calculate—taxes amounting to little or nothing, and wages averaging about a dollar a day.

Not only were these slender resources, but they were also of a kind not easily converted to the ready uses required for rapid development. Among the numerous difficulties with which the Union was to struggle, and which were to form the interest of American history, the disproportion between the physical obstacles and the material means for overcoming them was one of the most striking.

Popular Characteristics

THE growth of character, social and national—the formation of men's minds—more interesting than any territorial or industrial growth, defied the tests of censuses and surveys. No people could be expected, least of all when in infancy, to understand the intricacies of its own character, and rarely has a foreigner been gifted with insight to explain what natives did not comprehend. Only with diffidence could the best-informed Americans venture, in 1800, to generalize on the subject of their own national habits of life and thought. Of all American travellers President Dwight was the most experienced; yet his four volumes of travels were remarkable for no trait more uniform than their reticence in regard to the United States. Clear and emphatic wherever New England was in discussion, Dwight claimed no knowledge of other regions. Where so good a judge professed ignorance, other observers were likely to mislead; and Frenchmen like Liancourt, Englishmen like Weld, or Germans like Bülow, were almost equally worthless authorities on a subject which none understood. The newspapers of the time were little more trustworthy than the books of travel, and hardly so well written. The literature of a higher kind was chiefly limited to New England, New York, and Pennsylvania. From materials so poor no precision of result could be expected. A few customs, more or less local; a few prejudices, more or less popular; a few traits of thought, suggesting habits of mind—must form the entire material for a study more important than that of politics or economics.

The standard of comfort had much to do with the standard of character; and in the United States, except among the slaves, the laboring class enjoyed an ample supply of the necessaries of life. In this respect, as in some others, they claimed superiority over the laboring class in Europe, and the claim would have been still stronger had they shown more skill in using the abundance that surrounded them. The Duc de Liancourt,

among foreigners the best and kindest observer, made this
remark on the mode of life he saw in Pennsylvania—

There is a contrast of cleanliness with its opposite which to a
stranger is very remarkable. The people of the country are as
astonished that one should object to sleeping two or three in the
same bed and in dirty sheets, or to drink from the same dirty
glass after half a score of others, as to see one neglect to wash
one's hands and face of a morning. Whiskey diluted with water
is the ordinary country drink. There is no settler, however poor,
whose family does not take coffee or chocolate for breakfast, and
always a little salt meat; at dinner, salt meat, or salt fish, and
eggs; at supper again salt meat and coffee. This is also the common regime of the taverns.

An amusing, though quite untrustworthy Englishman named
Ashe, who invented an American journey in 1806, described the
fare of a Kentucky cabin—

The dinner consisted of a large piece of salt bacon, a dish of
hominy, and a tureen of squirrel broth. I dined entirely on the
last dish, which I found incomparably good, and the meat equal
to the most delicate chicken. The Kentuckian eat nothing but
bacon, which indeed is the favorite diet of all the inhabitants of
the State, and drank nothing but whiskey, which soon made
him more than two-thirds drunk. In this last practice he is also
supported by the public habit. In a country, then, where bacon
and spirits form the favorite summer repast, it cannot be just to
attribute entirely the causes of infirmity to the climate. No
people on earth live with less regard to regimen. They eat salt
meat three times a day, seldom or never have any vegetables,
and drink ardent spirits from morning till night. They have not
only an aversion to fresh meat, but a vulgar prejudice that it is
unwholesome. The truth is, their stomachs are depraved by
burning liquors, and they have no appetite for anything but
what is high-flavored and strongly impregnated by salt.

Salt pork three times a day was regarded as an essential part
of American diet. In the "Chainbearer," Cooper described what
he called American poverty as it existed in 1784. "As for bread,"
said the mother, "I count that for nothing. We always have
bread and potatoes enough; but I hold a family to be in a des-

perate way when the mother can see the bottom of the pork-barrel. Give me the children that's raised on good sound pork afore all the game in the country. Game's good as a relish, and so's bread; but pork is the staff of life. . . . My children I calker-late to bring up on pork."

Many years before the time to which Cooper referred, Poor Richard asked: "Maids of America, who gave you bad teeth?" and supplied the answer: "Hot soupings and frozen apples." Franklin's question and answer were repeated in a wider sense by many writers, but none was so emphatic as Volney—

I will venture to say [declared Volney] that if a prize were proposed for the scheme of a regimen most calculated to injure the stomach, the teeth, and the health in general, no better could be invented than that of the Americans. In the morning at breakfast they deluge their stomach with a quart of hot water, impregnated with tea, or so slightly with coffee that it is mere colored water; and they swallow, almost without chewing, hot bread, half baked, toast soaked in butter, cheese of the fattest kind, slices of salt or hung beef, ham, etc., all which are nearly insoluble. At dinner they have boiled pastes under the name of puddings, and the fattest are esteemed the most deli-cious; all their sauces, even for roast beef, are melted butter; their turnips and potatoes swim in hog's lard, butter, or fat; under the name of pie or pumpkin, their pastry is nothing but a greasy paste, never sufficiently baked. To digest these viscous substances they take tea almost instantly after dinner, making it so strong that it is absolutely bitter to the taste, in which state it affects the nerves so powerfully that even the English find it brings on a more obstinate restlessness than coffee. Supper again introduces salt meats or oysters. As Chastellux says, the whole day passes in heaping indigestions on one another; and to give tone to the poor, relaxed, and wearied stomach, they drink Madeira, rum, French brandy, gin, or malt spirits, which complete the ruin of the nervous system.

An American breakfast never failed to interest foreigners, on account of the variety and abundance of its dishes. On the main lines of travel, fresh meat and vegetables were invariably served at all meals; but Indian corn was the national crop, and Indian corn was eaten three times a day in another form as salt pork.

The rich alone could afford fresh meat. Ice-chests were hardly known. In the country fresh meat could not regularly be got, except in the shape of poultry or game; but the hog cost nothing to keep, and very little to kill and preserve. Thus the ordinary rural American was brought up on salt pork and Indian corn, or rye; and the effect of this diet showed itself in dyspepsia.

One of the traits to which Liancourt alluded marked more distinctly the stage of social development. By day or night, privacy was out of the question. Not only must all men travel in the same coach, dine at the same table, at the same time, on the same fare, but even beds were in common, without distinction of persons. Innkeepers would not understand that a different arrangement was possible. When the English traveller Weld reached Elkton, on the main road from Philadelphia to Baltimore, he asked the landlord what accommodation he had. "Don't trouble yourself about that," was the reply; "I have no less than eleven beds in one room alone." This primitive habit extended over the whole country from Massachusetts to Georgia, and no American seemed to revolt against the tyranny of innkeepers.

"At New York I was lodged with two others, in a back room on the ground floor," wrote, in 1796, the Philadelphian whose complaints have already been mentioned. "What can be the reason for that vulgar, hoggish custom, common in America, of squeezing three, six, or eight beds into one room?"

Nevertheless, the Americans were on the whole more neat than their critics allowed. "You have not seen the Americans," was Cobbett's reply, in 1819, to such charges; "you have not seen the nice, clean, neat houses of the farmers of Long Island, in New England, in the Quaker counties of Pennsylvania; you have seen nothing but the smoke-dried ultra-montanians." Yet Cobbett drew a sharp contrast between the laborer's neat cottage familiar to him in Surrey and Hampshire, and the "shell of boards" which the American occupied, "all around him as barren as a sea-beach." He added, too, that "the example of neatness was wanting;" no one taught it by showing its charm. Felix de Beaujour, otherwise not an enthusiastic American, paid a warm compliment to the country in this single respect, although he seemed to have the cities chiefly in mind—

American neatness must possess some very attractive quality, since it seduces every traveller; and there is no one of them who, in returning to his own country, does not wish to meet again there that air of ease and neatness which rejoiced his sight during his stay in the United States.

Almost every traveller discussed the question whether the Americans were a temperate people, or whether they drank more than the English. Temperate they certainly were not, when judged by a modern standard. Every one acknowledged that in the South and West drinking was occasionally excessive; but even in Pennsylvania and New England the universal taste for drams proved habits by no means strict. Every grown man took his noon toddy as a matter of course; and although few were seen publicly drunk, many were habitually affected by liquor. The earliest temperance movement, ten or twelve years later, was said to have had its source in the scandal caused by the occasional intoxication of ministers at their regular meetings. Cobbett thought drinking the national disease; at all hours of the day, he said, young men, "even little boys, at or under twelve years of age, go into stores and tip off their drams." The mere comparison with England proved that the evil was great, for the English and Scotch were among the largest consumers of beer and alcohol on the globe.

In other respects besides sobriety American manners and morals were subjects of much dispute, and if judged by the diatribes of travellers like Thomas Moore and H. W. Bülow, were below the level of Europe. Of all classes of statistics, moral statistics were least apt to be preserved. Even in England, social vices could be gauged only by the records of criminal and divorce courts; in America, police was wanting and a divorce suit almost, if not quite, unknown. Apart from some coarseness, society must have been pure; and the coarseness was mostly an English inheritance. Among New Englanders, Chief-Justice

Parsons was the model of judicial, social, and religious propriety; yet Parsons, in 1808, presented to a lady a copy of "Tom Jones," with a letter calling attention to the adventures of Molly Seagrim and the usefulness of describing vice. Among the social sketches in the "Portfolio" were many allusions to the coarseness of Philadelphia society, and the manners common to tea-parties. "I heard from married ladies," said a writer in February, 1803, "whose station as mothers demanded from them a guarded conduct—from young ladies, whose age forbids the audience of such conversation, and who using it modesty must disclaim—indecent allusions, indelicate expressions, and even at times immoral innuendoes. A loud laugh or a coarse exclamation followed each of these, and the young ladies generally went through the form of raising their fans to their faces."

Yet public and private records might be searched long, before they revealed evidence of misconduct such as filled the press and formed one of the commonest topics of conversation in the society of England and France. Almost every American family, however respectable, could show some victim to intemperance among its men, but few were mortified by a public scandal due to its women.

If the absence of positive evidence did not prove American society to be as pure as its simple and primitive condition implied, the same conclusion would be reached by observing the earnestness with which critics collected every charge that could be brought against it, and by noting the substance of the whole. Tried by this test, the society of 1800 was often coarse and sometimes brutal, but, except for intemperance, was moral. Indeed, its chief offence, in the eyes of Europeans, was dulness. The amusements of a people were commonly a fair sign of social development, and the Americans were only beginning to amuse themselves. The cities were small and few in number, and the diversions were such as cost little and required but elementary knowledge. In New England, although the theatre had gained a firm foothold in Boston, Puritan feelings still forbade the running of horses.

The principal amusements of the inhabitants [said Dwight]
are visiting, dancing, music, conversation, walking, riding, sailing, shooting at a mark, draughts, chess, and unhappily, in some
of the larger towns, cards and dramatic exhibitions. A considerable amusement is also furnished in many places by the
examination and exhibitions of the superior schools; and a more
considerable one by the public exhibitions of colleges. Our
countrymen also fish and hunt. Journeys taken for pleasure
are very numerous, and are a very favorite object. Boys and
young men play at foot-ball, cricket, quoits, and at many other
sports of an athletic cast, and in the winter are peculiarly fond
of skating. Riding in a sleigh, or sledge, is also a favorite diversion in New England.

President Dwight was sincere in his belief that college com-
mencements and sleigh-riding satisfied the wants of his people;
he looked upon whist as an unhappy dissipation, and upon the
theatre as immoral. He had no occasion to condemn horse-
racing, for no race-course was to be found in New England.
The horse and the dog existed only in varieties little suited
for sport. In colonial days New England produced one breed of
horses worth preserving and developing—the Narragansett
pacer; but, to the regret even of the clergy, this animal almost
disappeared, and in 1800 New England could show nothing to
take its place. The germ of the trotter and the trotting-match,
the first general popular amusement, could be seen in almost
any country village, where the owners of horses were in the
habit of trotting what were called scratch-races, for a quarter or
half a mile from the door of the tavern, along the public road.
Perhaps this amusement had already a right to be called a New-
England habit, showing defined tastes; but the force of the
popular instinct was not fully felt in Massachusetts, or even in
New York, although there it was given full play. New York
possessed a race-course, and made in 1792 a great stride toward
popularity by importing the famous stallion "Messenger" to become the source of endless interest for future generations; but
Virginia was the region where the American showed his true
character as a lover of sport. Long before the Revolution the

race-course was commonly established in Virginia and Maryland; English running-horses of pure blood—descendants of the Darley Arabian and the Godolphin Arabian—were imported, and racing became the chief popular entertainment. The long Revolutionary War, and the general ruin it caused, checked the habit and deteriorated the breed; but with returning prosperity Virginia showed that the instinct was stronger than ever. In 1798 "Diomed," famous as the sire of racers, was imported into the State, and future rivalry between Virginia and New York could be foreseen. In 1800 the Virginia race-course still remained at the head of American popular amusements.

In an age when the Prince of Wales and crowds of English gentlemen attended every prize-fight, and patronized Tom Crib, Dutch Sam, the Jew Mendoza, and the negro Molyneux, an Englishman could hardly have expected that a Virginia race-course should be free from vice; and perhaps travellers showed best the general morality of the people by their practice of dwelling on Virginia vices. They charged the Virginians with fondness for horse-racing, cock-fighting, betting, and drinking; but the popular habit which most shocked them, and with which books of travel filled pages of description, was the so-called rough-and-tumble fight. The practice was not one on which authors seemed likely to dwell; yet foreigners like Weld, and Americans like Judge Longstreet in "Georgia Scenes," united to give it a sort of grotesque dignity like that of a bull-fight, and under their treatment it became interesting as a popular habit. The rough-and-tumble fight differed from the ordinary prize-fight, or boxing-match, by the absence of rules. Neither kicking, tearing, biting, nor gouging was forbidden by the law of the ring. Brutal as the practice was, it was neither new nor exclusively Virginian. The English travellers who described it as American barbarism, might have seen the same sight in Yorkshire at the same date. The rough-and-tumble fight was English in origin, and was brought to Virginia and the Carolinas in early days, whence it spread to the Ohio and Mississippi. The habit attracted general notice because of its brutality

in a society that showed few brutal instincts. Friendly foreigners like Liancourt were honestly shocked by it; others
showed somewhat too plainly their pleasure at finding a vicious
habit which they could consider a natural product of democratic society. Perhaps the description written by Thomas Ashe
showed best not only the ferocity of the fight but also the
antipathies of the writer, for Ashe had something of the artist in
his touch, and he felt no love for Americans. The scene was at
Wheeling. A Kentuckian and a Virginian were the combatants.

Bulk and bone were in favor of the Kentuckian; science and
craft in that of the Virginian. The former promised himself
victory from his power; the latter from his science. Very few
rounds had taken place or fatal blows given, before the Virginian contracted his whole form, drew up his arms to his face, with
his hands nearly closed in a concave by the fingers being bent
to the full extension of the flexors, and summoning up all his
energy for one act of desperation, pitched himself into the
bosom of his opponent. Before the effects of this could be
ascertained, the sky was rent by the shouts of the multitude;
and I could learn that the Virginian had expressed as much
beauty and skill in his retraction and bound, as if he had been
bred in a menagerie and practised action and attitude among
panthers and wolves. The shock received by the Kentuckian,
and the want of breath, brought him instantly to the ground.
The Virginian never lost his hold. Like those bats of the South
who never quit the subject on which they fasten till they taste
blood, he kept his knees in his enemy's body; fixing his claws
in his hair and his thumbs on his eyes, gave them an instantaneous start from their sockets. The sufferer roared aloud, but
uttered no complaint. The citizens again shouted with joy.

Ashe asked his landlord whether this habit spread down the
Ohio.

I understood that it did, on the left-hand side, and that I
would do well to land there as little as possible. . . . I again
demanded how a stranger was to distinguish a good from a
vicious house of entertainment. "By previous inquiry, or, if
that was impracticable, a tolerable judgment could be formed
from observing in the landlord a possession or an absence of
ears."

The temper of the writer was at least as remarkable in this description as the scene he pretended to describe, for Ashe's Travels were believed to have been chiefly imaginary; but no one denied the roughness of the lower classes in the South and Southwest, nor was roughness wholly confined to them. No prominent man in Western society bore himself with more courtesy and dignity than Andrew Jackson of Tennessee, who in 1800 was candidate for the post of major-general of State militia, and had previously served as Judge on the Supreme Bench of his State; yet the fights in which he had been engaged exceeded belief.

Border society was not refined, but among its vices, as its virtues, few were permanent, and little idea could be drawn of the character that would at last emerge. The Mississippi boatman and the squatter on Indian lands were perhaps the most distinctly American type then existing, as far removed from the Old World as though Europe were a dream. Their language and imagination showed contact with Indians. A traveller on the levee at Natchez, in 1808, overheard a quarrel in a flatboat near by—

"I am a man; I am a horse; I am a team," cried one voice; "I can whip any man in all Kentucky, by God!" "I am an alligator," cried the other, "half man, half horse; can whip any man on the Mississippi, by God!" "I am a man," shouted the first; "have the best horse, best dog, best gun, and handsomest wife in all Kentucky, by God!" "I am a Mississippi snapping-turtle," rejoined the second; "have bear's claws, alligator's teeth, and the devil's tail; can whip *any* man, by God!"

And on this usual formula of defiance the two fire-eaters began their fight, biting, gouging, and tearing. Foreigners were deeply impressed by barbarism such as this, and orderly emigrants from New England and Pennsylvania avoided contact with Southern drinkers and fighters; but even then they knew that with a new generation such traits must disappear, and that little could be judged of popular character from the habits of frontiersmen. Perhaps such vices deserved more attention when found in the older communities, but even there they were rather survivals of English low-life than products of a new soil, and they were given too much consequence in the tales of foreign travellers.

This was not the only instance where foreigners were struck by what they considered popular traits, which natives rarely noticed. Idle curiosity was commonly represented as universal, especially in the Southern settler who knew no other form of conversation—

Frequently have I been stopped by one of them [said Weld], and without further preface asked where I was from, if I was acquainted with any news, where bound to, and finally my name. "Stop, Mister! why, I guess now you be coming from the new State?" "No, sir." "Why, then, I guess as how you be coming from Kentuck?" "No sir." "Oh, why, then, pray now where might you be coming from?" "From the low country." "Why, you must have heard all the news, then; pray now, Mister, what might the price of bacon be in those parts?" "Upon my word, my friend, I can't inform you." "Ay, ay; I see, Mister, you be'ent one of us. Pray now, Mister, what might your name be?"

Almost every writer spoke with annoyance of the inquisitorial habits of New England and the impertinence of American curiosity. Complaints so common could hardly have lacked foundation, yet the Americans as a people were never loquacious, but inclined to be somewhat reserved, and they could not recognize the accuracy of the description. President Dwight repeatedly expressed astonishment at the charge, and asserted that in his large experience it had no foundation. Forty years later, Charles Dickens found complaint with Americans for taciturnity. Equally strange to modern experience were the continual complaints in books of travel that loungers and loafers, idlers of every description, infested the taverns, and annoyed respectable travellers both native and foreign. Idling seemed to be considered a popular vice, and was commonly associated with tippling. So completely did the practice disappear in the course of another generation that it could scarcely be recalled as offensive; but in truth less work was done by the average man in 1800 than in aftertimes, for there was actually less work to do. "Good country this for lazy fellows," wrote Wilson from Kentucky; "they plant corn, turn their pigs into the woods, and in the autumn feed upon corn and pork. They lounge about the rest of the year." The roar of the steam-engine had never been heard in the land, and the carrier's wagon was three weeks between Philadelphia and Pittsburg. What need for haste when days counted for so little? Why not lounge about the tavern when life had no better amusement to offer? Why mind one's own business when one's business would take care of itself?

Yet however idle the American sometimes appeared, and however large the class of tavern loafers may have actually been, the true American was active and industrious. No immigrant came to America for ease or idleness. If an English farmer bought land near New York, Philadelphia, or Baltimore, and made the most of his small capital, he found that while he could earn more money than in Surrey or Devonshire, he worked harder and suffered greater discomforts. The climate was trying; fever was common; the crops ran new risks from strange insects, drought, and violent weather; the weeds were annoying; the flies and mosquitoes tormented him and his cattle; laborers were scarce and indifferent; the slow and magisterial ways of England, where everything was made easy, must be exchanged for quick and energetic action; the farmer's own eye must see to every detail, his own hand must hold the plough and the scythe. Life was more exacting, and every such man in America was required to do, and actually did, the work of two such men in Europe. Few English farmers of the conventional class took kindly to American ways, or succeeded in adapting themselves to the changed conditions. Germans were more successful and became rich; but the poorer and more adventurous class, who had no capital, and cared nothing for the comforts of civilization, went West, to find a harder lot. When, after toiling for weeks, they reached the neighborhood of Genessee or the

banks of some stream in southern Ohio or Indiana, they put up
a rough cabin of logs with an earthen floor, cleared an acre or
two of land, and planted Indian corn between the tree-stumps
—lucky if, like the Kentuckian, they had a pig to turn into
the woods. Between April and October, Albert Gallatin used to
say, Indian corn made the penniless immigrant a capitalist.
New settlers suffered many of the ills that would have afflicted
an army marching and fighting in a country of dense forest and
swamp, with one sore misery besides—that whatever trials the
men endured, the burden bore most heavily upon the women
and children. The chance of being shot or scalped by Indians
was hardly worth considering when compared with the certainty of malarial fever, or the strange disease called milk-sick-
ness, or the still more depressing home-sickness, or the misery
of nervous prostration, which wore out generation after generation of women and children on the frontiers, and left a tragedy
in every log-cabin. Not for love of ease did men plunge into the
wilderness. Few laborers of the Old World endured a harder lot,
coarser fare, or anxieties and responsibilities greater than those
of the Western emigrant. Not merely because he enjoyed the
luxury of salt pork, whiskey, or even coffee three times a day
did the American laborer claim superiority over the European.

A standard far higher than the average was common to the
cities; but the city population was so small as to be trifling.
Boston, New York, Philadelphia, and Baltimore together contained one hundred and eighty thousand inhabitants; and
these were the only towns containing a white population of
more than ten thousand persons. In a total population of more
than five millions, this number of city people, as Jefferson and
his friends rightly thought, was hardly American, for the true
American was supposed to be essentially rural. Their comparative luxury was outweighed by the squalor of nine hundred
thousand slaves alone.

From these slight notices of national habits no other safe
inference could be drawn than that the people were still simple.
The path their development might take was one of the many

problems with which their future was perplexed. Such few habits as might prove to be fixed, offered little clew to the habits that might be adopted in the process of growth, and speculation was useless where change alone could be considered certain.

If any prediction could be risked, an observer might have been warranted in suspecting that the popular character was likely to be conservative, for as yet this trait was most marked, at least in the older societies of New England, Pennsylvania, and Virginia. Great as were the material obstacles in the path of the United States, the greatest obstacle of all was in the human mind. Down to the close of the eighteenth century no change had occurred in the world which warranted practical men in assuming that great changes were to come. Afterward, as time passed, and as science developed man's capacity to control Nature's forces, old-fashioned conservatism vanished from society, reappearing occasionally, like the stripes on a mule, only to prove its former existence; but during the eighteenth century the progress of America, except in political paths, had been less rapid than ardent reformers wished, and the reaction which followed the French Revolution made it seem even slower than it was. In 1723 Benjamin Franklin landed at Philadelphia, and with his loaf of bread under his arm walked along Market Street toward an immortality such as no American had then conceived. He died in 1790, after witnessing great political revolutions; but the intellectual revolution was hardly as rapid as he must, in his youth, have hoped.

In 1732 Franklin induced some fifty persons to found a subscription library, and his example and energy set a fashion which was generally followed. In 1800 the library he founded was still in existence; numerous small subscription libraries on the same model, containing fifty or a hundred volumes, were scattered in country towns; but all the public libraries in the United States—collegiate, scientific, or popular, endowed or unendowed—could hardly show fifty thousand volumes, including duplicates, fully one third being still theological.

Half a century had passed since Franklin's active mind drew

the lightning from heaven, and decided the nature of electricity. No one in America had yet carried further his experiments in the field which he had made American. This inactivity was commonly explained as a result of the long Revolutionary War; yet the war had not prevented population and wealth from increasing, until Philadelphia in 1800 was far in advance of the Philadelphia which had seen Franklin's kite flying among the clouds.

In the year 1753 Franklin organized the postal system of the American colonies, making it self-supporting. No record was preserved of the number of letters then carried in proportion to the population, but in 1800 the gross receipts for postage were $320,000, toward which Pennsylvania contributed most largely —the sum of $55,000. From letters the Government received in gross $290,000. The lowest rate of letter-postage was then eight cents. The smallest charge for letters carried more than a hundred miles was twelve and a half cents. If on an average ten letters were carried for a dollar, the whole number of letters was 2,900,000—about one a year for every grown inhabitant.

Such a rate of progress could not be called rapid even by conservatives, and more than one stanch conservative thought it unreasonably slow. Even in New York, where foreign influence was active and the rewards of scientific skill were comparatively liberal, science hardly kept pace with wealth and population.

Noah Webster, who before beginning his famous dictionary edited the "New York Commercial Advertiser," and wrote on all subjects with characteristic confidence, complained of the ignorance of his countrymen. He claimed for the New Englanders an acquaintance with theology, law, politics, and light English literature; "but as to classical learning, history (civil and ecclesiastical), mathematics, astronomy, chemistry, botany, and natural history, excepting here and there a rare instance of a man who is eminent in some one of these branches, we may be said to have no learning at all, or a mere smattering." Although defending his countrymen from the criticisms of Dr.

Priestley, he admitted that "our learning is superficial in a shameful degree. . . . our colleges are disgracefully destitute of books and philosophical apparatus. . . . and I am ashamed to own that scarcely a branch of science can be fully investigated in America for want of books, especially original works. This defect of our libraries I have experienced myself in searching for materials for the History of Epidemic Diseases. . . . As to libraries, we have no such things. There are not more than three or four tolerable libraries in America, and these are extremely imperfect. Great numbers of the most valuable authors have not found their way across the Atlantic."

This complaint was made in the year 1800, and was the more significant because it showed that Webster, a man equally at home in Philadelphia, New York, and Boston, thought his country's deficiencies greater than could be excused or explained by its circumstances. George Ticknor felt at least equal difficulty in explaining the reason why, as late as 1814, even good schoolbooks were rare in Boston, and a copy of Euripides in the original could not be bought at any book-seller's shop in New England. For some reason, the American mind, except in politics, seemed to these students of literature in a condition of unnatural sluggishness; and such complaints were not confined to literature or science. If Americans agreed in any opinion, they were united in wishing for roads; but even on that point whole communities showed an indifference, or hostility, that annoyed their contemporaries. President Dwight was a somewhat extreme conservative in politics and religion, while the State of Rhode Island was radical in both respects; but Dwight complained with bitterness unusual in his mouth that Rhode Island showed no spirit of progress. The subject of his criticism was an unfinished turnpike-road across the State.

The people of Providence expended upon this road, as we are informed, the whole sum permitted by the Legislature. This was sufficient to make only those parts which I have mentioned. The turnpike company then applied to the Legislature for leave to expend such an additional sum as would complete the work.

The Legislature refused. The principal reason for the refusal, as alleged by one of the members, it is said, was the following: that turnpikes and the establishment of religious worship had their origin in Great Britain, the government of which was a monarchy and the inhabitants slaves; that the people of Massachusetts and Connecticut were obliged by law to support ministers and pay the fare of turnpikes, and were therefore slaves also; that if they chose to be slaves they undoubtedly had a right to their choice, but that free-born Rhode Islanders ought never to submit to be priest-ridden, nor to pay for the privilege of travelling on the highway. This demonstrative reasoning prevailed, and the road continued in the state which I have mentioned until the year 1805. It was then completed, and free-born Rhode Islanders bowed their necks to the slavery of travelling on a good road.

President Dwight seldom indulged in sarcasm or exaggeration such as he showed in this instance; but he repeated only matters of notoriety in charging some of the most democratic communities with unwillingness to pay for good roads. If roads were to exist, they must be the result of public or private enterprise; and if the public in certain States would neither construct roads nor permit corporations to construct them, the entire Union must suffer for want of communication. So strong was the popular prejudice against paying for the privilege of travelling on a highway that in certain States, like Rhode Island and Georgia, turnpikes were long unknown, while in Virginia and North Carolina the roads were little better than where the prejudice was universal.

In this instance the economy of a simple and somewhat rude society accounted in part for indifference; in other cases, popular prejudice took a form less easily understood. So general was the hostility to Banks as to offer a serious obstacle to enterprise. The popularity of President Washington and the usefulness of his administration were impaired by his support of a national bank and a funding system. Jefferson's hostility to all the machinery of capital was shared by a great majority of the Southern people and a large minority in the North. For seven years the New York legislature refused to charter the first banking company in the State; and when in 1791 the charter was obtained, and the Bank fell into Federalist hands, Aaron Burr succeeded in obtaining banking privileges for the Manhattan Company only by concealing them under the pretence of furnishing a supply of fresh water to the city of New York.

This conservative habit of mind was more harmful in America than in other communities, because Americans needed more than older societies the activity which could alone partly compensate for the relative feebleness of their means compared with the magnitude of their task. Some instances of sluggishness, common to Europe and America, were hardly credible. For more than ten years in England the steam-engines of Watt had been working, in common and successful use, causing a revolution in industry, that threatened to drain the world for England's advantage; yet Europe during a generation left England undisturbed to enjoy the monopoly of steam. France and Germany were England's rivals in commerce and manufactures, and required steam for self-defence; while the United States were commercial allies of England, and needed steam neither for mines nor manufactures, but their need was still extreme. Every American knew that if steam could be successfully applied to navigation, it must produce an immediate increase of wealth, besides an ultimate settlement of the most serious material and political difficulties of the Union. Had both the national and State Governments devoted millions of money to this object, and had the citizens wasted, if necessary, every dollar in their slowly filling pockets to attain it, they would have done no more than the occasion warranted, even had they failed; but failure was not to be feared, for they had with their own eyes seen the experiment tried, and they did not dispute its success. For America this question had been settled as early as 1789, when John Fitch—a mechanic, without education or wealth, but with the energy of genius—invented engine and paddles of his own, with so much success that during a whole summer Philadelphians watched his ferry-boat plying daily against the river current. No one denied that his boat was rapidly, steadily, and regularly moved against wind and tide, with as much certainty and convenience as could be expected in a first experiment; yet Fitch's company failed. He could raise no more money; the public refused to use his boat or to help him build a better; they did not want it, would not believe in it, and broke his heart by their contempt. Fitch struggled against failure, and invented another boat moved by a screw. The Eastern public still proving indifferent, he wandered to Kentucky, to try his fortune on the Western waters. Disappointed there, as in Philadelphia and New York, he made a deliberate attempt to end his life by drink; but the process proving too slow, he saved twelve opium pills from the physician's prescription, and was found one morning dead.

Fitch's death took place in an obscure Kentucky inn, three years before Jefferson, the philosopher president, entered the White House. Had Fitch been the only inventor thus neglected, his peculiarities and the defects of his steamboat might account for his failure; but he did not stand alone. At the same moment Philadelphia contained another inventor, Oliver Evans, a man so ingenious as to be often called the American Watt. He, too, invented a locomotive steam-engine which he longed to bring into common use. The great services actually rendered by this extraordinary man were not a tithe of those he would gladly have performed, had he found support and encouragement; but his success was not even so great as that of Fitch, and he stood aside while Livingston and Fulton, by their greater resources and influence, forced the steamboat on a sceptical public.

While the inventors were thus ready, and while State legislatures were offering mischievous monopolies for this invention, which required only some few thousand dollars of ready money, the Philosophical Society of Rotterdam wrote to the American Philosophical Society at Philadelphia, requesting to know what improvements had been made in the United States in the construction of steam-engines. The subject was referred to Benjamin H. Latrobe, the most eminent engineer in America, and his Report, presented to the Society in May, 1803, published in the Transactions, and transmitted abroad, showed the reasoning on which conservatism rested.

During the general lassitude of mechanical exertion which succeeded the American Revolution [said Latrobe] the utility of steam-engines appears to have been forgotten; but the subject afterward started into very general notice in a form in which it could not possibly be attended with much success. A sort of mania began to prevail, which indeed has not yet entirely subsided, for impelling boats by steam-engines. . . . For a short time a passage-boat, rowed by a steam-engine, was established between Bordentown and Philadelphia, but it was soon laid aside. . . . There are indeed general objections to the use of the steam-engine for impelling boats, from which no particular mode of application can be free. These are, first, the weight of the engine and of the fuel; second, the large space it occupies; third, the tendency of its action to rack the vessel and render it leaky; fourth, the expense of maintenance; fifth, the irregularity of its motion and the motion of the water in the boiler and cistern, and of the fuel-vessel in rough water; sixth, the difficulty arising from the liability of the paddles or oars to break if light, and from the weight, if made strong. Nor have I ever heard of an instance, verified by other testimony than that of the inventor, of a speedy and agreeable voyage having been performed in a steamboat of any construction. I am well aware that there are still many very respectable and ingenious men who consider the application of the steam-engine to the purpose of navigation as highly important and as very practicable, especially on the rapid waters of the Mississippi, and who would feel themselves almost offended at the expression of an opposite opinion. And perhaps some of the objections against it may be obviated. That founded on the expense and weight of the fuel may not for some years exist in the Mississippi, where there is a redundance of wood on the banks; but the cutting and loading will be almost as great an evil.

Within four years the steamboat was running, and Latrobe was its warmest friend. The dispute was a contest of temperaments, a divergence between minds, rather than a question of science; and a few visionaries such as those to whom Latrobe alluded—men like Chancellor Livingston, Joel Barlow, John Stevens, Samuel L. Mitchill, and Robert Fulton—dragged society forward. What but scepticism could be expected among a people thus asked to adopt the steamboat, when as yet the ordinary atmospheric steam-engine, such as had been in use in Europe for a hundred years, was practically unknown to them, and the engines of Watt were a fable? Latrobe's Report further said that in the spring of 1803, when he wrote, five steam-engines were at work in the United States—one lately set up by the Manhattan Water Company in New York to supply the city with water; another in New York for sawing timber; two in Philadelphia, belonging to the city, for supplying water and running a rolling and slitting mill; and one at Boston employed in some manufacture. All but one of these were probably constructed after 1800, and Latrobe neglected to say whether they belonged to the old Newcomen type, or to Watt's manufacture, or to American invention; but he added that the chief American improvement on the steam engine had been the construction of a wooden boiler, which developed sufficient power to work the Philadelphia pump at the rate of twelve strokes, of six feet, per minute. Twelve strokes a minute, or one stroke every five seconds, though not a surprising power, might have answered its purpose, had not the wooden boiler, as Latrobe admitted, quickly decomposed, and steam-leaks appeared at every bolt-hole.

If so eminent and so intelligent a man as Latrobe, who had but recently emigrated in the prime of life from England, knew little about Watt, and nothing about Oliver Evans, whose experience would have been well worth communicating to any philosophical society in Europe, the more ignorant and un-scientific public could not feel faith in a force of which they knew nothing at all. For nearly two centuries the Americans had struggled on foot or horseback over roads not much better than trails, or had floated down rushing streams in open boats momentarily in danger of sinking or upsetting. They had at length, in the Eastern and Middle States, reached the point of constructing turnpikes and canals. Into these undertakings they put sums of money relatively large, for the investment seemed safe and the profits certain. Steam as a locomotive power was still a visionary idea, beyond their experience, contrary to European precedent, and exposed to a thousand risks. They regarded it as a delusion.

About three years after Latrobe wrote his Report on the steam-engine, Robert Fulton began to build the boat which settled forever the value of steam as a locomotive power. According to Fulton's well-known account of his own experience, he suffered almost as keenly as Fitch, twenty years before, under the want of popular sympathy—

When I was building my first steamboat at New York [he said, according to Judge Story's report] the project was viewed by the public either with indifference or with contempt as a visionary scheme. My friends indeed were civil, but they were shy. They listened with patience to my explanations, but with a settled cast of incredulity upon their countenances. I felt the full force of the lamentation of the poet—

> Truths would you teach, or save a sinking land,
> All fear, none aid you, and few understand.

As I had occasion to pass daily to and from the building-yard while my boat was in progress, I have often loitered unknown near the idle groups of strangers gathering in little circles, and heard various inquiries as to the object of this new vehicle. The language was uniformly that of scorn, or sneer, or ridicule. The loud laugh often rose at my expense; the dry jest; the wise calculation of losses and expenditures; the dull but endless repetition of the Fulton Folly. Never did a single encouraging remark, a bright hope, or a warm wish cross my path.

Possibly Fulton and Fitch, like other inventors, may have exaggerated the public apathy and contempt; but whatever was the precise force of the innovating spirit, conservatism possessed the world by right. Experience forced on men's minds the conviction that what had ever been must ever be. At the close of the eighteenth century nothing had occurred which warranted the belief that even the material difficulties of America could be removed. Radicals as extreme as Thomas Jefferson and Albert Gallatin were contented with avowing no higher aim than that America should reproduce the simpler forms of European republican society without European vices; and even this their opponents thought visionary. The United States had thus far made a single great step in advance of the Old World—they had agreed to try the experiment of embracing half a continent in one republican system; but so little were they disposed to feel confidence in their success, that Jefferson himself did not look on this American idea as vital; he would not stake the future on so new an invention. "Whether we remain in one confederacy," he wrote in 1804, "or form into Atlantic and Mississippi confederations, I believe not very important to the happiness of either party." Even over his liberal mind history cast a spell so strong, that he thought the solitary American experiment of political confederation "not very important" beyond the Alleghanies.

The task of overcoming popular inertia in a democratic society was new, and seemed to offer peculiar difficulties. Without a scientific class to lead the way, and without a wealthy class to provide the means of experiment, the people of the United States were still required, by the nature of their problems, to become a speculating and scientific nation. They could do little without changing their old habit of mind, and without learning to love novelty for novelty's sake. Hitherto their timidity in using money had been proportioned to the scantiness of their means. Henceforward they were under every inducement to risk great stakes and frequent losses in order to win occasionally a thousand fold. In the colonial state they had naturally accepted old processes as the best, and European experience as final authority. As an independent people, with half a continent to civilize, they could not afford to waste time in following European examples, but must devise new processes of their own. A world which assumed that what had been must be, could not be scientific; yet in order to make the Americans a successful people, they must be roused to feel the necessity of scientific training. Until they were satisfied that knowledge was money, they would not insist upon high education; nor until they saw with their own eyes stones turned into gold, and vapor into cattle and corn, would they learn the meaning of science.

Intellect of New England

WHETHER the United States were to succeed or fail in their economical and political undertakings, the people must still develop some intellectual life of their own, and the character of this development was likely to interest mankind. New conditions and hopes could hardly fail to produce a literature and arts more or less original. Of all possible triumphs, none could equal that which might be won in the regions of thought if the intellectual influence of the United States should equal their social and economical importance. Young as the nation was, it had already produced an American literature bulky and varied enough to furnish some idea of its probable qualities in the future, and the intellectual condition of the literary class in the United States at the close of the eighteenth century could scarcely fail to suggest both the successes and the failures of the same class in the nineteenth.

In intellectual tastes, as in all else, the Union showed well-marked divisions between New England, New York, Pennsylvania, and the Southern States. New England was itself divided between two intellectual centres—Boston and New Haven. The Massachusetts and Connecticut schools were as old as the colonial existence; and in 1800 both were still alive, if not flourishing.

Society in Massachusetts was sharply divided by politics. In 1800 one half the population, represented under property qualifications by only some twenty thousand voters, was Republican. The other half, which cast about twenty-five thousand votes, included nearly every one in the professional and mercantile classes, and represented the wealth, social position, and education of the Commonwealth; but its strength lay in the Congregational churches and in the cordial union between the clergy, the magistracy, the bench and bar, and respectable society throughout the State. This union created what was unknown beyond New England—an organized social system, capable of acting at command either for offence or defence, and admirably adapted for the uses of the eighteenth century.

Had the authority of the dominant classes in Massachusetts depended merely on office, the task of overthrowing it would have been as simple as it was elsewhere; but the New England oligarchy struck its roots deep into the soil, and was supported by the convictions of the people. Unfortunately the system was not and could not be quickly adapted to the movement of the age. Its starting-point lay in the educational system, which was in principle excellent; but it was also antiquated. Little change had been made in it since colonial times. The common schools were what they had been from the first; the academies and colleges were no more changed than the schools. On an average of ten years, from 1790 to 1800, thirty-nine young men annually took degrees from Harvard College; while during the ten years, 1766–1776, that preceded the Revolutionary War, forty-three bachelors of arts had been annually sent into the world, and even in 1720–1730 the average number had been thirty-five. The only sign of change was that in 1720–1730 about one hundred and forty graduates had gone into the Church, while in 1790–1800 only about eighty chose this career. At the earlier period the president, a professor of theology, one of mathematics, and four tutors gave instruction to the under-graduates. In 1800 the president, the professor of theology, the professor of mathematics, and a professor of Hebrew, created in 1765, with the four tutors did the same work. The method of instruction had not changed in the interval, being suited to children fourteen years of age; the instruction itself was poor, and the discipline was indifferent. Harvard College had not in eighty years made as much progress as was afterward made in twenty. Life was quickening within it as within all mankind—the spirit and vivacity of the coming age could not be wholly shut out; but none the less the college resembled a priesthood which had lost the secret of its mysteries, and patiently stood holding the flickering torch before cold altars, until God should vouchsafe a new dispensation of sunlight.

Nevertheless, a medical school with three professors had been founded in 1783, and every year gave degrees to an average class of two doctors of medicine. Science had already a firm hold on the college, and a large part of the conservative clergy were distressed by the liberal tendencies which the governing body betrayed. This was no new thing. The college always stood somewhat in advance of society, and never joined heartily in dislike for liberal movements; but unfortunately it had been made for an instrument, and had never enjoyed the free use of its powers. Clerical control could not be thrown off, for if the college was compelled to support the clergy, on the other hand the clergy did much to support the college; and without the moral and material aid of this clerical body, which contained several hundred of the most respected and respectable citizens, clad in every town with the authority of spiritual magistrates, the college would have found itself bankrupt in means and character. The graduates passed from the college to the pulpit, and from the pulpit attempted to hold the college, as well as their own congregations, facing toward the past. "Let us guard against the insidious encroachments of *innovation*," they preached— "that evil and beguiling spirit which is now stalking to and fro through the earth, seeking whom he may destroy." These words were spoken by Jedediah Morse, a graduate of Yale in 1783, pastor of the church at Charlestown, near Boston, and still known in biographical dictionaries as "the father of American geography." They were contained in the Election Sermon of this worthy and useful man, delivered June 6, 1803; but the sentiment was not peculiar to him, or confined to the audience he was then addressing—it was the burden of a thousand discourses enforced by a formidable authority.

The power of the Congregational clergy, which had lasted unbroken until the Revolution, was originally minute and inquisitory, equivalent to a police authority. During the last quarter of the century the clergy themselves were glad to lay aside the more odious watchfulness over their parishes, and to welcome social freedom within limits conventionally fixed; but their old authority had not wholly disappeared. In country parishes they were still autocratic. Did an individual defy their authority, the minister put his three-cornered hat on his head, took his silver-topped cane in his hand, and walked down the village street, knocking at one door and another of his best parishioners, to warn them that a spirit of license and of French infidelity was abroad, which could be repressed only by a strenuous and combined effort. Any man once placed under this ban fared badly if he afterward came before a bench of magistrates. The temporal arm vigorously supported the ecclesiastical will. Nothing tended so directly to make respectability conservative, and conservatism a fetich of respectability, as this union of bench and pulpit. The democrat had no caste; he was not respectable; he was a Jacobin—and no such character was admitted into a Federalist house. Every dissolute intriguer, loose-liver, forger, false-coiner, and prison-bird; every harebrained, loud-talking demagogue; every speculator, scoffer, and atheist—was a follower of Jefferson; and Jefferson was himself the incarnation of their theories.

A literature belonging to this subject exists—stacks of newspapers and sermons, mostly dull, and wanting literary merit. In a few of them Jefferson figured under the well-remembered disguises of Puritan politics: he was Ephraim, and had mixed himself among the people; had apostatized from his God and religion; gone to Assyria, and mingled himself among the heathen; "gray hairs are here and there upon him, yet he knoweth not"; or he was Jeroboam, who drave Israel from following the Lord, and made them sin a great sin. He had doubted the authority of revelation, and ventured to suggest that petrified shells found embedded in rocks fifteen thousand feet above sea-level could hardly have been left there by the Deluge, because if the whole atmosphere were condensed as water, its weight showed that the seas would be raised only fifty-two and a half feet. Sceptic as he was, he could not accept the scientific theory that the ocean-bed had been uplifted by natural forces; but although he had thus instantly deserted this battery raised against revelation, he had still expressed the opinion that a universal deluge was *equally* unsatisfactory as an explanation, and had avowed preference for a profession of ignorance rather than a belief in error. He had said, "It does me no injury for my neighbors to say there are twenty gods, or no god," and that all the many forms of religious faith in the Middle States were "good enough, and sufficient to preserve peace and order." He was notoriously a deist; he probably ridiculed the doctrine of total depravity; and he certainly would never have part or portion in the blessings of the New Covenant, or be saved because of grace.

No abler or more estimable clergyman lived than Joseph Buckminster, the minister of Portsmouth, in New Hampshire, and in his opinion Jefferson was bringing a judgment upon the people.

I would not be understood to insinuate [said he in his sermon on Washington's death] that contemners of religious duties, and even men void of religious principle, may not have an attachment to their country and a desire for its civil and political prosperity—nay, that they may not even expose themselves to great dangers, and make great sacrifices to accomplish this object; but by their impiety . . . they take away the heavenly defence and security of a people, and render it necessary for him who ruleth among the nations in judgment to testify his displeasure against those who despise his laws and contemn his ordinances.

Yet the congregational clergy, though still greatly respected, has ceased to be leaders of thought. Theological literature no longer held the prominence it had enjoyed in the days of Edwards and Hopkins. The popular reaction against Calvinism, felt rather than avowed, stopped the development of doctrinal theology; and the clergy, always poor as a class, with no weapons but their intelligence and purity of character, commonly sought rather to avoid than to challenge hostility. Such literary activity as existed was not clerical but secular. Its field was the Boston press, and its recognized literary champion was Fisher Ames.

The subject of Ames's thought was exclusively political. At that moment every influence combined to maintain a stationary condition in Massachusetts politics. The manners and morals of the people were pure and simple; their society was democratic; in the worst excesses of their own revolution they had never become savage or bloodthirsty; their experience could not explain, nor could their imagination excuse, wild popular excesses; and when in 1793 the French nation seemed mad with the frenzy of its recovered liberties. New England looked upon the bloody and blasphemous work with such horror as religious citizens could not but feel. Thenceforward the mark of a wise and good man was that he abhorred the French Revolution, and believed democracy to be its cause. Like Edmund Burke, they listened to no argument: "It is a vile, illiberal school, this French Academy of the sans-culottes; there is nothing in it that is fit for a gentleman to learn." The answer to every democratic suggestion ran in a set phrase, "Look at France!" This idea became a monomania with the New England leaders, and took exclusive hold of Fisher Ames, their most brilliant writer and talker, until it degenerated into a morbid illusion. During the last few months of his life, even so late as 1808, this dying man could scarcely speak of his children without expressing his fears of their future servitude to the French. He believed his alarms to be shared by his friends. "Our days," he wrote, "are made heavy with the pressure of anxiety, and our nights restless with visions of horror. We listen to the clank of chains, and overhear the whispers of assassins. We mark the barbarous dissonance of mingled rage and triumph in the yell of an infuriated mob; we see the dismal glare of their burnings, and scent the loathsome steam of human victims offered in sacrifice." In theory the French Revolution was not an argument or a proof, but only an illustration, of the workings of divine law; and what had happened in France must sooner or later happen in America if the ignorant and vicious were to govern the wise and good.

The bitterness against democrats became intense after the

month of May, 1800, when the approaching victory of Jefferson was seen to be inevitable. Then for the first time the clergy and nearly all the educated and respectable citizens of New England began to extend to the national government the hatred which they bore to democracy. The expressions of this mixed antipathy filled volumes. "Our country," wrote Fisher Ames in 1803, "is too big for union, too sordid for patriotism, too democratic for liberty. What is to become of it, he who made it best knows. Its vice will govern it, by practising upon its folly. This is ordained for democracies." He explained why this inevitable fate awaited it. "A democracy cannot last. Its nature ordains that its next change shall be into a military despotism —of all known governments perhaps the most prone to shift its head, and the slowest to mend its vices. The reason is that the tyranny of what is called the people, and that by the sword, both operate alike to debase and corrupt, till there are neither men left with the spirit to desire liberty, nor morals with the power to sustain justice. Like the burning pestilence that destroys the human body, nothing can subsist by its dissolution but vermin." George Cabot, whose political opinions were law to the wise and good, held the same convictions. "Even in New England," wrote Cabot in 1840, "where there is among the body of the people more wisdom and virtue than in any other part of the United States, we are full of errors which no reasoning could eradicate, if there were a Lycurgus in every village. We are democratic altogether, and I hold democracy in its natural operation to be the government of the worst."

Had these expressions of opinion been kept to the privacy of correspondence, the public could have ignored them; but so strong were the wise and good in their popular following, that every newspaper seemed to exult in denouncing the people. They urged the use of force as the protection of wisdom and virtue. A paragraph from Dennie's "Portfolio," reprinted by all the Federalist newspapers in 1803, offered one example among a thousand of the infatuation which possessed the Federalist press, neither more extravagant nor more treasonable than the rest—

A democracy is scarcely tolerable at any period of national history. Its omens are always sinister, and its powers are unpropitious. It is on its trial here, and the issue will be civil war, desolation, and anarchy. No wise man but discerns its imperfections, no good man but shudders at its miseries, no honest man but proclaims its fraud, and no brave man but draws his swords against its force. The institution of a scheme of policy so radically contemptible and vicious is a memorable example of what the villany of some men can devise, the folly of others receive, and both establish in spite of reason, reflection, and sensation.

The Philadelphia grand jury indicted Dennie for this paragraph as a seditious libel, but it was not more expressive than the single word uttered by Alexander Hamilton, who owed no small part of his supremacy to the faculty of expressing the prejudices of his followers more tersely than they themselves could do. Compressing the idea into one syllable, Hamilton, at a New York dinner, replied to some democratic sentiment by striking his hand sharply on the table and saying, "Your people, sir—your people is a great *beast!*"

The political theories of these ultra-conservative New Englanders did not require the entire exclusion of all democratic influence from government. "While I hold," said Cabot, "that a government altogether popular is in effect a government of the populace, I maintain that no government can be relied on that has not a material portion of the democratic mixture in its composition." Cabot explained what should be the true portion of democratic mixture: "If no man in New England could vote for legislators who was not possessed in his own right of two thousand dollars' value *in land*, we could do something better." The Constitution of Massachusetts already restricted the suffrage to persons "having a freehold estate within the commonwealth of an annual income of three pounds, or any estate of the value of sixty pounds." A further restriction to freeholders whose estate was worth two thousand dollars would hardly have left a material mixture of any influence which democrats would have recognized as theirs.

Meanwhile even Cabot and his friends Ames and Colonel Hamilton recognized that the reform they wished could be effected only with the consent of the people; and firm in the conviction that democracy must soon produce a crisis, as in Greece and Rome, in England and France, when political power must revert to the wise and good, or to the despotism of a military chief, they waited for the catastrophe they foresaw. History and their own experience supported them. They were right, so far as human knowledge could make them so; but the old spirit of Puritan obstinacy was more evident than reason or experience in the simple-minded, overpowering conviction with which the clergy and serious citizens of Massachusetts and Connecticut, assuming that the people of America were in the same social condition as the contemporaries of Catiline and the adherents of Robespierre, sat down to bide their time until the tempest of democracy should drive the frail government so near destruction that all men with one voice should call on God and the Federalist prophets for help. The obstinacy of the race was never better shown than when, with the sunlight of the nineteenth century bursting upon them, these resolute sons of granite and ice turned their faces from the sight, and smiled in their sardonic way at the folly or wickedness of men who could pretend to believe the world improved because henceforth the ignorant and vicious were to rule the United States and govern the churches and schools of New England.

Even Boston, the most cosmopolitan part of New England, showed no tendency in its educated classes to become American in thought or feeling. Many of the ablest Federalists, and among the rest George Cabot, Theophilus Parsons, and Fisher Ames, shared few of the narrower theological prejudices of their time, but were conservatives of the English type, whose alliance with the clergy betrayed as much policy as religion, and whose intellectual life was wholly English. Boston made no strong claim to intellectual prominence. Neither clergy, lawyers, physicians, nor literary men were much known beyond the State. Fisher Ames enjoyed a wider fame; but Ames's best political writing was saturated with the despair of the tomb to which his wasting body was condemned. Five years had passed since he closed his famous speech on the British Treaty with the foreboding that if the treaty were not carried into effect, "even I, slender and almost broken as my hold upon life is, may outlive the government and constitution of my country." Seven years more were to pass in constant dwelling upon the same theme, in accents more and more despondent, before the long-expected grave closed over him, and his warning voice ceased to echo painfully on the air. The number of his thorough-going admirers was small, if his own estimate was correct. "There are," he said, "not many, perhaps not five hundred, even among the Federalists, who yet allow themselves to view the progress of licentiousness as so speedy, so sure, and so fatal as the deplorable experience of our country shows that it is, and the evidence of history and the constitution of human nature demonstrate that it must be." These five hundred, few as they were, comprised most of the clergy and the State officials, and overawed large numbers more.

Ames was the mouthpiece in the press of a remarkable group, of which George Cabot was the recognized chief in wisdom, and Timothy Pickering the most active member in national politics. With Ames, Cabot, and Pickering, joined in confidential relations, was Theophilus Parsons, who in the year 1800 left Newburyport for Boston. Parsons was an abler man than either Cabot, Ames, or Pickering, and his influence was great in holding New England fast to an independent course which could end only in the overthrow of the Federal constitution which these men had first pressed upon an unwilling people; but though gifted with strong natural powers, backed by laborious study and enlivened by the ready and somewhat rough wit native to New England, Parsons was not bold on his own account; he was felt rather than seen, and although ever ready in private to advise strong measures, he commonly let others father them before the world.

These gentlemen formed the Essex Junto, so called from the county of Essex where their activity was first felt. According to Ames, not more than five hundred men fully shared their opinions; but Massachusetts society was so organized as to make their influence great, and experience foretold that as the liberal Federalists should one by one wander to the Democratic camp where they belonged, the conservatism of those who remained would become more bitter and more absolute as the Essex Junto represented a larger and larger proportion of their numbers.

Nevertheless, the reign of old-fashioned conservatism was near its end. The New England Church was apparently sound; even Unitarians and Baptists were recognized as parts of one fraternity. Except a few Roman and Angelican bodies, all joined in the same worship, and said little on points of doctrinal difference. No one had yet dared to throw a firebrand into the temple; but Unitarians were strong among the educated and wealthy class, while the tendencies of a less doctrinal religious feeling were shaping themselves in Harvard College. William Ellery Channing took his degree in 1798, and in 1800 was a private tutor in Virginia. Joseph Stevens Buckminster, thought by his admirers a better leader than Channing, graduated in 1800, and was teaching boys to construe their Latin exercises at Exeter Academy. Only the shell of orthodoxy was left, but respectable society believed this shell to be necessary as an example of Christian unity and a safeguard against more serious innovations. No one could fail to see that the public had lately become restive under its antiquated discipline. The pulpits still fulminated against the fatal tolerance which within a few years had allowed theatres to be opened in Boston, and which scandalized God-fearing men by permitting public advertisements that "Hamlet" and "Othello" were to be performed in the town founded to protest against worldly pageants. Another innovation was more strenuously resisted. Only within the last thirty

years had Sunday travel been allowed even in England; in
Massachusetts and Connecticut it was still forbidden by law,
and the law was enforced. Yet not only travellers, but innkeepers and large numbers of citizens connived at Sunday
travel, and it could no longer be prevented. The clergy saw
their police authority weakening year by year, and understood,
without need of many words, the tacit warning of the city congregations that in this world they must be allowed to amuse
themselves, even though they were to suffer for it in the next.

The longing for amusement and freedom was a reasonable and
a modest want. Even the young theologians, the Buckminsters
and Channings, were hungry for new food. Boston was little
changed in appearance, habits, and style from what it had been
under its old king. When young Dr. J. C. Warren returned from
Europe about the year 1800, to begin practice in Boston, he
found gentlemen still dressed in colored coats and figured waist-
coats, short breeches buttoning at the knee, long boots with
white tops, ruffled shirts and wristbands, a white cravat filled
with what was called a "pudding," and for the elderly, cocked
hats, and wigs which once every week were sent to the barber's
to be dressed—so that every Saturday night the barbers' boys
were seen carrying home piles of wig-boxes in readiness for
Sunday's church. At evening parties gentlemen appeared in
white small-clothes, silk stockings and pumps, with a colored
or white waistcoat. There were few hackney-coaches, and ladies
walked to evening entertainments. The ancient minuet was
danced as late as 1806. The waltz was not yet tolerated.

Fashionable society was not without charm. In summer
Southern visitors appeared, and admired the town, with its
fashionable houses perched on the hillsides, each in its own
garden, and each looking seaward over harbor and islands. Boston was then what Newport afterward became, and its only
rival as a summer watering-place in the North was Ballston,
whither society was beginning to seek health before finding it
a little farther away at Saratoga. Of intellectual amusement
there was little more at once place than at the other, except that

the Bostonians devoted themselves more seriously to church-going and to literature. The social instinct took shape in varied forms, but was highly educated in none; while the typical entertainment in Boston, as in New York, Philadelphia, and Charleston, was the state dinner—not the light, feminine triviality which France introduced into an amusement-loving world, but the serious dinner of Sir Robert Walpole and Lord North, where gout and plethora waited behind the chairs; an effort of animal endurance.

There was the arena of intellectual combat, if that could be called combat where disagreement in principle was not tolerated. The talk of Samuel Johnson and Edmund Burke was the standard of excellence to all American society that claimed intellectual rank, and each city possessed its own circle of Federalist talkers. Democrats rarely figured in these entertainments, at least in fashionable private houses. "There was no exclusiveness," said a lady who long outlived the time; "but I should as soon have expected to see a cow in a drawing-room as a Jacobin." In New York, indeed, Colonel Burr and the Livingstons may have held their own, and the active-minded Dr. Mitchill there, like Dr. Eustis in Boston, was an agreeable companion. Philadelphia was comparatively cosmopolitan; in Baltimore the Smiths were a social power; and Charleston, after deserting Federal principles in 1800, could hardly ignore Democrats; but Boston society was still pure. The clergy took a prominent part in conversation, but Fisher Ames was the favorite of every intelligent company; and when Gouverneur Morris, another brilliant talker, visited Boston, Ames was pitted against him.

The intellectual wants of the community grew with the growing prosperity; but the names of half-a-dozen persons could hardly be mentioned whose memories survived by intellectual work made public in Massachusetts between 1783 and 1800. Two or three local historians might be numbered, including Jeremy Belknap, the most justly distinguished. Jedediah Morse the geographer was well known; but not a poet, a novelist, or a scholar could be named. Nathaniel Bowditch did not publish his "Practical Navigator" till 1800, and not till then did Dr. Waterhouse begin his struggle to introduce vaccination. With the exception of a few Revolutionary statesmen and elderly clergymen, a political essayist like Ames, and lawyers like Samuel Dexter and Theophilus Parsons, Massachusetts could show little that warranted a reputation for genius; and, in truth, the intellectual prominence of Boston began as the conservative system died out, starting with the younger Buckminster several years after the century opened.

The city was still poorer in science. Excepting the medical profession, which represented nearly all scientific activity, hardly a man in Boston got his living either by science or art. When in the year 1793 the directors of the new Middlesex Canal Corporation, wishing to bring the Merrimac River to Boston Harbor, required a survey of an easy route not thirty miles long, they could find no competent civil engineer in Boston, and sent to Philadelphia for an Englishman named Weston, engaged on the Delaware and Schuylkill Canal.

Possibly a few Bostonians could read and even speak French; but Germany was nearly as unknown as China, until Madame de Staël published her famous work in 1814. Even then young George Ticknor, incited by its account of German university education, could find neither a good teacher nor a dictionary, nor a German book in the shops or public libraries of the city or at the college in Cambridge. He had discovered a new world.

Pope, Addison, Akenside, Beattie, and Young were still the reigning poets. Burns was accepted by a few; and copies of a volume were advertised by booksellers, written by a new poet called Wordsworth. America offered a fair demand for new books, and anything of a light nature published in England was sure to cross the ocean. Wordsworth crossed with the rest, and his "Lyrical Ballads" were reprinted in 1802, not in Boston or New York, but in Philadelphia, where they were read and praised. In default of other amusements, men read what no one could have endured had a choice of amusements been open.

Neither music, painting, science, the lecture-room, nor even magazines offered resources that could rival what was looked upon as classical literature. Men had not the alternative of listening to political discussions, for stump-speaking was a Southern practice not yet introduced into New England, where such a political canvass would have terrified society with dreams of Jacobin license. The clergy and the bar took charge of politics; the tavern was the club and the forum of political discussion; but for those who sought other haunts, and especially for women, no intellectual amusement other than what was called "belles-lettres" existed to give a sense of occupation to an active mind. This keen and innovating people, hungry for the feast that was almost served, the Walter Scotts and Byrons so near at hand, tried meanwhile to nourish themselves with husks.

Afraid of Shakespeare and the drama, trained to the standards of Queen Anne's age, and ambitious beyond reason to excel, the New Englanders attempted to supply their own wants. Massachusetts took no lead in the struggle to create a light literature, if such poetry and fiction could be called light. In Connecticut the Muses were most obstinately wooed; and there, after the Revolutionary War, a persistent effort was made to give prose the form of poetry. The chief of the movement was Timothy Dwight, a man of extraordinary qualities, but one on whom almost every other mental gift had been conferred in fuller measure than poetical genius. Twenty-five years had passed since young Dwight, fresh from Yale College, began his career by composing an epic poem, in eleven books and near ten thousand lines, called "The Conquest of Canaan." In the fervor of patriotism, before independence was secured or the French Revolution imagined, he pictured the great Hebrew leader Joshua preaching the Rights of Man, and prophesying the spread of his "sons" over America—

> Then o'er wide lands, as blissful Eden bright,
> Type of the skies, and seats of pure delight,
> Our sons with prosperous course shall stretch their sway,

And claim an empire spread from sea to sea;
In one great whole th' harmonious tribes combine,
Trace Justice' path, and choose their chiefs divine;
On Freedom's base erect the heavenly plan,
Teach laws to reign, and save the Rights of Man.
Then smiling Art shall wrap the fields in bloom,
Fine the rich ore, and guide the useful loom;
Then lofty towers in golden pomp arise,
Then spiry cities meet auspicious skies;
The soul on Wisdom's wing sublimely soar,
New virtues cherish and new truths explore;
Through Time's long tract our name celestial run,
Climb in the east and circle with the sun;
And smiling Glory stretch triumphant wings
O'er hosts of heroes and o'er tribes of kings.

A world of eighteenth-century thought, peopled with personi-
fications, lay buried in the ten thousand lines of President
Dwight's youthful poem. Perhaps in the year 1800, after Jefferson's triumph, Dwight would have been less eager that his hero
should save the Rights of Man; by that time the phrase had
acquired a flavor of French infidelity which made it unpalatable
to good taste. Yet the same Jeffersonian spirit ran through
Dwight's famous national song, which was also written in the
Revolutionary War—

Columbia, Columbia, to glory arise,
The queen of the world and child of the skies!

. . . .

Thy heroes the rights of mankind shall defend,
And triumph pursue them, and glory attend.

. . . .

While the ensigns of union triumph unfurled
Hush the tumult of war and give peace to the world.

"Peace to the world" was the essence of Jeffersonian principles,
worth singing in something better than jingling metre and indifferent rhyme; but President Dwight's friends in 1800 no
longer sang this song. More and more conservative as he grew
older, he published in 1797 an orthodox "Triumph of Infidelity,"
introduced by a dedication to Voltaire. His rebuke to mild theology was almost as severe as that to French deism—

> There smiled the smooth divine, unused to wound
> The sinner's heart with Hell's alarming sound.

His poetical career reached its climax in 1794 in a clerical Connecticut pastoral in seven books, called "Greenfield Hill." Perhaps his verses were not above the level of the Beatties and
Youngs he imitated; but at least they earned for President
Dwight no mean reputation in days when poetry was at its lowest ebb, and made him the father of a school.

One quality gave respectability to his writing apart from
genius. He loved and believed in his country. Perhaps the uttermost depths of his nature were stirred only by affection for the
Connecticut Valley; but after all where was human nature
more respectable than in that peaceful region? What had the
United States then to show in scenery and landscape more beautiful or more willing than that country of meadow and mountain? Patriotism was no ardent feeling among the literary men
of the time, whose general sentiment was rather expressed by
Cliffton's lines—

> In these cold shades, beneath these shifting skies,
> Where Fancy sickens, and where Genius dies,
> Where few and feeble are the Muse's strains,
> And no fine frenzy riots in the veins,
> There still are found a few to whom belong
> The fire of virtue and the soul of song.

William Cliffton, a Pennsylvania Friend, who died in 1799
of consumption, in his twenty-seventh year, knew nothing of the
cold shades and shifting skies which chilled the genius of European poets; he knew only that America cared little for such
genius and fancy as he could offer, and he rebelled against the
neglect. He was better treated than Wordsworth, Keats, or
Shelley; but it was easy to blame the public for dulness and indifference, though readers were kinder than authors had a right
to expect. Even Cliffton was less severe than some of his contemporaries. A writer in the "Boston Anthology," for January,
1807 uttered in still stronger words the prevailing feeling of the
literary class—

We know that in this land where the spirit of democracy is everywhere diffused, we are exposed as it were to a poisonous atmosphere, which blasts everything beautiful in nature, and corrodes everything elegant in art; we know that with us 'the rose-leaves fall ungathered,' and we believe that there is little to praise and nothing to admire in most of the objects which would first present themselves to the view of a stranger.

Yet the American world was not unsympathetic toward Cliff-ton and his rivals, though they strained prose through their sieves of versification, and showed open contempt for their audience. Toward President Dwight the public was even generous; and he returned the generosity with parental love and condescension which shone through every line he wrote. For some years his patriotism was almost as enthusiastic as that of Joel Barlow. He was among the numerous rivals of Macaulay and Shelley for the honor of inventing the stranger to sit among the ruins of St. Paul's; and naturally America supplied the explorer who was to penetrate the forest of London and indulge his national self-complacency over ruined temples and towers.

> Some unknown wild, some shore without a name,
> In all thy pomp shall then majestic shine
> As silver-headed Time's slow years decline.
> Not ruins only meet th' inquiring eye;
> Where round yon mouldering oak vain brambles twine,
> The filial stem, already towering high,
> Erelong shall stretch his arms and nod in yonder sky.

From these specimens of President Dwight's poetry any critic, familiar with the time, could infer that his prose was sensible and sound. One of the few books of travel which will always retain value for New Englanders was written by President Dwight to describe his vacation rambles; and although in his own day no one would have ventured to insult him by calling these instructive volumes amusing, the quaintness which here and there gave color to the sober narrative had a charm of its own. How could the contrast be better expressed between volatile Boston and orthodox New Haven than in Dwight's quiet reproof, mixed with paternal tenderness? The Bostonians, he said, were distinguished by a lively imagination, ardor, and sensibility; they were "more like the Greeks than the Romans;" admired where graver people would only approve; applauded or hissed where another audience would be silent; their language was frequently hyperbolical, their pictures highly colored; the tea shipped to Boston was destroyed—in New York and Philadelphia it was stored; education in Boston was superficial, and Boston women showed the effects of this misfortune, for they practised accomplishments only that they might be admired, and were taught from the beginning to regard their dress as a momentous concern.

Under Dwight's rule the women of the Connecticut Valley were taught better; but its men set to the Bostonians an example of frivolity without a parallel, and they did so with the connivance of President Dwight and under the lead of his brother Theodore. The frivolity of the Hartford wits, as they were called, was not so light as that of Canning and the Anti-Jacobin," but had it been heavier than the "Conquest of Canaan" itself, it would still have found no literary rivalry in Boston. At about the time when Dwight composed his serious epic, another tutor at Yale, John Trumbull, wrote a burlesque epic in Hudibrastic verse, "McFingal," which his friend Dwight declared to be not inferior to "Hudibras" in wit and humor, and in every other respect superior. When "Hudibras" was published, more than a hundred years before, Mr. Pepys remarked: "It hath not a good liking in me, though I had tried but twice or three times reading to bring myself to think it witty." After the lapse of more than another century, the humor of neither poem may seem worth imitation; but to Trumbull in 1784 Butler was a modern classic, for the standard of taste between 1663 and 1784 changed less than in any twenty years of the following century. "McFingal" was a success, and laid a solid foundation for the coming school of Hartford wits. Posterity ratified the verdict of Trumbull's admirers by preserving for daily use a few of his lines quoted indiscriminately with Butler's best—

What has posterity done for us?

Optics sharp it needs, I ween,
To see what is not to be seen.

A thief ne'er felt the halter draw
With good opinion of the law.

Ten years after the appearance of "McFingal," and on the strength of its success, Trumbull, Lemuel Hopkins, Richard Alsop, Theodore Dwight, Joel Barlow, and others began a series of publications, "The Anarchiad," "The Echo," "The Guillotine," and the like, in which they gave tongue to their wit and sarcasm. As Alsop described the scene—

Begrimed with blood where erst the savage fell,
Shrieked the wild war-whoop with infernal yell,
The Muses sing; lo, Trumbull wakes the lyre.
. . . .
Majestic Dwight, sublime in epic strain,
Paints the fierce horrors of the crimson plain;
And in Virgilian Barlow's tuneful lines
With added splendor great Columbus shines.

Perhaps the Muses would have done better by not interrupting the begrimed savage; for Dwight, Trumbull, Alsop, and Hopkins, whatever their faults, were Miltonic by the side of Joel Barlow. Yet Barlow was a figure too important in American history to be passed without respectful attention. He expressed better than any one else that side of Connecticut character which roused at the same instant the laughter and the respect of men. Every human influence twined about his career and lent it interest; every forward movement of his time had his sympathy, and few steps in progress were made which he did not assist. His ambition, above the lofty ambition of Jefferson, made him aspire to be a Connecticut Maecenas and Virgil in one; to patronize Fulton and employ Smirke; counsel Jefferson and contend with Napoleon. In his own mind a figure such as the world rarely saw—a compound of Milton, Rousseau, and the Duke of Bridgewater—he had in him so large a share of conceit, that tragedy, which would have thrown a solemn shadow over another man's life, seemed to render his only more entertaining. As a poet, he undertook to do for his native land what Homer had done for Greece and Virgil for Rome, Milton for England and Camoens for Portugal—to supply America with a great epic, without which no country could be respectable; and his "Vision of Columbus," magnified afterward into the "Columbiad," with a magnificence of typography and illustration new to the United States, remained a monument of his ambition. In this vision Columbus was shown a variety of coming celebrities, including all the heroes of the Revolutionary War—

> Here stood stern Putnam, scored with ancient scars,
> The living records of his country's wars;
> Wayne, like a moving tower, assumes his post,
> Fires the whole field, and is himself a host;
> Undaunted Stirling, prompt to meet his foes,
> And Gates and Sullivan for action rose;
> Macdougal, Clinton, guardians of the State,
> Stretch the nerved arm to pierce the depth of fate;
> Moultrie and Sumter lead their banded powers;
> Morgan in front of his bold riflers towers,
> His host of keen-eyed marksmen, skilled to pour
> Their slugs unerring from the twisted bore;
> No sword, no bayonet they learn to wield,
> They gall the flank, they skirt the battling field,
> Cull out the distant foe in full horse speed,
> Couch the long tube and eye the silver bead,
> Turn as he turns, dismiss the whizzing lead,
> And lodge the death-ball in his heedless head.

More than seven thousand lines like these furnished constant pleasure to the reader, the more because the "Columbiad" was accepted by the public in a spirit as serious as that in which it was composed. The Hartford wits, who were bitter Federalists, looked upon Barlow as an outcast from their fold, a Jacobin in politics, and little better than a French atheist in religion; but they could not deny that his poetic garments were of a piece with their own. Neither could they without great ingratitude repudiate his poetry as they did his politics, for they themselves figured with Manco Capac, Montezuma, Raleigh, and Pocahontas before the eyes of Columbus; and the world bore witness that Timothy Dwight, "Heaven in his eye and rapture on his tongue," tuned his "high harp" in Barlow's inspired verses. Europe was as little disposed as America to cavil; and the Abbé Grégoire assured Barlow in a printed letter that this monument of genius and typography would immortalize the author and silence the criticisms of Pauw and other writers on the want of talent in America.

That the "Columbiad" went far to justify those criticisms was true; but on the other hand it proved something almost equivalent to genius. Dwight, Trumbull, and Barlow, whatever might be their differences, united in offering proof of the boundless ambition which marked the American character. Their aspirations were immense, and sooner or later such restless craving was sure to find better expression. Meanwhile Connecticut was a province by itself, a part of New England rather than of the United States. The exuberant patriotism of the Revolution was chilled by the steady progress of democratic principles in the Southern and Middle States, until at the election of Jefferson in 1800 Connecticut stood almost alone with no intellectual companion except Massachusetts, while the breach between them and the Middle States seemed to widen day by day. That the separation was only superficial was true; but the connection itself was not yet deep. An extreme Federalist partisan like Noah Webster did not cease working for his American language and literature because of the triumph of Jeffersonian principles elsewhere; Barlow became more American when his friends gained power; the work of the colleges went on unbroken; but prejudices, habits, theories, and laws remained what they had been in the past, and in Connecticut the influence of nationality was less active than ten, twenty, or even thirty years before. Yale College was but a reproduction of Harvard with stricter orthodoxy, turning out every year about thirty graduates, of whom nearly one fourth went into the Church.

For the last ten years the number tended rather to diminish than to increase.

Evidently an intellectual condition like that of New England could not long continue. The thoughts and methods of the eighteenth century held possession of men's minds only because the movement of society was delayed by political passions. Massachusetts, and especially Boston, already contained a younger generation eager to strike into new paths, while forcibly held in the old ones. The more decidedly the college graduates of 1800 disliked democracy and its habits of thought, the more certain they were to compensate for political narrowness by freedom in fields not political. The future direction of the New England intellect seemed already suggested by the impossibility of going further in the line of President Dwight and Fisher Ames. Met by a barren negation on that side, thought was driven to some new channel; and the United States were the more concerned in the result because, with the training and literary habits of New Englanders and the new models already established in Europe for their guidance, they were likely again to produce something that would command respect.

Intellect of the Middle States

BETWEEN New England and the Middle States was a gap like that between Scotland and England. The conceptions of life were different. In New England society was organized on a system—a clergy in alliance with a magistracy; universities supporting each, and supported in turn—a social hierarchy, in which respectability, education, property, and religion united to defeat and crush the unwise and vicious. In New York wisdom and virtue, as understood in New England, were but lightly esteemed. From an early moment no small number of those who by birth, education, and property were natural leaders of the wise and virtuous, showed themselves ready to throw in their lot with the multitude. Yet New York, much more than New England, was the home of natural leaders and family alliances. John Jay, the governor; the Schuylers, led by Philip Schuyler and his son-in-law Alexander Hamilton; the Livingstons, led by Robert R. Livingston the chancellor, with a promising younger brother Edward nearly twenty years his junior, and a brother-in-law John Armstrong, whose name and relationship will be prominent in this narrative, besides Samuel Osgood, Morgan Lewis, and Smith Thompson, other connections by marriage with the great Livingston stock; the Clintons, headed by Governor George Clinton, and supported by the energy of De Witt his nephew, thirty years of age, whose close friend Ambrose Spencer was reckoned as one of the family; finally, Aaron Burr, of pure Connecticut Calvinistic blood, whose two active lieutenants, William P. Van Ness and John Swartwout, were socially well connected and well brought up—all these Jays, Schuylers, Livingstons, Clintons, Burrs, had they lived in New England, would probably have united in the support of their class, or abandoned the country; but being citizens of New York they quarrelled. On one side Governor Jay, General Schuyler, and Colonel Hamilton were true to their principles. Rufus King, the American minister in London, by birth a New Englander,

Vol I, Chap. IV.

adhered to the same connection. On the other hand, George Clinton, like Samuel Adams in Boston, was a Republican by temperament, and his protest against the Constitution made him leader of the Northern Republicans long before Jefferson was mentioned as his rival. The rest were all backsliders from Federalism—and especially the Livingston faction, who, after carefully weighing arguments and interests, with one accord joined the mob of free-thinking democrats, the "great beast" of Alexander Hamilton. Aaron Burr, who prided himself on the inherited patrician quality of his mind and manners, coldly assuming that wisdom and virtue were powerless in a democracy, followed Chancellor Livingston into the society of Cheetham and Paine. Even the influx of New Englanders into the State could not save the Federalists; and in May, 1800, after a sharp struggle, New York finally enrolled itself on the side of Jefferson and George Clinton.

Fortunately for society, New York possessed no church to overthrow, or traditional doctrines to root out, or centuries of history to disavow. Literature of its own it had little; of intellectual unity, no trace. Washington Irving was a boy of seventeen wandering along the banks of the river he was to make famous; Fenimore Cooper was a boy of eleven playing in the primitive woods of Otsego, or fitting himself at Albany for entrance to Yale College; William Cullen Bryant was a child of six in the little village of Cummington, in western Massachusetts.

Political change could as little affect the educational system as it could affect history, church, or literature. In 1795, at the suggestion of Governor Clinton, an attempt had been made by the New York legislature to create a common-school system, and a sum of fifty thousand dollars was for five years annually applied to that object; but in 1800 the appropriation was exhausted, and the thirteen hundred schools which had been opened were declining. Columbia College, with a formidable array of unfilled professorships, and with fifteen or twenty annual graduates, stood apart from public affairs, although one of its professors, Dr. Samuel L. Mitchill, gave scientific reputation to the whole State. Like the poet Barlow, Mitchill was a universal genius—a chemist, botanist, naturalist, physicist, and politician, who, to use the words of a shrewd observer, supported the Republican party because Jefferson was its leader, and supported Jefferson because he was a philosopher. Another professor of Columbia College, Dr. David Hosack, was as active as Dr. Mitchill in education, although he contented himself with private life, and did not, like Mitchill, reach the dignity of congressman and senator.

Science and art were still less likely to be harmed by a democratic revolution. For scientific work accomplished before 1800 New York might claim to excel New England; but the result was still small. A little botany and mineralogy, a paper on the dispute over yellow fever or vaccination, was the utmost that medicine could show; yet all the science that existed was in the hands of the medical faculty. Botany, chemistry, mineralogy, midwifery, and surgery were so closely allied that the same professor might regard them all as within the range of his instruction; and Dr. Mitchill could have filled in succession, without much difficulty, every chair in Columbia College as well as in the Academy of Fine Arts about to be established. A surgeon was assumed to be an artist. The Capitol at Washington was designed, in rivalry with a French architect, by Dr. William Thornton, an English physician, who in the course of two weeks' study at the Philadelphia Library gained enough knowledge of architecture to draw incorrectly an exterior elevation. When Thornton was forced to look for some one to help him over his difficulties, Jefferson could find no competent native American, and sent for Latrobe. Jefferson considered himself a better architect than either of them, and had he been a professor of materia medica at Columbia College, the public would have accepted his claim as reasonable.

The intellectual and moral character of New York left much to be desired; but on the other hand, had society adhered stiffly to what New England thought strict morals, the difficulties in the path of national development would have been increased. Innovation was the most useful purpose which New York could serve in human interests, and never was a city better fitted for its work. Although the great tide of prosperity had hardly begun to flow, the political character of city and State was already well defined in 1800 by the election which made Aaron Burr vice-president of the United States, and brought De Witt Clinton into public life as Burr's rival. De Witt Clinton was hardly less responsible than Burr himself for lowering the standard of New York politics, and indirectly that of the nation; but he was foremost in creating the Erie Canal. Chancellor Livingston was frequently charged with selfishness as great as that of Burr and Clinton; but he built the first steamboat, and gave immortality to Fulton. Ambrose Spencer's politics were inconsistent enough to destroy the good name of any man in New England; but he became a chief-justice of ability and integrity. Edward Livingston was a defaulter under circumstances of culpable carelessness, as the Treasury thought; but Gallatin, who dismissed him from office, lived to see him become the author of a celebrated code of civil law, and of the still more celebrated Nullification Proclamation. John Armstrong's character was so little admired that his own party could with difficulty be induced to give him high office; yet the reader will judge how Armstrong compared in efficiency of public service with the senators who distrusted him.

New York cared but little for the metaphysical subtleties of Massachusetts and Virginia, which convulsed the nation with spasms almost as violent as those that, fourteen centuries before, distracted the Eastern Empire in the effort to establish the double or single nature of Christ. New York was indifferent whether the nature of the United States was single or multiple, whether they were a nation or a league. Leaving this class of questions to other States which were deeply interested in them, New York remained constant to no political theory. There society, in spite of its aristocratic mixture, was democratic by instinct; and in abandoning its alliance with New England in order to join Virginia and elect Jefferson to the Presidency, it pledged itself to principles of no kind, least of all to Virginia doctrines. The Virginians aimed at maintaining a society so simple that purity should suffer no danger, and corruption gain no foothold; and never did America witness a stranger union than when Jefferson, the representative of ideal purity, allied himself with Aaron Burr, the Livingstons and Clintons, in the expectation of fixing the United States in a career of simplicity and virtue. George Clinton indeed, a States-rights Republican of the old school, understood and believed the Virginia doctrines; but as for Aaron Burr, Edward Livingston, De Witt Clinton, and Ambrose Spencer—young men whose brains were filled with dreams of a different sort—what had such energetic democrats to do with the plough, or what share had the austerity of Cato and the simplicity of Ancus Martius in their ideals? The political partnership between the New York Republicans and the Virginians was from the first that of a business firm; and no more curious speculation could have been suggested to the politicians of 1800 than the question whether New York would corrupt Virginia, or Virginia would check the prosperity of New York.

In deciding the issue of this struggle, as in every other issue that concerned the Union, the voice which spoke in most potent tones was that of Pennsylvania. This great State, considering its political importance, was treated with little respect by its neighbors; and yet had New England, New York, and Virginia been swept out of existence in 1800, democracy could have better spared them all than have lost Pennsylvania. The only true democratic community then existing in the eastern States, Pennsylvania was neither picturesque nor troublesome. The State contained no hierarchy like that of New England; no great families like those of New York; no oligarchy like the planters of Virginia and South Carolina. "In Pennsylvania," said Albert Gallatin, "not only we have neither Livingstons nor Rensselaers, but from the suburbs of Philadelphia to the banks of the Ohio I do not know a single family that has any extensive influence. An equal distribution of property has rendered every individual independent, and there is among us true and real equality." This was not all. The value of Pennsylvania to the Union lay not so much in the democratic spirit of society as in the rapidity with which it turned to national objects. Partly for this reason the State made an insignificant figure in politics. As the nation grew, less and less was said in Pennsylvania of interests distinct from those of the Union. Too thoroughly democratic to fear democracy, and too much nationalized to dread nationality, Pennsylvania became the ideal American State, easy, tolerant, and contented. If its soil bred little genius, it bred still less treason. With twenty different religious creeds, its practice could not be narrow, and a strong Quaker element made it humane. If the American Union succeeded, the good sense, liberality, and democratic spirit of Pennsylvania had a right to claim credit for the result; and Pennsylvanians could afford to leave power and patronage to their neighbors, so long as their own interests were to decide the path of administration.

The people showed little of that acuteness which prevailed to the eastward of the Hudson. Pennsylvania was never smart, yet rarely failed to gain her objects, and never committed serious follies. To politics the Pennsylvanians did not take kindly. Perhaps their democracy was so deep an instinct that they knew not what to do with political power when they gained it; as though political power were aristocratic in its nature, and democratic power a contradiction in terms. On this ground rested the reputation of Albert Gallatin, the only Pennsylvanian who made a mark on the surface of national politics. Gallatin's celebrated financial policy carried into practice the doctrine that the powers of government, being necessarily irresponsible, and therefore hostile to liberty, ought to be exercised only within the narrowest bounds, in order to leave democracy free to develop itself without interference in its true social, intellectual, and economical strength. Unlike Jefferson and the Virginians, Gallatin never hesitated to claim for government all the powers necessary for whatever object was in hand; but he agreed with

them in checking the practical use of power, and this he did
with a degree of rigor which has been often imitated but never
equalled. The Pennsylvanians followed Gallatin's teachings.
They indulged in endless factiousness over offices, but they
never attempted to govern, and after one brief experience they
never rebelled. Thus holding abstract politics at arm's length,
they supported the national government with a sagacious sense
that their own interests were those of the United States.

Although the State was held by the New Englanders and Virginians in no high repute for quickness of intellect, Philadelphia
in 1800 was still the intellectual centre of the nation. For ten
years the city had been the seat of national government, and at
the close of that period had gathered a more agreeable society,
fashionable, literary, and political, than could be found anywhere, except in a few capital cities of Europe. This Quaker
city of an ultra-democratic State startled travellers used to
luxury, by its extravagance and display. According to the Duc
de Liancourt, writing in 1797—

The profusion and luxury of Philadelphia on great days, at
the tables of the wealthy, in their equipages, and the dresses of
their wives and daughters, are extreme. I have seen balls on the
President's birthday where the splendor of the rooms and the
variety and richness of the dresses did not suffer in comparison
with Europe; and it must be acknowledged that the beauty of
the American ladies has the advantage in the comparison. The
young women of Philadelphia are accomplished in different
degrees, but beauty is general with them. They want the ease
and fashion of French women, but the brilliancy of their complexion is infinitely superior. Even when they grow old they
are still handsome; and it would be no exaggeration to say, in
the numerous assemblies of Philadelphia it is impossible to
meet with what is called a plain woman. As to the young men,
they for the most part seem to belong to another species.

For ten years Philadelphia had attracted nearly all the intelligence and cultivation that could be detached from their native
stocks. Stagnation was impossible in this rapid current of men
and ideas. The Philadelphia press showed the effect of such un-

usual movement. There Cobbett vociferated libels against democrats. His career was cut short by a blunder of his own; for he quitted the safe field of politics in order to libel the physicians, and although medical practice was not much better than when it had been satirized by Le Sage some eighty years before, the physicians had not become less sensitive. If ever medical practice deserved to be libelled, the bleeding which was the common treatment not only for fevers but for consumption, and even for old age, warranted all that could be said against it; but Cobbett found to his cost that the Pennsylvanians were glad to bleed, or at least to seize the opportunity for silencing the libeller. In 1800 he returned to England; but the style of political warfare in which he was so great a master was already established in the Philadelphia press. An Irish-American named Duane, who had been driven from England and India for expressing opinions too liberal for the time and place, came to Philadelphia and took charge of the opposition newspaper, the "Aurora," which became in his hands the most energetic and slanderous paper in America. In the small society of the time libels rankled, and Duane rivalled Cobbett in the boldness with which he slandered. Another point of resemblance existed between the two men. At a later stage in his career Duane, like Cobbett, disregarded friend as well as foe; he then attacked all who offended him, and denounced his party leaders as bitterly as did his opponents; but down to the year 1800 he reserved his abuse for his enemies, and the "Aurora" was the nearest approach to a modern newspaper to be found in the country.

Judged by the accounts of his more reputable enemies, Duane seemed beneath forbearance; but his sins, gross as they were, found abettors in places where such conduct was less to be excused. He was a scurrilous libeller; but so was Cobbett; so was William Coleman, who in 1801 became editor of the New York "Evening Post" under the eye of Alexander Hamilton; so was the refined Joseph Dennie, who in the same year established at Philadelphia the "Portfolio," a weekly paper devoted to literature, in which for years to come he was to write literary essays, diversified by slander of Jefferson. Perhaps none of these habitual libellers deserved censure so much as Fisher Ames, the idol of respectability, who cheered on his party to vituperate his political opponents. He saw no harm in showing "the knaves," Jefferson and Gallatin, "the cold-thinking villains who lead, 'whose black blood runs temperately bad,'" the motives of "their own base hearts. . . . The vain, the timid, and trimming must be made by examples to see that scorn smites and blasts and withers like lightning the knaves that mislead them." Little difference could be seen between the two parties in their use of such weapons, except that democrats claimed a right to slander opponents because they were monarchists and aristocrats, while Federalists thought themselves bound to smite and wither with scorn those who, as a class, did not respect established customs.

Of American newspapers there was no end; but the education supposed to have been widely spread by eighteenth-century newspapers was hardly to be distinguished from ignorance. The student of history might search forever these storehouses of political calumny for facts meant to instruct the public in any useful object. A few dozen advertisements of shipping and sales; a marine list; rarely or never a price-list, unless it were European; copious extracts from English newspapers, and long columns of political disquisition—such matter filled the chief city newspapers, from which the smaller sheets selected what their editors thought fit. Reporters and regular correspondents were unknown. Information of events other than political—the progress of the New York or Philadelphia water-works, of the Middlesex Canal, of Fitch's or Fulton's voyages, or even the commonest details of a Presidential inauguration—could rarely be found in the press. In such progress as newspapers had made Philadelphia took the lead, and in 1800 was at the height of her influence. Not until 1801 did the extreme Federalists set up the "Evening Post" under William Coleman, in New York, where at about the same time the Clinton interest put an English refugee named Cheetham in charge of their new paper, the "American Citizen and Watchtower," while Burr's friends established the "Morning Chronicle," edited by Dr. Peter Irving. Duane's importance was greatly reduced by this outburst of journalism in New York, and by the rise of the "National Intelligencer" at Washington, semi-official organ of Jefferson's administration. After the year 1800 the "Aurora" languished; but between 1795 and 1800 it was the leading newspaper of the United States, and boasted in 1802 of a circulation of four thousand copies, at least half of which its rivals declared to be imaginary.

Although Philadelphia was the literary as well as the political capital of America, nothing proved the existence of a highly intellectual society. When Joseph Dennie, a graduate of Harvard College, quitted Boston and established his "Portfolio" in Philadelphia in 1801, he complained as bitterly as the Pennsylvanian Cliffton against the land "where Genius sickens and where Fancy dies;" but he still thought Philadelphia more tolerable than any other city in the United States. With a little band of literary friends he passed his days in defying the indifference of his countrymen. "In the society of Mr. Dennie and his friends at Philadelphia I passed the few agreeable moments which my tour through the States afforded me," wrote in 1804 the British poet whom all the world united in calling by the familiar name of Tom Moore. "If I did not hate as I ought the rabble to which they are opposed, I could not value as I do the spirit with which they defy it; and in learning from them what Americans *can be*, I but see with the more indignation what Americans *are*."

> Yet, yet forgive me, O you sacred few,
> Whom late by Delaware's green banks I knew;
> Whom, known and loved, through many a social eve
> 'T was bliss to live with, and 't was pain to leave.
> Oh, but for *such*, Columbia's days were done!
> Rank without ripeness, quickened without sun,
> Crude at the surface, rotten at the core,
> Her fruits would fall before her spring were o'er.

If Columbia's days were to depend on "*such*," they were scarcely worth prolonging; for Dennie's genius was but the thin echo of an English classicism thin at its best. Yet Moore's words had value, for they gave a lifelike idea of the "sacred few" who sat with him, drinking deep, and reviling America because she could not produce poets like Anacreon and artists like Phidias, and still more because Americans cared little for Addisonian essays. An adventurer called John Davis, who published in London a book of American travels, mentioned in it that he too met the Philadelphia authors. "Dennie passed his mornings in the shop of Mr. Dickens, which I found the rendezvous of the Philadelphia sons of literature—Blair [Linn], author of a poem called the 'Powers of Genius'; Ingersoll, known by a tragedy of which I forget the title; Stock, celebrated for his dramatic criticisms." C. J. Ingersoll did in fact print a tragedy called "Edwy and Elgiva," which was acted in 1801, and John Blair Linn's "Powers of Genius" appeared in the same year; but Dennie's group boasted another member more notable than these. Charles Brockden Brown, the first American novelist of merit, was a Philadelphian. Davis called upon Brown. " He occupied a dismal room in a dismal street. I asked him whether a view of Nature would not be more propitious to composition, or whether he should not write with more facility were his window to command the prospect of the Lake of Geneva. 'Sir,' said he, 'good pens, thick paper, and ink well diluted would facilitate my composition more than the prospect of the broadest ex- panse of water or mountains rising against the clouds.' "

Pennsylvania was largely German and the Moravians were not without learning, yet no trace of German influence showed itself in the educated and literary class. Schiller was at the end of his career, and Goethe at the zenith of his powers; but neither was known in Pennsylvania, unless it might be by translations of the "Robbers," or the "Sorrows of Werther." As for deeper studies, search in America would be useless for what was rare or unknown either in England or France. Kant had closed and

Hegel was beginning his labors; but the Western nations knew no more of German thought than of Egyptian hieroglyphics, and America had not yet reached the point of understanding that metaphysics apart from theology could exist at all. Locke was a college text-book, and possibly a few clergymen had learned to deride the idealism of Berkeley; but as an interest which concerned life, metaphysics, apart from Calvinism, had no existence in America, and was to have none for another generation. The literary labors of Americans followed easier paths, and such thought as prevailed was confined within a narrow field—yet within this limit Pennsylvania had something to show, even though it failed to please the taste of Dennie and Moore.

Not far from the city of Philadelphia, on the banks of the Schuylkill, lived William Bartram, the naturalist, whose "Travels" through Florida and the Indian country, published in 1791, were once praised by Coleridge, and deserved reading both for the matter and the style. Not far from Bartram, and his best scholar, was Alexander Wilson, a Scotch poet of more than ordinary merit, gifted with a dogged enthusiasm, which in spite of obstacles gave to America an ornithology more creditable than anything yet accomplished in art or literature. Beyond the mountains, at Pittsburg, another author showed genuine and original qualities. American humor was not then so marked as it afterward became, and good-nature was rarer; but H. H. Brackenridge set an example of both in a book once universally popular throughout the South and West. A sort of prose "Hudibras," it had the merit of leaving no sting, for this satire on democracy was written by a democrat and published in the most democratic community of America. "Modern Chivalry" told the adventures of a militia captain, who riding about the country with a raw Irish servant, found this red-headed, ignorant bog-trotter, this Sancho Panza, a much more popular person than himself, who could only with difficulty be restrained from becoming a clergyman, an Indian chief, a member of the legislature, of the philosophical society, and of Congress. At

length his employer got for him the appointment of excise officer in the Alleghanies, and was gratified at seeing him tarred
and feathered by his democratic friends. "Modern Chivalry"
was not only written in good last-century English, none too
refined for its subject, but was more thoroughly American than
any book yet published, or to be published until the "Letters of
Major Jack Downing" and the "Georgia Scenes" of forty years
later. Never known, even by title, in Europe, and little enjoyed in the seaboard States, where bog-trotters and weavers
had no such prominence, Judge Brackenridge's book filled the
place of Don Quixote on the banks of the Ohio and along the
Mississippi.

Another man whose literary merits were not to be overlooked,
had drifted to Philadelphia because of its varied attractions. If
in the last century America could boast of a poet who shared
some of the delicacy if not the grandeur of genius, it was Philip
Freneau; whose verses, poured out for the occasion, ran freely,
good and bad, but the bad, as was natural, much more freely
than the good. Freneau proved his merit by an experience
unique in history. He was twice robbed by the greatest English
poets of his day. Among his many slight verses were some pleasing lines called "The Indian Burying Ground"—

> His bow for action ready bent,
>   And arrows with a head of stone,
> Can only mean that life is spent,
>   And not the finer essence gone.
>
> By midnight moons, o'er moistening dews,
>   In vestments for the chase arrayed,
> The hunter still the deer pursues,
>   The hunter and the deer—a shade.

The last line was taken by the British poet Campbell for his
own poem called "O'Connor's Child," and Freneau could afford
to forgive the theft which thus called attention to the simple
grace of his melody; but although one such compliment might
fall to the lot of a common man, only merit could explain a
second accident of the same kind. Freneau saw a greater genius

than Campbell borrow from his modest capital. No one complained of Walter Scott for taking whatever he liked wherever he chose, to supply that flame of genius which quickened the world; but Freneau had the right to claim that Scott paid him the highest compliment one poet could pay another. In the Introduction to the third canto of "Marmion" stood and still stands a line taken directly from the verse in Freneau's poem on the Heroes of Eutaw—

They took the spear—but left the shield.

All these men—Wilson, Brackenridge, Freneau—were democrats, and came not within the Federalist circle where Moore could alone see a hope for Columbia. Yet the names of Federalists also survived in literature. Alexander Graydon's pleasant Memoirs could never lose interest. Many lawyers, clergymen, and physicians left lasting records. Dallas was bringing out his reports; Duponceau was laboring over jurisprudence and languages; William Lewis, William Rawle, and Judge Wilson were high authorities at the bar; Dr. Wistar was giving reputation to the Philadelphia Medical School, and the famous Dr. Physic was beginning to attract patients from far and near as the best surgeon in America. Gilbert Stuart, the best painter in the country, came to Philadelphia, and there painted portraits equal to the best that England or France could produce—for Reynolds and Gainsborough were dead, and Sir Thomas Lawrence ruled the fashion of the time. If Franklin and Rittenhouse no longer lived to give scientific fame to Philadelphia, their liberal and scientific spirit survived. The reputation of the city was not confined to America, and the accident that made a Philadelphian, Benjamin West, President of the Royal Academy in succession to Sir Joshua Reynolds, was a tacit compliment, not undeserved, to the character of the American metropolis.

There manners were milder and more humane than elsewhere. Societies existed for lessening the hardship of the unfortunate. A society labored for the abolition of slavery without exciting popular passion, although New York contained more than twenty thousand slaves, and New Jersey more than twelve thousand. A society for alleviating the miseries of prisons watched the progress of experiments in the model jail, which stood alone of its kind in America. Elsewhere the treatment of criminals was such as it had ever been. In New Haven they were still confined under-ground, in the shafts of an abandoned copper-mine. The Memoirs of Stephen Burroughs gave some idea of the prisons and prison discipline of Massachusetts. The Pennsylvania Hospital was also a model, for it contained a department for the insane, the only one of the sort in America except the Virginia Lunatic Asylum at Williamsburg. Even there the treatment of these beings, whom a later instinct of humanity thought peculiarly worthy of care and lavish expenditure, was harsh enough—strait-jackets, whippings, chains, and dark-rooms being a part of the prescribed treatment in every such hospital in the world; but where no hospitals existed, as in New England, New York, and elsewhere, the treatment was apt to be far worse. No horror of the Middle Ages wrung the modern conscience with a sense of disgust more acute than was felt in remembering the treatment of the insane even within recent times. Shut in attics or cellars, or in cages outside a house, without warmth, light, or care, they lived in filth, with nourishment such as was thrown to dogs. Philadelphia led the way in humanitarian efforts which relieved man from incessant contact with these cruel and coarsening associations.

The depth of gratitude due to Pennsylvania as the model democratic society of the world was so great as to risk overestimating what had been actually done. As yet no common-school system existed. Academies and colleges were indifferent. New Jersey was no better provided than Pennsylvania. The Englishman Weld, a keen if not a friendly critic, visited Princeton—

A large college [he said] held in much repute by the neighboring States. The number of students amounts to upwards of seventy; from their appearance, however, and the course of studies they seem to be engaged in, like all the other American colleges I ever saw, it better deserves the title of a grammar school than of a college. The library which we were shown is most wretched, consisting for the most part of old theological books not even arranged with any regularity. An orrery contrived by Mr. Rittenhouse stands at one end of the apartment, but it is quite out of repair, as well as a few detached parts of a philosophical apparatus enclosed in the same glass-case. At the opposite end of the room are two small cupboards which are shown as the museum. These contain a couple of small stuffed alligators and a few singular fishes in a miserable state of preservation, from their being repeatedly tossed about.

Philadelphia made no claim to a wide range of intellectual interests. As late as 1811, Latrobe, by education an architect and by genius an artist, wrote to Volney in France—

Thinking only of the profession and of the affluence which it yields in Europe to all who follow it, you forget that I am an engineer in America; that I am neither a mechanic nor a merchant, nor a planter of cotton, rice, or tobacco. You forget— for you know it as well as I do—that with us the labor of the hand has precedence over that of the mind; that an engineer is considered only as an overseer of men who dig, and an architect as one that watches others who hew stone or wood.

The labor of the hand had precedence over that of the mind throughout the United States. If this was true in the city of Franklin, Rittenhouse, and West, the traveller who wandered farther toward the south felt still more strongly the want of intellectual variety, and found more cause for complaint.

Intellect of the Southern States

BETWEEN Pennsylvania and Virginia stretched no barrier of mountains or deserts. Nature seemed to mean that the northern State should reach toward the Chesapeake, and embrace its wide system of coasts and rivers. The Susquehanna, crossing Pennsylvania from north to south, rolled down wealth which in a few years built the city of Baltimore by the surplus of Pennsylvania's resources. Any part of Chesapeake Bay, or of the streams which flowed into it, was more easily accessible to Baltimore than any part of Massachusetts or Pennsylvania to New York. Every geographical reason argued that the Susquehanna, the Potomac, and the James should support one homogenous people; yet the intellectual difference between Pennsylvania and Virginia was already more sharply marked than that between New England and the Middle States.

The old Virginia society was still erect, priding itself on its resemblance to the society of England, which had produced Hampden and Chatham. The Virginia gentleman, wherever met, was a country gentleman or a lawyer among a society of planters. The absence of city life was the sharpest characteristic of Virginia, even compared with South Carolina. In the best and greatest of Virginians, the virtues which always stood in most prominence were those of the field and farm—the simple and straightforward mind, the notions of courage and truth, the absence of mercantile sharpness and quickness, the rusticity and open-handed hospitality, which could exist only where the struggle for life was hardly a struggle at all. No visitor could resist the charm of kindly sympathy which softened the asperities of Virginian ambition. Whether young Albert Gallatin went there, hesitating between Europe and America, or the still younger William Ellery Channing, with all New England on his active conscience, the effect was the same—

I blush for my own people [wrote Channing from Richmond in 1799] when I compare the selfish prudence of a Yankee with

Vol. I, Chap. V.

the generous confidence of a Virginian. Here I find great vices, but greater virtues than I left behind me. There is one single trait which attaches me to the people I live with more than all the virtues of New England—they *love money less* than we do; they are more disinterested; their patriotism is not tied to their purse-strings. Could I only take from the Virginians their sensuality and their slaves, I should think them the greatest people in the world. As it is, with a few great virtues, they have innumerable vices.

Even forty years afterward, so typical a New Englander as the poet Bryant acknowledged that "whatever may be the comparison in other respects, the South certainly has the advantage over us in point of manners." Manners were not all their charm; for the Virginians at the close of the eighteenth century were inferior to no class of Americans in the sort of education then supposed to make refinement. The Duc de Liancourt bore witness—

In spite of the Virginian love for dissipation, the taste for reading is commoner there among men of the first class than in any other part of America; but the populace is perhaps more ignorant there than elsewhere.

Those whom Liancourt called "men of the first class" were equal to any standard of excellence known to history. Their range was narrow, but within it they were supreme. The traditions of high breeding were still maintained, and a small England, much as it existed in the time of the Commonwealth, was perpetuated in the Virginia of 1800. Social position was a birthright, not merely of the well born, but of the highly gifted. Nearly all the great lawyers of Virginia were of the same social stock as in New England—poor and gifted men, welcomed into a landed aristocracy simple in tastes and genial in temper. Chief-Justice Marshall was such a man, commanding respect and regard wherever he was seen—perhaps most of all from New Englanders, who were least familiar with the type. George Mason was an ideal republican—a character as strong in its way as Washington or Marshall. George Wythe the Chancellor stood in the same universal esteem; and even his young clerk

Henry Clay, "the mill-boy of the slashes," who had lately left
Chancellor Wythe's office to set up one of his own at Lexington
in Kentucky, inherited that Virginia geniality which, as it rip-
ened with his years, made him an idol among Northern and
Western multitudes who knew neither the source nor secret of
his charm. Law and politics were the only objects of Virginian
thought; but within these bounds the Virginians achieved triumphs. What could America offer in legal literature that
rivalled the judicial opinions of Chief-Justice Marshall? What
political essay equalled the severe beauty of George Mason's
Virginia Bill of Rights? What single production of an American pen reached the fame of Thomas Jefferson's Declaration of
Independence? "The Virginians are the best orators I ever
heard," wrote the young Channing; although Patrick Henry,
the greatest of them all, was no longer alive.

Every one admitted that Virginia society was ill at ease. In
colonial days it rested on a few great props, the strongest being
its close connection with England; and after this had been cut
away by the Revolutionary War, primogeniture, the Church, ex-
emption of land from seizure for debt, and negro slavery remained to support the oligarchy of planters. The momentum
given by the Declaration of Independence enabled Jefferson and
George Wythe to sweep primogeniture from the statute book.
After an interval of several years, Madison carried the law
which severed Church from State. There the movement ended.
All the great Virginians would gladly have gone on, but the
current began to flow against them. They suggested a bill for
emancipation, but could find no one to father it in the legislature, and they shrank from the storm it would excite.

President Washington, in 1796, in a letter already quoted,
admitted that land in Virginia was lower in price than land of
the same quality in Pennsylvania. For this inferiority he suggested, among other reasons, the explanation that Pennsylvania had made laws for the gradual abolition of slavery, and he
declared nothing more certain than that Virginia must adopt
similar laws at a period not remote. Had the Virginians seen a

sure prospect that such a step would improve their situation,
they would probably have taken it; but the slave-owners were
little pleased at the results of reforms already effected, and
they were in no humor for abolishing more of their old institutions. The effects of disestablishing the Church were calculated
to disgust them with all reform. From early times the colony
had been divided into parishes, and each parish owned a church
building. The system was the counterpart of that established
in New England. The church lands, glebes, and endowments
were administered by the clergyman, wardens, and vestry. Good
society in Virginia recognized no other religion than was taught
in this branch of English episcopacy. "Sure I am of one thing,"
was the remark in the Virginia legislature of an old-fashioned
Federalist, with powdered hair, three-cornered hat, long queue,
and white top-boots—"Sure I am of one thing, that no *gentleman* would choose any road to heaven but the Episcopal."
Every plantation was attached to a parish, and the earliest associations of every well-bred man and woman in Virginia were
connected with the Church service. In spite of all this, no sooner
had Madison and his friends taken away the support of the
State than the Church perished. They argued that freedom of
religion worked well in Pennsylvania, and therefore must succeed in Virginia; but they were wrong. The Virginia gentry
stood by and saw their churches closed, the roofs rot, the aisles
and pews become a refuge for sheep and foxes, the tombstones
of their ancestry built into strange walls or turned into flagging
to be worn by the feet of slaves. By the year 1800, Bishop Madison found his diocese left so nearly bare of clergy and com-
municants that after a few feeble efforts to revive interest he
abandoned the struggle, and contented himself with the hum-
bler task of educating boys at the ancient College of William
and Mary in the deserted colonial capital of Williamsburg.
There the English traveller Weld visited him about the year
1797, and gave a curious picture of his establishment—

The Bishop [he said] is president of the college, and has
apartments in the building. Half-a-dozen or more of the stu-

dents, the eldest about twelve years old, dined at his table one day that I was there. Some were without shoes or stockings, others without coats. During dinner they constantly rose to help themselves at the sideboard. A couple of dishes of salted meat and some oyster-soup formed the whole of the dinner.

Such a state of society was picturesque, but not encouraging. An aristocracy so lacking in energy and self-confidence was a mere shell, to be crushed, as one might think, by a single vigorous blow. Nevertheless, Jefferson and Madison, after striking it again and again with the full force of Revolutionary violence, were obliged to desist, and turned their reforming axes against the Church and hierarchy of New England. There they could do nothing but good, for the society of New England was sound, whatever became of the Church or of slavery; but in Virginia the gap which divided gentry from populace was enormous; and another gap, which seemed impassable, divided the populace from the slaves. Jefferson's reforms crippled and impoverished the gentry, but did little for the people, and for the slaves nothing.

Nowhere in America existed better human material than in the middle and lower classes of Virginians. As explorers, adventurers, fighters—wherever courage, activity, and force were wanted—they had no equals; but they had never known discipline, and were beyond measure jealous of restraint. With all their natural virtues and indefinite capacities for good, they were rough and uneducated to a degree that shocked their own native leaders. Jefferson tried in vain to persuade them that they needed schools. Their character was stereotyped, and development impossible; for even Jefferson, with all his liberality of ideas, was Virginian enough to discourage the introduction of manufactures and the gathering of masses in cities, without which no new life could grow. Among the common people, intellectual activity was confined to hereditary commonplaces of politics, resting on the axiom that Virginia was the typical society of a future Arcadian America. To escape the tyranny of Cæsar by perpetuating the simple and isolated lives of their fathers was the sum of their political philosophy; to fix upon the national government the stamp of their own idyllic conservatism was the height of their ambition.

Debarred from manufacturing, possessed of no shipping, and enjoying no domestic market, Virginian energies necessarily knew no other resource than agriculture. Without church, university, schools, or literature in any form that required or fostered intellectual life, the Virginians concentrated their thoughts almost exclusively upon politics; and this concentration produced a result so distinct and lasting, and in character so respectable, that American history would lose no small part of its interest in losing the Virginia school.

No one denied that Virginia, like Massachusetts, in the War of Independence, believed herself competent to follow independently of other provinces whatever path seemed good. The Constitution of Virginia did not, like that of Massachusetts, authorize the governor to "be the commander-in-chief of the army and navy," in order "to take and surprise, by all ways and means whatsoever, all and every such person or persons (with their ships, arms, ammunition, and other goods) as shall in a hostile manner invade or attempt the invading, conquering, or annoying this Commonwealth"; but although Massachusetts expressed the power in language more detailed, Virginia held to its essence with equal tenacity. When experience showed the necessity of "creating a more perfect union," none of the great States were unanimous for the change. Massachusetts and New York were with difficulty induced to accept the Constitution of 1787. Their final assent was wrung from them by the influence of the cities and of the commercial class; but Virginia contained no cities and few merchants. The majority by which the State Convention of Virginia, after an obstinate contest, adopted the Constitution, was influenced by pure patriotism as far as any political influence could be called pure; but the popular majority was probably hostile to the Constitution, and certainly remained hostile to the exercise of its powers. From the first the State took an attitude of opposition to the national government, which became more and more decided, until in 1798 it found expression in a formal announcement, through the legislature and governor, that the limit of further obedience was at hand. The General Assembly adopted Resolutions promising support to the government of the United States in all measures warranted by the Constitution, but declaring the powers of the federal government "no further valid than they are authorized by the grants enumerated in that compact; and that in case of a deliberate, palpable, and dangerous exercise of other powers, not granted by said compact, the States who are parties thereto have the right, and are in duty bound, to interpose, for arresting the progress of the evil and for maintaining within their respective limits the authorities, rights, and liberties appertaining to them."

Acting immediately on this view, the General Assembly did interpose by declaring certain laws, known as the Alien and Sedition Laws, unconstitutional, and by inviting the other States to concur, in confidence "that the necessary and proper measures will be taken by each for co-operating with this State in maintaining unimpaired the authorities, rights, and liberties reserved to the States respectively or to the people."

These Virginia Resolutions, which were drawn by Madison, seemed strong enough to meet any possible aggression from the national government; but Jefferson, as though not quite satisfied with these, recommended the Kentucky legislature to adopt still stronger. The draft of the Kentucky Resolutions, whether originally composed or only approved by him, representing certainly his own convictions, declared that "where powers are assumed which have not been delegated a nullification of the Act is the rightful remedy," and "that every State has a natural right, in cases not within the compact, to nullify of their own authority all assumptions of power by others within their limits." Jefferson did not doubt "that the co-States, recurring to their natural right in cases not made federal, will concur in declaring these acts void and of no force, and will each take measures of its own for providing that neither these acts, nor any others of the federal government not plainly and intentionally authorized by the Constitution, shall be exercised within their respective territories."

In the history of Virginia thought, the personal opinions of Jefferson and Madison were more interesting, if not more important, than the official opinion of State legislatures. Kentucky shrank from using language which seemed unnecessarily violent, but still declared, with all the emphasis needed, that the national government was not "the exclusive or final judge of the extent of the powers delegated to itself, since that would have made its discretion, and not the Constitution, the measure of its powers," but that each party had an equal right to judge for itself as to an infraction of the compact, and the proper redress; that in the case of the Alien and Sedition Laws the compact had been infringed, and that these Acts, being unconstitutional and therefore void, "may tend to drive these States into revolution and blood;" finally, the State of Kentucky called for an expression of sentiment from other States, like Virginia not doubting "that the co-States, recurring to their natural right in cases not made federal, will concur in declaring these Acts void and of no force."

These famous Resolutions of Virginia and Kentucky, historically the most interesting of all the intellectual products of the Virginia school, were adopted in 1798 and 1799. In 1800, Jefferson their chief author was chosen President of the United States, and Madison became his Secretary of State. Much discussion then and afterward arose over the Constitutional theory laid down by Virginia and Kentucky, and thus apparently adopted by the Union; but in such cases of disputed powers that theory was soundest which was backed by the strongest force, for the sanction of force was the most necessary part of law. The United States government was at that time powerless to enforce its theories; while, on the other hand, Virginia had all the power necessary for the object desired. The Republican leaders believed that the State was at liberty to withdraw from the Union if it should think that an infraction of the Constitution had taken place; and Jefferson in 1798 preferred to go on by way of Resolution rather than by way of Secession, not because of any doubt as to the right, but because, "if we now reduce our Union to Virginia and North Carolina, immediately the conflict will be established between those two States, and they will end by breaking into their simple units." In other letters he explained that the Kentucky Resolutions were intended "to leave the matter in such a train as that we may not be committed absolutely to push the matter to extremities, and yet may be free to push as far as events will render prudent." Union was a question of expediency, not of obligation. This was the conviction of the true Virginia school, and of Jefferson's opponents as well as his supporters; of Patrick Henry, as well as John Taylor of Caroline and John Randolph of Roanoke.

The Virginia and Kentucky Resolutions, giving form to ideas that had not till then been so well expressed, left a permanent mark in history, and fixed for an indefinite time the direction and bounds of Virginia politics; but if New England could go no further in the lines of thought pursued by Fisher Ames and Timothy Dwight, Virginia could certainly expect no better results from those defined by Jefferson and Madison. The science of politics, if limited by the Resolutions of Virginia and Kentucky, must degenerate into an enumeration of powers reserved from exercise. Thought could find little room for free development where it confined its action to narrowing its own field.

This tendency of the Virginia school was the more remarkable because it seemed little suited to the tastes and instincts of the two men who gave it expression and guided its course. By common consent Thomas Jefferson was its intellectual leader. According to the admitted standards of greatness, Jefferson was a great man. After all deductions on which his enemies might choose to insist, his character could not be denied elevation, versatility, breadth, insight, and delicacy; but neither as a politician nor as a political philosopher did he seem at ease in the atmosphere which surrounded him. As a leader of democracy he appeared singularly out of place. As reserved as President Washington in the face of popular familiarities, he never showed himself in crowds. During the last thirty years of his life he was not seen in a Northern city, even during his Presidency; nor indeed was he seen at all except on horseback, or by his friends and visitors in his own house. With manners apparently popular and informal, he led a life of his own, and allowed few persons to share it. His tastes were for that day excessively refined. His instincts were those of a liberal European nobleman, like the Duc de Liancourt, and he built for himself at Monticello a château above contact with man. The rawness of political life was an incessant torture to him, and personal attacks made him keenly unhappy. His true delight was in an intellectual life of science and art. To read, write, speculate in new lines of thought, to keep abreast of the intellect of Europe, and to feed upon Homer and Horace, were pleasures more to his mind than any to be found in a public assembly. He had some knowledge of mathematics, and a little acquaintance with classical art; but he fairly revelled in what he believed to be beautiful, and his writings often betrayed subtle feeling for artistic form—a sure mark of intellectual sensuousness. He shrank from whatever was rough or coarse, and his yearning for sympathy was almost feminine. That such a man should have ventured upon the stormy ocean of politics was surprising, the more because he was no orator, and owed nothing to any magnetic influence of voice or person. Never effective in debate, for seventeen years before his Presidency he had not appeared in a legislative body except in the chair of the Senate. He felt a nervous horror for the contentiousness of such assemblies, and even among his own friends he sometimes abandoned for the moment his strongest convictions rather than support them by an effort of authority.

If Jefferson appeared ill at ease in the position of a popular leader, he seemed equally awkward in the intellectual restraints of his own political principles. His mind shared little in common with the provincialism on which the Virginia and Kentucky Resolutions were founded. His instincts led him to widen rather than to narrow the bounds of every intellectual exercise; and if vested with political authority, he could no more resist the temptation to stretch his powers than he could abstain from using his mind on any subject merely because he might be drawn upon ground supposed to be dangerous. He was a deist, believing that men could manage their own salvation without the help of a state church. Prone to innovation, he sometimes generalized without careful analysis. He was a theorist, prepared to risk the fate of mankind on the chance of reasoning far from certain in its details. His temperament was sunny and sanguine, and the atrabilious philosophy of New England was intolerable to him. He was curiously vulnerable, for he seldom wrote a page without exposing himself to attack. He was superficial in his knowledge, and a martyr to the disease of omniscience. Ridicule of his opinions and of himself was an easy task, in which his Federalist opponents delighted, for his English was often confused, his assertions inaccurate, and at times of excitement he was apt to talk with indiscretion; while with all his extraordinary versatility of character and opinions, he seemed during his entire life to breathe with perfect satisfaction nowhere except in the liberal, literary, and scientific air of Paris in 1789.

Jefferson aspired beyond the ambition of a nationality, and embraced in his view the whole future of man. That the United States should become a nation like France, England, or Russia, should conquer the world like Rome, or develop a typical race like the Chinese, was no part of his scheme. He wished to begin a new era. Hoping for a time when the world's ruling interests should cease to be local and should become universal; when questions of boundary and nationality should become insignificant; when armies and navies should be reduced to the work of police, and politics should consist only in nonintervention—he set himself to the task of governing, with this golden age in view. Few men have dared to legislate as though

eternal peace were at hand, in a world torn by wars and convulsions and drowned in blood; but this was what Jefferson
aspired to do. Even in such dangers, he believed that Americans
might safely set an example which the Christian world should
be led by interest to respect and at length to imitate. As he
conceived a true American policy, war was a blunder, an unnecessary risk; and even in case of robbery and aggression the
United States, he believed, had only to stand on the defensive
in order to obtain justice in the end. He would not consent to
build up a new nationality merely to create more navies and
armies, to perpetuate the crimes and follies of Europe; the
central government at Washington should not be permitted
to indulge in the miserable ambitions that had made the Old
World a hell, and frustrated the hopes of humanity.

With these humanitarian ideas which passed beyond the
bounds of nationality, Jefferson held other views which seemed
narrower than ordinary provincialism. Cities, manufactures,
mines, shipping, and accumulation of capital led, in his opinion,
to corruption and tyranny.

Generally speaking [said he, in his only elaborate work, the
Notes on Virginia] the proportion which the aggregate of the
other classes of citizens bears in any State to that of its hus-
bandmen is the proportion of its unsound to its healthy parts,
and is a good enough barometer whereby to measure its degree
of corruption. . . . Those who labor in the earth are the chosen
people of God if ever he had a chosen people, whose breasts
he has made his peculiar deposit for substantial and genuine
virtue.

This doctrine was not original with Jefferson, but its application to national affairs on a great scale was something new
in the world, and the theory itself clashed with his intellectual
instincts of liberality and innovation.

A school of political thought, starting with postulates like
these, was an interesting study, and would have been more
interesting had Jefferson's friends undertaken to develop his
ideas in the extent he held them. Perhaps this was impossible.

At all events, Madison, although author of the Virginia Resolutions, showed little earnestness in carrying out their principles either as a political or as a literary task; and John Taylor of Caroline, the only consistent representative of the school, began his writings only when political power had established precedents inconsistent with their object.

With such simple conceptions as their experience gave them in politics, law, and agriculture, the Virginians appeared to be satisfied; and whether satisfied or not, they were for the time helpless to produce other literature, science, or art. From the three States lying farther south, no greater intellectual variety could be expected. In some respects North Carolina, though modest in ambition and backward in thought, was still the healthiest community south of the Potomac. Neither aristocratic like Virginia and South Carolina, nor turbulent like Georgia, nor troubled by a sense of social importance, but above all thoroughly democratic, North Carolina tolerated more freedom of political action and showed less family and social influence, fewer vested rights in political power, and less tyranny of slaveholding interests and terrors than were common elsewhere in the South. Neither cultivated nor brilliant in intellect, nor great in thought, industry, energy, or organization, North Carolina was still interesting and respectable. The best qualities of the State were typified in its favorite representative, Nathaniel Macon.

The small society of rice and cotton planters at Charleston, with their cultivated tastes and hospitable habits, delighted in whatever reminded them of European civilization. They were travellers, readers, and scholars; the society of Charleston compared well in refinement with that of any city of its size in the world, and English visitors long thought it the most agreeable in America. In the southern wilderness which stretched from the Appomattox to the St. Mary's, Charleston was the only oasis. The South Carolinians were ambitious for other distinctions than those which could be earned at the bar or on the plantation. From there Washington Allston went to study at

Harvard College, and after taking his degree in the same class with young Buckminster, sailed in the same year, 1800, for Europe with his friend Malbone, to learn to express in color and form the grace and dignity of his imagination. In South Carolina were felt the instincts of city life. During two or three weeks of the winter, the succession of dinners, balls, and races at Charleston rivalled the gayety of Philadelphia itself; and although the city was dull during the rest of the year, it was not deserted even in the heat of summer, for the sea-breeze made it a watering-place, like Boston, and the deadly fevers sure to kill the white man who should pass a night on one bank of the Ashley River were almost unknown on the other. In the summer, therefore, the residents remained or returned; the children got their schooling, and business continued. For this reason South Carolina knew less of the country hospitality which made Virginia famous; city life had the larger share in existence, although in the hot weather torpor and languor took the place of gayety. In certain respects Charleston was more Northern in habits than any town of the North. In other warm countries, the summer evening was commonly the moment when life was best worth living; music, love-making, laughter, and talk turned night into day; but Charleston was Puritanic in discipline. Every night at ten o'clock the slamming of window-blinds and locking of doors warned strangers and visitors to go not only to their houses, but to their beds. The citizens looked with contempt on the gayety of Spanish or Italian temper. Beneath all other thoughts, the care of the huge slave population remained constant. The streets were abandoned at an early hour to the patrol, and no New England village was more silent.

Confident as the Carolinian was in the strength of the slave-system, and careless as he seemed and thought himself to be on that account, the recent fate of St. Domingo gave him cause for constant anxiety; but even without anxiety, he would have been grave. The gentry of the lower country belonged to the same English class which produced the gentry of Virginia and

Massachusetts. The austerity of the Puritan may have been an exaggerated trait, but among the Middletons, Pinkneys, Rutledges, and Lowndeses the seriousness of the original English stock was also not without effect in the habit of their minds. They showed it in their treatment of the slave-system, but equally in their churches and houses, their occupations and prejudices, their races and sports, the character of their entertainments, the books they read, and the talk at their tables. No gentleman belonged to any church but the Anglican, or connected himself with trade. No court departed from the practice and precedents of English law, however anomalous they might be. Before the Revolution large numbers of young men had been educated in England, and their influence was still strong in the society of Charleston. The younger generation inherited similar tastes. Of this class the best-known name which will appear in this narrative was that of William Lowndes; and no better example could be offered of the serious temper which marked Carolinian thought, than was given by the career of this refined and highly educated gentleman, almost the last of his school.

Charleston was more cosmopolitan than any part of Virginia, and enjoyed also a certain literary reputation on account of David Ramsay, whose works were widely read; and of Governor Drayton, whose "Letters written during a Tour through the Northern and Eastern States," and "View of South Carolina," gave an idea of the author as well as of the countries he described. Charleston also possessed a library of three or four thousand well-selected books, and maintained a well-managed theatre. The churches were almost as strictly attended as those in Boston. The fashionable wine-party was even more common, and perhaps the guests took pride in drinking deeper than they would have been required to do in New York or Philadelphia.

Politics had not mastered the thought of South Carolina so completely as that of Virginia, and the natural instincts of Carolinian society should have led the gentry to make common cause with the gentry of New England and the Middle States against democratic innovations. The conservative side in politics seemed to be that which no Carolinian gentleman could fail to support. The oligarchy of South Carolina, in defiance of democratic principles, held the political power of the State, and its interests could never harmonize with those of a theoretic democracy, or safely consent to trust the national government in the hands of Jefferson and his friends, who had founded their power by breaking down in Virginia an oligarchy closely resembling that of the Carolinian rice-planters. Yet in 1800 enough of these gentlemen, under the lead of Charles Pinckney, deserted their Northern friends, to secure the defeat of the Federalist candidates, and to elect Jefferson as President. For this action, no satisfactory reason was ever given. Of all States in the Union, South Carolina, under its actual system of politics, was the last which could be suspected of democratic tendencies.

Such want of consistency seemed to show some peculiarity of character. Not every educated and privileged class has sacrificed itself to a social sentiment, least of all without understanding its object. The eccentricity was complicated by another peculiar element of society. In South Carolina the interesting union between English tastes and provincial prejudices, which characterized the wealthy planters of the coast, was made more striking by contrast with the character of the poor and hardy yeomanry of the upper country. The seriousness of Charleston society changed to severity in the mountains. Rude, ignorant, and in some of its habits half barbarous, this population, in the stiffness of its religious and social expression, resembled the New England of a century before rather than the liberality of the Union. Largely settled by Scotch and Irish emigrants, with the rigid Presbyterian doctrine and conservatism of their class, they were democratic in practice beyond all American democrats, and were more conservative in thought than the most aristocratic Europeans. Though sharply divided both socially and by interest from the sea-coast planters, these up-country farmers had one intellectual sympathy with their fellow-citizens in Charleston—a sympathy resting on their common dislike for change, on the serious element which lay at the root of their common characters; and this marriage of two widely divergent minds produced one of the most extraordinary statesmen of America. In the year 1800 John Caldwell Calhoun, a boy of eighteen, went from the upper country to his brother-in-law's academy in Georgia. Grown nearly to manhood without contact with the world, his modes of thought were those of a Connecticut Calvinist; his mind was cold, stern, and metaphysical; but he had the energy and ambition of youth, the political fervor of Jeffersonian democracy, and little sympathy with slavery or slave-owners. At this early age he, like many other Republicans, looked on slavery as a "scaffolding," to be taken down when the building should be complete. A radical democrat, less liberal, less cultivated, and much less genial than Jefferson, Calhoun was the true heir to his intellectual succession; stronger in logic, bolder in action. Upon him was to fall the duty of attempting to find for Carolina an escape from the logical conclusions of those democratic principles which Jefferson in 1800 claimed for his own, but which in the full swing of his power, and to the last day of his life, he shrank from pressing to their results.

Viewed from every side by which it could be approached, the society of South Carolina, more than that of any other portion of the Union, seemed to bristle with contradictions. The elements of intellectual life existed without a sufficient intellectual atmosphere. Society, colonial by origin and dependent by the conditions of its existence, was striving to exist without external support. Whether it would stand or fall, and whether, either standing or falling, it could contribute any new element to American thought, were riddles which, with so many others, American history was to answer.

American Ideals

NEARLY every foreign traveller who visited the United States during these early years, carried away an impression sober if not sad. A thousand miles of desolate and dreary forest, broken here and there by settlements; along the sea-coast a few flourishing towns devoted to commerce; no arts, a provincial literature, a cancerous disease of negro slavery, and differences of political theory fortified within geographical lines—what could be hoped for such a country except to repeat the story of violence and brutality which the world already knew by heart, until repetition for thousands of years had wearied and sickened mankind? Ages must probably pass before the interior could be thoroughly settled; even Jefferson, usually a sanguine man, talked of a thousand years with acquiescence, and in his first Inaugural Address, at a time when the Mississippi River formed the Western boundary, spoke of the country as having "room enough for our descendants to the hundredth and thousandth generation." No prudent person dared to act on the certainty that when settled, one government could comprehend the whole; and when the day of separation should arrive, and America should have her Prussia, Austria, and Italy, as she already had her England, France, and Spain, what else could follow but a return to the old conditions of local jealousies, wars, and corruption which had made a slaughter-house of Europe?

The mass of Americans were sanguine and self-confident, partly by temperament, but partly also by reason of ignorance; for they knew little of the difficulties which surrounded a complex society. The Duc de Liancourt, like many critics, was struck by this trait. Among other instances, he met with one in the person of a Pennsylvania miller, Thomas Lea, "a sound American patriot, persuading himself that nothing good is done, and that no one has any brains, except in America; that the wit, the imagination, the genius of Europe are already in

Vol. I, Chap. VI.

decrepitude"; and the duke added: "This error is to be found in almost all Americans—legislators, administrators, as well as millers, and is less innocent there." In the year 1796 the House of Representatives debated whether to insert in the Reply to the President's Speech a passing remark that the nation was "the freest and most enlightened in the world"—a nation as yet in swaddling-clothes, which had neither literature, arts, sciences, nor history; nor even enough nationality to be sure that it was a nation. The moment was peculiarly ill-chosen for such a claim, because Europe was on the verge of an outburst of genius. Goethe and Schiller, Mozart and Haydn, Kant and Fichte, Cavendish and Herschel were making way for Walter Scott, Wordsworth, and Shelley, Heine and Balzac, Beethoven and Hegel, Oersted and Cuvier, great physicists, biologists, geologists, chemists, mathematicians, metaphysicians, and historians by the score. Turner was painting his earliest landscapes, and Watt completing his latest steam-engine; Napoleon was taking command of the French armies, and Nelson of the English fleets; investigators, reformers, scholars, and philosophers swarmed, and the influence of enlightenment, even amid universal war, was working with an energy such as the world had never before conceived. The idea that Europe was in her decrepitude proved only ignorance and want of enlightenment, if not of freedom, on the part of Americans, who could only excuse their error by pleading that notwithstanding these objections, in matters which for the moment most concerned themselves Europe was a full century behind America. If they were right in thinking that the next necessity of human progress was to lift the average man upon an intellectual and social level with the most favored, they stood at least three generations nearer than Europe to their common goal. The destinies of the United States were certainly staked, without reserve or escape, on the soundness of this doubtful and even improbable principle, ignoring or overthrowing the institutions of church, aristocracy, family, army, and political intervention, which long experience had shown to be needed for the safety of society. Europe might be right in thinking that without such safeguards society must come to an end; but even Europeans must concede that there was a chance, if no greater than one in a thousand, that America might, at least for a time, succeed. If this stake of temporal and eternal welfare stood on the winning card; if man actually should become more virtuous and enlightened, by mere process of growth, without church or paternal authority; if the average human being could accustom himself to reason with the logical processes of Descartes and Newton!—what then?

Then, no one could deny that the United States would win a stake such as defied mathematicians. With all the advantages of science and capital, Europe must be slower than America to reach the common goal. American society might be both sober and sad, but except for negro slavery it was sound and healthy in every part. Stripped for the hardest work, every muscle firm and elastic, every ounce of brain ready for use, and not a trace of superfluous flesh on his nervous and supple body, the American stood in the world a new order of man. From Maine to Florida, society was in this respect the same, and was so organized as to use its human forces with more economy than could be approached by any society of the world elsewhere. Not only were artificial barriers carefully removed, but every influence that could appeal to ordinary ambition was applied. No brain or appetite active enough to be conscious of stimulants could fail to answer the intense incentive. Few human beings, however sluggish, could long resist the temptation to acquire power; and the elements of power were to be had in America almost for the asking. Reversing the old-world system, the American stimulant increased in energy as it reached the lowest and most ignorant class, dragging and whirling them upward as in the blast of a furnace. The penniless and homeless Scotch or Irish immigrant was caught and consumed by it; for every stroke of the axe and the hoe made him a capitalist, and made gentlemen of his children. Wealth was the strongest agent for moving the mass of mankind; but political power was hardly less tempting to the more intelligent and better-educated swarms of American-born citizens, and the instinct of activity, once created, seemed heritable and permanent in the race.

Compared with this lithe young figure, Europe was actually in decrepitude. Mere class distinctions, the *patois* or dialect of the peasantry, the fixity of residence, the local costumes and habits marking a history that lost itself in the renewal of identical generations, raised from birth barriers which paralyzed half the population. Upon this mass of inert matter rested the Church and the State, holding down activity of thought. Endless wars withdrew many hundred thousand men from production, and changed them into agents of waste; huge debts, the evidence of past wars and bad government, created interests to support the system and fix its burdens on the laboring class; courts, with habits of extravagance that shamed common-sense, helped to consume private economies. All this might have been borne; but behind this stood aristocracies, sucking their nourishment from industry, producing nothing themselves, employing little or no active capital or intelligent labor, but pressing on the energies and ambition of society with the weight of an incubus. Picturesque and entertaining as these social anomalies were, they were better fitted for the theatre or for a museum of historical costumes than for an active workshop preparing to compete with such machinery as America would soon command. From an economical point of view, they were as incongruous as would have been the appearance of a mediaeval knight in helmet and armor, with battle-axe and shield, to run the machinery of Arkwright's cotton-mill; but besides their bad economy they also tended to prevent the rest of society from gaining a knowledge of its own capacities. In Europe, the conservative habit of mind was fortified behind power. During nearly a century Voltaire himself—the friend of kings, the wit and poet, historian and philosopher of his age—had carried on, in daily terror, in exile and excommunication, a protest against an intellectual despotism contemptible even to its own supporters. Hardly was Voltaire dead, when Priestley, as great a man if not so great a wit, trying to do for England what Voltaire tried to do for France, was mobbed by the people of Birmingham and driven to America. Where Voltaire and Priestley failed, common men could not struggle; the weight of society stifled their thought. In America the balance between conservative and liberal forces was close; but in Europe conservatism held the physical power of government. In Boston a young Buckminster might be checked for a time by his father's prayers or commands in entering the path that led toward freer thought; but youth beckoned him on, and every reward that society could offer was dangled before his eyes. In London or Paris, Rome, Madrid, or Vienna, he must have sacrificed the worldly prospects of his life.

Granting that the American people were about to risk their future on a new experiment, they naturally wished to throw aside all burdens of which they could rid themselves. Believing that in the long run interest, not violence, would rule the world, and that the United States must depend for safety and success on the interests they could create, they were tempted to look upon war and preparations for war as the worst of blunders; for they were sure that every dollar capitalized in industry was a means of overthrowing their enemies more effective than a thousand dollars spent on frigates or standing armies. The success of the American system was, from this point of view, a question of economy. If they could relieve themselves from debts, taxes, armies, and government interference with industry, they must succeed in outstripping Europe in economy of production; and Americans were even then partly aware that if their machine were not so weakened by these economies as to break down in the working, it must of necessity break down every rival. If their theory was sound, when the day of competition should arrive, Europe might choose between American and Chinese institutions, but there would be no middle path; she might become a confederated democracy, or a wreck.

Whether these ideas were sound or weak, they seemed self-evident to those Northern democrats who, like Albert Gallatin, were comparatively free from slave-owning theories, and understood the practical forces of society. If Gallatin wished to reduce the interference of government to a minimum, and cut down expenditures to nothing, he aimed not so much at saving money as at using it with the most certain effect. The revolution of 1800 was in his eyes chiefly political, because it was social; but as a revolution of society, he and his friends hoped to make it the most radical that had occurred since the downfall of the Roman empire. Their ideas were not yet cleared by experience, and were confused by many contradictory prejudices, but wanted neither breadth nor shrewdness.

Many apparent inconsistencies grew from this undeveloped form of American thought, and gave rise to great confusion in the different estimates of American character that were made both at home and abroad.

That Americans should not be liked was natural; but that they should not be understood was more significant by far. After the downfall of the French republic they had no right to expect a kind word from Europe, and during the next twenty years they rarely received one. The liberal movement of Europe was cowed, and no one dared express democratic sympathies until the Napoleonic tempest had passed. With this attitude Americans had no right to find fault, for Europe cared less to injure them than to protect herself. Nevertheless, observant readers could not but feel surprised that none of the numerous Europeans who then wrote or spoke about America seemed to study the subject seriously. The ordinary traveller was apt to be little more reflective than a bee or an ant, but some of these critics possessed powers far from ordinary; yet Talleyrand alone showed that had he but seen America a few years later than he did, he might have suggested some sufficient reason for apparent contradictions that perplexed him in the national character. The other travellers—great and small, from the Duc de Liancourt to Basil Hall, a long and suggestive list —were equally perplexed. They agreed in observing the contradictions, but all, including Talleyrand, saw only sordid motives. Talleyrand expressed extreme astonishment at the apathy of Americans in the face of religious sectarians; but he explained it by assuming that the American ardor of the moment was absorbed in money-making. The explanation was evidently insufficient, for the Americans were capable of feeling and showing excitement, even to their great pecuniary injury, as they frequently proved; but in the foreigner's range of observation, love of money was the most conspicuous and most common trait of American character. "There is, perhaps, no civilized country in the world," wrote Felix de Beaujour, soon after 1800, "where there is less generosity in the souls, and in the heads fewer of those illusions which make the charm or the consolation of life. Man here weighs everything, calculates everything, and sacrifices everything to his interest." An Englishman named Fearon, in 1818, expressed the same idea with more distinctness: "In going to America, I would say generally, the emigrant must expect to find, not an economical or cleanly people; not a social or generous people; not a people of enlarged ideas; not a people of liberal opinions, or toward whom you can express your thoughts free as air; not a people friendly to the advocates of liberty in Europe; not a people who understand liberty from investigation and principle; not a people who comprehend the meaning of the words 'honor' and 'generosity.' " Such quotations might be multiplied almost without limit. Rapacity was the accepted explanation of American peculiarities; yet every traveller was troubled by inconsistencies that required explanations of a different kind. "It is not in order to hoard that the Americans are rapacious," observed Liancourt as early as 1796. The extravagance, or what economical Europeans thought extravagance, with which American women were allowed and encouraged to spend money, was as notorious in 1790 as a century later; the recklessness with which Americans often risked their money, and the liberality with which they used it, were marked even then, in comparison with the ordinary European habit. Europeans saw such contradictions, but made no attempt to reconcile them. No foreigner of that day—neither poet, painter, nor philosopher—could detect in American life any-

thing higher than vulgarity; for it was something beyond the
range of their experience, which education and culture had not
framed a formula to express. Moore came to Washington, and
found there no loftier inspiration than any Federalist rhymester
of Dennie's school.

> Take Christians, Mohawks, democrats and all,
> From the rude wigwam to the Congress hall—
> From man the savage, whether slaved or free,
> To man the civilized, less tame than he:
> 'T is one dull chaos, one unfertile strife
> Betwixt half-polished and half-barbarous life;
> Where every ill the ancient world can brew
> Is mixed with every grossness of the new;
> Where all corrupts, though little can entice,
> And nothing 's known of luxury but vice.

Moore's two small volumes of Epistles, printed in 1807, contained much more so-called poetry of the same tone—poetry
more polished and less respectable than that of Barlow and
Dwight; while, as though to prove that the Old World knew
what grossness was, he embalmed in his lines the slanders which
the Scotch libeller Callender invented against Jefferson—

> The weary statesman for repose hath fled
> From halls of council to his negro's shed;
> Where, blest, he woos some black Aspasia's grace,
> And dreams of freedom in his slave's embrace.

To leave no doubt of his meaning, he explained in a footnote
that his allusion was to the President of the United States;
and yet even Moore, trifler and butterfly as he was, must have
seen, if he would, that between the morals of politics and society in America and those then prevailing in Europe, there
was no room for comparison—there was room only for contrast.

Moore was but an echo of fashionable England in his day.
He seldom affected moral sublimity; and had he in his wan-
derings met a race of embodied angels, he would have sung
of them or to them in the slightly erotic notes which were so
well received in the society he loved to frequent and flatter.

His remarks upon American character betrayed more temper than truth; but even in this respect he expressed only the common feeling of Europeans, which was echoed by the Federalist society of the United States. Englishmen especially indulged in unbounded invective against the sordid character of American society, and in shaping their national policy on this contempt they carried their theory into practice with so much energy as to produce its own refutation. To their astonishment and anger, a day came when the Americans, in defiance of self-interest and in contradiction of all the qualities ascribed to them, insisted on declaring war; and readers of this narrative will be surprised at the cry of incredulity, not unmixed with terror, with which Englishmen started to their feet when they woke from their delusion on seeing what they had been taught to call the meteor flag of England, which had burned terrific at Copenhagen and Trafalgar, suddenly waver and fall on the bloody deck of the "Guerriere." Fearon and Beaujour, with a score of other contemporary critics, could see neither generosity, economy, honor, nor ideas of any kind in the American breast; yet the obstinate repetition of these denials itself betrayed a lurking fear of the social forces whose strength they were candid enough to record. What was it that, as they complained, turned the European peasant into a new man within half an hour after landing at New York? Englishmen were never at a loss to understand the poetry of more prosaic emotions. Neither they nor any of their kindred failed in later times to feel the "large excitement" of the country boy, whose "spirit leaped within him to be gone before him," when the lights of London first flared in the distance; yet none seemed ever to feel the larger excitement of the American immigrant. Among the Englishmen who criticised the United States was one greater than Moore—one who thought himself at home only in the stern beauty of a moral presence. Of all poets, living or dead, Wordsworth felt most keenly what he called the still, sad music of humanity; yet the highest conception he could create of America was not more poetical than that of any Cumberland beggar he might have met in his morning walk—

> Long-wished-for sight, the Western World appeared;
> And when the ship was moored, I leaped ashore
> Indignantly—resolved to be a man,
> Who, having o'er the past no power, would live
> No longer in subjection to the past,
> With abject mind—from a tyrannic lord
> Inviting penance, fruitlessly endured.
> So, like a fugitive whose feet have cleared
> Some boundary which his followers may not cross
> In prosecution of their deadly chase,
> Respiring, I looked round. How bright the sun,
> The breeze how soft! Can anything produced
> In the Old World compare, thought I, for power
> And majesty, with this tremendous stream
> Sprung from the desert? And behold a city
> Fresh, youthful, and aspiring! . . .
>   Sooth to say,
> On nearer view, a motley spectacle
> Appeared, of high pretensions—unreproved
> But by the obstreperous voice of higher still;
> Big passions strutting on a petty stage,
> Which a detached spectator may regard
> Not unamused. But ridicule demands
> Quick change of objects; and to laugh alone,
> . . . in the very centre of the crowd
> To keep the secret of a poignant scorn,
>   . . . is least fit
> For the gross spirit of mankind.

Thus Wordsworth, although then at his prime, indulging in what sounded like a boast that he alone had felt the sense sublime of something interfused, whose dwelling is the light of setting suns, and the round ocean, and the living air, and the blue sky, and in the mind of man—even he, to whose moods the heavy and the weary weight of all this unintelligible world was lightened by his deeper sympathies with nature and the soul, could do no better, when he stood in the face of American democracy, than "keep the secret of a poignant scorn."

Possibly the view of Wordsworth and Moore, of Weld, Dennie, and Dickens was right. The American democrat possessed little art of expression, and did not watch his own emotions with a view of uttering them either in prose or verse; he never told more of himself than the world might have assumed without listening to him. Only with diffidence could history attribute to such a class of men a wider range of thought or feeling than they themselves cared to proclaim. Yet the difficulty of denying or even ignoring the wider range was still greater, for no one questioned the force or the scope of an emotion which caused the poorest peasant in Europe to see what was invisible to poet and philosopher—the dim outline of a mountain-summit across the ocean, rising high above the mist and mud of American democracy. As though to call attention to some such difficulty, European and American critics, while affirming that Americans were a race without illusions or enlarged ideas, declared in the same breath that Jefferson was a visionary whose theories would cause the heavens to fall upon them. Year after year, with endless iteration, in every accent of contempt, rage, and despair, they repeated this charge against Jefferson. Every foreigner and Federalist agreed that he was a man of illusions, dangerous to society and unbounded in power of evil; but if this view of his character was right, the same visionary qualities seemed also to be a national trait, for every one admitted that Jefferson's opinions, in one form or another, were shared by a majority of the American people.

Illustrations might be carried much further, and might be drawn from every social class and from every period in national history. Of all presidents, Abraham Lincoln has been considered the most typical representative of American society, chiefly because his mind, with all its practical qualities, also inclined, in certain directions, to idealism. Lincoln was born in 1809, the moment when American character stood in lowest esteem. Ralph Waldo Emerson, a more distinct idealist, was born in 1803. William Ellery Channing, another idealist, was born in 1780. Men like John Fitch, Oliver Evans, Robert Fulton, John Barlow, John Stevens, and Eli Whitney were all classed among visionaries. The whole society of Quakers belonged in the same category. The records of the popular religious sects abounded in examples of idealism and illusion to such an extent that the masses seemed hardly to find comfort or hope in any authority, however old or well established. In religion as in politics, Americans seemed to require a system which gave play to their imagination and their hopes.

Some misunderstanding must always take place when the observer is at cross-purposes with the society he describes. Wordsworth might have convinced himself by a moment's thought that no country could act on the imagination as America acted upon the instincts of the ignorant and poor, without some quality that deserved better treatment than poignant scorn; but perhaps this was only one among innumerable cases in which the unconscious poet breathed an atmosphere which the self-conscious poet could not penetrate. With equal reason he might have taken the opposite view—that the hard, practical, money-getting American democrat, who had neither generosity nor honor nor imagination, and who inhabited cold shades where fancy sickened and where genius died, was in truth living in a world of dream, and acting a drama more instinct with poetry than all the avatars of the East, walking in gardens of emerald and rubies, in ambition already ruling the world and guiding Nature with a kinder and wiser hand than had ever yet been felt in human history. From this point his critics never approached him—they stopped at a stone's throw; and at the moment when they declared that the man's mind had no illusions, they added that he was a knave or a lunatic. Even on his practical and sordid side, the American might easily have been represented as a victim to illusion. If the Englishman had lived as the American speculator did—in the future—the hyperbole of enthusiasm would have seemed less monstrous. "Look at my wealth!" cried the American to his foreign visitor. "See these solid mountains of salt and iron, of lead, copper, silver, and gold! See these mag-

nificent cities scattered broadcast to the Pacific! See my cornfields rustling and waving in the summer breeze from ocean to
ocean, so far that the sun itself is not high enough to mark
where the distant mountains bound my golden seas! Look at
this continent of mine, fairest of created worlds, as she lies
turning up to the sun's never-failing caress her broad and exuberant breasts, overflowing with milk for her hundred million
children! See how she glows with youth, health, and love!"
Perhaps it was not altogether unnatural that the foreigner, on
being asked to see what needed centuries to produce, should
have looked about him with bewilderment and indignation.
"Gold! cities! cornfields! continents! Nothing of the sort! I see
nothing but tremendous wastes, where sickly men and women
are dying of home-sickness or are scalped by savages! moun-
tain-ranges a thousand miles long, with no means of getting to
them, and nothing in them when you get there! swamps and
forests choked with their own rotten ruins! nor hope of better
for a thousand years! Your story is a fraud, and you are a liar
and swindler!"

Met in this spirit, the American, half perplexed and half
defiant, retaliated by calling his antagonist a fool, and by
mimicking his heavy tricks of manner. For himself he cared
little, but his dream was his whole existence. The men who
denounced him admitted that they left him in his forest-swamp
quaking with fever, but clinging in the delirium of death to
the illusions of his dazzled brain. No class of men could be
required to support their convictions with a steadier faith, or
pay more devotedly with their persons for the mistakes of
their judgment. Whether imagination or greed led them to
describe more than actually existed, they still saw no more
than any inventor or discoverer must have seen in order to
give him the energy of success. They said to the rich as to the
poor, "Come and share our limitless riches! Come and help
us bring to light these unimaginable stores of wealth and
power!" The poor came, and from them were seldom heard
complaints of deception or delusion. Within a moment, by the

mere contact of a moral atmosphere, they saw the gold and jewels, the summer cornfields and the glowing continent. The rich for a long time stood aloof—they were timid and narrow-minded; but this was not all—between them and the American democrat was a gulf.

The charge that Americans were too fond of money to win the confidence of Europeans was a curious inconsistency; yet this was a common belief. If the American deluded himself and led others to their death by baseless speculations; if he buried those he loved in a gloomy forest where they quaked and died while he persisted in seeing there a splendid, healthy, and well-built city—no one could deny that he sacrificed wife and child to his greed for gain, that the dollar was his god, and a sordid avarice his demon. Yet had this been the whole truth, no European capitalist would have hesitated to make money out of his grave; for, avarice against avarice, no more sordid or meaner type existed in America than could be shown on every 'Change in Europe. With much more reason Americans might have suspected that in America Englishmen found everywhere a silent influence, which they found nowhere in Europe, and which had nothing to do with avarice or with the dollar, but, on the contrary, seemed likely at any moment to sacrifice the dollar in a cause and for an object so illusory that most Englishmen could not endure to hear it discussed. European travellers who passed through America noticed that everywhere, in the White House at Washington and in log-cabins beyond the Alleghanies, except for a few Federalists, every American, from Jefferson and Gallatin down to the poorest squatter, seemed to nourish an idea that he was doing what he could to overthrow the tyranny which the past had fastened on the human mind. Nothing was easier than to laugh at the ludicrous expressions of this simple-minded conviction, or to cry out against its coarseness, or grow angry with its prejudices; to see its nobler side, to feel the beating of a heart underneath the sordid surface of a gross humanity, was not so easy. Europeans seemed seldom or never conscious that the sentiment could possess a noble side, but found only matter for complaint in the remark that every American democrat believed himself to be working for the overthrow of tyranny, aristocracy, hereditary privilege, and priesthood, wherever they existed. Even where the American did not openly proclaim this conviction in words, he carried so dense an atmosphere of the sentiment with him in his daily life as to give respectable Europeans an uneasy sense of remoteness.

Of all historical problems, the nature of a national character is the most difficult and the most important. Readers will be troubled, at almost every chapter of the coming narrative, by the want of some formula to explain what share the popular imagination bore in the system pursued by government. The acts of the American people during the administrations of Jefferson and Madison were judged at the time by no other test. According as bystanders believed American character to be hard, sordid, and free from illusion, they were severe and even harsh in judgment. This rule guided the governments of England and France. Federalists in the United States, knowing more of the circumstances, often attributed to the democratic instinct a visionary quality which they regarded as sentimentality, and charged with many bad consequences. If their view was correct, history could occupy itself to no better purpose than in ascertaining the nature and force of the quality which was charged with results so serious; but nothing was more elusive than the spirit of American democracy. Jefferson, the literary representative of the class, spoke chiefly for Virginians, and dreaded so greatly his own reputation as a visionary that he seldom or never uttered his whole thought. Gallatin and Madison were still more cautious. The press in no country could give shape to a mental condition so shadowy. The people themselves, although millions in number, could not have expressed their finer instincts had they tried, and might not have recognized them if expressed by others.

In the early days of colonization, every new settlement rep-

resented an idea and proclaimed a mission. Virginia was
founded by a great, liberal movement aiming at the spread of
English liberty and empire. The Pilgrims of Plymouth, the
Puritans of Boston, the Quakers of Pennsylvania, all avowed
a moral purpose, and began by making institutions that consciously reflected a moral idea. No such character belonged to
the colonization of 1800. From Lake Erie to Florida, in long,
unbroken line, pioneers were at work, cutting into the forests
with the energy of so many beavers, and with no more express
moral purpose than the beavers they drove away. The civilization they carried with them was rarely illumined by an idea;
they sought room for no new truth, and aimed neither at creating, like the Puritans, a government of saints, nor, like the
Quakers, one of love and peace; they left such experiments behind them, and wrestled only with the hardest problems of
frontier life. No wonder that foreign observers, and even the
educated, well-to-do Americans of the sea-coast, could seldom
see anything to admire in the ignorance and brutality of frontiersmen, and should declare that virtue and wisdom no longer
guided the United States! What they saw was not encouraging.
To a new society, ignorant and semi-barbarous, a mass of dema-
gogues insisted on applying every stimulant that could inflame
its worst appetites, while at the same instant taking away every
influence that had hitherto helped to restrain its passions.
Greed for wealth, lust for power, yearning for the blank void
of savage freedom such as Indians and wolves delighted in—
these were the fires that flamed under the caldron of American
society, in which, as conservatives believed, the old, well-proven,
conservative crust of religion, government, family, and even
common respect for age, education, and experience was rapidly
melting away, and was indeed already broken into fragments,
swept about by the seething mass of scum ever rising in greater
quantities to the surface.

Against this Federalist and conservative view of democratic
tendencies, democrats protested in a thousand forms, but never

in any mode of expression which satisfied them all, or explained their whole character. Probably Jefferson came nearest to the mark, for he represented the hopes of science as well as the prejudices of Virginia; but Jefferson's writings may be searched from beginning to end without revealing the whole measure of the man, far less of the movement. Here and there in his letters a suggestion was thrown out, as though by chance, revealing larger hopes—as in 1815, at a moment of despondency, he wrote: "I fear from the experience of the last twenty-five years that morals do not of necessity advance hand in hand with the sciences." In 1800, in the flush of triumph, he believed that his task in the world was to establish a democratic republic, with the sciences for an intellectual field, and physical and moral advancement keeping pace with their advance. Without an excessive introduction of more recent ideas, he might be imagined to define democratic progress, in the somewhat affected precision of his French philosophy: "Progress is either physical or intellectual. If we can bring it about that men are on the average an inch taller in the next generation than in this; if they are an inch larger round the chest; if their brain is an ounce or two heavier, and their life a year or two longer—that is progress. If fifty years hence the average man shall invariably argue from two ascertained premises where he now jumps to a conclusion from a single supposed revelation—that is progress! I expect it to be made here, under our democratic stimulants, on a great scale, until every man is potentially an athlete in body and an Aristotle in mind." To this doctrine the New Englander replied, "What will you do for moral progress?" Every possible answer to this question opened a chasm. No doubt Jefferson held the faith that men would improve morally with their physical and intellectual growth; but he had no idea of any moral improvement other than that which came by nature. He could not tolerate a priesthood, a state church, or revealed religion. Conservatives, who could tolerate no society without such pillars of order, were, from their point of view, right in answering. "Give us rather the worst despotism of Europe—there our souls at least may have a chance of salvation!" To their minds vice and virtue were not relative, but fixed terms. The Church was a divine institution. How could a ship hope to reach port when the crew threw overboard sails, spars, and compass, unshipped their rudder, and all the long day thought only of eating and drinking. Nay, even should the new experiment succeed in a worldly sense, what was a man profited if he gained the whole world, and lost his own soul? The Lord God was a jealous God, and visited the sins of the parents upon the children; but what worse sin could be conceived than for a whole nation to join their chief in chanting the strange hymn with which Jefferson, a new false prophet, was deceiving and betraying his people: "It does me no injury for my neighbor to say there are twenty Gods or no God!"

On this ground conservatism took its stand, as it had hitherto done with success in every similar emergency in the world's history, and fixing its eyes on moral standards of its own, refused to deal with the subject as further open to argument. The two parties stood facing opposite ways, and could see no common ground of contact.

Yet even then one part of the American social system was proving itself to be rich in results. The average American was more intelligent than the average European, and was becoming every year still more active-minded as the new movement of society caught him up and swept him through a life of more varied experiences. On all sides the national mind responded to its stimulants. Deficient as the American was in the machinery of higher instruction; remote, poor; unable by any exertion to acquire the training, the capital, or even the elementary textbooks he needed for a fair development of his natural powers —his native energy and ambition already responded to the spur applied to them. Some of his triumphs were famous throughout the world; for Benjamin Franklin had raised high the reputation of American printers, and the actual President of the United States, who signed with Franklin the treaty of peace with Great Britain, was the son of a small farmer, and had himself kept school in his youth. In both these cases social recognition followed success; but the later triumphs of the American mind were becoming more and more popular. John Fitch was not only one of the poorest, but one of the least-educated Yankees who ever made a name; he could never spell with tolerable correctness, and his life ended as it began—in the lowest social obscurity. Eli Whitney was better educated than Fitch, but had neither wealth, social influence, nor patron to back his ingenuity. In the year 1800 Eli Terry, another Connecticut Yankee of the same class, took into his employ two young men to help him make wooden clocks, and this was the capital on which the greatest clock-manufactory in the world began its operations. In 1797 Asa Whittemore, a Massachusetts Yankee, invented a machine to make cards for carding wool, which "operated as if it had a soul," and became the foundation for a hundred subsequent patents. In 1790 Jacob Perkins, of Newburyport, invented a machine capable of cutting and turning out two hundred thousand nails a day; and then invented a process for transferring engraving from a very small steel cylinder to copper, which revolutionized cotton-printing. The British traveller Weld, passing through Wilmington, stopped, as Liancourt had done before him, to see the great flour-mills on the Brandywine. "The improvements," he said, "which have been made in the machinery of the flour-mills in America are very great. The chief of these consist in a new application of the screw, and the introduction of what are called elevators, the idea of which was evidently borrowed from the chain-pump." This was the invention of Oliver Evans, a native of Delaware, whose parents were in very humble life, but who was himself, in spite of every disadvantage, an inventive genius of the first order. Robert Fulton, who in 1800 was in Paris with Joel Barlow, sprang from the same source in Pennsylvania. John Stevens, a native of New York, belonged to a more favored class, but followed the same impulses. All these men were the outcome of typical American society, and all their inventions transmuted the democratic instinct into a practical and tangible shape. Who would undertake to say that there was a limit to the fecundity of this teeming source? Who that saw only the narrow, practical, money-getting nature of these devices could venture to assert that as they wrought their end and raised the standard of millions, they would not also raise the creative power of those millions to a higher plane? If the priests and barons who set their names to Magna Charta had been told that in a few centuries every swine-herd and cobbler's apprentice would write and read with an ease such as few kings could then command, and reason with better logic than any university could then practise, the priest and baron would have been more incredulous than any man who was told in 1800 that within another five centuries the ploughboy would go a-field whistling a sonata of Beethoven, and figure out in quaternions the relation of his furrows. The American democrat knew so little of art that among his popular illusions he could not then nourish artistic ambition; but leaders like Jefferson, Gallatin, and Barlow might without extravagance count upon a coming time when diffused ease and education should bring the masses into familiar contact with higher forms of human achievement, and their vast creative power, turned toward a nobler culture, might rise to the level of that democratic genius which found expression in the Parthenon; might revel in the delights of a new Buonarotti and a richer Titian; might create for five hundred million people the America of thought and art which alone could satisfy their omnivorous ambition.

Whether the illusions, so often affirmed and so often denied to the American people, took such forms or not, these were in effect the problems that lay before American society: Could it transmute its social power into the higher forms of thought? Could it provide for the moral and intellectual needs of mankind? Could it take permanent political shape? Could it give new life to religion and art? Could it create and maintain in the mass of mankind those habits of mind which had hitherto belonged to men of science alone? Could it physically develop the convolutions of the human brain? Could it produce, or was it compatible with, the differentiation of a higher variety of the human race? Nothing less than this was necessary for its complete success.

Narrative

WITH *chapter 7 Adams begins his narrative.*

The Inauguration

THE man who mounted the steps of the Capitol, March 4, 1801, to claim the place of an equal between Pitt and Bonaparte, possessed a character which showed itself in acts; but person and manner can be known only by contemporaries, and the liveliest description was worth less than a moment of personal contact. Jefferson was very tall, six feet two-and-a-half inches in height; sandy-complexioned; shy in manner, seeming cold; awkward in attitude, and with little in his bearing that suggested command. Senator Maclay of Pennsylvania described him in 1790, when he had returned from France to become Secretary of State, and appeared before a Committee of the Senate to answer questions about foreign relations.

Jefferson is a slender man [wrote the senator]; has rather the air of stiffness in his manner. His clothes seem too small for him. He sits in a lounging manner, on one hip commonly, and with one of his shoulders elevated much above the other. His face has a sunny aspect. His whole figure has a loose, shackling air. He had a rambling, vacant look, and nothing of the firm collected deportment which I expected would dignify the presence of a secretary or minister. I looked for gravity, but a laxity of manner seemed shed about him. He spoke almost without ceasing; but even his discourse partook of his personal demeanor. It was loose and rambling; and yet he scattered information wherever he went, and some even brilliant sentiments sparkled from him.

Maclay was one of the earliest members of the Republican party, and his description was not unfriendly. Augustus Foster, Secretary of the British Legation, described Jefferson as he appeared in 1804—

He was a tall man, with a very red freckled face, and gray neglected hair; his manners good-natured, frank, and rather friendly, though he had somewhat of a cynical expression of countenance. He wore a blue coat, a thick gray-colored hairy waistcoat, with a red under-waistcoat lapped over it, green velveteen breeches with pearl buttons, yarn stockings, and

Vol. I, Chap. VII.

slippers down at the heels—his appearance being very much like that of a tall, large-boned farmer.

In the middle of the seventeenth century the celebrated Cardinal de Retz formed a judgment of the newly-elected Pope from his remark, at a moment when minds were absorbed in his election, that he had for two years used the same pen. "It is only a trifle," added De Retz, "but I have often observed that the smallest things are sometimes better marks than the greatest." Perhaps dress could never be considered a trifle. One of the greatest of modern writers first made himself famous by declaring that society was founded upon *cloth;* and Jefferson, at moments of some interest in his career as President, seemed to regard his peculiar style of dress as a matter of political importance, while the Federalist newspapers never ceased ridiculing the corduroy small-clothes, red-plush waistcoat, and sharp-toed boots with which he expressed his contempt for fashion.

For eight years this tall, loosely built, somewhat stiff figure, in red waistcoat and yarn stockings, slippers down at the heel, and clothes that seemed too small for him, may be imagined as Senator Maclay described him, sitting on one hip, with one shoulder high above the other, talking almost without ceasing to his visitors at the White House. His skin was thin, peeling from his face on exposure to the sun, and giving it a tettered appearance. This sandy face, with hazel eyes and sunny aspect; this loose, shackling person; this rambling and often brilliant conversation, belonged to the controlling influences of American history, more necessary to the story than three-fourths of the official papers, which only hid the truth. Jefferson's personality during these eight years appeared to be the government, and impressed itself, like that of Bonaparte, although by a different process, on the mind of the nation. In the village simplicity of Washington he was more than a king, for he was alone in social as well as in political pre-eminence. Except the British Legation, no house in Washington was open to general society; the whole mass of politicians, even the Federalists, were dependent

on Jefferson and "The Palace" for amusement; and if they refused to go there, they "lived like bears, brutalized and stupe-
fied."

Jefferson showed his powers at their best in his own house,
where among friends as genial and cheerful as himself his ideas
could flow freely, and could be discussed with sympathy. Such
were the men with whom he surrounded himself by choice, and
none but such were invited to enter his Cabinet. First and oldest of his political associates was James Madison, about to become Secretary of State, whose character also described itself,
and whose personality was as distinct as that of his chief. A
small man, quiet, somewhat precise in manner, pleasant, fond
of conversation, with a certain mixture of ease and dignity in
his address, Madison had not so much as Jefferson of the commanding attitude which imposed respect on the world. "He has
much more the appearance of what I have imagined a Roman
cardinal to be," wrote Senator Mills of Massachusetts in 1815.
An imposing presence had much to do with political influence,
and Madison labored under serious disadvantage in the dryness
of his personality. Political opponents of course made fun of
him. "As to Jemmy Madison—oh, poor Jemmy!—he is but a
withered little apple-john," wrote Washington Irving in 1812,
instinctively applying the Knickerbocker view of history to
national concerns.

In his dress [said one who knew him] he was not at all ec-
centric or given to dandyism, but always appeared neat and
genteel, and in the costume of a well-bred and tasty old-school
gentleman. I have heard in early life he sometimes wore light-
colored clothes; but from the time I first knew him . . . never
any other color than black, his coat being cut in what is termed
dress-fashion; his breeches short, with buckles at the knees,
black silk stockings, and shoes with strings, or long fair top-
boots when out in cold weather, or when he rode on horseback,
of which he was fond. . . . He wore powder on his hair, which
was dressed full over the ears, tied behind, and brought to a
point above the forehead, to cover in some degree his baldness,
as may be noticed in all the likenesses taken of him.

Madison had a sense of humor, felt in his conversation, and detected in the demure cast of his flexible lips, but leaving no trace in his published writings. Small in stature, in deportment modest to the point of sensitive reserve, in address simple and pleasing, in feature rather thoughtful and benevolent than strong, he was such a man as Jefferson, who so much disliked contentious and self-asserting manners, loved to keep by his side. Sir Augustus Foster liked Mr. Madison, although in 1812 Madison sent him out of the country—

I thought Mr. Jefferson more of a statesman and man of the world than Mr. Madison, who was rather too much the disputatious pleader; yet the latter was better informed, and moreover a social, jovial, and good-humored companion, full of anecdote, sometimes rather of a loose description, but oftener of a political and historical interest. He was a little man with small features, rather wizened when I saw him, but occasionally lit up with a good-natured smile. He wore a black coat, stockings with shoes buckled, and had his hair powdered, with a tail.

The third aristocrat in this democratic triumvirate was Albert Gallatin, marked by circumstances even more than by the President's choice for the post of Secretary of the Treasury. Like the President and the Secretary of State, Gallatin was born and bred a gentleman; in person and manners he was well fitted for the cabinet-table over which Jefferson presided. Gallatin possessed the personal force which was somewhat lacking in his two friends. His appearance impressed by-standers with a sense of strength. His complexion was dark; his eyes were hazel and full of expression; his hair black, and like Madison he was becoming bald. From long experience, at first among the democrats of western Pennsylvania, and afterward as a leader in the House of Representatives, he had lost all shyness in dealing with men. His long prominent nose and lofty forehead showed character, and his eyes expressed humor. A slight foreign accent betrayed his Genevan origin. Gallatin was also one of the best talkers in America, and perhaps the best-informed man in the country; for his laborious mind had studied

America with infinite care, and he retained so much knowledge of European affairs as to fit him equally for the State Department or the Treasury. Three more agreeable men than Jefferson, Madison, and Gallatin were never collected round the dinner-table of the White House; and their difference in age was enough to add zest to their friendship; for Jefferson was born in 1743, Madison in 1751, and Gallatin in 1761. While the President was nearly sixty years old, his Secretary of the Treasury had the energy and liberality of forty.

Jefferson was the first President inaugurated at Washington, and the ceremony, necessarily simple, was made still simpler for political reasons. The retiring President was not present at the installation of his successor. In Jefferson's eyes a revolution had taken place as vast as that of 1776; and if this was his belief, perhaps the late President was wise to retire from a stage where everything was arranged to point a censure upon his principles, and where he would have seemed, in his successor's opinion, as little in place as George III. would have appeared at the installation of President Washington. The collapse of government which marked the last weeks of February, 1801, had been such as to leave of the old Cabinet only Samuel Dexter of Massachusetts, the Secretary of the Treasury, and Benjamin Stoddert of Maryland, the Secretary of the Navy, still in office. John Marshall, the late Secretary of State, had been appointed, six weeks before, Chief-Justice of the Supreme Court.

In this first appearance of John Marshall as Chief-Justice, to administer the oath of office, lay the dramatic climax of the inauguration. The retiring President, acting for what he supposed to be the best interests of the country, by one of his last acts of power, deliberately intended to perpetuate the principles of his administration, placed at the head of the judiciary, for life, a man as obnoxious to Jefferson as the bitterest New England Calvinist could have been; for he belonged to that class of conservative Virginians whose devotion to President Washington, and whose education in the common law, caused them to hold Jefferson and his theories in antipathy. The new President and his two Secretaries were political philanthropists, bent on restricting the powers of the national government in the interests of human liberty. The Chief-Justice, a man who in grasp of mind and steadiness of purpose had no superior, perhaps no equal, was bent on enlarging the powers of government in the interests of justice and nationality. As they stood face to face on this threshhold of their power, each could foresee that the contest between them would end only with life.

If Jefferson and his two friends were the most aristocratic of democrats, John Marshall was of all aristocrats the most democratic in manners and appearance.

A tall, slender figure [wrote Joseph Story in 1808], not graceful or imposing, but erect and steady. His hair is black, his eyes small and twinkling, his forehead rather low; but his features are in general harmonious. His manners are plain yet dignified, and an unaffected modesty diffuses itself through all his actions. His dress is very simple yet neat; his language chaste, but hardly elegant; it does not flow rapidly, but it seldom wants precision. In conversation he is quite familiar, but is occasionally embarrassed by a hesitancy and drawling. . . . I love his laugh—it is too hearty for an intriguer; and his good temper and unwearied patience are equally agreeable on the bench and in the study.

The unaffected simplicity of Marshall's life was delightful to all who knew him, for it sprang from the simplicity of his mind. Never self-conscious, his dignity was never affected by his situation. Bishop Meade, who was proud of the Chief-Justice as one of his flock, being in a street near Marshall's house one morning between daybreak and sunrise, met the Chief-Justice on horseback, with a bag of clover-seed lying before him, which he was carrying to his little farm at seed-time. Simple as American life was, his habits were remarkable for modest plainness; and only the character of his mind, which seemed to have no flaw, made his influence irresistible upon all who were brought within its reach.

Nevertheless this great man nourished one weakness. Pure

in life; broad in mind, and the despair of bench and bar for the unswerving certainty of his legal method; almost idolized by those who stood nearest him, and loving warmly in return—this excellent and amiable man clung to one rooted prejudice: he detested Thomas Jefferson. He regarded with quiet, unspoken, but immovable antipathy the character and doings of the philosopher standing before him, about to take the oath to preserve, protect, and defend the Constitution. No argument or entreaty affected his conviction that Jefferson was not an honest man. "By weakening the office of President he will increase his personal power," were Marshall's words, written at this time; "the morals of the author of the letter to Mazzei cannot be pure." Jefferson in return regarded Marshall with a repugnance tinged by a shade of some deeper feeling, almost akin to fear. "The judge's inveteracy is profound," he once wrote, "and his mind of that gloomy malignity which will never let him forego the opportunity of satiating it on a victim."

Another person, with individuality not less marked, took the oath of office the same day. When the Senate met at ten o'clock on the morning of March 4, 1801, Aaron Burr stood at the desk, and having duly sworn to support the Constitution, took his seat in the chair as Vice-President. This quiet, gentlemanly, and rather dignified figure, hardly taller than Madison, and dressed in much the same manner, impressed with favor all who first met him. An aristocrat imbued in the morality of Lord Chesterfield and Napoleon Bonaparte, Colonel Burr was the chosen head of Northern democracy, idol of the wards of New York city, and aspirant to the highest offices he could reach by means legal or beyond the law; for as he pleased himself with saying, after the manner of the First Consul of the French Republic, "Great souls care little for small morals." Among the other party leaders who have been mentioned—Jefferson, Madison, Gallatin, Marshall—not one was dishonest. The exaggerations or equivocations that Jefferson allowed himself, which led to the deep-rooted conviction of Marshall that he did not tell the truth and must therefore be dangerous, amounted to nothing when compared with the dishonesty of a corrupt man. Had the worst political charges against Jefferson been true, he would not have been necessarily corrupt. The self-deception inherent in every struggle for personal power was not the kind of immorality which characterized Colonel Burr. Jefferson, if his enemies were to be believed, might occasionally make misstatements of fact; yet he was true to the faith of his life, and would rather have abdicated his office and foregone his honors than have compassed even an imaginary wrong against the principles he professed. His life, both private and public, was pure. His associates, like Madison, Gallatin, and Monroe, were men upon whose reputations no breath of scandal rested. The standard of morality at Washington, both in private society and in politics, was respectable. For this reason Colonel Burr was a new power in the government; for being in public and in private life an adventurer of the same school as scores who were then seeking fortune in the antechambers of Bonaparte and Pitt, he became a loadstone for every other adventurer who frequented New York or whom the chances of politics might throw into office. The Vice-President wielded power, for he was the certain centre of corruption.

Thus when the doors of the Senate chamber were thrown open, and the new President of the United States appeared on the threshold; when the Vice-President rose from his chair, and Jefferson sat down in it, with Aaron Burr on his right hand and John Marshall on his left, the assembled senators looked up at three men who profoundly disliked and distrusted each other.

John Davis, one of many Englishmen who were allowed by Burr to attach themselves to him on the chance of some future benefit to be derived from them, asserted in a book of American travels published in London two years afterward, that he was present at the inauguration, and that Jefferson rode on horseback to the Capitol, and after hitching his horse to the palings, went in to take the oath. This story, being spread by the

Federalist newspapers, was accepted by the Republicans and became a legend of the Capitol. In fact Davis was not then at Washington, and his story was untrue. Afterward as President, Jefferson was in the habit of going on horseback, rather than in a carriage, wherever business called him, and the Federalists found fault with him for doing so. "He makes it a point," they declared, "when he has occasion to visit the Capitol to meet the representatives of the nation on public business, to go on a single horse, which he leads into the shed and hitches to a peg." Davis wished to write a book that should amuse Englishmen, and in order to give an air of truth to invention, he added that he was himself present at the ceremony. Jefferson was then living as Vice-President at Conrad's boarding-house, within a stone's throw of the Capitol. He did not mount his horse only to ride across the square and dismount in a crowd of observers. Doubtless he wished to offer an example of republican simplicity, and he was not unwilling to annoy his opponents; but the ceremony was conducted with proper form.

Edward Thornton, then in charge of the British Legation at Washington, wrote to Lord Grenville, then Foreign Secretary in Pitt's administration, a despatch enclosing the new President's Inaugural Address, with comments upon its democratic tendencies; and after a few remarks on this subject, he added—

The same republican spirit which runs through this performance, and which in many passages discovers some bitterness through all the sentiments of conciliation and philanthropy with which it is overcharged, Mr. Jefferson affected to display in performing the customary ceremonies. He came from his own lodgings to the House where the Congress convenes, and which goes by the name of the Capitol, on foot, in his ordinary dress, escorted by a body of militia artillery from the neighboring State, and accompanied by the Secretaries of the Navy and the Treasury, and a number of his political friends in the House of Representatives. He was received by Mr. Burr, the Vice-President of the United States, who arrived a day or two ago at the seat of government, and who was previously admitted this morning to the chair of the Senate; and was afterward complimented at his own lodgings by the very few foreign agents who reside at this place, by the members of Congress, and other public officials.

Only the north wing of the Capitol had then been so far completed as to be occupied by the Senate, the courts, and the small library of Congress. The centre rose not much above its foundations; and the south wing, some twenty feet in height, contained a temporary oval brick building, commonly called the "Oven," in which the House of Representatives sat in some peril of their lives, for had not the walls been strongly shored up from without, the structure would have crumbled to pieces. In the north wing the new President went, accompanied by the only remaining secretaries, Dexter and Stoddert, and by his friends from the House. Received by Vice-President Burr, and seated in the chair between Burr and Marshall, after a short pause Jefferson rose, and in a somewhat inaudible voice began his Inaugural Address.

Time, which has laid its chastening hand on many reputations, and has given to many once famous formulas a meaning unsuspected by their authors, has not altogether spared Jefferson's first Inaugural Address, although it was for a long time almost as well known as the Declaration of Independence; yet this Address was one of the few State Papers which should have lost little of its interest by age. As the starting-point of a powerful party, the first Inaugural was a standard by which future movements were measured, and it went out of fashion only when its principles were universally accepted or thrown aside. Even as a literary work, it possessed a certain charm of style peculiar to Jefferson, a flavor of Virginia thought and manners, a Jeffersonian ideality calculated to please the ear of later generations forced to task their utmost powers in order to carry the complex trains of their thought.

The chief object of the Address was to quiet the passions which has been raised by the violent agitation of the past eight years. Every interest of the new Administration required that the extreme Federalists should be disarmed. Their temper was such as to endanger both Administration and Union; and their power was still formidable, for they controlled New England and contested New York. To them, Jefferson turned—

Let us unite with one heart and one mind [he entreated]; let us restore to social intercourse that harmony and affection without which liberty and even life itself are but dreary things. And let us reflect, that, having banished from our land that religious intolerance under which mankind so long bled and suffered, we have yet gained little if we countenance a political intolerance as despotic, as wicked, and capable of as bitter and bloody persecutions. During the throes and convulsions of the ancient world, during the agonizing spasms of infuriated man, seeking through blood and slaughter his long-lost liberty, it was not wonderful that the agitation of the billows should reach even this distant and peaceful shore; that this should be more felt and feared by some than by others; that this should divide opinions as to measures of safety. But every difference of opinion is not a difference of principle. We are all Republicans, we are all Federalists.

The Federalist newspapers never ceased laughing at the "spasms" so suddenly converted into "billows," and at the orthodoxy of Jefferson's Federalism; but perhaps his chief fault was to belittle the revolution which had taken place. In no party sense was it true that all were Republicans or all Federalists. As will appear, Jefferson himself was far from meaning what he seemed to say. He wished to soothe the great body of his opponents, and if possible to win them over; but he had no idea of harmony or affection other than that which was to spring from his own further triumph; and in representing that he was in any sense a Federalist, he did himself a wrong.

I know, indeed [he continued], that some honest men fear that a republican government cannot be strong; that this government is not strong enough. But would the honest patriot in the full tide of successful experiment, abandon a government which has so far kept us free and firm, on the theoretic and visionary fear that this government, the world's best hope, may by possibility want energy to preserve itself? I trust not. I believe this, on the contrary, the strongest government on earth. I believe it is the only one where every man, at the call of the laws, would fly to the standard of the law, and would meet invasions of the public order as his own personal concern. Sometimes it is said that man cannot be trusted with the government of himself. Can he then be trusted with the government of others? Or have we found angels in the forms of kings to govern him? Let history answer this question!

That the government, the world's best hope, had hitherto kept the country free and firm, in the full tide of successful experiment, was a startling compliment to the Federalist party, coming as it did from a man who had not been used to compliment his political opponents; but Federalists, on the other hand, might doubt whether this government would continue to answer the same purpose when administered for no other avowed object than to curtail its powers. Clearly, Jefferson credited government with strength which belonged to society; and if he meant to practise upon this idea, by taking the tone of "the strongest government on earth" in the face of Bonaparte and Pitt, whose governments were strong in a different sense, he might properly have developed this idea at more length, for it was likely to prove deeply interesting. Moreover, history, if asked, must at that day have answered that no form of government, whether theocratic, autocratic, aristocratic, democratic, or mixed, had ever in Western civilization lasted long, without change or need of change. History was not the witness to which Republicans could with entire confidence appeal, even against kings.

The Address next enumerated the advantages which America enjoyed, and those which remained to be acquired—

With all these blessings, what more is necessary to make us a happy and prosperous people? Still one thing more, fellow-citizens—a wise and frugal government, which shall restrain men from injuring one another, which shall leave them otherwise free to regulate their own pursuits of industry and improvement, and shall not take from the mouth of labor the bread it has earned. This is the sum of good government, and this is necessary to close the circle of our felicities.

A government restricted to keeping the peace, which should

raise no taxes except for that purpose, seemed to be simply a judicature and a police. Jefferson gave no development to the idea further than to define its essential principles, and those which were to guide his Administration. Except the Kentucky and Virginia Resolutions of 1798, this short passage was the only official gloss ever given to the Constitution by the Republican party; and for this reason students of American history who would understand the course of American thought should constantly carry in mind not only the Constitutions of 1781 and of 1787, but also the Virginia and Kentucky resolutions, and the following paragraph of Jefferson's first Inaugural Address—

I will compress them [said the President], within the narrowest compass they will bear, stating the general principle, but not all its limitations. Equal and exact justice to all men, of whatever state or persuasion, religious or political; peace, commerce, and honest friendship with all nations, entangling alliances with none; the support of the State governments in all their rights, as the most competent administrations for our domestic concerns and the surest bulwarks against anti-republican tendencies; the preservation of the general government in its whole Constitutional vigor, as the sheet-anchor of our peace at home and safety abroad; a jealous care of the right of election by the People—a mild and safe corrective of abuses which are lopped by the sword of revolution where peaceable remedies are unprovided; absolute acquiescence in the decisions of the majority—the vital principle of republics, from which there is no appeal but to force, the vital principle and immediate parent of despotism; a well-disciplined militia—our best reliance in peace and for the first moments of war, till regulars may relieve them; the supremacy of the civil over the military authority; economy in the public expense, that labor may be lightly burdened; the honest payment of our debts, and sacred preservation of the public faith; encouragement of agriculture, and of commerce as its handmaid; the diffusion of information, and arraignment of all abuses at the bar of public reason; freedom of religion, freedom of the press, and freedom of person under the protection of the *habeas corpus;* and trial by juries impartially selected—these principles form the bright constellation which has gone before us and guided our steps through an age of revolution and reformation. The wisdom of our sages and the blood of our

heroes have been devoted to their attainment; they should be
the creed of our political faith, the text of civic instruction, the
touchstone by which to try the services of those we trust; and
should we wander from them in moments of error or alarm, let
us hasten to retrace our steps and to regain the road which alone
leads to peace, liberty, and safety.

From the metaphors in which these principles appeared as
a constellation, a creed, a text, a touchstone, and a road, the
world learned that they had already guided the American people through an age of revolution. In fact, they were mainly the
principles of President Washington, and had they been announced by a Federalist President, would have created little
remonstrance or surprise. In Jefferson's mouth they sounded
less familiar, and certain phrases seemed even out of place.

Among the cardinal points of republicanism thus proclaimed
to the world was one in particular, which as a maxim of government seemed to contradict cherished convictions and the fixed
practice of the Republican party. "Absolute acquiescence" was
required "in the decisions of the majority—the vital principle
of republics, from which there is no appeal but to force, the
vital principle and immediate parent of despotism." No principle was so thoroughly entwined in the roots of Virginia republicanism as that which affirmed the worthlessness of decisions made by a majority of the United States, either as a nation or a confederacy, in matters which concerned the exercise
of doubtful powers. Not three years had passed since Jefferson
himself penned the draft of the Kentucky Resolutions, in
which he declared "that in cases of an abuse of the delegated
powers, the members of the general government being chosen
by the people, a change by the people would be the Constitutional remedy; but where powers are assumed which have not
been delegated, a nullification of the act is the rightful remedy;
that every State has a natural right, in cases not within the
compact, to nullify of their own authority all assumptions of
power by others within their limits; that without this right they
would be under the dominion, absolute and unlimited, of whoso-

ever might exercise this right of judgment for them." He went so far as to advise that every State should forbid, within its borders, the execution of any act of the general government "not plainly and intentionally authorized by the Constitution;" and although the legislatures of Kentucky and Virginia softened the language, they acted on the principle so far as to declare certain laws of the United States unconstitutional, with the additional understanding that whatever was unconstitutional was void. So far from accepting with "absolute acquiescence" the decisions of the majority, Jefferson and his followers held that freedom could be maintained only by preserving inviolate the right of every State to judge for itself what was, and what was not, lawful for a majority to decide.

What, too, was meant by the words which pledged the new Administration to preserve the general government "in its whole Constitutional vigor"? The two parties were divided by a bottomless gulf in their theories of Constitutional powers; but until the precedents established by the Federalists should be expressly reversed, no one could deny that those precedents, to be treated as acts of the majority with absolute acquiescence, were a measure of the vigor which the President pledged himself to preserve. Jefferson could not have intended such a conclusion; for how could he promise to "preserve" the powers assumed in the Alien and Sedition laws, which then represented the whole vigor of the general government in fact if not in theory, when he had himself often and bitterly denounced those powers, when he had been a party to their nullification, and when he and his friends had actually prepared to resist by arms their enforcement? Undoubtedly Jefferson meant no more than to preserve the general government in such vigor as in his opinion was Constitutional, without regard to Federalist precedents; but his words were equivocal, and unless they were to be defined by legislation, they identified him with the contrary legislation of his predecessors. In history and law they did so. Neither the Alien nor the Sedition Act, nor any other Federalist precedent, was ever declared unconstitutional by any department of the general government; and Jefferson's pledge to preserve that government in its full Constitutional vigor was actually redeemed with no exception or limitation on the precedents established. His intention seemed to be different; but the sweeping language of his pledge was never afterward restricted or even more exactly defined while he remained in power.

Hence arose a sense of disappointment for future students of the Inaugural Address. A revolution had taken place; but the new President seemed anxious to prove that there had been no revolution at all. A new experiment in government was to be tried, and the philosopher at its head began by pledging himself to follow in the footsteps of his predecessors. Americans ended by taking him at his word, and by assuming that there was no break of continuity between his ideas and those of President Washington; yet even at the moment of these assurances he was writing privately in an opposite sense. In his eyes the past was wrong, both in method and intention; its work must be undone and its example forgotten. His conviction of a radical difference between himself and his predecessors was expressed in the strongest language. His predecessors, in his opinion, had involved the government in difficulties in order to destroy it, and to build up a monarchy on its ruins. "The tough sides of our Argosie," he wrote two days after his inauguration, "have been thoroughly tried. Her strength has stood the waves into which she was steered with a view to sink her. We shall put her on her Republican tack, and she will now show by the beauty of her motion the skill of her builders." "The Federalists," said he at one moment, "wished for everything which would approach our new government to a monarchy; the Republicans, to preserve it essentially republican. . . . The real difference consisted in their different degrees of inclination to monarchy or republicanism." "The revolution of 1800," he wrote many years afterward, "was as real a revolution in the principles of our government as that of 1776 was in its form."

Not, therefore, in the Inaugural Address, with its amiable

professions of harmony, could President Jefferson's full view of his own reforms be discovered. Judged by his inaugural addresses and annual messages, Jefferson's Administration seemed a colorless continuation of Washington's; but when seen in the light of private correspondence, the difference was complete. So strong was the new President's persuasion of the monarchical bent of his predecessors, that his joy at obtaining the government was mingled with a shade of surprise that his enemies should have handed to him, without question, the power they had so long held. He shared his fears of monarchy with politicians like William B. Giles, young John Randolph, and many Southern voters; and although neither Madison nor Gallatin seemed to think monarchists formidable, they gladly encouraged the President to pursue a conservative and conciliatory path. Jefferson and his Southern friends took power as republicans opposed to monarchists, not as democrats opposed to oligarchy. Jefferson himself was not in a social sense a democrat, and was called so only as a term of opprobrium. His Northern followers were in the main democrats; but he and most of his Southern partisans claimed to be republicans, opposed by secret monarchists.

The conflict of ideas between Southern republicanism, Northern democracy, and Federal monarchism marked much of Jefferson's writing; but especially when he began his career as President his mind was filled with the conviction that he had wrung power from monarchy, and that in this sense he was the founder of a new republic. Henceforward, as he hoped, republicanism was forever safe; he had but to conciliate the misguided, and give an example to the world, for centralization was only a monarchical principle. Nearly twenty years passed before he woke to a doubt on this subject; but even then he did not admit a mistake. In the tendency to centralization he still saw no democratic instinct, but only the influence of monarchical Federalists "under the pseudo-republican mask."

The republic which Jefferson believed himself to be founding or securing in 1801 was an enlarged Virginia—a society to be kept pure and free by the absence of complicated interests, by the encouragement of agriculture and of commerce as its handmaid, but not of industry in a larger sense. "The agricultural capacities of our country," he wrote long afterward, "constitute its distinguishing feature; and the adapting our policy and pursuits to that is more likely to make us a numerous and happy people than the mimicry of an Amsterdam, a Hamburg, or a city of London." He did not love mechanics or manufactures, or the capital without which they could not exist. "Banking establishments are more dangerous than standing armies," he said; and added, "that the principle of spending money to be paid by posterity, under the name of funding, is but swindling futurity on a large scale." Such theories were republican in the Virginia sense, but not democratic; they had nothing in common with the democracy of Pennsylvania and New England, except their love of freedom; and Virginia freedom was not the same conception as the democratic freedom of the North.

In 1801 this Virginia type was still the popular form of republicanism. Although the Northern democrat has already developed a tendency toward cities, manufactures, and "the mimicry of an Amsterdam, a Hamburg, or a city of London," while the republican of the South was distinguished by his dislike of every condition except that of agriculture, the two wings of the party had so much in common that they could afford to disregard for a time these divergencies of interest; and if the Virginians cared nothing for cities, banks, and manufactures, or if the Northern democrats troubled themselves little about the dangers of centralization, they could unite with one heart in overthrowing monarchy, and in effecting a social revolution.

Henceforward, as Jefferson conceived, government might act directly for the encouragement of agriculture and of commerce as its handmaid, for the diffusion of information and the arraignment of abuses; but there its positive functions stopped. Beyond that point only negative action remained—respect for States' rights, preservation of constitutional powers, economy, and the maintenance of a pure and simple society such as already existed. With a political system which would not take from the mouth of labor the bread it had earned, and which should leave men free to follow whatever paths of industry or improvement they might find most profitable, "the circle of felicities" was closed.

The possibility of foreign war alone disturbed this dream. President Washington himself might have been glad to accept these ideas of domestic politics, had not France, England, and Spain shown an unequivocal wish to take advantage of American weakness in arms in order to withhold rights vital to national welfare. How did Jefferson propose to convert a government of judiciary and police into the strongest government on earth? His answer to this question, omitted from the Inaugural Address, was to be found in his private correspondence and in the speeches of Gallatin and Madison as leaders of the opposition. He meant to prevent war. He was convinced that governments like human beings, were on the whole controlled by their interests, and that the interests of Europe required peace and free commerce with America. Believing a union of European Powers to be impossible, he was willing to trust their jealousies of each other to secure their good treatment of the United States. Knowing that Congress could by a single act divert a stream of wealth from one European country to another, foreign Governments would hardly challenge the use of such a weapon, or long resist their own overpowering interests. The new President found in the Constitutional power "to regulate commerce with foreign nations" the machinery for doing away with navies, armies, and wars.

During eight years of opposition the Republican party had matured its doctrines on this subject. In 1797, in the midst of difficulties with France, Jefferson wrote—

If we weather the present storm, I hope we shall avail ourselves of the calm of peace to place our foreign connections under a new and different arrangement. We must make the interest of every nation stand surety for their justice, and their own loss to follow injury to us, as effect follows its cause. As to everything except commerce, we ought to divorce ourselves from them all.

A few months before the inauguration, he wrote in terms more general—

The true theory of our Constitution is surely the wisest and best, that the States are independent as to everything within themselves, and united as to everything respecting foreign nations. Let the general government be reduced to foreign concerns only, and let our affairs be disentangled from those of all other nations, except as to commerce, which the merchants will manage the better the more they are free to manage for themselves, and our general government may be reduced to a very simple organization and a very unexpensive one—a few plain duties to be performed by a few servants.

Immediately after the inauguration the new President explained his future foreign policy to correspondents, who, as he knew, would spread his views widely throughout both continents. In a famous letter to Thomas Paine—a letter which was in some respects a true inaugural address—Jefferson told the thought he had but hinted in public. "Determined as we are to avoid, if possible, wasting the energies of our people in war and destruction, we shall avoid implicating ourselves with the Powers of Europe, even in support of principles which we mean to pursue. They have so many other interests different from ours that we must avoid being entangled in them. We believe we can enforce those principles as to ourselves by peaceable means, now that we are likely to have our public counsels detached from foreign views." A few days later, he wrote to the well-known Pennsylvania peacemaker, Dr. Logan, and explained the process of enforcing against foreign nations "principles as to ourselves by peaceable means." "Our commerce," said he, "is so valuable to them that they will be glad to purchase it, when the only price we ask is to do us justice. I believe we have in our own hands the means of peaceable coercion; and that the moment they see our government so united as that we can make use of it, they will for their own interest be disposed to do us justice."

To Chancellor Livingston, in September, 1801, the President wrote his views of the principles which he meant to pursue: "Yet in the present state of things," he added, "they are not worth a war; nor do I believe war the most certain means of enforcing them. Those peaceable coercions which are in the power of every nation, if undertaken in concert and in time of peace, are more likely to produce the desired effect."

That these views were new as a system in government could not be denied. In later life Jefferson frequently asserted, and took pains to impress upon his friends, the difference between his opinions and those of his Federalist opponents. The radical distinction lay in their opposite conceptions of the national government. The Federalists wished to extend its functions; Jefferson wished to exclude its influence from domestic affairs—

The people [he declared in 1821], to whom all authority belongs, have divided the powers of government into two distinct departments, the leading characters of which are foreign and domestic; and they have appointed for each a distinct set of functionaries. These they have made co-ordinate, checking and balancing each other, like the three cardinal departments in the individual States—each equally supreme as to the powers delegated to itself, and neither authorized ultimately to decide what belongs to itself or to its coparcener in government. As independent, in fact, as different nations, a spirit of forbearance and compromise, therefore, and not of encroachment and usurpation, is the healing balm of such a Constitution.

In the year 1824 Jefferson still maintained the same doctrine, and expressed it more concisely than ever—

The federal is in truth our foreign government, which department alone is taken from the sovereignty of the separate States. I recollect no case where a question simply between citizens of the same State has been transferred to the foreign department, except that of inhibiting tenders but of metallic money, and *ex post facto* legislation.

These expressions, taken together, partly explain why Jefferson thought his assumption of power to be "as real a revolution in the principles of our government as that of 1776 was in its form." His view of governmental functions was simple and clearly expressed. The national government, as he conceived it, was a foreign department as independent from the domestic department, which belonged to the States, as though they were governments of different nations. He intended that the general government should "be reduced to foreign concerns only"; and his theory of foreign concerns was equally simple and clear. He meant to enforce against foreign nations such principles as national objects required, not by war, but by "peaceable coercion" through commercial restrictions. "Our commerce is so valuable to them that they will be glad to purchase it, when the only price we ask is to do us justice."

The history of his Administration will show how these principles were applied, and what success attended the experiment.

IN *spite of Jefferson's great personal power and popularity he was unable to carry out in any substantial manner the anti-Federalist reforms to which the Republican party was committed. The promotion of states' rights was cardinal Virginia doctrine, to be accomplished by reducing the responsibilities of the central government and by stringent economy. Jefferson was committed to this doctrine; yet almost at the very outset, he found "a war and a navy fastened on his resources," to suppress the Barbary pirates in the Mediterranean. As a result, a much-heralded economy measure—abolition of internal taxes—quickly proved to be illusory. A further obstacle to decentralization lay in the fact that the Federalists retained control of the Supreme Court as a result of the appointment of Chief Justice Marshall by President Adams. Marshall promptly asserted the supremacy of the court in* Marbury v. Madison *by holding that it had the right to pass on the constitutionality of acts of congress. Between the internecine feuds within Jefferson's own party, arising chiefly from the efforts of Governor Clinton's New York faction to destroy Vice-President Burr's influence over the patronage, and the virulent hostility of the New England Federalists, the impulse toward fundamental reform quietly abated. The atmosphere of repose and judicious inaction, however, was deceptive, for "complications of a new and unexpected kind began, which henceforward caused the chief interest of politics to center in foreign affairs." These complications involved the imperial schemes of Napoleon Bonaparte. The following chapter opens "the rapid and half-understood drama" in international intrigue which centered on the Louisiana Purchase.*

Spain's secret retrocession of Louisiana to France in 1800 brought to a head the clamor of the Southern and Western states to be free of the threat of interference with American commerce on the Mississippi by either Spain or France. Faced with the demand for action—either war or purchase—Jefferson dispatched Monroe as a special envoy to buy the territory. Fortunately for American ambitions, Napoleon's hand was forced by the bloody rebellion on the island of Santo Domingo under Toussaint L'Ouverture. The rebellion reduced the island to a savage ruin in which the French army was consumed, and it spoiled Napoleon's plan to establish a base for exploiting Louisiana. The narrative of the Louisiana negotiation in the following two chapters shows "the comic muse" of Henry Adams at its best. It is also a remarkable example of his skill in dramatizing his historical sources.

The Retrocession

IN July, 1797, eight months before Godoy's retirement from power at Madrid, Talleyrand became Minister of Foreign Affairs to the French Directory. If the Prince of Peace was a man of no morals, the ex-Bishop of Autun was one of no morality. Colder than Pitt, and hardly less corrupt than Godoy, he held theories in regard to the United States which differed from those of other European statesmen only in being more aggressive. Chateaubriand once said "When M. Talleyrand is not conspiring, he traffics." The epigram was not an unfair description of Talleyrand's behavior toward the United States. He had wandered through America in the year 1794, and found there but one congenial spirit. "Hamilton *avait deviné l'Europe*," was his phrase: Hamilton had felt by instinct the problem of European conservatives. After returning from America and obtaining readmission to France, Talleyrand made almost his only appearance as an author by reading to the Institute, in April, 1797, a memoir upon America and the Colonial System. This paper was the clew to his ambition, preparing his return to power by laying the foundation for a future policy. The United States, it said, were wholly English, both by tastes and by commercial necessity; from them France could expect nothing; she must build up a new colonial system of her own—but "to announce too much of what one means to do, is the way not to do it at all." In October Bonaparte announced a part of it in sending to the Directory the Treaty of Campo Formio as a step, he wrote, to the destruction of England, and "the re-establishment of our commerce and our marine."

France still coveted Louisiana, the creation of Louis XIV., whose name it bore, which remained always French at heart, although in 1763 France ceded it to Spain in order to reconcile the Spanish government to sacrifices in the treaty of Paris. By the same treaty Florida was given by Spain to England, and remained twenty years in English hands, until the close of the Revolutionary War, when the treaty of 1783 restored it to Spain. The Spanish government of 1783, in thus gaining possession of Florida and Louisiana together, aimed at excluding the United States, not France, from the Gulf. Indeed, when the Count de Vergennes wished to recover Louisiana for France, Spain was willing to return it, but asked a price which, although the mere reimbursement of expenses, exceeded the means of the French treasury, and only for that reason Louisiana remained a Spanish province. After Godoy's war with France, at the Peace of Bâle the French Republic again tried to obtain the retrocession of Louisiana, but in vain. Nevertheless some progress was made, for by that treaty, July 22, 1795, Spain consented to cede to France the Spanish, or eastern, part of St. Domingo—the cradle of her Transatlantic power, and the cause of yearly deficits to the Spanish treasury. Owing to the naval superiority of England, the French republic did not ask for immediate possession. Fearing Toussaint Louverture, whose personal authority in the French part of the island already required forbearance, France retained the title, and waited for peace. Again, in 1797, Carnot and Barthelemy caused the Directory to offer the King of Spain a magnificent bribe for Louisiana. They proposed to take the three legations just wrung from the Pope, and joining them with the Duchy of Parma, make a principality for the son of the Duke of Parma, who had married a daughter of Don Carlos IV. Although this offer would have given his daughter a splendid position, Charles refused it, because he was too honest a churchman to share in the spoils of the Church.

These repeated efforts proved that France, and especially the Foreign Office, looked to the recovery of French power in America. A strong party in the Government aimed at restoring peace in Europe and extending French empire abroad. Of this party Talleyrand was, or aspired to be, the head; and his memoir, read to the Institute in April and July, 1797, was a cautious announcement of the principles to be pursued in the administration of foreign affairs which he immediately afterward assumed.

July 24, 1797, commissioners arrived from the United States to treat for a settlement of the difficulties then existing between the two countries; but Talleyrand refused to negotiate without a gift of twelve hundred thousand francs—amounting to about two hundred and fifty thousand dollars. Two of the American commissioners, in the middle of April, 1798, returned home, and war seemed inevitable.

Thus the month of April, 1798, was a moment of crisis in American affairs. Talleyrand had succeeded in driving Godoy from office, and in securing greater subservience from his successor, Don Mariano Luis de Urquijo, who had been chief clerk in the Foreign Department, and who acted as Minister for Foreign Affairs. Simultaneously Talleyrand carried his quarrel with the United States to the verge of rupture; and at the same time Godoy's orders compelled Governor Gayoso of Louisiana to deliver Natchez to the United States. The actual delivery of Natchez was hardly yet known in Europe; and the President of the United States at Philadelphia had but lately heard that the Spaniards were fairly gone, when Talleyrand drafted instructions for the Citizen Guillemardet, whom he was sending as minister to Madrid. These instructions offered a glimpse into the heart of Talleyrand's policy.

The Court of Madrid [said he], ever blind to its own interests, and never docile to the lessons of experience, has again quite recently adopted a measure which cannot fail to produce the worst effects upon its political existence and on the preservation of its colonies. The United States have been put in possession of the forts situated along the Mississippi which the Spaniards had occupied as posts essential to arrest the progress of the Americans in those countries.

The Americans, he continued, meant at any cost to rule alone in America, and to exercise a preponderating influence in the political system of Europe, although twelve hundred leagues of ocean rolled between.

Moreover, their conduct ever since the moment of their independence is enough to prove this truth: the Americans are devoured by pride, ambition, and cupidity; the mercantile spirit of the city of London ferments from Charleston to Boston, and the Cabinet of St. James directs the Cabinet of the Federal Union.

Chateaubriand's epigram came here into pointed application. Down to the moment of writing this despatch, Talleyrand had for some months been engaged in trafficking with these Americans, who were devoured by cupidity, and whom he had required to pay him two hundred and fifty thousand dollars for peace. He next conspired.

There are [he continued] no other means of putting an end to the ambition of the Americans than that of shutting them up within the limits which Nature seems to have traced for them; but Spain is not in a condition to do this great work alone. She cannot, therefore, hasten too quickly to engage the aid of a preponderating Power, yielding to it a small part of her immense domains in order to preserve the rest.

This small gratuity consisted of the Floridas and Louisiana.

Let the Court of Madrid cede these districts to France, and from that moment the power of America is bounded by the limit which it may suit the interests and the tranquillity of France and Spain to assign her. The French Republic, mistress of these two provinces, will be a wall of brass forever impenetrable to the combined efforts of England and America. The Court of Madrid has nothing to fear from France.

This scheme was destined to immediate failure, chiefly through the mistakes of its author; for not only had Talleyrand, a few weeks before, driven the United States to reprisals, and thus sacrificed what was left of the French colonies in the West Indies, but at the same moment he aided and encouraged young Bonaparte to carry a large army to Egypt, with the idea, suggested by the Duc de Choiseul many years before, that France might find there compensation for the loss of her colonies in America. Two years were consumed in retrieving these mistakes. Talleyrand first discovered that he could not afford a war with the United States; and even at the moment of writing these instructions to his minister at Madrid, he was engaged in conciliating the American commissioner who still remained unwillingly at Paris. The unexpected revelation by the United States government of his demands for money roused him, May 30, to consciousness of his danger. He made an effort to recover his lost ground. "I do not see what delay I could have prevented. I am mortified that circumstances have not rendered our progress more rapid." When Gerry coldly refused to hear these entreaties, and insisted upon receiving his passport, Talleyrand was in genuine despair. "You have not even given me an opportunity of proving what liberality the executive Directory would use on the occasion." He pursued Gerry with entreaties to use his influence on the President for peace; he pledged himself that no obstacle should be put in the path of negotiation if the American government would consent to renew it. At first the Americans were inclined to think his humility some new form of insult; but it was not only real, it was unexampled. Talleyrand foresaw that his blunder would cost France her colonies, and this he could bear; but it would also cost himself his office, and this was more than he could endure. His fears proved true. A year later, July 20, 1799, he was forced to retire, with little hope of soon recovering his character and influence, except through subservience to some coming adventurer.

Thus occurred a delay in French plans. By a sort of common agreement among the discontented factions at Paris, Bonaparte was recalled from Egypt. Landing at Fréjus early in October, 1799, a month afterward, November 9, he effected the *coup d'état* of the 18th Brumaire. He feared to disgust the public by replacing Talleyrand immediately in the office of foreign minister, and therefore delayed the appointment. "The place was naturally due to Talleyrand," said Napoleon in his memoirs, "but in order not too much to shock public opinion, which was very antagonistic to him, especially on account of American affairs, Reinhard was kept in office for a short time." The delay was of little consequence, for internal reorganization preceded the establishment of a new foreign policy; and Talleyrand was in no haste to recall the blunders of his first experiment.

Although Talleyrand had mismanaged the execution of his plan, the policy itself was a great one. The man who could pacify Europe and turn the energies of France toward the creation of an empire in the New World was the more sure of success because, in the reactionary spirit of the time, he commanded the sympathies of all Europe in checking the power of republicanism in its last refuge. Even England would see with pleasure France perform this duty, and Talleyrand might safely count upon a tacit alliance to support him in curbing American democracy. This scheme of uniting legitimate governments in peaceful combination to crush the spirit of license ran through the rest of Talleyrand's political life, and wherever met, whether in France, Austria, or England, was the mark of the school which found its ablest chief in him.

The first object of the new policy was to restore the peace of Europe; and the energy of Bonaparte completed this great undertaking within two years after the 18th Brumaire. France was at variance with the United States, Great Britain, and Austria. Peace with Austria could be obtained only by conquering it; and after passing a winter in organizing his government, Bonaparte sent Moreau to attack the Austrians on the line of the Danube, while he himself was to take command in Italy. As yet diplomacy could not act with effect; but early in the spring, March 1, 1800, before campaigning began, new American commissioners reached Paris, rather as dictators than as suppliants, and informed Talleyrand that the President of the United States was still ready to take him at his word. They were received with marked respect, and were instantly met by French commissioners, at whose head was Joseph Bonaparte, the First Consul's brother. While their negotiations were beginning, Bonaparte left Paris, May 20, crossed the Alps, and wrung from the Austrians, June 14, a victory at Marengo, while Moreau on the Danube pressed from one brilliant success to another. Hurrying back to Paris, July 2, Bonaparte instantly began the negotiations for peace with Austria; and thus two problems were solved.

Yet Talleyrand's precipitation in pledging France to prompt negotiation with the United States became a source of annoyance to the First Consul, whose shrewder calculation favored making peace first with Europe, in order to deal with America alone, and dictate his own terms. His brother Joseph, who was but an instrument in Napoleon's hands, but who felt a natural anxiety that his first diplomatic effort should succeed, became alarmed at the First Consul's coldness toward the American treaty, and at the crisis of negotiation, when failure was imminent, tried to persuade him that peace with the United States was made necessary by the situation in Europe. Napoleon met this argument by one of his characteristic rebuffs. "You understand nothing of the matter," he said; "within two years we shall be masters of the world." Within two years, in fact, the United States were isolated. Nevertheless Joseph was allowed to have his way. The First Consul obstinately refused to admit in the treaty any claim of indemnity for French spoliations on American commerce; and the American commissioners as resolutely refused to abandon the claim. They in their turn insisted that the new treaty should abrogate the guaranties and obligations imposed on the United States government by the old French treaty of alliance in 1778; and although Bonaparte cared nothing for the guaranty of the United States, he retained this advantage in order that he might set it off against the claims. Thus the negotiators were at last obliged to agree, by the second article of the treaty, that these two subjects should be reserved for future negotiation; and Sept. 30, 1800, the Treaty of Morfontaine, as Joseph Bonaparte wished to call it, was signed. It reached America in the confusion of a presidential election which threatened to overthrow the government; but the Senate voted, Feb. 3, 1801, to ratify it, with the omission of the second article. The instrument, with this change, was then sent back to Paris, where Bonaparte in his turn set terms upon his ratification. He agreed to omit the second article, as the Senate wished, "provided that by this retrenchment the two States renounced the respective pretensions which are the object of the said article." The treaty returned to America with this condition imposed upon it, and Jefferson submitted it to the Senate, which gave its final approval Dec. 19, 1801.

Thus Bonaparte gained his object, and won his first diplomatic success. He followed an invariable rule to repudiate debts and claims wherever repudiation was possible. For such demands he had one formula: "Give them a very civil answer—that I will examine the claim, etc.; but of course one never pays that sort of thing." In this case he meant to extinguish the spoliation claims; and nothing could be more certain than that he would thenceforward peremptorily challenge and resist any claim, direct or indirect, founded on French spoliations before 1800, and would allege the renunciation of Article II. in the treaty of Morfontaine as his justification. Equally certain was it that he had offered, and the Senate had approved his offer, to set off the guaranties of the treaty of alliance against the spoliation claims—which gave him additional reason for rejecting such claims in future. The United States had received fair consideration from him for whatever losses American citizens had suffered.

Meanwhile the First Consul took action which concerned America more closely than any of the disputes with which Joseph Bonaparte was busied. However little admiration a bystander might feel for Napoleon's judgment or morals, no one could deny the quickness of his execution. Within six weeks after the battle of Marengo, without waiting for peace with the United States, England, or Austria, convinced that he held these countries in the hollow of his hand, he ordered Talleyrand to send a special courier to the Citizen Alquier, French minister at Madrid, with powers for concluding a treaty by which Spain should retrocede Louisiana to France, in return for an equivalent aggrandizement of the Duchy of Parma. The courier was at once despatched, and returned with a promptitude and success which ought to have satisfied even the restlessness of Bonaparte. The Citizen Alquier no sooner received his orders than he went to Señor Urquijo, the Spanish Secretary for Foreign Relations, and passing abruptly over the well-worn arguments in favor of retrocession, he bluntly told Urquijo to oppose it if he dared.

France expects from you [I said to him] what she asked in vain from the Prince of Peace. I have dispersed the prejudice which had been raised against you in the mind of the French government. You are to-day distinguished by its esteem and its consideration. Do not destroy my work; do not deprive yourself of the only counterpoise which you can oppose to the force of your enemies. The Queen, as you know, holds by affection as much as by vanity to the aggrandizement of her house; she will never forgive you if you oppose an exchange which can alone realize the projects of her ambition—for I declare to you formally that your action will decide the fate of the Duke of Parma, and should you refuse to cede Louisiana you may count on getting nothing for that Prince. You must bear in mind, too, that your refusal will necessarily change my relations with you. Obliged to serve the interests of my country and to obey the orders of the First Consul, who attaches the highest value to this retrocession, I shall be forced to receive for the first time the offers of service that will inevitably be made to me; for you may be sure that your enemies will not hesitate to profit by that occasion to increase their strength—already a very real force— by the weight of the French influence; they will do what you will not do, and you will be abandoned at once by the Queen and by us.

Urquijo's reply measured the degradation of Spain:

Eh! who told you that I would not give you Louisiana? But we must first have an understanding, and you must help me to convince the King.

At this reply, which sounded like Beaumarchais' comedies, Alquier saw that his game was safe. "Make yourself easy on that score," he replied; "the Queen will take that on herself." So the conference ended.

Alquier was right. The Queen took the task on herself, and Urquijo soon found that both King and Queen were anxious to part with Louisiana for their daughter's sake. They received the offer with enthusiasm, and lavished praises upon Bonaparte. The only conditions suggested by Urquijo were that the new Italian principality should be clearly defined, and that Spain should be guaranteed against the objections that might be made by other Governments.

Meanwhile Bonaparte reiterated his offer on a more definite scale. August 3, immediately after the interview with Urquijo, Alquier put the first demand on record in a note important chiefly because it laid incidental stress on Talleyrand's policy of restraining the United States—

The progress of the power and population of America, and her relations of interest always maintained with England, may and must some day bring these two powers to concert together the conquest of the Spanish colonies. If national interest is the surest foundation for political calculations, this conjecture must appear incontestable. The Court of Spain will do, then, at once a wise and great act if it calls the French to the defence of its colonies by ceding Louisiana to them, and by replacing in their hands this outpost of its richest possessions in the New World.

Before this note was written, the First Consul had already decided to supersede Alquier by a special agent who should take entire charge of this negotiation. July 28 he notified Talleyrand that General Berthier, Bonaparte's right hand in matters of secrecy and importance, was to go upon the mission.

Talleyrand drafted the necessary instructions, which were framed to meet the fears of Spain lest the new arrangement should cause complications with other Powers; and toward the end of August Berthier started for Madrid, carrying a personal letter of introduction from the First Consul to King Charles and the *projet* of a treaty of retrocession drawn by Talleyrand. This *projet* differed in one point from the scheme hitherto put forward, and, if possible, was still more alarming to the United States.

The French Republic [it ran] pledges itself to procure for the Duke of Parma in Italy an aggrandizement of territory to contain at least one million inhabitants; the Republic charges itself with procuring the consent of Austria and the other States interested, so that the Duke may be put in possession of his new territory at the coming peace between France and Austria. Spain on her side pledges herself to retrocede to the French Republic the colony of Louisiana, with the same extent it actually has in the hands of Spain, and such as it should be according to the treaties subsequently passed between Spain and other States. Spain shall further join to this cession that of the two Floridas, eastern and western, with their actual limits.

Besides Louisiana and the two Floridas, Spain was to give France six ships of war, and was to deliver the provinces to France whenever the promised territory for the Duke of Parma should be delivered by France to Spain. The two Powers were further to make common cause against any person or persons who should attack or threaten them in consequence of executing their engagement.

In the history of the United States hardly any document, domestic or foreign, to be found in their archives has greater interest than this *projet;* for from it the United States must trace whatever legal title they obtained to the vast region west of the Mississippi. The treaties which followed were made merely in pursuance of this engagement, with such variations as seemed good for the purpose of carrying out the central idea of restoring Louisiana to France.

That the recovery of colonial power was the first of all Bonaparte's objects was proved not only by its being the motive of his earliest and most secret diplomatic step, but by the additional evidence that every other decisive event in the next three years of his career was subordinated to it. Berthier hastened to Madrid, and consumed the month of September, 1800, in negotiations. Eager as both parties were to conclude their bargain, difficulties soon appeared. So far as these concerned America, they rose in part from the indiscretion of the French Foreign Office, which announced the object of Berthier's mission in a Paris newspaper, and thus brought on Urquijo a demand from the American minister at Madrid for a categorical denial. Urquijo and Alquier could silence the attack only by denials not well calculated to carry conviction. This was not all. Alquier had been told to ask for Louisiana; Berthier was instructed to demand the Floridas and six ships of war in addition. The demand for the Floridas should have been made at first, if Bonaparte expected it to be successful. King Charles was willing to give back to France a territory which was French in character, and had come as the gift of France to his father; but he was unwilling to alienate Florida, which was a part of the national domain. Urquijo told Berthier that "for the moment the King had pronounced himself so strongly against the cession of any portion whatever of Florida as to make it both useless and impolitic to talk with him about it;" but he added that, "after the general peace, the King might decide to cede a part of the Floridas between the Mississippi and the Mobile, on the special demand which the First Consul might make for it." Berthier was embarrassed, and yielded.

Thus at last the bargain was put in shape. The French government held out the hope of giving Tuscany as the equivalent for Louisiana and six seventy-fours. If not Tuscany, the three legations, or their equivalent, were stipulated. The suggestion of Tuscany delighted the King and Queen. Thus far the secret was confined to the parties directly interested; but after the principle had been fixed, another person was intrusted with it. The Prince of Peace was suddenly called to the Palace by a message marked *"luego, luego, luego!"*—the sign of triple haste. He found Don Carlos in a paroxysm of excitement; joy sparkled in his eyes. "Congratulate me," he cried, "on this brilliant beginning of Bonaparte's relations with Spain! The Prince-presumptive of Parma, my son-in-law and nephew, a Bourbon, is invited by France to reign, on the delightful banks of the Arno, over a people who once spread their commerce through the known world, and who were the controlling power of Italy—a people mild, civilized, full of humanity; the classical land of science and art!" The Prince of Peace could only offer congratulations; his opinion was asked without being followed, and a few days later the treaty was signed.

On the last day of September, 1800, Joseph Bonaparte signed the so-called Treaty of Morfontaine, which restored relations between France and the United States. The next day, October 1, Berthier signed at San Ildefonso the treaty of retrocession, which was equivalent to a rupture of the relations established four-and-twenty hours earlier. Talleyrand was aware that one of these treaties undid the work of the other. The secrecy in which he enveloped the treaty of retrocession, and the pertinacity with which he denied its existence showed his belief that Bonaparte had won a double diplomatic triumph over the United States.

Moreau's great victory at Hohenlinden, December 3, next brought Austria to her knees. Joseph Bonaparte was sent to Lunéville in Lorraine, and in a few weeks negotiated the treaty which advanced another step the cession of Louisiana. The fifth article of this treaty, signed Feb. 9, 1801, deprived the actual Grand Duke of his Grand Duchy, and established the young Duke of Parma in Tuscany. To complete the transaction, Lucien Bonaparte was sent as ambassador to Madrid.

Lucien had the qualities of his race. Intelligent, vivacious, vain, he had been a Jacobin of the deepest dye; and yet his hands were as red with the crime of the 18th Brumaire as those of his brother Napoleon. Too troublesome at Paris to suit the First Consul's arbitrary views, he was sent to Spain, partly to

remove him, partly to flatter Don Carlos IV. The choice was
not wise; for Lucien neither could nor would execute in good
faith the wishes of his dictatorial brother, and had no idea of
subordinating his own interests to those of the man whose
blunders on the 18th Brumaire, in his opinion, nearly cost the
lives of both, and whose conduct since had turned every democrat in France into a conspirator. To make the selection still
more dangerous, Lucien had scarcely reached Madrid before
Urquijo was sent into retirement and Godoy restored to power
in some anomalous position of general superintendence, supporting the burden, but leaving to Don Pedro Cevallos the title
of Foreign Secretary. The secret of this restoration was told
by Godoy himself with every appearance of truth. The King
insisted on his return, because Godoy was the only man who
could hold his own against Bonaparte; and at that moment
Bonaparte was threatening to garrison Spain with a French
army, under pretence of a war with Portugal. The measure
showed that Charles IV. was not wanting in shrewdness, for
Godoy was well suited to deal with Lucien. He was more subtle,
and not less corrupt.

Lucien's first act was to negotiate a new treaty closing the
bargain in regard to Parma and Tuscany. Here Godoy offered
no resistance. The Prince of Parma was created King of Tuscany, and the sixth article provided that the retrocession of
Louisiana should at once be carried out. This treaty was signed
at Madrid, March 21, 1801. The young King and Queen of
Tuscany—or, according to their title, of Etruria—were despatched to Paris. Lucien remained to overlook the affair of
Portugal. To the extreme irritation of Napoleon, news soon
came that the Prince of Peace had signed at Badajos, June 5,
1801, a treaty with Portugal, to which Lucien had put his
name as ambassador of France, and which baffled Napoleon's
military designs in the Peninsula.

Lucien, with inimitable effrontery, wrote to his brother two
days later: "For the treaty of Tuscany I have received twenty
good pictures out of the Gallery of the Retiro for my gallery,

and diamonds to the value of one hundred thousand crowns have been set for me. I shall receive as much more for the Peace of Portugal." Two hundred thousand crowns and twenty pictures from the Retiro, besides flattery that would have turned the head of Talleyrand himself, were what Lucien acknowledged receiving; but there was reason to believe that this was not all, and that the Prince of Peace gorged him with spoil, until he carried back to France wealth which made him the richest member of his family, and gave him an income of sixty or eighty thousand dollars a year. Godoy paid this price to save Spain for seven years.

The treaty of Badajos into which Godoy thus drew Lucien not only checked Napoleon's schemes, but came on the heels of other reverses which threatened to place the First Consul in an awkward position, unless he should hasten the general pacification to which he was tending. The assassination of his ally, the Czar Paul I. March 23, 1801, cost him the aid of Russia, as Godoy's return to power cost him the control of Spain. A few days after Paul's murder, April 9, 1801, Nelson crushed the Danish fleet at Copenhagen, and tore Denmark from his grasp. More serious than all, the fate of the French army which Bonaparte had left in Egypt could not be long delayed, and its capitulation would give a grave shock to his credit. All these reasons forced the First Consul to accept the check he had received from Godoy and Lucien, and to hasten peace with England; but he yielded with a bad grace. He was furious with Godoy. "If this prince, bought by England, draws the King and Queen into measures contrary to the honor and interests of the republic, the last hour of the Spanish monarchy will have sounded." So he wrote to Talleyrand in anger at finding himself checked, and Talleyrand instructed Lucien accordingly. Within a fortnight Bonaparte sent orders to London which rendered peace with England certain; and without waiting to hear further, acting at length on the conviction that nothing could be gained by delay, he ordered Talleyrand to demand of the Court of Spain the authority to take possession of Louisiana.

Supple and tenacious as any Corsican, Godoy's temper was perfect and his manners charming; he eluded Bonaparte with the skill and coolness of a picador. After causing the First Consul to stumble and fall on the very threshold of Portugal, Godoy kept Louisiana out of his control. As the affair then stood, surrender of Louisiana except at the sword's point would have been inexcusable. The young King of Etruria had been entertained at Paris by the First Consul with a patronizing hospitality that roused more suspicion than gratitude; he had been sent to Italy, and had there been told that he possessed a kingdom and wore a crown—but French armies occupied the territory; French generals administered the government; no foreign Power recognized the new kingdom, and no vestige of royal authority went with the royal title. Godoy and Cevallos gave it to be understood that they did not consider the First Consul to have carried out his part of the bargain in such a sense as to warrant Charles IV. in delivering Louisiana. They were in the right; but Bonaparte was angrier than ever at their audacity, and drafted with his own hand the note which Talleyrand was to send in reply.

It is at the moment when the First Consul gives such strong proofs of his consideration for the King of Spain, and places a prince of his house on a throne which is fruit of the victories of French arms, that a tone is taken toward the French Republic such as might be taken with impunity toward the Republic of San Marino. The First Consul, full of confidence in the personal character of his Catholic Majesty, hopes that from the moment he is made aware of the bad conduct of some of his ministers, he will look to it, and will recall them to the sentiments of esteem and consideration which France does not cease to entertain for Spain. The First Consul will never persuade himself that his Catholic Majesty wishes to insult the French people and their Government at the moment when these are doing so much for Spain. This would suit neither his heart nor his loyalty, nor the interest of his crown.

In a note written the same day to Talleyrand, Bonaparte spoke in a still stronger tone of the *"misérable"* who was thus crossing his path, and he ordered that Lucien should let the King and Queen know "that I am long-suffering, but that already I am warmly affected by this tone of contempt and de-consideration which is taken at Madrid; and that if they continue to put the republic under the necessity either of enduring the shame of the outrages publicly inflicted on it, or of avenging them by arms, they may see things they do not expect."

Nevertheless Godoy held his ground, well aware that the existence of Spain was at stake, but confident that concession would merely tempt encroachment. History might render what judgment it would of Godoy's character or policy—with this moral or political question the United States had nothing to do; but Bonaparte's hatred of Godoy and determination to crush him were among the reasons why Louisiana fell at a sudden and unexpected moment into the hands of Jefferson, and no picture of American history could be complete which did not show in the background the figures of Bonaparte and Godoy, locked in struggle over Don Carlos IV.

The Louisiana Treaty

MONROE arrived in sight of the French coast April 7, 1803; but while he was still on the ocean, Bonaparte without reference to him or his mission, opened his mind to Talleyrand in regard to ceding Louisiana to the United States. The First Consul a few days afterward repeated to his Finance Minister, Barbé Marbois, a part of the conversation with Talleyrand; and his words implied that Talleyrand opposed Bonaparte's scheme, less because it sacrificed Louisiana than because its true object was not a war with England, but conquest of Germany. "He alone knows my intentions," said Bonaparte to Marbois. "If I attended to his advice, France would confine her ambition to the left bank of the Rhine, and would make war only to protect the weak States and to prevent any dismemberment of her possessions; but he also admits that the cession of Louisiana is not a dismemberment of France." In reality, the cession of Louisiana meant the overthrow of Talleyrand's influence and the failure of those hopes which had led to the coalition of the 18th Brumaire.

Easter Sunday, April 10, 1803, arrived, and Monroe was leaving Havre for Paris, when Bonaparte, after the religious ceremonies of the day at St. Cloud, called to him two of his ministers, of whom Barbé Marbois was one. He wished to explain his intention of selling Louisiana to the United States; and he did so in his peculiar way. He began by expressing the fear that England would seize Louisiana as her first act of war. "I think of ceding it to the United States. I can scarcely say that I cede it to them, for it is not yet in our possession. If, however, I leave the least time to our enemies, I shall only transmit an empty title to those republicans whose friendship I seek. They ask of me only one town in Louisiana; but I already consider the colony as entirely lost; and it appears to me that in the hands of this growing Power it will be more useful to the policy, and even to the commerce, of France than if I should attempt to keep it."

To this appeal the two ministers replied by giving two opposite opinions. Marbois favored the cession, as the First Consul probably expected him to do; for Marbois was a republican who had learned republicanism in the United States, and whose attachment to that country was secured by marriage to an American wife. His colleague, with equal decision, opposed the scheme. Their arguments were waste of breath. The First Consul said no more, and dismissed them; but the next morning, Monday, April 11, at daybreak, summoning Marbois, he made a short oration of the kind for which he was so famous—

Irresolution and deliberation are no longer in season; I renounce Louisiana. It is not only New Orleans that I cede; it is the whole colony, without reserve. I know the price of what I abandon. I have proved the importance I attach to this province, since my first diplomatic act with Spain had the object of recovering it. I renounce it with the greatest regret; to attempt obstinately to retain it would be folly. I direct you to negotiate the affair. Have an interview this very day with Mr. Livingston.

The order so peremptorily given was instantly carried out; but not by Marbois. Talleyrand, in an interview a few hours afterward, startled Livingston with the new offer.

M. Talleyrand asked me this day, when pressing the subject, whether we wished to have the whole of Louisiana. I told him no; that our wishes extended only to New Orleans and the Floridas; that the policy of France, however, should dictate (as I had shown in an official note) to give us the country above the River Arkansas, in order to place a barrier between them and Canada. He said that if they gave New Orleans the rest would be of little value, and that he would wish to know "what we would give for the whole." I told him it was a subject I had not thought of, but that I supposed we should not object to twenty millions [francs], provided our citizens were paid. He told me that this was too low an offer, and that he would be glad if I would reflect upon it and tell him to-morrow. I told him that as Mr. Monroe would be in town in two days, I would delay my further offer until I had the pleasure of introducing him. He added that he did not speak from authority, but that the idea had struck him.

The suddenness of Bonaparte's change disconcerted Livingston. For months he had wearied the First Consul with written and verbal arguments, remonstrances, threats—all intended to prove that there was nothing grasping or ambitious in the American character; that France should invite the Americans to protect Louisiana from the Canadians; that the United States cared nothing for Louisiana, but wanted only West Florida and New Orleans—"barren sands and sunken marshes," he said; "a small town built of wood; . . . about seven thousand souls;" a territory important to the United States because it contained "the mouths of some of their rivers," but a mere drain of resources to France. To this rhapsody, repeated day after day for weeks and months, Talleyrand had listened with his imperturbable silence, the stillness of a sceptical mind into which such professions fell meaningless; until he suddenly looked into Livingston's face and asked: "What will you give for the whole?" Naturally Livingston for a moment lost countenance.

The next day, Tuesday, April 12, Livingston, partly recovered from his surprise, hung about Talleyrand persistently, for his chance of reaping alone the fruit of his labors vanished with every minute that passed. Monroe had reached St. Germain late Monday night, and at one o'clock Tuesday afternoon descended from his postchaise at the door of his Paris hotel. From the moment of his arrival he was sure to seize public attention at home and abroad. Livingston used the interval to make one more effort with Talleyrand—

He then thought proper to declare that his proposition was only personal, but still requested me to make an offer; and upon my declining to do so, as I expected Mr. Monroe the next day, he shrugged up his shoulders and changed the conversation. Not willing, however, to lose sight of it, I told him I had been long endeavoring to bring him to some point, but unfortunately without effect; and with that view had written him a note which contained that request. . . . He told me he would answer my note, but that he must do it evasively, because Louisiana was not theirs. I smiled at this assertion, and told him that I had seen the treaty recognizing it. . . . He still persisted that they had it in contemplation to obtain it, but had it not.

An hour or two afterward came a note from Monroe announcing that he would wait upon Livingston in the evening. The two American ministers passed the next day together, examining papers and preparing to act whenever Monroe could be officially presented. They entertained a party at dinner that afternoon in Livingston's apartments, and while sitting at table Livingston saw Barbé Marbois strolling in the garden outside. Livingston sent to invite Marbois to join the party at table. While coffee was served, Marbois came in and entered into conversation with Livingston, who began at once to tell him of Talleyrand's "extraordinary conduct." Marbois hinted that he knew something of the matter, and that Livingston had better come to his house as soon as the dinner company departed. The moment Monroe took leave, Livingston acted on Marbois's hint, and in a midnight conversation the bargain was practically made. Marbois told a story, largely of his own invention, in regard to the First Consul's conduct on Easter Sunday, three days before. Bonaparte mentioned fifty million francs as his price for Louisiana; but as Marbois reported the offer to Livingston, Bonaparte said: "Well! you have charge of the Treasury. Let them give you one hundred millions of francs, and pay their own claims, and take the whole country." The American claims were estimated at about twenty-five millions, and therefore Marbois's price amounted to at least one hundred and twenty-five million francs.

Yet twenty-four or twenty-five million dollars for the whole west bank of the Mississippi, from the Lake of the Woods to the Gulf of Mexico, and indefinitely westward, was not an extortionate price, especially since New Orleans was thrown into the bargain, and indirect political advantages which could

not be valued at less than the cost of a war, whatever it might
be. Five million dollars were to be paid in America to American
citizens, so that less than twenty millions would come to
France. Livingston could hardly have been blamed for closing
with Marbois on the spot, especially as his instructions warranted him in offering ten millions for New Orleans and the
Floridas alone; but Livingston still professed that he did not
want the west bank. "I told him that the United States were
anxious to preserve peace with France; that for that reason
they wished to remove them to the west side of the Mississippi;
that we would be perfectly satisfied with New Orleans and the
Floridas, and had no disposition to extend across the river;
that of course we would not give any great sum for the purchase. . . . He then pressed me to name the sum." After a little
more fencing, Marbois dropped at once from one hundred millions to sixty, with estimated claims to the amount of twenty
millions more. "I told him that it was vain to ask anything
that was so greatly beyond our means; that true policy would
dictate to the First Consul not to press such a demand; that he
must know it would render the present government unpopular."
The conversation closed by Livingston's departure at midnight
with a final protest: "I told him that I would consult Mr.
Monroe, but that neither he nor I could accede to his ideas
on the subject." Then he went home; and sitting down to his
desk wrote a long despatch to Madison, to record that without
Monroe's help he had won Louisiana. The letter closed with
some reflections—

As to the quantum, I have yet made up no opinion. The field
open to us is infinitely larger than our instructions contemplated, the revenue increasing, and the land more than adequate to sink the capital, should we even go the sum proposed
by Marbois—nay, I persuade myself that the whole sum may
be raised by the sale of the territory west of the Mississippi,
with the right of sovereignty, to some Power in Europe whose
vicinity we should not fear. I speak now without reflection and
without having seen Mr. Monroe, as it was midnight when I
left the Treasury Office, and it is now near three o'clock. It is

so very important that you should be apprised that a negotiation is actually opened, even before Mr. Monroe has been presented, in order to calm the tumult which the news of war will renew, that I have lost no time in communicating it. We shall do all we can to cheapen the purchase; but my present sentiment is that we shall buy.

A week was next passed in haggling over the price. Livingston did his utmost to beat Marbois down, but without success. Meanwhile he ran some risk of losing everything; for when Bonaparte offered a favor suitors did well to waste no time in acceptance. A slight weight might have turned the scale; a divulgence of the secret, a protest from Spain, a moment of irritation at Jefferson's coquetry with England or at the vaporings of the American press, a sudden perception of the disgust which every true Frenchman was sure sooner or later to feel at this squandering of French territory and enterprise—any remonstrance that should stir the First Consul's pride or startle his fear of posterity, might have cut short the thread of negotiation. Livingston did not know the secrets of the Tuileries, or he would not have passed time in cheapening the price of his purchase. The voice of opposition was silenced in the French people, but was still so high in Bonaparte's family as to make the Louisiana scheme an occasion for scenes so violent as to sound like the prelude to a tragedy.

One evening when Talma was to appear in a new *rôle*, Lucien Bonaparte, coming home to dress for the theatre, found his brother Joseph waiting for him. "Here you are at last!" cried Joseph; "I was afraid you might not come. This is no time for theatre-going; I have news for you that will give you no fancy for amusement. The General wants to sell Louisiana."

Lucien, proud of having made the treaty which secured the retrocession, was for a moment thunderstruck; then recovering confidence, he said, "Come, now! if he were capable of wishing it, the Chambers would never consent."

"So he means to do without their consent," replied Joseph. "This is what he answered me, when I said to him, like you, that the Chambers would not consent. What is more, he added that this sale would supply him the first funds for the war. Do you know that I am beginning to think he is much too fond of war?"

History is not often able to penetrate the private lives of famous men, and catch their words as they were uttered. Although Lucien Bonaparte's veracity was not greatly superior to that of his brother Napoleon, his story agreed with the known facts. If his imagination here and there filled in the gaps of memory—if he was embittered and angry when he wrote, and hated his brother Napoleon with Corsican passion, these circumstances did not discredit his story, for he would certainly have told the truth against his brother under no other conditions. The story was not libellous, but Napoleonic; it told nothing new of the First Consul's character, but it was honorable to Joseph, who proposed to Lucien that they should go together and prevent their brother from committing a fault which would rouse the indignation of France, and endanger his own safety as well as theirs.

The next morning Lucien went to the Tuileries; by his brother's order he was admitted, and found Napoleon in his bath, the water of which was opaque with mixture of *eau de Cologne.* They talked for some time on indifferent matters. Lucien was timid, and dared not speak until Joseph came. Then Napoleon announced his decision to sell Louisiana, and invited Lucien to say what he thought of it.

"I flatter myself," replied Lucien, "that the Chambers will not give their consent."

"You flatter yourself!" repeated Napoleon in a tone of surprise; then murmuring in a lower voice, "that is precious, in truth!" (*c'est précieux, en vérité!*)

"And I too flatter myself, as I have already told the First Consul," cried Joseph.

"And what did I answer?" said Napoleon warmly, glaring from his bath at the two men.

"That you would do without the Chambers."

"Precisely! That is what I have taken the great liberty to tell Mr. Joseph, and what I now repeat to the Citizen Lucien —begging him at the same time to give me his opinion about it, without taking into consideration his parental tenderness for his diplomatic conquest." Then, not satisfied with irony, he continued in a tone of exasperating contempt: "And now, gentlemen, think of it what you will; but both of you go into mourning about this affair—you, Lucien, for the sale itself; you, Joseph, because I shall do without the consent of any one whomsoever. Do you understand?"

At this Joseph came close to the bath, and rejoined in a vehement tone: "And you will do well, my dear brother, not to expose your project to parliamentary discussion; for I declare to you that if necessary I will put myself first at the head of the opposition which will not fail to be made against you."

The First Consul burst into a peal of forced laughter, while Joseph, crimson with anger and almost stammering his words, went on: "Laugh, laugh, laugh, then! I will act up to my promise; and though I am not fond of mounting the tribune, this time you will see me there!"

Napoleon, half rising from the bath, rejoined in a serious tone: "You will have no need to lead the opposition, for I repeat that there will be no debate, for the reason that the project which has not the fortune to meet your approval, conceived by me, negotiated by me, shall be ratified and executed by me alone, do you comprehend?—by me, who laugh at your opposition!"

Hereupon Joseph wholly lost his self-control, and with flashing eyes shouted: "Good! I tell you, General, that you, I, and all of us, if you do what you threaten, may prepare ourselves soon to go and join the poor innocent devils whom you so legally, humanely, and especially with such justice, have transported to Sinnamary."

At this terrible rejoinder Napoleon half started up, crying out: "You are insolent! I ought—" then threw himself violently back in the bath with a force which sent a mass of perfumed

water into Joseph's flushed face, drenching him and Lucien, who had the wit to quote, in a theatrical tone, the words which Virgil put into the mouth of Neptune reproving the waves—
   "Quos ego . . ."
Between the water and the wit the three Bonapartes recovered their tempers, while the valet who was present, overcome by fear, fainted and fell on the floor. Joseph went home to change his clothes, while Lucien remained to pass through another scene almost equally amusing. A long conversation followed after the First Consul's toilet was finished. Napoleon spoke of St. Domingo. "Do you want me to tell you the truth?" said he. "I am to-day more sorry than I like to confess for the expedition to St. Domingo. Our national glory will never come from our marine." He justified what he called, in jest at Lucien, his "Louisianicide," by the same reasons he gave to Marbois and Talleyrand, but especially by the necessity of providing funds for the war not yet declared. Lucien combated his arguments as Joseph had done, until at last he reached the same point. "If, like Joseph, I thought that this alienation of Louisiana without the assent of the Chambers might be fatal to me —to me alone—I would consent to run all risks in order to prove the devotion you doubt; but it is really too unconstitutional and—"

"Ah, indeed!" burst out Napoleon with another prolonged, forced laugh of derisive anger. "You lay it on handsomely! Unconstitutional is droll from you. Come now, let me alone! How have I hurt your Constitution? Answer!"

Lucien replied that the intent to alienate any portion whatever of territory belonging to the Republic without the consent of the Chambers was an unconstitutional project. "In a word, the Constitution—"

"Go about your business!" broke in the guardian of the Constitution and of the national territory. Then he quickly and vehemently went on: "Constitution! unconstitutional! republic! national sovereignty!—big words! great phrases! Do you think yourself still in the club of St. Maximin? We are no longer there, mind that! Ah, it becomes you well, Sir Knight of the Constitution, to talk so to me! You had not the same respect for the Chambers on the 18th Brumaire!"

Nothing exasperated Lucien more than any allusion to the part he took in the *coup d'état* of the 18th Brumaire, when he betrayed the Chamber over which he presided. He commanded himself for the moment; but when Napoleon went on to say with still more contempt, "I laugh at you and your national representation," Lucien answered coldly, "I do not laugh at you, Citizen Consul, but I know well what I think about it."

"Parbleu!" said Napoleon, "I am curious to know what you think of me: say it, quick!"

"I think, Citizen Consul, that having given your oath to the Constitution of the 18th Brumaire into my own hands as President of the Council of Five Hundred, seeing you despise it thus, if I were not your brother I would be your enemy."

"My enemy! ah, I would advise you! My enemy! That is a trifle strong!" cried Napoleon, advancing as though to strike his younger brother. "You my enemy! I would break you, look, like this box!" And so saying he flung his snuff-box violently on the floor.

In these angry scenes both parties knew that Napoleon's bravado was not altogether honest. For once, Lucien was in earnest; and had his brother left a few other men in France as determined as he and his friend Bernadotte, the First Consul would have defied public opinion less boldly. Joseph, too, although less obstinate than his brothers, was not easily managed. According to Lucien there were further scenes between them, at one of which Joseph burst into such violence that the First Consul took refuge in Josephine's room. These stories contained nothing incredible. The sale of Louisiana was the turning-point in Napoleon's career; no true Frenchman forgave it. A second betrayal of France, it announced to his fellow conspirators that henceforward he alone was to profit by the treason of the 18th Brumaire.

Livingston and Monroe knew nothing of all this; they even

depended upon Joseph to help their negotiation. Monroe fell ill and could not act. Over the negotiation of the treaty has always hung a cloud of mystery such as belonged to no other measure of equal importance in American history. No official report showed that the commissioners ever met in formal conference; no protocol of their proceedings, no account of their discussions, no date when their agreement was made, was left on record. Both the treaty itself and the avowals of Livingston gave evidence that at the end all parties acted in haste. If it were not for a private memorandum by Monroe—not sent to the Government, but preserved among his private papers—the course of negotiation could not be followed.

A fortnight passed after Monroe's arrival without advancing matters a step. This period of inaction seems to have been broken by the First Consul. April 23 he drew up a *"Projet* of a Secret Convention,"* which he gave to Marbois and which set forth that to prevent misunderstandings about the matters of discussion mentioned in Articles II. and V. of the Morfontaine treaty, and also to strengthen friendly relations, the French republic was to cede its rights over Louisiana; and "in consequence of the said cession, Louisiana, its territory, and its proper dependencies shall become part of the American Union, and shall form successively one or more States on the terms of the Federal Constitution"; in return the United States were to favor French commerce in Louisiana, and give it all the rights of American commerce, with perpetual *entrepôts* at six points on the Mississippi, and a corresponding perpetual right of navigation; further, they were to assume all debts due to American citizens under the treaty of Morfontaine; and, finally, were to pay a hundred million francs to France. With this *projet* Marbois went by appointment, at two o'clock, April 27, to Monroe's lodgings, where the three gentlemen had an informal meeting, of which no other record is known to exist than Monroe's memoranda. Monroe himself was too unwell to sit at the table, and reclined on a sofa throughout the discussion. Marbois produced Bonaparte's *projet*, and after admitting that it was hard and unreasonable, presented a substitute of his own which he thought the First Consul would accept.

Livingston tried to give precedence to the claims; he wanted to dispose of them first, in case the cession should fail; but after pressing the point as far as he could, he was overruled by Monroe, and Livingston took Marbois's project for consideration. The two American commissioners passed a day in working over it. Livingston drafted a claims convention, and it was drawn, as he thought, "with particular attention." Monroe thought differently. "My colleague took Mr. Marbois's project with him, and brought me one, very loosely drawn, founded on it." Monroe made a draft of his own which was certainly not creditable to his legal or diplomatic skill, and which began by adopting an oversight contained in Bonaparte's draft, according to which the cancelled Article II. of the treaty of Morfontaine was made a foundation of the new convention. "We called on Mr. Marbois the 29th, and gave him our project, which was read to him and discussed. We proposed to offer fifty millions to France, and twenty millions on account of her debt to the citizens of the United States, making seventy in the whole." Marbois replied that he would proceed only on the condition that eighty millions were accepted as the price. Then at last the American commissioners gave way; and with this change Marbois took their *projet* for reference to the First Consul the next morning.

The 30th of April was taken by Marbois for consultation with the First Consul. May 1 Monroe was presented at the Tuileries, and dined there with Livingston; but Bonaparte said nothing of their business, except that it should be settled. The same evening the two envoys had a final discussion with Marbois. "May 2, we actually signed the treaty and convention for the sixty million francs to France, in the French language; but our copies in English not being made out, we could not sign in our language. They were however prepared, and signed in two or three days afterward. The convention respecting American claims took more time, and was not signed till about the 8th or 9th." All these documents were antedated to the 30th April.

The first object of remark in this treaty was the absence of any attempt to define the property thus bought and sold. "Louisiana with the same extent that is now in the hands of Spain, and that it had when France possessed it, and such as it should be after the treaties subsequently entered into between Spain and other States"—these words, taken from Berthier's original treaty of retrocession, were convenient for France and Spain, whose governments might be supposed to know their own boundaries; but all that the United States government knew upon the subject was that Louisiana, as France possessed it, had included a part of Florida and the whole Ohio Valley as far as the Alleghany Mountains and Lake Erie. The American commissioners at first insisted upon defining the boundaries, and Marbois went to the First Consul with their request. He refused. "If an obscurity did not already exist, it would perhaps be good policy to put one there." He intentionally concealed the boundary he had himself defined, a knowledge of which would have prevented a long and mortifying dispute. Livingston went to Talleyrand for the orders given by Spain to the Marquis of Somoruelo, by France to Victor and Laussat. "What are the eastern bounds of Louisiana?" asked Livingston. "I do not know," replied Talleyrand; "you must take it as we received it." "But what did you mean to take?" urged Livingston. "I do not know," repeated Talleyrand. "Then you mean that we shall construe it our own way?" "I can give you no direction. You have made a noble bargain for yourselves, and I suppose you will make the most of it," was the final reply of Talleyrand. Had Livingston known that Victor's instructions, which began by fixing the boundaries in question, were still in Talleyrand's desk, the answer would have been the same.

One point alone was fixed—the Floridas were not included in the sale; this was conceded on both sides. In his first conversation with Marbois, Livingston made a condition that France should aid him in procuring these territories from Spain. "I asked him, in case of purchase, whether they would stipulate that France would never possess the Floridas, and that she would aid us to procure them, and relinquish all right that she might have to them. He told me that she would go thus far." Several days later, Marbois repeated this assurance to Monroe, saying that the First Consul authorized him, besides offering Louisiana, "to engage his support of our claim to the Floridas with Spain." Yet when the American commissioners tried to insert this pledge into the treaty, they failed. Bonaparte would give nothing but a verbal promise to use his good offices with Spain.

Besides the failure to dispose of these two points, which were in reality but one, the treaty contained a positive provision, Article III., taken from Bonaparte's *projet*, with slight alteration, that "the inhabitants of the ceded territory shall be incorporated in the Union of the United States, and admitted as soon as possible, according to the principles of the Federal Constitution, to the enjoyment of all the rights, advantages, and immunities of citizens of the United States." On republican principles of the Virginian school, only the States themselves could by a new grant of power authorize such an incorporation. Article III. violated Madison's instructions, which forbade the promise. "To incorporate the inhabitants of the hereby-ceded territory with the citizens of the United States," said these instructions, "being a provision which cannot now be made, it is to be expected, from the character and policy of the United States, that such incorporation will take place without unnecessary delay." The provision, which Madison said could not be made, was nevertheless made by Livingston and Monroe.

Embarrassing as these omissions or provisions were, they proved not so much that the treaty was carelessly drawn, as that the American negotiators were ready to stipulate whatever was needed for their purpose. Other portions of the treaty were not to be defended on that excuse. The price stipulated for Louisiana was sixty million francs, in the form of United States six-per-cent bonds, representing a capital of $11,250,000. Besides this sum of eleven and a quarter million dollars, the

United States government was to assume and pay the debts due by France to American citizens, estimated at twenty million francs, or, at the same rate of exchange, $3,750,000—making fifteen million dollars in all as the price to be paid. Livingston himself drew the claims convention with what he supposed to be particular attention; but it was modified by Monroe, and still further altered by Marbois. "The moment was critical; the question of peace or war was in the balance; and it was important to come to a conclusion before either scale preponderated. I considered the convention as a trifle compared with the other great object," avowed Livingston; "and as it had already delayed us many days, I was ready to take it under any form." The claims convention was not signed till nearly a week after the signature of the treaty of cession. The form in which Livingston took it showed that neither he nor Monroe could have given careful attention to the subject; for not only did the preamble declare that the parties were acting in compliance with Article II. of the treaty of Morfontaine—an Article which had been formally struck out by the Senate, cancelled by Bonaparte, and the omission ratified by the Senate and President since Livingston's residence at Paris; not only did the claims specified fail to embrace all the cases provided for by the treaty of 1800, which this convention was framed to execute; not only were the specifications arbitrary, and even self-contradictory—but the estimate of twenty million francs was far below the amount of the claims admitted in principle; no rule of apportionment was provided, and, worst of all, the right of final decision in every case was reserved to the French government. The meaning of this last provision might be guessed from the notorious corruption of Talleyrand and his band of confidential or secret agents.

Doubtless Livingston was right in securing his main object at any cost; but could he have given more time to his claims convention, he would perhaps have saved his own reputation and that of his successor from much stain, although he might have gained no more than he did for his Government. In the two conventions of 1800 and 1803 the United States obtained two objects of the utmost value—by the first, a release from treaty obligations which, if carried out, required war with England; by the second, the whole west bank of the Mississippi River and the island of New Orleans, with all the incidental advantages attached. In return for these gains the United States government promised not to press the claims of its citizens against the French government beyond the amount of three million seven hundred and fifty thousand dollars, which was one fourth part of the price paid for Louisiana. The legitimate claims of American citizens against France amounted to many million dollars; in the result, certain favored claimants received three million seven hundred and fifty thousand dollars less their expenses, which reduced the sum about one half.

The impression of diplomatic oversight was deepened by the scandals which grew out of the distribution of the three million seven hundred and fifty thousand dollars which the favored claimants were to receive. Livingston's diplomatic career was poisoned by quarrels over this money. That the French government acted with little concealment of venality was no matter of surprise; but that Livingston should be officially charged by his own associates with favoritism and corruption—"imbecility of mind and a childish vanity, mixed with a considerable portion of duplicity"—injured the credit of his Government; and the matter was not bettered when he threw back similar charges on the Board of Commissioners, or when at last General Armstrong, coming to succeed him, was discredited by similar suspicions. Considering how small was the amount of money distributed, the scandal and corruption surpassed any other experience of the national government.

Livingston's troubles did not end there. He could afford to suffer some deduction from his triumph; for he had achieved the greatest diplomatic success recorded in American history. Neither Franklin, Jay, Gallatin, nor any other American diplomatist was so fortunate as Livingston for the immensity of his results compared with the paucity of his means. Other treaties of immense consequence have been signed by American representatives—the treaty of alliance with France; the treaty of peace with England which recognized independence; the treaty of Ghent; the treaty which ceded Florida; the Ashburton treaty; the treaty of Guadalupe Hidalgo—but in none of these did the United States government get so much for so little. The annexation of Louisiana was an event so portentous as to defy measurement; it gave a new face to politics, and ranked in historical importance next to the Declaration of Independence and the adoption of the Constitution—events of which it was the logical outcome; but as a matter of diplomacy it was unparalleled, because it cost almost nothing.

The scandalous failure of the claims convention was a trifling drawback to the enjoyment of this unique success; but the success was further embittered by the conviction that America would give the honor to Monroe. Virginia was all-powerful. Livingston was unpopular, distrusted, not liked even by Madison; while Monroe, for political reasons, had been made a prominent figure. Public attention had been artificially drawn upon his mission; and in consequence, Monroe's name grew great, so as almost to overshadow that of Madison, while Livingston heard few voices proclaiming his services to the country. In a few weeks Livingston began to see his laurels wither, and was forced to claim the credit that he thought his due. Monroe treated him less generously than he might have done, considering that Monroe gained the political profit of the success. Acknowledging that his own share was next to nothing in the negotiation, he still encouraged the idea that Livingston's influence had been equally null. This view was doubtless correct, but if universally applied in history, would deprive many great men of their laurels. Monroe's criticism helped only to diminish the political chances of a possible rival who had no Virginia behind him to press his preferment and cover his mistakes.

NEITHER *the cabinet nor the congress shared Jefferson's scruples about the constitutionality of the purchase, and his proposal for a constitutional amendment received short shrift. Reluctantly he acquiesced in their theory of broad construction although he knew it must be ultimately fatal to states' rights. He had to accept the fact, as Adams puts it, that both the Republican and the Federalist parties "agreed that the moment had come when the old Union must change its character." The government at Washington could not avoid exercising all the rights inherent in sovereignty. Ironically, his own party, the party of strict construction, was the author of the change. The old established constitutional balances were further shaken by the adoption of the twelfth amendment requiring the separate election of the President and the Vice-President. The measure closed the door to the kind of intrigue which had troubled the election of Jefferson and Burr, but it further diminished the influence of the small states in the Electoral College.*

Although the government had demonstrated that it was prepared to govern with the requisite energy, the New England Federalists were alarmed by the assaults of the Republicans upon the judiciary, as shown in their successful impeachment of Judge Pickering and the threatened impeachment of Justice Chase under the management of John Randolph of Roanoke. Forming the Essex Junto they allied themselves with Burr, the "Mephistopheles of politics," and supported him in his unsuccessful bid for the governorship of New York against Hamilton's strong objection. Hamilton, though an avowed enemy of democratic principles, was opposed to the Federalist extremists who talked of separation, and he had only contempt for Burr. The duel in which Hamilton was killed ended Burr's influence.

The extremist Republicans for their part failed in their attempt to remove Justice Chase. Henceforth, Chief Justice Marshall could safely assert the authority of the Supreme Court to interpret the constitution according to Federalist and centralizing principles.

Adams's richly detailed narrative now turns to the complex diplomatic jockeying by which Jefferson tried to maintain neutrality in the struggle between France and England and of how he tried to profit from the controversy between France and her unhappy ally, Spain. His expansionist advisers soon persuaded him to adopt the theory that West Florida was part of the Louisiana Purchase. He pressed the claim over Spanish protests, mistakenly expecting that since Spain would be drawn into the war with England she would yield the point to avoid further struggle with the United States. Napoleon, who saw the value of the ambiguity in the Louisiana Treaty as a lever in managing his relations with America, unexpectedly came to the defense of the Spanish government. More serious embarrassments, however, now began to confront the pacific Jefferson, as a result of the renewed war and the strain it put on the relations of the United States with England by reopening all the old subjects of controversy. To provide the background for that change, Adams reviews the history of the relations with England.

Relations with England

FOR eighteen years after 1783 William Pitt guided England through peace and war with authority almost as absolute as that of Don Carlos IV. or Napoleon himself. From him and from his country President Jefferson had much to fear and nothing to gain beyond a continuance of the good relations which President Washington, with extreme difficulty, had succeeded in establishing between the two peoples. So far as England was concerned, this understanding had been the work of Pitt and Lord Grenville, who rather imposed it on their party than accepted it as the result of any public will. The extreme perils in which England then stood inspired caution; and of this caution the treaty of 1794 was one happy result. So long as the British government remained in a cautious spirit, America was safe; but should Pitt or his successors throw off the self-imposed restraints on England's power, America could at the utmost, even by a successful war, gain nothing materially better than a return to the arrangements of 1794.

The War of Independence, which ended in the definitive treaty of 1783, naturally left the English people in a state of irritation and disgust toward America; and the long interregnum of the Confederation, from 1783 to 1789, allowed this disgust to ripen into contempt. When at length the Constitution of 1789 restored order in the American chaos, England felt little faith in the success of the experiment. She waited for time to throw light on her interests.

This delay was natural; for American independence had shattered into fragments the commercial system of Great Britain, and powerful interests were combined to resist further concession. Before 1776 the colonies of England stretched from the St. Lawrence to the Mississippi, and across the Gulf of Mexico to the coast of South America, mutually supporting and strengthening each other. Jamaica and the other British islands of the West Indies drew their most necessary supplies from the Delaware and the Hudson. Boston and New York were in some respects more important to them than London itself. The timber, live-stock, and provisions which came from the neighboring continent were essential to the existence of the West Indian planters and negroes. When war cut off these supplies, famine and pestilence followed. After the peace of 1783 even the most conservative English statesmen were obliged to admit that the strictness of their old colonial system could not be maintained, and that the United States, though independent, must be admitted to some of the privileges of a British colony. The government unwillingly conceded what could not be refused, and the West Indian colonists compelled Parliament to relax the colonial system so far as to allow a restricted intercourse between their islands and the ports of the United States. The relaxation was not a favor to the United States—it was a condition of existence to the West Indies; not a boon, but a right which the colonists claimed and an Act of Parliament defined.

The right was dearly paid for. The islands might buy American timber and grain, but they were allowed to make return only in molasses and rum. Payment in sugar would have been cheaper for the colonists, and the planters wished for nothing more earnestly than to be allowed this privilege; but as often as they raised the prayer, English shipowners cried that the navigation laws were in peril, and a chorus of familiar phrases filled the air, all carrying a deep meaning to the English people. "Nursery of seamen" was one favorite expression; "Neutral frauds" another; and all agreed in assuming that at whatever cost, and by means however extravagant, the navy must be fed and strengthened. Under the cover of supporting the navy any absurdity could be defended; and in the case of the West Indian trade, the British shipowner enjoyed the right to absurdities sanctioned by a century and a half of law and custom. The freight on British sugars belonged of right to British shippers, who could not be expected to surrender of their own accord, in obedience to any laws of political economy, a property which was the source of their incomes. The colonists asked permission to refine their own sugar; but their request not only roused strong opposition from the shipowners who wanted the bulkier freight, but started the home sugar-refiners to their feet, who proved by Acts of Parliament that sugar-refining was a British and not a colonial right. The colonists then begged a reduction of the heavy duty on sugar; but English country gentlemen cried against a measure which might lead to an increase of the income-tax or the imposition of some new burden on agriculture. In this dilemma the colonists frankly said that only their weakness, not their will, prevented them from declaring themselves independent, like their neighbors at Charleston and Philadelphia.

Even when the qualified right of trade was conceded, the colonists were not satisfied; and the concession itself laid the foundation of more serious changes. From the moment that American produce was admitted to be a necessity for the colonists, it was clear that the Americans must be allowed a voice in the British system. Discussion whether the Americans had or had not a right to the colonial trade was already a long step toward revolution. One British minister after another resented the idea that the Americans had any rights in the matter; yet when they came to practical arrangements the British statesmen were obliged to concede that they were mistaken. From the necessity of the case, the Americans had rights which never could be successfully denied. Parliament struggled to prevent the rebel Americans from sharing in the advantages of the colonial system from which they had rebelled; but unreasonable as it was that the United States should be rewarded for rebellion by retaining the privileges of subjects, this was the inevitable result. Geography and Nature were stronger than Parliament and the British navy.

At first Pitt hoped that the concession to the colonists might entail no concession to the United States; while admitting a certain hiatus in the colonial system, he tried to maintain the navigation laws in their integrity. The admission of American produce into the West Indies was no doubt an infraction of the protectionist principle on which all the civilized world, except America, founded its economical ideas; but in itself it was not serious. To allow the flour, potatoes, tobacco, timber, and horses of the American continent to enter the harbors of Barbadoes and Jamaica; to allow in turn the molasses and rum of the islands to be sent directly to New York and Boston—harmed no one, and was advantageous to all parties, so long as British ships were employed to carry on the trade. At first this was the case. The Act of Parliament allowed only British subjects, in British-built ships, to enter colonial ports with American produce. Whether the United States government would long tolerate such legislation without countervailing measures was a question which remained open for a time, while the system itself had a chance to prove its own weakness. The British shipping did not answer colonial objects. Again and again the colonists found themselves on the verge of starvation; and always in this emergency the colonial governors threw open their ports by proclamation to American shipping, while with equal regularity Parliament protected the governors by Acts of Indemnity. To this extent the navigation system suffered together with the colonial system, but in theory it was intact. Ministry, Parliament, and people clung to the navigation laws as their ark of safety; and even the colonists conceded that although they had a right to eat American wheat and potatoes, they had no right to eat those which came to them in the hold of a Marblehead schooner.

Such a principle, however convenient to Great Britain, was not suited to the interests of New England shippers. In peace their chances were comparatively few, and the chief diplomatic difficulties between European governments and the United States had their source in the American attempt to obtain legal recognition of trade which America wished to maintain with the colonies; but in war the situation changed, and more serious disputes occurred. Then the French and Spanish West Indian ports were necessarily thrown open to neutral commerce, because their own ships were driven from the ocean by the superiority of the British navy. Besides the standing controversy about the admission of American produce to British islands, the British government found itself harassed by doubts to what extent it might safely admit the Americans into the French or Spanish West Indies, and allow them to carry French property, as though their flag were competent to protect whatever was under it. Granting that an article like French sugar might be carried in a neutral vessel, there were still other articles, called contraband, which ought not to be made objects of neutral commerce; and England was obliged to define the nature of contraband. She was also forced to make free use of the right of blockade. These delicate questions were embittered by another and more serious quarrel. The European belligerents claimed the right to the military service of their subjects, and there was no doubt that their right was perfect. In pursuance of the claim they insisted upon taking their seamen from American merchant-vessels wherever met on the high seas. So far as

France was concerned, the annoyance was slight; but the identity of race made the practice extremely troublesome as concerned England.

At the outbreak of the French wars, Nov. 6, 1793, the British government issued instructions directing all British armed vessels to seize every neutral ship they should meet, loaded with the produce of a French colony or carrying supplies for its use. These orders were kept secret for several weeks, until the whole American commerce with the Antilles, and all American ships found on the ocean, laden in whole or in part with articles of French colonial produce or for French colonial use, were surprised and swept into British harbors, where they were condemned by British admiralty courts, on the ground known as the "Rule of the War of 1756"—that because trade between the French colonies and the United States was illegal in peace, it was illegal in war. From the point of view in which European Powers regarded their colonies, much could be said in support of this rule. A colony was almost as much the property of its home government as a dockyard or a military station. France and Spain could hardly complain if England chose to treat the commerce of such government-stations as contraband; but a rule which might perhaps be applied by European governments to each other worked with great injustice when applied to the United States, who had no colonies, and made no attempt to build up a navy or support an army by such means. Taken in its broadest sense, the European colonial system might be defined by the description which the best of British commentators gave to that of England—a "policy pursued for rendering the foreign trade of the whole world subservient to the increase of her shipping and navigation." American Independence was a protest against this practice; and the first great task of the United States was to overthrow and destroy the principle, in order to substitute freedom of trade. America naturally objected to becoming a martyr to the rules of a system which she was trying to revolutionize.

When these British instructions of Nov. 26, 1793, became

known in the United States, the Government of President Washington imposed an embargo, threatened retaliation, and sent Chief-Justice Jay to London as a last chance of maintaining peace. On arriving there, Jay found that Pitt had already voluntarily retreated from his ground, and that new Orders, dated Jan. 8, 1794, had been issued, exempting from seizure American vessels engaged in the direct trade from the United States to the French West Indies. In the end, the British government paid the value of the confiscated vessels. The trade from the United States to Europe was not interfered with; and thus American ships were allowed to carry French colonial produce through an American port to France, while Russian or Danish ships were forbidden by England to carry such produce to Europe at all, although their flags and harbors were as neutral as those of the United States. America became suddenly a much favored nation, and the enemies of England attributed this unexpected kindness to fear. In truth it was due to a natural mistake. The British Treasury calculated that the expense and trouble of carrying sugar and coffee from Martinique or St. Domingo to Boston, of landing it, paying duties, re-embarking it, receiving the drawback, and then carrying it to Bordeaux or Brest, would be such as to give ample advantages to English vessels which could transship more conveniently at London. The mistake soon became apparent. The Americans quickly proved that they could under these restrictions carry West Indian produce to Europe not only more cheaply than British ships could do it, but almost as quickly; while it was a positive advantage on the return voyage to make double freight by stopping at an American port. The consequence of this discovery was seen in the sudden increase of American shipping, and was largely due to the aid of British seamen, who found in the new service better pay, food, and treatment than in their own, and comparative safety from the press-gang and the lash. At the close of the century the British flag seemed in danger of complete exclusion from the harbors of the United States. In 1790 more than 550 British ships, with a capacity of more than 115,000 tons, had entered inward and outward, representing about half that number of actual vessels; in 1799 the custom-house returns showed not 100 entries, and in 1800 about 140, representing a capacity of 40,000 tons. In the three years 1790–1792, the returns showed an average of some 280 outward and inward entries of American ships with a capacity of 54,000 tons; in 1800 the entries were 1,057, with a capacity of 236,000 tons. The Americans were not only beginning to engross the direct trade between their own ports and Europe, but were also rapidly obtaining the indirect carrying-trade between the West Indies and the European continent, and even between one European country and another. The British government began to feel seriously uneasy. At a frightful cost the people of England were striving to crush the navies and commerce of France and Spain, only to build up the power of a dangerous rival beyond the ocean.

Doubtless the British government would have taken measures to correct its mistake, if the political situation had not hampered its energies. Chief-Justice Jay, in 1794, negotiated a treaty with Lord Grenville which was in some respects very hard upon the United States, but was inestimably valuable to them, because it tied Pitt's hands and gave time for the new American Constitution to acquire strength. Ten years of steady progress were well worth any temporary concessions, even though these concessions exasperated France, and roused irritation between her and the United States which in 1798 became actual hostility. The prospect that the United States would become the ally of England was so fair that Pitt dared not disturb it. His government was in a manner forced to give American interests free play, and to let American shipping gain a sudden and unnatural enlargement. His liberality was well paid. For a moment France drove the United States to reprisals; and as the immediate consequence, St. Domingo became practically independent, owing to the support given by the United States to Toussaint. Even the reconciliation of France with America effected by Bonaparte and Talleyrand in 1800 did not at first redress the balance. Not till the Peace of Amiens, in 1802, did France recover her colonies; and not till a year later did Bonaparte succeed, by the sacrifice of Louisiana, in bringing the United States back to their old attitude of jealousy toward England.

Nevertheless, indications had not been wanting that England was aware of the advantage she had given to American commerce, and still better of the advantages which had been given it by Nature. All the Acts of Parliament on the statute-book could not prevent the West Indies from being largely dependent on the United States; yet the United States need not be allowed the right to carry West Indian produce to France—a right which depended only on so-called international law, and was worthless unless supported by the stronger force. A new Order was issued, Jan. 25, 1798, which admitted European neutrals to enemies' colonies, and allowed them to bring French colonial produce to England or to their own ports. This Order was looked upon as a side-blow at American shipping, which was not allowed the same privilege of sailing direct from the Antilles to Europe. The new Order was justified on the ground that the old rule discriminated in favor of American merchants, whose competition might be injurious to the commercial interests of England.

Further than this the British government did not then go; on the contrary, it officially confirmed the existing arrangement. The British courts of admiralty conformed closely to the rules of their political chiefs. Sir William Scott, better known as Lord Stowell, whose great reputation as a judge was due to the remarkable series of judgments in which he created a new system of admiralty law, announced with his usual clearness the rules by which he meant to be guided. In the case of the "Emmanuel," in November, 1799, he explained the principle on which the law permitted neutrals to carry French produce from their own country to France. "By importation," he said, "the produce became part of the national stock of the neutral country; the inconveniences of aggravated delay and expense were a safeguard against this right becoming a special convenience to France or a serious abridgement of belligerent rights." Soon afterward, in the case of the "Polly," April 29, 1800, he took occasion to define what he meant by importation into a neutral country. He said it was not his business to decide what was universally the test of a *bona fide* importation; but he was strongly disposed to hold that it would be sufficient if the goods were proved to have been landed and the duties paid; and he did accordingly rule that such proof was sufficient to answer the fair demands of his court.

Rufus King, then American minister in London, succeeded in obtaining from Pitt an express acceptance of this rule as binding on the government. On the strength of a report from the King's Advocate, dated March 16, 1801, the British Secretary of State notified the American minister that what Great Britain considered as the general principle of colonial trade had been relaxed in a certain degree in consideration of the present state of commerce. Neutrals might import French colonial produce, and convey it by re-exportation to France. Landing the goods and paying the duties in America legalized the trade, even though these goods were at once re-shipped and forwarded to France on account of the same owners.

With this double guaranty Jefferson began his administration, and the American merchants continued their profitable business. Not only did they build and buy large numbers of vessels, and borrow all the capital they could obtain, but doubtless some French and Spanish merchants, besides a much greater number of English, made use of the convenient American flag. The Yankees exulted loudly over the decline of British shipping in the harbors; the British masters groaned to see themselves sacrificed by their own government; and the British admirals complained bitterly that their prize-money was cut off, and that they were wearing out their lives in the hardest service, in order to foster a commerce of smugglers and perjurers, whose only protection was the flag of a country that had not a single line-of-battle ship to fly it.

Yet President Jefferson had reason to weigh long and soberly the pointed remark with which the King's Advocate began his report—that the general principle with respect to the colonial trade had been to a certain extent relaxed in consideration of the present state of commerce. No doubt the British pretension, as a matter of international law, was outrageous. The so-called rule of 1756 was neither more nor less than a rule of force; but when was international law itself anything more than a law of force? The moment a nation found itself unable to show some kind of physical defence for its protection, the wisdom of Grotius and Bynkershoek could not prevent it from being plundered; and how could President Jefferson complain merely because American ships were forbidden by England to carry French sugars to France, when he looked on without a protest while England and France committed much greater outrages on every other country within their reach?

President Jefferson believed that the United States had ample means to resist any British pretension. As his letters to Paine and Logan showed, he felt that European Powers could be controlled through the interests of commerce. He was the more firmly convinced by the extraordinary concessions which Pitt had made, and by the steady encouragement he gave to the American merchant. Jefferson felt sure that England could not afford to sacrifice a trade of some forty million dollars, and that her colonies could not exist without access to the American market. What need to spend millions on a navy, when Congress, as Jefferson believed, already grasped England by the throat, and could suffocate her by a mere turn of the wrist!

This reasoning had much in its favor. To Pitt the value of the American trade at a time of war with France and Spain was immense; and when taken in connection with the dependence of the West Indian colonies on America, it made a combination of British interests centering in the United States which much exceeded the entire value of all England's other branches of foreign commerce. Its prospective value was still greater if things should remain as they were, and if England should continue to undersell all rivals in articles of general manufacture. England could well afford to lose great sums of money in the form of neutral freights rather than drive Congress to a protective system which should create manufactures of cotton, woollen, and iron. These were motives which had their share in the civility with which England treated America; and year by year their influence should naturally have increased.

Of all British markets the American was the most valuable; but next to the American market was that of the West Indies. In some respects the West Indian was of the two the better worth preserving. From head to foot the planters and their half-million negroes were always clad in cottons or linens made by the clothiers of Yorkshire, Wiltshire, or Belfast. Every cask and hoop, every implement and utensil, was supplied from the British islands. The sailing of a West Indian convoy was "an epoch in the diary of every shop and warehouse throughout the Kingdom." The West Indian colonies employed, including the fisheries, above a thousand sail of shipping and twenty-five thousand seamen. While America might, and one day certainly would, manufacture for herself, the West Indies could not even dream of it; there the only profitable or practicable industry was cultivation of the soil, and the chief article of cultivation was the sugar-cane. Rival industries to those of Great Britain were impossible; the only danger that threatened British control was the loss of naval supremacy or the revolt of the negroes.

A great majority of British electors would certainly have felt no hesitation in deciding, as between the markets of the United States and of the West Indies, that if a choice must be made, good policy required the government to save at all hazards the West Indies. Both as a permanent market for manufactures and as a steady support for shipping, the West Indian commerce held the first place in British interests. This fact needed to be taken into account by the United States government before relying with certainty on the extent to which Great Britain could be controlled by the interests involved in the American trade. At the most critical moment all Jefferson's calculations might be upset by the growth of a conviction in England that the colonial system was in serious danger; and to make this chance stronger, another anxiety was so closely connected with it as to cause incessant alarm in the British mind.

The carrying-trade between the French West Indies and Europe which had thus fallen into American hands, added to the natural increase of national exports and imports, required a large amount of additional shipping; and what was more directly hostile to English interests, it drew great numbers of British sailors into the American merchant-service. The desertion of British seamen and the systematic encouragement offered to deserters in every seaport of the Union were serious annoyances, which the American government was unable to excuse or correct. Between 1793 and 1801 they reached the proportions of a grave danger to the British service. Every British government packet which entered the port of New York during the winter before Jefferson's accession to power lost almost every seaman in its crew; and neither people nor magistrates often lent help to recover them. At Norfolk the crew of a British ship deserted to an American sloop-of-war, whose commander, while admitting the fact, refused to restore the men, alleging his construction of official orders in his excuse. In most American harbors such protection as the British shipmaster obtained sprang from the personal good-will of magistrates, who without strict legal authority consented to apply, for the benefit of the foreign master, the merchant-shipping law of the United States; but in one serious case even this voluntary assistance was stopped by the authority of a State government.

This interference was due to the once famous dispute over Jonathan Robbins, which convulsed party politics in America during the heated election of 1800. Thomas Nash, a boatswain on the British frigate "Hermione," having been ringleader in conspiracy and murder on the high seas, was afterward identified in the United States under the name and with the papers of Jonathan Robbins of Danbury, in Connecticut. On a requisition from the British minister, dated June 3, 1799, he was delivered under the extradition clause of Jay's treaty, and was hung. The Republican party, then in opposition, declared that Robbins, or Nash, was in their belief an American citizen whose surrender was an act of base subservience to Great Britain. An effigy of Robbins hanging to a gibbet was a favorite electioneering device at public meetings. The State of Virginia, having a similar grievance of its own, went so far as to enact a law which forbade, under the severest penalties, any magistrate who acted under authority of the State to be instrumental in transporting any person out of its jurisdiction. As citizens of the Union, sworn to support the Constitution, such magistrates were equally bound with the Federal judges to grant warrants of commitment, under the Twenty-seventh Article of Jay's treaty, against persons accused of specified crimes. The Virginia Act directly contravened the treaty; while indirectly it prevented magistrates from granting warrants against deserters and holding them in custody, so that every English vessel which entered a Virginia port was at once abandoned by her crew, who hastened to enter the public or private ships of the United States.

The captain of any British frigate which might happen to run into the harbor of New York, if he went ashore, was likely to meet on his return to the wharf some of his boat's crew strolling about the town, every man supplied with papers of American citizenship. This was the more annoying, because American agents in British ports habitually claimed and received the benefit of the British law; while so far as American papers were concerned, no pretence was made of concealing the fraud, but they were issued in any required quantity, and were transferred for a few dollars from hand to hand.

Not only had the encouragement to desertion a share in the decline of British shipping in American harbors, but it also warranted, and seemed almost to render necessary, the only countervailing measure the British government could employ. Whatever happened to the merchant-service, the British navy could not be allowed to suffer. England knew no conscription for her armies, because for centuries she had felt no need of general military service; but at any moment she might compel her subjects to bear arms, if circumstances required it. Her necessities were greater on the ocean. There, from time immemorial, a barbarous sort of conscription, known as impressment, had been the ordinary means of supplying the royal navy in emergencies; and every seafaring man was liable to be dragged at any moment from his beer-cellar or coasting-vessel to man the guns of a frigate on its way to a three-years' cruise in the West Indies or the Mediterranean. Mere engagement in a foreign merchant-service did not release the British sailor from his duty. When the captain of a British frigate overhauled an American merchant-vessel for enemy's property or contraband of war, he sent an officer on board who mustered the crew, and took out any seamen whom he believed to be British. The measure as the British navy regarded it, was one of self-protection. If the American government could not or would not discourage desertion, the naval commander would recover his men in the only way he could. Thus a circle of grievances was established on each side. Pitt's concessions to the United States irritated the British navy and merchant-marine, while they gave great profits to American shipping; the growth of American shipping stimulated desertions from the British service to the extent of injuring its efficiency; and these desertions in their turn led to a rigorous exercise of the right of impressment. To find some point at which this vicious circle could be broken was a matter of serious consequence to both countries, but most so to the one which avowed that it did not mean to protect its interests by force.

Great Britain could have broken the circle by increasing the pay and improving the condition of her seamen; but she was excessively conservative, and the burdens already imposed on her commerce were so great that she could afford to risk nothing. In the face of a combined navy like that of Spain and France, her control of the seas at any given point, such as the West Indies, was still doubtful; and in the face of American competition, her huge convoys suffered under great disadvantage. Conscious of her own power, she thought that the United States should be first to give way. Had the American government been willing to perform its neutral obligations strictly, the circle might have been broken without much trouble; but the United States wished to retain their advantage, and preferred to risk whatever England might do rather than discourage desertion, or enact and enforce a strict naturalization law, or punish fraud. The national government was too weak to compel the States to respect neutral obligations, even if it had been disposed to make the attempt.

The practice of impressment brought the two governments to a deadlock on an issue of law. No one denied that every government had the right to command the services of its native subjects, and as yet no one ventured to maintain that a merchant-ship on the high seas could lawfully resist the exercise of this right; but the law had done nothing to define the rights of naturalized subjects or citizens. The British government might, no doubt, impress its own subjects; but almost every British sailor in the American service carried papers of American citizenship, and although some of these were fraudulent, many were genuine. The law of England, as declared from time out of mind by every generation of her judges, held that the allegiance of a subject was indefeasible, and therefore that naturalization was worthless. The law of the United States, as declared by Chief-Justice Ellsworth in 1799, was in effect the same; he held that no citizen could dissolve the compact of protection and defence between himself and society without the consent or default of the community. On both sides the law was emphatic to the point that naturalization could not bind the government which did not consent to it; and the United States could hardly require England to respect naturalization papers which the Supreme Court of the United States declared itself unable to respect in a similar case. Nevertheless, while courts and judges declare what the law is or ought to be, they bind only themselves, and their decisions have no necessary effect on the co-ordinate branches of government. While the judges laid down one doctrine in Westminster Hall, Parliament laid down another in St. Stephen's chapel; and no one could say whether the law or the statute was final. The British statute-book contained Acts of Parliament as old as the reign of Queen Anne to encourage the admission of foreign seamen into the British navy, offering them naturalization as an inducement. American legislation went not quite so far, but by making naturalization easy it produced worse results. A little perjury, in no wise unsafe, was alone required in order to transform British seamen into American citizens; and perjury was the commonest commodity in a seaport. The British government was forced to decide whether papers so easily obtained and transferred should be allowed to bar its claims on the services of its subjects, and whether it could afford to become a party to the destruction of its own marine, even though the United States should join with France and carry on endless war.

That there were some points which not even the loss of American trade would bring England to concede was well known to Jefferson; and on these points he did not mean to insist. Setting the matter of impressment aside, the relations between England and America had never been better than when the new President took office March 4, 1801. The British government seemed earnest in conciliation, and lost no opportunity of showing its good-will. Under the Sixth Article of Jay's treaty, a commission had been appointed to settle long-standing debts due to British subjects, but held in abeyance by State legislation in contravention of the treaty of 1783. After long delays the commission met at Philadelphia and set to work, but had made little progress when the two American commissioners, with the President's approval, in the teeth of the treaty which created the Board, refused to accept its decisions, and seceded. This violent measure was not taken by the Administration without uneasiness, for England might reasonably have resented it; but after some further delay the British government consented to negotiate again, and at last accepted a round sum of three million dollars in full discharge of the British claim. This was a case in which England was the aggrieved party; she behaved equally well in other cases where the United States were aggrieved. Rufus King complained that her admiralty courts in the West Indies and at Halifax were a scandal; in deference to his remonstrances these courts were thoroughly reformed by Act of Parliament. The vice-admiralty court at Nassau condemned the American brigantine "Leopard," engaged in carrying Malaga wine from the United States to the Spanish West Indies. The American minister complained of the decision, and within three days the King's Advocate reported in his favor. The report was itself founded on Sir William Scott's favorable decision in the case of the "Polly." Soon afterward the American minister complained that Captain Pellew, of the "Cleopatra," and Admiral Parker had not effectually restrained their subordinates on the American station; both officers were promptly recalled. Although the Ministry had not yet consented to make any arrangement on the practice of impressment, Rufus King felt much hope that they might consent even to this reform; meanwhile Lord Grenville checked the practice, and professed a strong wish to find some expedient that should take its place.

There was no reason to doubt the sincerity of the British Foreign Office in wishing friendship. Its policy was well expressed in a despatch written from Philadelphia by Robert Liston, the British minister, shortly before he left the United States to return home—

The advantages to be ultimately reaped from a perseverance in the line of conduct which Great Britain has adopted for the last four years appear to my mind to be infallible and of infinite magnitude; the profitable consequences of a state of hostility, small and uncertain. I have been pleasing my imagination with looking forward to the distant spectacle of all the northern continent of America covered with friendly though not subject States, consuming our manufactures, speaking our language, proud of their parent State, attached to her prosperity.

War must bring with it extensive damage to our navigation, the probable loss of Canada, and the *world* behind it, the propagation of enmity and prejudices which it may be impossible to eradicate. The system of the American government does not strike me, with the near view I have of it, as being in so perilous a situation as is imagined in Europe. I am willing to avoid political prophecies, but I confess I think it will get on well enough if the country remains in peace; and if they go to war, the fabric may acquire strength. God forbid that it should be to our detriment, and to the triumph of our enemies!

In 1803, as a result of the violation of the Treaty of Amiens of the preceding year, neutral powers were again placed at the mercy of the two great belligerents. For Americans the question of impressments became more urgent as increasing numbers of British sailors deserted to American ships and the British navy insisted on its right of search to reclaim them, even to the point of blockading New York for that purpose. Determined to avoid war, Jefferson countered the seizures of ships by securing the passage early in 1806 of the Non-Importation Act as a weapon of peaceable coercion against England. But a new threat to neutral commerce arose in May when a British Order in Council declared a blockade of portions of the Continent. Then Napoleon, flushed with his victory at Jena, retaliated with the famous Berlin Decree forbidding all neutral trade with England. This was followed in turn by a new Order of Council, which compounded old injuries by prohibiting European coastal commerce to neutrals. Blockade-running continued to be highly profitable though increasingly costly in impounded American ships and cargoes.

Suddenly in June, 1807, came the murderous attack of the British frigate Leopard on the American warship Chesapeake when the American captain refused to submit to search. England disavowed the attack but not the principle. A still further restraint was imposed on commerce in November, 1807, by an Order in Council imposing a licensing scheme that in effect made American commerce a part of British commerce. Since the milder Non-Importation Act had produced no effect upon English policy, congress thereupon adopted Jefferson's permanent Embargo Act on December 21, 1807, as the final instrument of his foreign policy. The following chapter narrates the disastrous domestic effects of that policy.

The Cost of the Embargo

THE embargo was an experiment in politics well worth making. In the scheme of President Jefferson's statesmanship, non-

Vol. IV, Chap. XII.

intercourse was the substitute for war—the weapon of defence
and coercion which saved the cost and danger of supporting
army or navy, and spared America the brutalities of the Old
World. Failure of the embargo meant in his mind not only a
recurrence to the practice of war, but to every political and
social evil that war had always brought in its train. In such a
case the crimes and corruptions of Europe, which had been the
object of his political fears, must, as he believed, sooner or
later teem in the fat soil of America. To avert a disaster so vast,
was a proper motive for statesmanship, and justified disregard
for smaller interests. Jefferson understood better than his
friends the importance of his experiment; and when in pursuing
his object he trampled upon personal rights and public principles, he did so, as he avowed in the Louisiana purchase, because he believed that a higher public interest required the
sacrifice—

My principle is, that the conveniences of our citizens shall
yield reasonably, and their taste greatly, to the importance of
giving the present experiment so fair a trial that on future
occasions our legislators may know with certainty how far they
may count on it as an engine for national purposes.

Hence came his repeated entreaties for severity, even to the
point of violence and bloodshed—

I do consider the severe enforcement of the embargo to be of
an importance not to be measured by money, for our future government as well as present objects.

Everywhere, on all occasions, he proclaimed that embargo
was the alternative to war. The question next to be decided
was brought by this means into the prominence it deserved.
Of the two systems of statesmanship, which was the most costly
—which the most efficient?

The dread of war, radical in the Republican theory, sprang
not so much from the supposed waste of life or resources as from
the retroactive effects which war must exert upon the form of
government; but the experience of a few months showed that

the embargo as a system was rapidly leading to the same effects. Indeed, the embargo and the Louisiana purchase taken together were more destructive to the theory and practice of a Virginia republic than any foreign war was likely to be. Personal liberties and rights of property were more directly curtailed in the United States by embargo than in Great Britain by centuries of almost continuous foreign war. No one denied that a permanent embargo strained the Constitution to the uttermost tension; and even the Secretary of the Treasury and the President admitted that it required the exercise of most arbitrary, odious, and dangerous powers. From this point of view the system was quickly seen to have few advantages. If American liberties must perish, they might as well be destroyed by war as be stifled by non-intercourse.

While the constitutional cost of the two systems was not altogether unlike, the economical cost was a point not easily settled. No one could say what might be the financial expense of embargo as compared with war. Yet Jefferson himself in the end admitted that the embargo had no claim to respect as an economical measure. The Boston Federalists estimated that the net American loss of income, exclusive of that on freights, could not be less than ten per cent for interest and profit on the whole export of the country—or ten million eight hundred thousand dollars on a total export value of one hundred and eight millions. This estimate was extravagant, even if the embargo had been wholly responsible for cutting off American trade; it represented in fact the loss resulting to America from Napoleon's decrees, the British orders, and the embargo taken together. Yet at least the embargo was more destructive than war would have been to the interests of foreign commerce. Even in the worst of foreign wars American commerce could not be wholly stopped—some outlet for American produce must always remain open, some inward bound ships would always escape the watch of a blockading squadron. Even in 1814, after two years of war, and when the coast was stringently blockaded, the American Treasury collected six million dollars from imports; but in 1808, after the embargo was in full effect, the customs yielded only a few thousand dollars on cargoes that happened to be imported for some special purpose. The difference was loss, to the disadvantage of embargo. To this must be added loss of freight, decay of ships and produce, besides enforced idleness to a corresponding extent; and finally the cost of a war if the embargo system should fail.

In other respects the system was still costly. The citizen was not killed, but he was partially paralyzed. Government did not waste money or life, but prevented both money and labor from having their former value. If long continued, embargo must bankrupt the government almost as certainly as war; if not long continued, the immediate shock to industry was more destructive than war would have been. The expense of war proved, five years afterward, to be about thirty million dollars a year, and of this sum much the larger portion was pure loss; but in 1808, owing to the condition of Europe, the expense need not have exceeded twenty millions, and the means at hand were greater. The effect of the embargo was certainly no greater than the effect of war in stimulating domestic industry. In either case the stimulus was temporary and ineffective; but the embargo cut off the resources of credit and capital; while war gave both an artificial expansion. The result was that while embargo saved perhaps twenty millions of dollars a year and some thousands of lives which war would have consumed, it was still an expensive system, and in some respects more destructive than war itself to national wealth.

The economical was less serious than the moral problem. The strongest objection to war was not its waste of money or even of life; for money and life in political economy were worth no more than they could be made to produce. A worse evil was the lasting harm caused by war to the morals of mankind, which no system of economy could calculate. The reign of brute force and brutal methods corrupted and debauched society, making it blind to its own vices and ambitious only for mischief. Yet even on that ground the embargo had few advantages. The peaceable coercion which Jefferson tried to substitute for war was less brutal, but hardly less mischievous, than the evil it displaced. The embargo opened the sluice-gates of social corruption. Every citizen was tempted to evade or defy the laws. At every point along the coast and frontier the civil, military, and naval services were brought in contact with corruption; while every man in private life was placed under strong motives to corrupt. Every article produced or consumed in the country became an object of speculation; every form of industry became a form of gambling. The rich could alone profit in the end; while the poor must sacrifice at any loss the little they could produce.

If war made men brutal, at least it made them strong; it called out the qualities best fitted to survive in the struggle for existence. To risk life for one's country was no mean act even when done for selfish motives; and to die that others might more happily live was the highest act of self-sacrifice to be reached by man. War, with all its horrors, could purify as well as debase; it dealt with high motives and vast interests; taught courage, discipline, and stern sense of duty. Jefferson must have asked himself in vain what lessons of heroism or duty were taught by his system of peaceable coercion, which turned every citizen into an enemy of the laws—preaching the fear of war and of self-sacrifice, making many smugglers and traitors, but not a single hero.

If the cost of the embargo was extravagant in its effects on the Constitution, the economy, and the morals of the nation, its political cost to the party in power was ruinous. War could have worked no more violent revolution. The trial was too severe for human nature to endure. At a moment's notice, without avowing his true reasons, President Jefferson bade foreign commerce to cease. As the order was carried along the seacoast, every artisan dropped his tools, every merchant closed his doors, every ship was dismantled. American produce—wheat, timber, cotton, tobacco, rice—dropped in value or became unsalable; every imported article rose in price; wages stopped;

swarms of debtors became bankrupt; thousands of sailors hung idle round the wharves trying to find employment on coasters, and escape to the West Indies or Nova Scotia. A reign of idleness began; and the men who were not already ruined felt that their ruin was only a matter of time.

The British traveller, Lambert, who visited New York in 1808, described it as resembling a place ravaged by pestilence—

The port indeed was full of shipping, but they were dismantled and laid up; their decks were cleared, their hatches fastened down, and scarcely a sailor was to be found on board. Not a box, bale, cask, barrel, or package was to be seen upon the wharves. Many of the counting-houses were shut up, or advertised to be let; and the few solitary merchants, clerks, porters, and laborers that were to be seen were walking about with their hands in their pockets. The coffee-houses were almost empty; the streets, near the water-side, were almost deserted; the grass had begun to grow upon the wharves.

In New England, where the struggle of existence was keenest, the embargo struck like a thunderbolt, and society for a moment thought itself at an end. Foreign commerce and shipping were the life of the people—the ocean, as Pickering said, was their farm. The outcry of suffering interests became every day more violent, as the public learned that this paralysis was not a matter of weeks, but of months or years. New Englanders as a class were a law-abiding people; but from the earliest moments of their history they had largely qualified their obedience to the law by the violence with which they abused and the ingenuity with which they evaded it. Against the embargo and Jefferson they concentrated the clamor and passion of their keen and earnest nature. Rich and poor, young and old, joined in the chorus; and one lad, barely in his teens, published what he called "The Embargo: a Satire"—a boyish libel on Jefferson, which the famous poet and Democrat would afterward have given much to recall—

> And thou, the scorn of every patriot name,
> Thy country's ruin, and her councils' shame.
>
> .   .   .   .

> Go, wretch! Resign the Presidential chair,
> Disclose thy secret measures, foul or fair;
> Go search with curious eye for horned frogs
> 'Mid the wild waste of Louisiana bogs;
> Or where Ohio rolls his turbid stream
> Dig for huge bones, thy glory and thy theme. *

The belief that Jefferson, sold to France, wished to destroy American commerce and to strike a deadly blow at New and Old England at once, maddened the sensitive temper of the people. Immense losses, sweeping away their savings and spreading bankruptcy through every village, gave ample cause for their complaints. Yet in truth, New England was better able to defy the embargo than she was willing to suppose. She lost nothing except profits which the belligerents had in any case confiscated; her timber would not harm for keeping, and her fish were safe in the ocean. The embargo gave her almost a monopoly of the American market for domestic manufactures; no part of the country was so well situated or so well equipped for smuggling. Above all, she could easily economize. The New Englander knew better than any other American how to cut down his expenses to the uttermost point of parsimony; and even when he became bankrupt he had but to begin anew. His energy, shrewdness, and education were a capital which the embargo could not destroy, but rather helped to improve.

The growers of wheat and live stock in the Middle States were more hardly treated. Their wheat, reduced in value from two dollars to seventy-five cents a bushel, became practically unsalable. Debarred a market for their produce at a moment when every article of common use tended to rise in cost, they were reduced to the necessity of living on the produce of their farms; but the task was not then so difficult as in later times, and the cities still furnished local markets not to be despised. The manufacturers of Pennsylvania could not but feel the stimulus of the new demand; so violent a system of protection was never applied to them before or since. Probably for that reason

* The Embargo; or Sketches of the Times. A Satire. By William Cullen Bryant. 1808.

the embargo was not so unpopular in Pennsylvania as elsewhere, and Jefferson had nothing to fear from political revolution in this calm and plodding community.

The true burden of the embargo fell on the Southern States,
but most severely upon the great State of Virginia. Slowly
decaying, but still half patriarchal, Virginia society could
neither economize nor liquidate. Tobacco was worthless; but
four hundred thousand negro slaves must be clothed and fed,
great establishments must be kept up, the social scale of living
could not be reduced, and even bankruptcy could not clear a
large landed estate without creating new encumbrances in a
country where land and negroes were the only forms of property
on which money could be raised. Stay-laws were tried, but
served only to prolong the agony. With astonishing rapidity
Virginia succumbed to ruin, while continuing to support the
system that was draining her strength. No episode in American
history was more touching than the generous devotion with
which Virginia clung to the embargo, and drained the poison
which her own President held obstinately to her lips. The cotton and rice States had less to lose, and could more easily bear
bankruptcy; ruin was to them—except in Charleston—a word
of little meaning; but the old society of Virginia could never be
restored. Amid the harsh warnings of John Randolph it saw its
agonies approach; and its last representative, heir to all its honors and dignities, President Jefferson himself woke from his
long dream of power only to find his own fortunes buried in the
ruin he had made.

Except in a state of society verging on primitive civilization,
the stoppage of all foreign intercourse could not have been attempted by peaceable means. The attempt to deprive the laborer of sugar, salt, tea, coffee, molasses, and rum; to treble
the price of every yard of coarse cottons and woollens; to reduce
by one half the wages of labor, and to double its burdens—this
was a trial more severe than war; and even when attempted by
the whole continent of Europe, with all the resources of manufactures and wealth which the civilization of a thousand years

had supplied, the experiment required the despotic power of Napoleon and the united armies of France, Austria, and Russia to carry it into effect. Even then it failed. Jefferson, Madison, and the Southern Republicans had no idea of the economical difficulties their system created, and were surprised to find American society so complex even in their own Southern States that the failure of two successive crops to find a sale threatened beggary to every rich planter from the Delaware to the Sabine. During the first few months, while ships continued to arrive from abroad and old stores were consumed at home, the full pressure of the embargo was not felt; but as the summer of 1808 passed, the outcry became violent. In the Southern States, almost by common consent debts remained unpaid, and few men ventured to oppose a political system which was peculiarly a Southern invention; but in the Northern States, where the bankrupt laws were enforced and the habits of business were comparatively strict, the cost of the embargo was soon shown in the form of political revolution.

The relapse of Massachusetts to Federalism and the overthrow of Senator Adams in the spring of 1808 were the first signs of the political price which President Jefferson must pay for his passion of peace. In New York the prospect was little better. Governor Morgan Lewis, elected in 1804 over Aaron Burr by a combination of Clintons and Livingstons, was turned out of office in 1807 by the Clintons. Governor Daniel D. Tompkins, his successor, was supposed to be a representative of De Witt Clinton and Ambrose Spencer. To De Witt Clinton the State of New York seemed in 1807 a mere appendage—a political property which he could control at will; and of all American politicians next to Aaron Burr none had shown such indifference to party as he. No one could predict his course, except that it would be shaped according to what seemed to be the interests of his ambition. He began by declaring himself against the embargo, and soon afterward declared himself for it. In truth, he was for or against it as the majority might decide; and in New York a majority could hardly fail to decide against the embargo. At the spring election of 1808, which took place about May 1, the Federalists made large gains in the legislature. The summer greatly increased their strength, until Madison's friends trembled for the result, and their language became despondent beyond reason. Gallatin, who knew best the difficulties created by the embargo, began to despair. June 29 he wrote: "From present appearances the Federalists will turn us out by 4th of March next." Ten days afterward he explained the reason of his fears: "I think that Vermont is lost; New Hampshire is in a bad neighborhood; and Pennsylvania is extremely doubtful." In August he thought the situation so serious that he warned the President—

There is almost an equal chance that if propositions from Great Britain, or other events, do not put it in our power to raise the embargo before the 1st of October, we will lose the Presidential election. I think that at this moment the Western States, Virginia, South Carolina, and perhaps Georgia are the only sound States, and that we will have a doubtful contest in every other.

Two causes saved Madison. In the first place, the opposition failed to concentrate its strength. Neither George Clinton nor James Monroe could control the whole body of opponents to the embargo. After waiting till the middle of August for some arrangement to be made, leading Federalists held a conference at New York, where they found themselves obliged, by the conduct of De Witt Clinton, to give up the hope of a coalition. Clinton decided not to risk his fortunes for the sake of his uncle the Vice-President; and this decision obliged the Federalists to put a candidate of their own in the field. They named C. C. Pinckney of South Carolina for President, and Rufus King of New York for Vice-President, as in 1804.

From the moment his opponents divided themselves among three candidates, Madison had nothing to fear; but even without this good fortune he possessed an advantage that weighed decisively in his favor. The State legislatures had been chosen chiefly in the spring or summer, when the embargo was still comparatively popular; and in most cases, but particularly in New York, the legislature still chose Presidential electors. The people expressed no direct opinion on national politics, except in regard to Congressmen. State after State deserted the Federalists without affecting the general election. Early in September Vermont elected a Federalist governor, but the swarm of rotten boroughs in the State secured a Republican legislature, which immediately chose electors for Madison. The revolution in Vermont surrendered all New England to the Federalists. New Hampshire chose Presidential electors by popular vote; Rhode Island did the same—and both States, by fair majorities, rejected Madison and voted for Pinckney. In Massachusetts and Connecticut the legislatures chose Federalist electors. Thus all New England declared against the Administration; and had Vermont been counted as she voted in September, the opposition would have received forty-five electoral votes from New England, where in 1804 it had received only nine. In New York the opponents of the embargo were very strong, and the nineteen electoral votes of that State might in a popular election have been taken from Madison. In this case Pennsylvania would have decided the result. Eighty-eight electoral votes were needed for a choice. New England, New York, and Delaware represented sixty-seven. Maryland and North Carolina were so doubtful that if Pennsylvania had deserted Madison, they would probably have followed her, and would have left the Republican party a wreck.

The choice of electors by the legislatures of Vermont and New York defeated all chance of overthrowing Madison; but apart from these accidents of management the result was already decided by the people of Pennsylvania. The wave of Federalist success and political revolution stopped short in New York, and once more the Democracy of Pennsylvania steadied and saved the Administration. At the October election of 1808— old Governor McKean having at last retired—Simon Snyder was chosen governor by a majority of more than twenty thousand votes. The new governor was the candidate of Duane and the extreme Democrats; his triumph stopped the current of Federalist success, and enabled Madison's friends to drive hesitating Republicans back to their party. In Virginia, Monroe was obliged to retire from the contest, and his supporters dwindled in numbers until only two or three thousand went to the polls. In New York, De Witt Clinton contented himself with taking from Madison six of the nineteen electoral votes and giving them to Vice-President Clinton. Thus the result showed comparatively little sign of the true Republican loss; yet in the electoral college where in 1804 Jefferson had received the voices of one hundred and sixty-two electors, Madison in 1808 received only one hundred and twenty-two votes. The Federalist minority rose from fourteen to forty-seven.

In the elections to Congress the same effects were shown. The Federalists doubled their number of Congressmen, but the huge Republican majority could well bear reduction. The true character of the Eleventh Congress could not be foretold by the party vote. Many Northern Republicans chosen to Congress were as hostile to the embargo as though they had been Federalists. Elected on the issue of embargo or anti-embargo, the Congress which was to last till March 5, 1811, was sure to be factious; but whether factious or united, it could have neither policy nor leader. The election decided its own issue. The true issue thenceforward was that of war; but on this point the people had not been asked to speak, and their representatives would not dare without their encouragement to act.

The Republican party by a supreme effort kept itself in office; but no one could fail to see that if nine months of embargo had so shattered Jefferson's power, another such year would shake the Union itself. The cost of this "engine for national purposes" exceeded all calculation. Financially, it emptied the Treasury, bankrupted the mercantile and agricultural class, and ground the poor beyond endurance. Constitutionally, it overrode every specified limit on arbitrary power and made Congress despotic, while it left no bounds to the authority which might be vested by Congress in the President. Morally, it sapped the nation's vital force, lowering its courage, paralyzing its energy, corrupting its principles, and arraying all the active elements of society in factious opposition to government or in secret paths of treason. Politically, it cost Jefferson the fruits of eight years painful labor for popularity, and brought the Union to the edge of a precipice.

Finally, frightful as the cost of this engine was, as a means of coercion the embargo evidently failed. The President complained of evasion, and declared that if the measure were faithfully executed it would produce the desired effect; but the people knew better. In truth, the law was faithfully executed. The price-lists of Liverpool and London, the published returns from Jamaica and Havana, proved that American produce was no longer to be bought abroad. On the continent of Europe commerce had ceased before the embargo was laid, and its coercive effects were far exceeded by Napoleon's own restrictions; yet not a sign came from Europe to show that Napoleon meant to give way. From England came an answer to the embargo, but not such as promised its success. On all sides evidence accumulated that the embargo, as an engine of coercion, needed a long period of time to produce a decided effect. The law of physics could easily be applied to politics; force could be converted only into its equivalent force. If the embargo—an exertion of force less violent than war—was to do the work of war, it must extend over a longer time the development of an equivalent energy. Wars lasted for many years, and the embargo must be calculated to last much longer than any war; but meanwhile the morals, courage, and political liberties of the American people must be perverted or destroyed; agriculture and shipping must perish; the Union itself could not be preserved.

Under the shock of these discoveries Jefferson's vast popularity vanished, and the labored fabric of his reputation fell in sudden and general ruin. America began slowly to struggle, under the consciousness of pain, toward a conviction that she must bear the common burdens of humanity, and fight with the weapons of other races in the same bloody arena; that she could not much longer delude herself with hopes of evading laws of Nature and instincts of life; and that her new statesmanship which made peace a passion could lead to no better result than had been reached by the barbarous system which made war a duty.

THE embargo fitted so neatly into Napoleon's schemes that many critics charged that Jefferson was a tool of Napoleon. Napoleon was not one to be gratified easily, however, and he continued to dangle before Americans, with maddening uncertainty, the possibility of acquiring West Florida, hoping to lure Jefferson into an alliance. Meanwhile, to further his grand plan of conquest, Napoleon now moved to complete the subjugation of Spain and her colonies, intending to rebuild his fleets in her harbors, bar the Mediterranean to British commerce, and challenge England's control of the oceans. On February 21, 1808, he marched against Spain. The complaisant Spanish monarchy, already rendered impotent by Napoleon's ruthless diplomacy, collapsed at the touch; and in Adams's phrase, the "Bourbon rubbish" was swept from Madrid and replaced by a new king, Napoleon's brother Joseph. On May 2 the people of Madrid rose in revolt against the usurper. Although Murat crushed the insurrection, the revolutionary impulse toward freedom from foreign rule attracted the support of the monarchies of England and the Continent and thus in one of the recurring ironies of history opened the way for the spread of democracy among the Spanish colonies and ultimately among the nations of Europe itself.

To Adams, May 2 was therefore one of the great turning points of world history. It was a major illustration of the determinist thesis of the entire History. "The workings of human development were never more strikingly shown than in the helplessness with which the strongest political and social forces in the world followed or resisted at haphazard the necessities of a movement which they could not control or comprehend. Spain, France, Germany, England, were swept into a vast and bloody torrent which dragged America, from Montreal to Valparaiso, slowly into its movement; while the familiar figures of famous men—Napoleon, Alexander, Canning, Godoy, Jefferson, Madison, Talleyrand; emperors, generals, presidents, conspirators, patriots, tyrants, and martyrs by the thousand were borne away by the stream . . . all helping more or less unconsciously to reach the new level which society was obliged to seek."

Although America did not support the cause of Spanish freedom, the "revolution opened an endless vista of democratic ambition," a vista whose grand dimensions would soon be delimited by the Monroe Doctrine. Jefferson may have realized the implications of the fall of the Spanish empire; nevertheless, his detestation of war bound him ever more closely to the embargo as an instrument of foreign policy.

There could be no question that in spite of denials the embargo hurt British industry and stifled trade with America. Jefferson, hoping to capitalize on that fact, authorized Pinkney, the American envoy, to offer to withdraw the embargo if England would revoke the Orders in Council. The offer came at an unpropitious moment, for the English government was so elated by the developments in Spain that it contemptuously rejected the offer. Congress wrangled over what measures to be taken but feared to take the step urged by Gallatin—armed defense of American neutrality against both belligerents—in short, war. In this climate of fear and anxiety, Madison was elected President. Adams's narrative records the final repudiation of Jefferson's foreign policy of "peaceful coercion."

Repeal of the Embargo

EARLY in January the intended policy of Madison became known. As the story has already told, Madison and Gallatin decided to retain the embargo until June, but to call the new Congress together May 22, and then to declare war, unless Erskine could make concessions. President Jefferson was chiefly interested in maintaining the embargo until after March 4, and the despotism he had so long maintained over Congress seemed still to exasperate his enemies. By common consent, attack upon the embargo was regarded as attack upon the President: and the Northern Democrats had so far lost respect for their old leader as to betray almost a passion for telling him unpleasant truths.

Vol. IV, Chap. XIX.

Joseph Story, who took the lead in this party rebellion, came to Congress determined to overthrow the embargo, and found Ezekiel Bacon—another Massachusetts member—equally determined with himself. In after years Justice Story told the tale as he remembered it—

The whole influence of the Administration was directly brought to bear upon Mr. Ezekiel Bacon and myself to seduce us from what we considered a great duty to our country, and especially to New England. We were scolded, privately consulted, and argued with by the Administration and its friends on that occasion. I knew at the time that Mr. Jefferson had no ulterior measure in view, and was determined on protracting the embargo for an indefinite period, even for years. I was well satisfied that such a course would not and could not be borne by New England, and would bring on a direct rebellion. It would be ruin to the whole country. Yet Mr. Jefferson, with his usual visionary obstinacy, was determined to maintain it; and the New England Republicans were to be made the instruments. Mr. Bacon and myself resisted; and measures were concerted by us, with the aid of Pennsylvania, to compel him to abandon his mad scheme. For this he never forgave me.

Joseph Story, with very high and amiable qualities, was quick in temper; and in regard to Jefferson he let his temper master his memory.

One thing I did learn while I was a member of Congress [he continued], and that was that New England was expected, so far as the Republicans were concerned, to do everything and to have nothing. They were to obey, but not to be trusted. This, in my humble judgment, was the steady policy of Mr. Jefferson at all times. We were to be kept divided, and thus used to neutralize each other.

In this spirit toward his own President Story came to Washington, and joined hands with Timothy Pickering, John Randolph, and George Canning in the attempt "to lower and degrade" Jefferson in the eyes of his own people. Jefferson asked only to be spared the indignity of signing with his own hand the unconditional repeal of the embargo; while the single point on which Story, Bacon, Pickering, and Canning were agreed was that the repeal should be the act of the man who made the law. On one side Jefferson, Madison, Gallatin, and their friends entreated Congress to stand firm; to maintain the ground already solemnly taken; to leave the embargo until June, and then to declare war if they pleased. On the other hand, Pickering, Bacon, Story, the Clintons, and the Pennsylvanians demanded immediate repeal—partly to pacify New England, but quite as much for the reason, which Pickering urged, that immediate repeal would prevent war. That it would in fact prevent war was obvious. Repeal was submission.

Story took no part in the public struggle, for he left Washington about January 20, and the great debate began ten days afterward; but although he held his peace in public, and his friends made no open display of their anger, the temper in which they acted was notorious, and the breach between them and Jefferson was never healed. They could not forgive him: that Jefferson should ever forget the wound they inflicted, required magnanimity beyond that of any philosopher known in politics.

As soon as the naval and military bills and the extra session for May 22 were at last fairly determined and every detail decided, Wilson Cary Nicholas took the lead of the House, and January 30 called up a Resolution intended to settle the policy of embargo and war. The words of this Resolve were too serious not to have received very careful attention:

Resolved, As the opinion of this House, that the United States ought not to delay beyond the ——— day of ——— to resume, maintain, and defend the navigation of the high seas; and that provision ought to be made by law for repealing on the ——— day of ——— the several embargo laws, and for authorizing at the same time letters of marque and reprisal against Great Britain and France, provided on that day their Orders or Edicts violating the lawful commerce and neutral rights of the United States shall be in force; or against either of those nations having in force such Orders or Edicts.

Nicholas agreed to divide the Resolution so that a test vote might first be taken on the repeal of the embargo; and he then

moved to fill the blank with the words, "the first day of June."
The House was thus asked to pledge itself that on June 1 the
embargo should cease. On this question the debate began.

David R. Williams was a typical Carolinian. With something
of the overbearing temper which marked his class, he had also
the independence and the honesty which went far to redeem
their failings. He had stood for years, with his friend Macon,
proof against the influence of patronage and power; he supported the embargo, and was not ashamed to avow his dread
of war; but since his favorite measure was to be thrown aside,
he stood by his character, and made an appeal to the House,
giving at once to the debate an air of dignity which it never
wholly lost—

Will you drive us to a repeal of the embargo, and make no
resistance? Are you ready to lie down quietly under the im-
positions laid upon you? You have driven us from the embargo.
The excitements in the East render it necessary that we should
enforce the embargo with the bayonet or repeal it. I will repeal
it—and I could weep over it more than over a lost child. If you
do not resist, you are no longer a nation; you dare not call yourself so; you are the merest vassals conceivable. . . . I appeal to
the minority, who hold the destinies of the nation in their grasp
—for they can enforce embargo without the bayonet—I beg
them, if they will not declare war, that they will do the best
they can for their country.

No one then wondered to see South Carolina almost on her
knees before Massachusetts, beseeching her, on her own terms,
for her own honor, to do the best she could for the common
country; but Massachusetts had no voice to respond. Dryly,
in the caustic tone of Connecticut austerity, Samuel Dana
replied that the days of ancient chivalry had not yet returned.
When Massachusetts at last found a spokesman, she gave her
answer through the mouth of Ezekiel Bacon—a man second to
none in respectability, but not one whom, in a moment of
supreme crisis, the State would naturally have chosen among
all her citizens to pronounce her will. Bacon had carefully collected advice from the men in his State who were most com-

petent to give counsel; but in Massachusetts affairs at Washington were little understood. Bent only on saving the Union by forcing a repeal of the embargo, and hampered by alliance with Federalists and Pennsylvanians, Bacon could not afford to show a sense of national self-respect.

He began by admitting that the discontents in New England made immediate repeal necessary—

It surely could not be sound policy, by adhering to this system beyond the measure of absolute necessity, to risk in the hands of any faction which might be disposed to wield it an instrument by which they may endanger the union of our country, and raise themselves to power on the ruins of liberty and the Constitution.

Such a beginning, offering a reward for threats of disunion, and conceding to traitors what would have been refused to good citizens, was an evil augury; and the rest of Bacon's speech carried out the promise. As he refused to prolong the embargo, so he refused to vote for war. "In every point of view, the policy of declaring offensive war against any nation four months in advance is to me wholly objectionable." The conclusion was as feeble as was required by the premises; but only some demon of bad taste could have inspired an orator at such a moment to use the language of Falstaff—

We choose not to take measures any more than to give reasons "upon compulsion," and we will not so take them. We will, however, I trust, defend ourselves against the depredations of both [belligerents]; and if they both or either choose to persevere in the execution of their lawless aggressions, we shall, it is hoped, become more united in our determination and our efforts to vindicate our rights, if they shall continue to be assailed. At any rate, I am for leaving it to the wisdom of the ensuing Congress, which is to meet at an early day, to determine upon that position which the nation shall take in relation to such a state of things as may grow out of the course which I propose.

Between the Federalists and the Republicans of Massachusetts Congress was left under no illusions. Bacon expressed in these vacillating phrases the true sense of the country. On the evening of February 2, after four days of debate, the committee, by seventy-three votes against forty, rejected Wilson Cary Nicholas's motion to fix June 1 as the date for removing the embargo; and the next day, by an affirmative vote of seventy, with no negatives, March 4 was fixed as the term.

Immediately after this decisive division John Randolph took the floor. Discord had become his single object in public life. The Federalists at least had a purpose in their seditiousness, and were honest in preferring the British government to their own; the Republicans of all shades, however weak in will or poor in motive, were earnest in their love of country; but Randolph was neither honest nor earnest, neither American nor English nor truly Virginian. Disappointed ambition had turned him into a mere egoist; his habits had already become intemperate, and his health was broken; but he could still charge upon Jefferson all the disasters of the country, and could delight in the overwhelming ruin which had fallen upon his former chief. Randolph's speech of February 3 was stale and tedious. Except on the single point of raising the embargo he was spiritless; and his only positive idea, borrowed from the Federalists, consisted in a motion that, instead of issuing letters of marque, Government should authorize merchant-vessels to arm and defend themselves from seizure. If the scheme had a meaning, it meant submission to the British Orders, and was suggested by the Federalists for no other object; but in Randolph's mind such a plan carried no definite consequence.

On Randolph's motion the debate continued until February 7. The Republicans, disconcerted and disheartened by the conduct of their friends from New England and New York, made little show of energy, and left to David R. Williams the task of expressing the whole ignominy of their defeat. Williams struggled manfully. Randolph's fears for the Constitution were answered by the South Carolinian in a few words, which condensed into a single paragraph the results of his party theories—

If the Constitution is made of such brittle stuff as not to stand a single war; if it is only to be preserved by submission to foreign taxation—I shall very soon lose all solicitude for its preservation.

With more than Federalist bitterness he taunted the hesitation of the Democrats—"contemptible cowardice," he called it. "It is time we should *assume*, if it is not in our natures, nerve enough to decide whether we will go to war or submit." The House replied by striking out the recommendation of reprisals, by a vote of fifty-seven to thirty-nine.

These two votes rendered the Administration for the moment powerless to make head against the sweeping Federalist victory. Josiah Quincy, who watched every symptom of democratic disaster, wrote as early as February 2, before the first defeat of the Administration: "There is dreadful distraction in the enemy's camp on the subject of removing the embargo. Jefferson and his friends are obstinate. Bacon and the Northern Democrats are equally determined that it shall be raised in March." The next day Quincy added: "Jefferson is a host; and if the wand of that magician is not broken, he will yet defeat the attempt."

The contest had become personal; to break the "wand of the magician" was as much the object of Democrats as of Federalists, and neither Madison nor Gallatin could restore discipline. February 4 the Secretary of the Treasury wrote: "As far as my information goes, everything grows more quiet in Massachusetts and Maine. All would be well if our friends remained firm here."

The attempt to hold the friends of the Administration firm brought only greater disaster. The vote in committee refusing to recommend reprisals took place February 7; and the next day Quincy wrote again: "Great caucusing is the order of the day and the night here. The Administration is determined to rally its friends, and postpone the removal of the embargo till May. But I think they cannot succeed. Bacon, I am told, stands firm and obstinate against all their solicitations and even almost denunciations. However, they had another caucus last night. The event is unknown. Jefferson has prevailed."

February 9 the result of the caucus was shown by a vote of the House discharging the Committee of the Whole, and referring the subject to the Committee of Foreign Relations, whose chairman was G. W. Campbell—which amounted to a public admission that Madison's plan had failed, and that some new expedient for uniting the party must be invented. Ezekiel Bacon refused to obey the caucus, and voted with the Federalists against the reference.

President Jefferson, though his name was still a terror to his enemies, accepted whatever decision his Cabinet advised. Till the day of his death he never forgot the violence of these last weeks of his administration, or the outcry of the New England towns. "How powerfully did we feel the energy of this organization in the case of the embargo," he wrote long afterward. "I felt the foundations of the government shaken under my feet by the New England townships." He showed the same lack of interest in February which had marked his conduct in November; not even the certainty of his own overthrow called out the familiar phrases of vexation. February 7 he wrote to his son-in-law, Thomas Mann Randolph—

I thought Congress had taken their ground firmly for continuing their embargo till June, and then war. But a sudden and unaccountable revolution of opinion took place the last week, chiefly among the New England and New York members, and in a kind of panic they voted the 4th of March for removing the embargo, and by such a majority as gave all reason to believe they would not agree either to war or non-intercourse. This, too, was after we had become satisfied that the Essex Junto had found their expectation desperate, of inducing the people there either to separation or forcible opposition. The majority of Congress, however, has now rallied to the removing the embargo on the 4th of March, non-intercourse with France and Great Britain, trade everywhere else, and continuing war preparations. The further details are not yet settled, but I believe it is perfectly certain that the embargo will be taken off the 4th of March.

As the President became more subdued, Senator Pickering became more vehement; his hatred for Jefferson resembled the hatred of Cotton Mather for a witch. February 4 he wrote to his nephew in Boston—

I entertain no doubt that Jefferson stands pledged to Bonaparte to maintain the embargo until a non-intercourse or war shall succeed; and he dreads the explosion justly to be apprehended by him from the disappointment and passion of Bonaparte, should the embargo be removed without a substitute as well or better comporting with his views. Upon this aspect of things it behooves our State legislature to advance with a firm step in defence of the rights of our citizens and of the Constitution. The palatines tremble at their posts. The least relaxation or wavering in the councils of New England would give them fresh courage, and hazard the most disastrous consequences.

Another observer wrote comments, serious in a different sense. Erskine watched with extreme interest every detail of this complicated struggle, and reported to Canning both facts and speculations which could not fail to affect the British government. Aware that Canning had won a brilliant success, Erskine labored to profit by his triumph, and to turn it in the interests of peace. A vast majority of Americans, he said, wanted only some plausible excuse to justify them in resenting Napoleon's conduct; but "they naturally wish to be saved the complete humiliation of being obliged avowedly to recant all their violent declarations of their determination never to submit to the Orders in Council of Great Britain." He speculated "how far it might be possible still further to bend the spirit of that part of the people of the United States until they should be forced to single out France to be resisted as the original aggressors while his Majesty's Orders in Council continued to be enforced." After the repeal of the embargo and the refusal to make war, but one remnant of American protest against British aggressions remained. The Republican caucus, February 7, de-

cided in favor of returning to Jefferson's pacific non-intercourse
—the system which had been, by common consent, thrown
aside as insufficient even before the embargo. February 10
Erskine gave an account of the new measure, and of its probable effect on American politics—

It is true that a non-intercourse law may be considered by
the Eastern States very objectionable; but as it would be rather
a nominal prohibition than a rigorous enforcement, a resistance
to it would be less likely to be made, and of less importance if
it should take place. The ultimate consequences of such differences and jealousies arising between the Southern and Eastern
States would inevitably tend to a dissolution of the Union,
which has been for some time talked of, and has of late, as I
have heard, been seriously contemplated by many of the leading people in the Eastern division.

The Non-intercourse Bill, which Erskine described February
10 as likely to be no more than a nominal prohibition of commerce, was reported February 11 to the House from the Committee of Foreign Relations. The bill excluded all public and
private vessels of France and England from American waters;
forbade under severe penalties the importation of British or
French goods; repealed the embargo laws, "except so far as they
relate to Great Britain or France or their colonies or dependencies, or places in the actual possession of either"; and gave the
President authority to reopen by proclamation the trade with
France or England in case either of these countries should cease
to violate neutral rights. That the proposed non-intercourse was
in truth submission to the Orders in Council, no one denied.

I conceive that great advantages may be reaped from it by
England [wrote Erskine] as she has the command of the seas,
and can procure through neutrals any of the produce of this
country, besides the immense quantity which will be brought
direct to Great Britain under various pretences; whereas France
will obtain but little, at a great expense and risk.

Such a non-intercourse merely sanctioned smuggling, and
was intended for no other purpose. Gallatin in his disgust

flung open the doors to illicit commerce. When Erskine went to him to ask what was meant by "France, England, and their dependencies," Gallatin replied that only places in actual possession of England and France were intended; that it was impossible to say what nations had decrees in force infringing neutral rights, but that even Holland would be considered an independent country.

The intention of this indefinite description [continued Erskine] is undoubtedly to leave open as many places for their commerce as they can, consistently with keeping up an appearance of resistance to the belligerent restrictions; but it is thoroughly understood that the whole measure is a mere subterfuge to extricate themselves from the embarrassments of the embargo system, and is never intended to be enforced.

When this bill came before the House, another long debate arose. Hardly a trace of national pride remained. No one approved the bill, but no one struggled longer against submission. Josiah Quincy and many of the Federalists held that the surrender was not yet complete enough, and that total submission to Great Britain must precede the return of Massachusetts to harmony with the Union, or to a share in measures of government. His words were worth noting—

He wished peace if possible; if war, union in that war. For this reason he wished a negotiation to be opened, unshackled with those impediments to it which now existed. As long as they remained, the people in the portion of country whence he came would not deem an unsuccessful attempt at negotiation to be cause for war. If they were removed, and an earnest attempt at negotiation was made, unimpeded with these restrictions, and should not meet with success, they would join heartily in a war.

Doubtless Quincy believed the truth of what he said; but as though to prove him mistaken in claiming even the modest amount of patriotism which he asserted for his party, Barent Gardenier immediately followed with a declaration that Great Britain was wholly in the right, and that America should not only submit to the Orders in Council, but should take pride in submission—

I do not say that the orders were lawful, or that they were not infringements of our rights as a neutral nation—as it might offend the prejudices of the House. But I may be permitted to say that if they were unlawful, I have proved that they are not hurtful; that the British Orders in Council only supplied to that which our sense of honor would lead us to do, their sanction.

Gardenier's views roused no longer much outward irritation. The war Republicans liked honest avowals better than sham patriotism; but John Randolph, unwilling to be embarrassed with allies so candid, rated Gardenier sharply—

I looked at the gentleman from New York at that moment with the sort of sensation which we feel in beholding a sprightly child meddling with edged tools—every moment expecting, what actually happened, that he will cut his fingers. . . . The gentleman's friends, if any he have—and I have no right to presume that he has none, but the contrary—will do well to keep such dangerous implements out of his way for the future.

Randolph himself persisted in the scheme of withdrawing all restrictions on commerce, and allowing merchant-vessels to arm—a measure which had the advantage of being warlike or pacific, according as he should prefer in the future to represent it. David R. Williams hit upon an idea more sensible, and likely to prove more effective. "If the embargo is to be taken off, and war not to be substituted—if the nation is to submit —I wish to do it profitably." He proposed to shut out the shipping of England and France, but to admit their manufactures, under a duty of fifty per cent when imported in American vessels. A number of Southern Republicans approved this plan.

Much the strongest speech against the bill was that of George W. Campbell, who made no attempt to hide his mortification at seeing the House desert him, its leader, and turn its back upon the pledge it had solemnly given in accepting his Report only two months before—

At the very time when your own people are rallying round the standard of their government; when they are about to shake off that timidity, that alarm, that restless disposition, which the first pressure occasioned by the suspension of commerce naturally produced; when they are, in almost every quarter of the Union, declaring their determination and solemnly pledging themselves to support your measures, to maintain the embargo, or go to war if necessary—to do anything but submit: at that very moment, instead of being invited by a similar patriotic enthusiasm to throw yourselves in front, and to lead them on to the honorable contest, you abandon the ground you have already occupied, you check their generous enthusiasm, and leave them the mortification of seeing their country disgraced by a timid, temporizing policy that must, if persevered in, ruin the nation.

Although events had already proved that no appeal to self-respect called out a response from this Congress, Campbell might reasonably suppose that arguments of self-interest would be heard; and he pressed one objection to the bill which, in theory, should have been decisive—

The non-intercourse would press most severely on the Southern and Western States, who depend chiefly on the immediate exchange of their productions for foreign goods, and would throw almost the whole commerce of the nation into the hands of the Eastern States, without competition, and also add a premium on their manufactures at the expense of the agricultural interest to the South and West. Foreign goods being excluded, the manufacturing States would furnish the rest of the Union with their manufactured goods at their own prices.

A moment's reflection must have satisfied the Republicans that this argument against the bill was fatal. Non-intercourse must ruin the South, in order to offer an immense bribe to the shipping and manufactures of New England as an inducement for New England to remain in the Union. The manufacturing interests never ventured to ask such extravagant protection as was thrust upon them in 1809 by the fears of the agricultural States; the greed of corporate capital never suggested the monopoly created for Eastern ships and factories by a measure which shut from America all ships and manufactures but theirs. Even if but partially enforced, such legislation was ruinous to agriculture.

Entreaty and argument were thrown away. The House lost discipline, self-respect, and party character. No one felt responsible for any result, no majority approved any suggestion. As the last days of the session drew near, the machinery of legislation broke down, and Congress became helpless. So strange and humiliating a spectacle had not before been seen. The nation seemed sinking into the weakness of dissolution.

The paralysis came in a form that could not be disguised. While the House disputed over one Non-intercourse Bill, the Senate passed another; and February 22 the House laid aside its own measure in order to take up that of the Senate, which contained the disputed clause authorizing letters of marque and reprisal against nations that should continue their unlawful edicts after repeal of the embargo. In pursuance of its vote of February 7, the House in committee promptly struck out the reprisal clause. Next it rejected David R. Williams's motion for discriminating duties. Ezekiel Bacon, perhaps somewhat scandalized at the legislation he had chiefly caused, suggested the Federalist plan of authorizing merchant-vessels to resist seizure; and February 25 a struggle occurred on the question of permitting forcible resistance by merchant-vessels. The minority was deeply agitated as the act of complete submission became imminent. David R. Williams cried that if the House could so abandon national rights, they deserved to be scoffed by all the world; John W. Eppes declared himself compelled to believe Josiah Quincy's assertion that the majority could not be kicked into a war; even the peaceable Macon moved a warlike amendment. Vote after vote was taken; again and again the ayes and noes were called on dilatory motions of adjournment; but every motion looking toward war was steadily voted down, and in the end, February 27, the Non-intercourse Bill in its most unresisting shape received the approval of the House. Not a speaker defended it; at the last moment the charge was freely made that the bill had not a single friend. The members who voted for it declared in doing so that the measure was a weak and wretched expedient, that they detested it, and took it merely as a choice of evils; but eighty-one members voted in its favor, and only forty in the negative. More extraordinary still, this non-intercourse, which bound the South to the feet of New England, was supported by forty-one Southern members, while but twelve New England representatives recorded their names in its favor.

Three months afterward, at a moment when the danger of war seemed to have vanished, John Randolph recalled the memory of this confused struggle, and claimed for President Jefferson and himself the credit for having prevented a declaration of war. He had voted against the non-intercourse, he said, because he had believed that he could get rid of the embargo on still better terms; others had voted against it because they thought it absolute disgrace—

The fact is that nobody would advocate it; that though it was carried by a majority of two to one, those who finally voted for it condemned it, and all parties seemed ashamed of it; and that . . . all the high-toned men and high-toned presses in this country denounced the majority of this House for passing that law, as having utterly disgraced themselves. . . . If the great leaders could have been gratified, according to their own showing they would have dragged this country into a war with Great Britain. . . . Now to be sure, sir, those persons who undertook to stop their wild career were composed of heterogeneous materials; . . . there were minority men, caucus men, protesters —in fact, sir, all parties, Catholics, Protestants, Seceders—and all were united in the effort to prevent the leaders of both Houses from plunging the nation into a war with one Power and knuckling to the other; from riveting the chains of French influence, perhaps of French alliance upon us. Thank God that their designs were proclaimed to the nation, that the President did not give his consent, which would have made us kick the beam. Yes, sir! Federalists, minority men, protesters, and all would have kicked the beam if it had ever emanated from the Cabinet that the President was for war.

If Randolph was right, the "wand of the magician" had not been broken; and other observers besides Randolph held the same opinion. "Jefferson has triumphed," wrote Josiah Quincy, February 27, immediately after the repeal; "his intrigues have prevailed."

In a spirit widely different from that of Randolph and Quincy, Nathaniel Macon, February 28, wrote to his friend Nicholson—

Otis, the Secretary of the Senate, has this moment informed the House of Representatives that the Senate have agreed to the amendments made by the House to the Bill to repeal the embargo.

The Lord, the mighty Lord, must come to our assistance, or I fear we are undone as a nation!

THE *failure of the embargo and Jefferson's stubborn refusal to acknowledge that failure cost him whatever popularity still clung to him, and he retired from office a bitterly disappointed man. He insisted that the embargo had failed through evasions and domestic opposition but had to acknowledge that from a purely economic point of view war would have been cheaper. One of his last official acts was to sign the repeal bill which reinstated the innocuous Non-Importation Act, whose vague prohibitions, as everyone knew, encouraged illicit trade with England. Jefferson was glad to escape to Monticello even though faced with heavy private debts.*

Madison took office on March 4, 1809, inheriting the factionalism and intrigues of the preceding administration—intrigues that Adams traces with exhaustive thoroughness. The inevitable political bargaining yielded, as Adams says, one of the least satisfactory cabinets that "any President had known." Gallatin survived as Secretary of the Treasury but with much reduced influence. Although commerce had suffered from the embargo, New England manufacturing received a tremendous stimulus, and the flood of profits quieted the Federalists. Once again Adams points out the irony of events. The embargo, which had been the work of Jefferson and the Virginians, had given New England an economic monopoly of manufacturing—a monopoly of which the South and West were the victims.

Since the Non-Importation Act repealing the embargo threatened French ships with confiscation, Napoleon retaliated with the secret Decree of Vienna of August, 1809, authorizing the seizure of American vessels entering French ports. He offered to revoke his retaliatory decrees if England would revoke its blockade and the Orders in Council. As neither side dared yield, the impasse continued for two more years.

The intricate maneuverings on both sides of the Atlantic, the diplomatic intrigues and conspiracies that marked the two following years, the struggles between the partisans of France and England, the inability of the congress and the executive to force concessions from either belligerent as the unpredictable fortunes of war in Europe rose and fell, and the passionate con-

troversies over enlarging the military establishment fill nearly two volumes of the History *and defy any comprehensive summary. Each side alternately issued its menaces or deluded the Americans with insubstantial promises of relief. Napoleon, a master at double-dealing, cynically tricked Madison into believing that his decrees had been revoked at the very moment that French cruisers were sailing under secret orders to destroy ships that violated the decrees. The ironic end of this long, confusing, and irresolute chapter in American history is told in the following narrative.*

Repeal of the Orders in Council

WHILE Napoleon thus tried the temper of America, the Government of England slowly and with infinite reluctance yielded to American demands. Not for the first time experience showed that any English minister whose policy rested on jealousy of America must sooner or later come to ruin and disgrace.

After the departure of Pinkney and Foster in May, 1811, diplomatic action was for a time transferred to Washington. The young American *chargé* in London, John Spear Smith, could only transmit news that came officially to his hands. The Marquess Wellesley, still struggling to reorganize the Ministry, found the Prince Regent less and less inclined to assist him, until at last he despaired. American affairs resumed their old position. In June, 1811, Sir William Scott, after some months of hesitation, rendered final decision that the French Decrees were still in force, and that in consequence all American vessels falling within the range of the British Orders in Council were liable to condemnation. In the Cabinet, Wellesley urged his colleagues either to negotiate with America or to show themselves prepared for war; but his colleagues would do neither. Convinced that the United States would not and could not fight, Perceval and Eldon, Bathurst and Liverpool, were indifferent to Wellesley's discomfort. In the autumn of 1811 nothing in the attitude of the British government, except its previous hesitation, held out a hope of change.

Yet many reasons combined to show that concessions were inevitable. The sweeping ruin that overwhelmed British commerce and industry in 1810 sank deep among the laboring classes in 1811. The seasons doubled the distress. The winter had been intense, the summer was unfavorable; wheat rose in the autumn to one hundred and forty-five shillings, or about thirty-six dollars the quarter, and as the winter of 1811 began, disorders broke out in the manufacturing districts. The inland counties reached a state of actual insurrection which no exercise of force seemed to repress. The American non-importation aggravated the trouble, and worked unceasingly to shake the authority of Spencer Perceval, already one of the most unpopular ministers England had ever seen.

Popular distress alone could hardly have effected a change in Perceval's system; so great a result was not to be produced by means hitherto so little regarded. The moment marked an era in English history, for the new class of laborers, the mill-operatives and other manufacturing workmen, took for the first time an active share in shaping legislation. In their hostility to Perceval's policy they were backed by their employers; but the united efforts of employers and workmen were not yet equal to controlling the Government, even though they were aided by the American non-importation. They worried Perceval, but did not break him down. At the close of 1811 he showed still no signs of yielding; but news then arrived that the American Congress had met, and that the President's Message, the debates in the House, the tone of the press, and the feelings of the American people announced war. This was a new force with which Perceval could not deal.

No man of common-sense could charge England with want of courage, for if ever a nation had fought its way, England had a right to claim whatever credit such a career bestowed; but England lived in war, she knew its exact cost, and at that moment she could not afford it. The most bigoted Tory could see that if Napoleon succeeded in his coming attack on Russia, as he had hitherto succeeded in every war he had undertaken in Europe even when circumstances were less favorable, he would need only the aid of America to ruin beyond redemption the trade and finances of Great Britain. Little as Englishmen believed in the military capacity of the United States, they needed too much the markets and products of America to challenge war.

The gradual decline of the domineering tone which Canning had made fashionable offered a curious study in politics. In 1807 the affair of the "Little Belt" would have caused violent anger; in 1812 it created hardly a flurry. The Tory "Courier" talked wildly, but the "Times" took the matter with calmness; the Ministry showed no offence, and within a few weeks the affair was forgotten. Even after this irritation, the British public seemed pleased rather than angered to learn that Lord Wellesley had yielded complete apology and redress to America for the "Chesapeake" outrage. The commercial class for many months expected energetic retaliation by their government against the American Non-importation Act; but in September this idea was laid aside, and no one complained. Little by little the press took a defensive tone. In the place of threats the newspapers were filled with complaints. America was unfair, unreasonable, unjust; she called on England to admit that the French Decrees were repealed when in fact they were still in force; she threatened war; she hectored and bullied—but the more dignified course required England to be temperate though firm.

Parliament met Jan. 7, 1812, and the Prince Regent's speech was studiously moderate in its reference to the United States. In the Commons, January 8, Whitbread attacked ministers for their failure to conciliate America; and Spencer Perceval replied in a manner that could hardly have satisfied himself.

He would allow [he said] that a war with America would be an evil to Great Britain, but he also knew that such a war would be a greater evil to America. As an evil to America he was anxious to avert it; he looked upon America as accessory to the prosperity and welfare of Great Britain, and would be sorry to see her impoverished, crushed, or destroyed. . . . Sure he was that no one could construe those truly conciliatory dispositions of England into fear; but he was of the opinion that England, conscious of her own dignity, could bear more from America for peace's sake than from any other Power on earth.

This sentiment was the more significant because the latest news showed that England in the immediate future would be obliged to bear a great deal from America. The news became every day more and more alarming, and was reinforced by steadily increasing outcry from Birmingham, Liverpool, Nottingham, Hull, ending in a general agitation organized by active radicals, with Brougham at their head. So rapidly was one attack followed by another, that Perceval and his lieutenants—George Rose and James Stephen—could no longer carry their points by mere weight of office. The Marquess Wellesley, refusing to serve longer under Perceval, resigned from the Cabinet January 16, and no one felt confident that Perceval could supply his place. During more than a month negotiations continued without result, until, February 22, Lord Castlereagh received the appointment of Foreign Secretary.

During this interval the movement against the Orders in Council gained strength. In the Commons, February 13, another debate occurred when Whitbread, in a strong American speech, moved for the diplomatic correspondence with the United States, and was answered with some temper by Stephen and Perceval. Stephen went so far as to declare—and whatever he declared he certainly believed—that "nothing but the utmost aversion to a quarrel with America would have enabled this country to have borne so much. So far from having done anything to provoke a rupture with America, the strongest, most persevering, and almost even humiliating means had been employed to avoid it"; but he would not surrender to her the carrying and coasting trade of Europe even to prevent a war. Perceval spoke more evasively than usual, defending his commercial system as one that had been begun by his Whig predecessors, and throwing the blame for its irregularities on Napoleon's decrees; but although that day he was supposed to be in extreme peril of losing his majority, he closed his speech by declaring that sooner than yield to the repeal of the Orders in Council he would refuse share in any Administration. Alexander Baring answered that in this case war could hardly be avoided, and made an earnest appeal, founded on the distress of the manufacturing towns, in favor of the direct interference of Parliament to overrule the minister. Even William Wilberforce, whose speeches sometimes recalled those of Polonius, and whose hesitations generally marked the decline rather than the rise of a Ministry in power, felt himself constrained to say that "there was not at all times a sufficient attention in this country to the spirit of conciliation toward other countries, and particularly toward America. It would be well if persons in high situations in government had been more abundant in their civilities to that nation."

Again, five days afterward, Baring attacked Perceval by an embarrassing motion on the subject of licenses. No such scandal as the license system had been known in England since the monopolies of the Tudors and Stuarts. Most of the trade between Great Britain and the Continent was conducted by the Board of Trade on one side and Napoleon on the other, under special licenses issued for the carriage of specified articles. In 1807 the number of such licenses amounted to sixteen hundred; in 1810 they reached eighteen thousand. Owing to practical difficulties and to Napoleon's dislike, American vessels took few licenses. A nondescript class of so-called neutrals under the flags of Pappenberg, Kniphausen, and Varel, carrying double licenses and double sets of papers, served as the agents for this curious commerce which reeked with fraud and perjury. In the case of the "Aeolus," Aug. 8, 1810, the Court said: "It is a matter perfectly notorious that we are carrying on the trade of the whole world under simulated and disguised papers. The commerce of the world unavoidably assumes a disguise; these disguises we ourselves are under the necessity of employing, with simulation and dissimulation." Dr. Joseph Phillimore, perhaps the highest authority on civil law in England, in two strong pamphlets declared that ancient rules and practices had been rendered obsolete, so that the Admiralty Courts were no longer occupied with the law of nations, but only with the interpretation of licenses; and while the property of enemies was as invariably restored as formerly it had been condemned, the condemnation of true neutral property had become as much a matter of course as had been its restitution a few years before. No one, even among the sternest supporters of the Orders in Council, ventured to defend the licenses on any other ground than that of their necessity.

Baring's motion called up Perceval again. "The only principle on which Government acted," said he, "was to secure to the natives of England that trade by means of licenses, the profits of which without them would devolve to the hands of aliens." This admission, or avowal, seemed to yield the whole ground of complaint which America had taken; neither Perceval nor Rose ventured to defend the licenses as in themselves deserving support; they stood only by the system. Their attitude led to another and more famous debate, which added an interesting chapter to the history of England.

In the Lords, February 28, the Marquess of Lansdowne moved for a committee to consider the subject of the Orders in Council. Like all that Lord Lansdowne did, his speech was temperate and able; but his arguments were the same that have been so often repeated. Lord Bathurst, President of the Board of Trade, replied. Bathurst's argument was singularly free from the faults of Perceval and Rose; and he went to the verge of destroying his own case by avowing that in the clamor raised about the Orders in Council no one could say what those orders were, or what would be the consequences of yielding to American demands. He was sure that France had suffered from the effect of the system, but he was not so certain that England had been also a sufferer, while he maintained that the licenses tended to diminish the spirit of perjury, and that the aban-

donment of licenses would only place an additional obstacle
in the way of trade. "Were they to put restraints on the freedom
of British commerce for the simple purpose of giving the trade
of Europe to the Americans?" This avowal, like those made by
Perceval and Stephen, seemed to concede the justice of American complaints; but perhaps it admitted only the reply made
by Lord Holland, who said in plain words that the choice lay
between the orders and war, and that he could not suppose the
orders to be their Lordships' preference. Lansdowne's motion
was rejected by a vote of one hundred and thirty-five to seventy-
one.

In the Commons the great debate took place March 3, when
Henry Brougham repeated Lansdowne's motion for a committee, after a speech showing as much self-restraint as clearness
and force. In reply, George Rose offered a general denial of the
facts which Brougham alleged. He denied that the orders injured the British export trade; that the license system injured
British shipping or increased perjury; or that the orders caused
manufacturing distress. On all these points he arrayed statistics
in his support; but toward the close of his speech he made a
remark—such as had been made many times by every defender
of the system—surrendering in effect the point in diplomatic
dispute between England and the United States. "The honorable gentleman," he said, "had not been correct in calling these
orders a system of retaliation; they were rather a system of
self-defence, a plan to prevent the whole trade of the world
from being snatched away from her." He was followed by Alexander Baring, who condemned the policy which built up the
shipping of France at the cost of American shipping, and manufactures in Massachusetts at the cost of British manufactures;
and after Baring came James Stephen, who repeated his old
arguments without essential change. Then toward midnight,
after these four long, serious, statistical speeches, such as usually emptied the House, George Canning rose; and so keen was
the interest and anxiety of the moment that more than four
hundred members crowded in, curious to learn by what in-

genuity Canning would defend a threatened vote against those Orders in Council of which he had been so long the champion.

For these Orders in Council [he said], so far as he had been connected with their adoption, he was ready to take his full share of responsibility. What orders were truly meant? Why, they were the Orders in Council which, until he had heard the speech of the right honorable gentleman (Mr. Rose), he had always looked upon as retaliatory upon the enemy; which had been so understood in every instance, until the Vice-President of the Board of Trade, in contradiction to every statement which had hitherto been given to the public on the subject—in contradiction to every document in office respecting these Orders—in contradiction to every communication which he (Mr. Canning) had made, and every despatch written in his official character explanatory of their nature and spirit—in contradiction to every speech which had been made in Parliament in defence of them —had thought proper to represent them not as measures retaliatory upon the enemy, but as measures of self-defence. Self-defence, but not retaliatory! . . . If they were to be in no larger a sense retaliatory than as self-defensive—if they were not to retaliate directly against the enemy, but to be defensive against a rival in trade—if they were not to be belligerent measures, but purely defensive—then all the arguments by which they had hitherto been supported would fail to apply.

Again and again Canning returned to this slip of the tongue by which Rose had given him pretext for turning against the Administration.

If at any time it should appear that these orders did not retort his aggression upon the enemy, but operated solely to the injury of the neutrals; if even the British government should appear to have interfered to relieve their pressure upon the enemy—they would stand upon far different principles than those upon which he had supported them, and would in his opinion be very proper objects for examination and revision. . . . Were he called upon to state his opinion of what he conceived the Orders in Council should be, he could not do it more fully than by saying that they were most perfect as they approached toward a belligerent measure and receded from a commercial one. Let them have for their object the pressure and distress of the enemy, for the purpose of compelling him to listen to terms of accommodation, and not for the narrow policy of wringing temporary concessions from him with which they might go to his own market.

To the amazement of friend and foe Canning next attacked the license system as one of which he had little knowledge, but whose details required investigation. As for America, as he was the last man who would lay the honor of the country at her feet, so would he be among the first to go far in the work of honorable conciliation, and he would not oppose the motion before the House because it might have incidentally the effect of conciliating her. Finally, if the account of Plumer Ward be true, "he concluded the first dull and flat speech I ever heard him make, without the smallest support from the House, and sat down without a cheer and almost without its being known that he had finished."

Plumer Ward was a passionate admirer of Spencer Perceval, and his anger with Canning showed the soreness caused by Canning's sudden change of front. Perceval was obliged to rescue Rose, but in doing so made the case worse rather than better as far as regarded America. Having declared that the orders were strictly retaliatory, he added, in the same breath, that "the object of Government was to protect and to force the trade of this country. . . . The object of the Orders in Council was not to destroy the trade of the Continent, but to force the Continent to trade with us." Had this assertion been made by Madison or Brougham it would have been instantly contradicted; but Perceval's silence was still less creditable than his avowals. No one knew so well as Perceval where to strike with effect at Canning; for not only could he show that from the first Canning was privy to the system of forcing commerce upon France, but he had preserved the letter in which Canning at the outset advised him to keep out of sight the exceptions which gave the measure the air of a commercial rather than a political transaction. Never had a distinguished man exposed himself with less caution than Canning, by declaring that in his opinion the orders required revision from the moment the

British government should appear to intervene to relax their pressure upon the enemy; for during two years of his official life he had given steady though silent support to the Board of Trade in its persistent efforts to supply France, by means of licenses in thousands and smuggling without limit, with every product known to commerce. Such conduct challenged the severest retort, but Perceval made none. He would have been superior to the statesmen of his time had he felt the true nature of that sleight-of-hand which he and Canning practised, and which, like the trick of blacklegs on the race-course, consisted in shuffling together the two words, "Retaliation—Self-defence! Self-defence—Retaliation!" but he could at least understand the impossibility of exposing Canning without also exposing himself.

The debate ended in a division. One hundred and forty-four members, including Canning and Wilberforce, went into the lobby with Brougham. Only a majority of seventy-two remained to be overcome; and to Brougham's energetic nature such a majority offered an incentive to exertion. Perceval's friends, on the other hand, exulted because this majority of seventy-two stood by him against the combined forces of Wellesley, Canning, the Radicals, and the Whigs. Except for one danger, Perceval and his system were still secure; but the fear that the Americans meant at last to fight gave him no rest—it dogged his steps, and galled him at every motion. Neither Rose nor James Stephen could prove, by any statistics under the control of the Board of Trade, that their system would benefit British commerce if it produced an American war. Already the north and west of England, the inland counties, the seaports, had risen in insurrection against the orders. Stephen and Rose exhausted themselves and the House to prove that the balance of profit was still in England's favor; but what would become of their balance-sheet if they were obliged to add the cost of an American war to the debtor side of their account?

In the effort to strengthen his Ministry Perceval persuaded Lord Sidmouth to enter the Cabinet, but only on condition that the orders should be left an open question. Sidmouth plainly said that he would rather give up the orders than face an American war. He also asked that the license system should be renounced. Perceval replied that this would be a greater sacrifice than if the licenses had never been granted. Lord Sidmouth was not a great man—Canning despised his abilities, and the Prince of Wales called him a blockhead; but he was, except Lord Castlereagh, the only ally to be found, and Perceval accepted him on his own terms. The new Cabinet at once took the American question in hand, and Castlereagh then wrote his instructions of April 10 to Foster, making use of Bassano's report to justify England's persistence in the orders; but besides this despatch Castlereagh wrote another of the same date, in which Sidmouth's idea took shape. If the United States would restore intercourse with Great Britain, the British government would issue no more licenses and would resort to rigorous blockades. This great concession showed how rapidly Perceval lost ground; but this was not yet all. April 21 the Prince Regent issued his formal declaration that whenever the French government should publish an authentic Act expressly and unconditionally repealing the Berlin and Milan Decrees, the Orders in Council, including that of Jan. 7, 1807, should be wholly and absolutely revoked.

Had the United States at that moment been so fortunate as to enjoy the services of Pinkney in London, or of any man whose position and abilities raised him above the confusion of party politics, he might have convinced them that war was unnecessary. The mere threat was sufficient. Sidmouth's entrance into the Cabinet showed the change of current, and once Perceval began to give way, he could not stop. Unfortunately the United States had no longer a minister in England. In July, 1811, the President ordered Jonathan Russell to London to act as *chargé* until a minister should be appointed, which he added would be done as soon as Congress met; but he changed his mind and appointed no minister, while Jonathan Russell, seeing that Perceval commanded a majority and was determined to maintain his system, reported the situation as hopeless.

Brougham, without taking the precaution of giving Russell the daily information he so much needed, devoted all his energies to pressing the popular movement against the Orders in Council. Petition after petition was hurried to Parliament, and almost every petition caused a new debate. George Rose, who possessed an unhappy bluntness, in conversation with a Birmingham committee said that the two countries were like two men with their heads in buckets of water, whose struggle was which of the two could hold out longest before suffocation. The phrase was seized as a catchword, and helped agitation. April 28 Lord Stanley, in the House, renewed the motion for a committee on the petitions against the orders. Perceval had been asked whether he would consent to the committee, and had refused; but on consulting his followers he found such symptoms of disaffection as obliged him to yield rather than face a defeat. George Rose then announced, greatly against his will, that as a matter of respect to the petitioners he would no longer oppose their request; Castlereagh and Perceval, cautioning the House that nothing need be expected from the investigation, followed Rose; while Stephen, after denouncing as a foul libel the charge that the orders had been invented to extend the commerce of Great Britain, also yielded to the committee "as a negative good, and to prevent misconstruction."

Stimulated by the threatening news from America, Brougham pressed with his utmost energy the victory he had won. The committee immediately began its examination of witnesses, who appeared from every quarter to prove that the Orders in Council and the subsequent non-importation had ruined large branches of British trade, and had lopped away a market that consumed British products to the value of more than ten million pounds sterling a year. Perceval and Stephen did their best to stem the tide, but were slowly overborne, and seemed soon to struggle only for delay.

Then followed a melodramatic change. May 11, as the prime minister entered the House to attend the investigation, persons about the door heard the report of a pistol, and saw Spencer Perceval fall forward shot through the heart. By the hand of a

lunatic moved only by imaginary personal motives, this minister, who seemed in no way a tragical figure, became the victim
of a tragedy without example in modern English history; but
although England had never been in a situation more desperate,
the true importance of Spencer Perceval was far from great,
and when he vanished in the flash of a pistol from the stage
where he seemed to fill the most considerable part, he stood
already on the verge of overthrow. His death relieved England
of a burden. Brougham would not allow his inquiry to be
suspended, and the premier's assassination rather concealed
than revealed the defeat his system must have suffered.

During the negotiations which followed, in the midst of difficulties in forming a new Ministry, Castlereagh received from
Jonathan Russell Napoleon's clandestine Decree of Repeal.
Brougham asked, May 22, what construction was to be put by
ministers on this paper. Castlereagh replied that the decree
was a trick disgraceful to any civilized government, and contained nothing to satisfy the conditions required by England.
Apart from the subordinate detail that his view of the decree
was correct, his remarks meant nothing. The alarm caused by
news that Congress had imposed an embargo as the last step
before war, the annoyance created by John Henry's revelations
and Castlereagh's lame defence, the weight of evidence pressing
on Parliament against the Orders in Council, the absence of a
strong or permanent Ministry—these influences, gaining from
day to day, forced the conviction that a change of system must
take place. June 8 Lord Liverpool announced that he had
formed an Administration, and would deal in due course with
the Orders in Council. June 16 Brougham made his motion
for a repeal of the orders. When he began his speech he did not
know what part the new Ministry would take, but while he
unfolded his long and luminous argument he noticed that James
Stephen failed to appear in the House. This absence could
mean only that Stephen had been deserted by ministers; and
doubt ceased when Brougham and Baring ended, for then Lord
Castlereagh—after Perceval's death the leader of the House—

rose and awkwardly announced that the Government, though till within three or four days unable to deliberate on the subject, had decided to suspend immediately the Orders in Council.

Thus ended the long struggle waged for five years by the United States against the most illiberal Government known in England within modern times. Never since the Definitive Treaty of Peace had America won so complete a triumph, for the surrender lacked on England's part no element of defeat. Canning never ceased taunting the new Ministry with their want of courage in yielding without a struggle. The press submitted with bad grace to the necessity of holding its tongue. Every one knew that the danger, already almost a certainty, of an American war chiefly caused the sudden and silent surrender, and that the Ministry like the people shrank from facing the consequences of their own folly. Every one cried that England should not suffer herself to be provoked by the irritating conduct of America; and at a moment when every word and act of the American government announced war in the rudest terms, not a voice was heard in England for accepting the challenge, nor was a musket made ready for defence. The new Ministry thought the war likely to drive them from office, for they were even weaker than when Spencer Perceval led them. The "Times" of June 17 declared that whatever might be the necessity of defending British rights by an American war, yet it would be the most unpopular war ever known, because every one would say that with happier talents it might have been avoided. "Indeed," it added, "every one is so declaring at the present moment; so that we who have ever been the most strenuous advocates of the British cause in this dispute are really overwhelmed by the general clamor." Bitter as the mortification was, the headlong abandonment of the Orders in Council called out reproaches only against the ministers who originally adopted them. "We are most surprised," said the "Times" of June 18, "that such acts could ever have received the sanction of the Ministry when so little was urged in their defence."

Such concessions were commonly the result rather than the prelude of war; they were not unlike those by which Talley-rand succeeded, in 1799, in restoring friendly relations between France and America. Three months earlier they would have answered their purpose; but the English were a slow and stub-born race. Perhaps that they should have repealed the orders at all was more surprising than that they should have waited five years; but although they acted more quickly and decidedly than was their custom, Spencer Perceval lived three months too long. The Orders in Council were abandoned at Westminster June 17; within twenty-four hours at Washington war was declared; and forty-eight hours later Napoleon, about to enter Russia, issued the first bulletin of his Grand Army.

THE war started off badly, for military preparations had been inadequate, being much too little and much too late; the army was pitifully small and poorly led. Hence the grandiose plan for the conquest of Canada ended in General Hull's ignominious surrender at Detroit. The Niagara campaign under General Smyth was another fiasco. On the sea, however, Americans showed their inherent superiority. Part of that stirring record is given in the following chapters, which display Adams's expert grasp of naval tactics and his pride in American seamanship.

Naval Battles

CULPABLE as was the helplessness of the War Department in 1812, the public neither understood nor knew how to enforce responsibility for disasters which would have gone far to cost a European war minister his life, as they might have cost his nation its existence. By fortune still kinder, the Navy Department escaped penalty of any sort for faults nearly as serious as those committed by its rival. The navy consisted, besides gunboats, of three heavy frigates rated as carrying forty-four guns; three lighter frigates rated at thirty-eight guns; one of thirty-two, and one of twenty-eight; besides two ships of eighteen guns, two brigs of sixteen, and four brigs of fourteen and twelve—in all sixteen sea-going vessels, twelve of which were probably equal to any vessels afloat of the same class. The eight frigates were all built by Federalist Congresses before President Jefferson's time; the smaller craft, except one, were built under the influence of the war with Tripoli. The Administration which declared war against England did nothing to increase the force. Few of the ships were in first-rate condition. The officers complained that the practice of laying up the frigates in port hastened their decay, and declared that hardly a frigate in the service was as sound as she should be. For this negligence Congress was alone responsible; but the Department perhaps shared the blame for want of readiness when war was declared.

The only ships actually ready for sea, June 18, were the "President," 44, commanded by Commodore Rodgers, at New York, and the "United States," 44, which had cruised to the southward with the "Congress," 38, and "Argus," 16, under the command of Commodore Decatur. Secretary Hamilton, May 21, sent orders to Decatur to prepare for war, and June 5 wrote more urgently: "Have the ships under your command immediately ready for extensive active service, and proceed with them to New York, where you will join Commodore Rodgers and wait further orders. Prepare for battle, which I hope will add to your fame." To Rodgers he wrote on the same day in much the same words: "Be prepared in all respects for extensive service." He asked both officers for their advice how to make the navy most useful. Rodgers's reply, if he made one, was not preserved; but Decatur answered from Norfolk, June 8—

The plan which appears to me to be the best calculated for our little navy . . . would be to send them out with as large a supply of provisions as they can carry, distant from our coast and singly, or not more than two frigates in company, without giving them any specific instructions as to place of cruising, but to rely on the enterprise of the officers.

The Department hesitated to adopt Decatur's advice, and began by an effort to concentrate all its ships at New York—an attempt in which Secretary Hamilton could not wholly succeed, for the "Constellation" and the "Chesapeake," 38-gun frigates, and the "Adams," 28, were not in condition for sea; the "Essex," 32, was not quite ready, and the "Wasp," 18, was bringing despatches from Europe, while the "Constitution," 44, detained at Annapolis by the difficulty of shipping a new crew, could not sail within three weeks. The secretary ordered Captain Hull, who commanded the "Constitution," to make his way to New York with the utmost speed, and if his crew were in proper condition, to look for the British frigate "Belvidera" on the way. The only ships that could be brought to

New York without delay were those of Decatur at Norfolk. To him the secretary, on the declaration of war, sent orders to proceed with all despatch northwards, and "to notice the British flag if it presents itself" on the way. "The 'Belvidera' is said to be on our coast," added the secretary. Before this letter reached Norfolk, Decatur and his squadron sailed from the Chesapeake and were already within sight of Sandy Hook; so that the only orders from the Navy Department which immediately affected the movement of the frigates were those sent to New York for Commodore Rodgers and the frigate "President," but which included Decatur's squadron when it should arrive.

For the present [wrote the secretary to Rodgers], it is desirable that with the force under your command you remain in such position as to enable you most conveniently to receive further more extensive and more particular orders, which will be conveyed to you through New York. But as it is understood that there are one or more British cruisers on the coast in the vicinity of Sandy Hook, you are at your discretion free to strike them, returning immediately after into port. You are free to capture or destroy them.

These orders reached New York June 21. Rodgers in his fine frigate the "President," with the "Hornet," 18, was eager to sail. The hope of capturing the "Belvidera," which had long been an intolerable annoyance to New York commerce, was strong both in the Navy Department and in the navy; but the chance of obtaining prize money from the British West India convoy, just then passing eastward only a few days' sail from the coast, added greatly to the commodore's impatience. Decatur's squadron arrived off Sandy Hook June 19. June 21, within an hour after receiving the secretary's orders of June 18, the whole fleet, including two forty-four and one thirty-eight-gun frigates, with the "Hornet" and the "Argus," stood out to sea.

The secretary might have spared himself the trouble of giving further orders, for many a week passed before Rodgers and Decatur bethought themselves of his injunction to return immediately into port after striking the "Belvidera." They struck the "Belvidera" within forty-eight hours, and lost her; partly on account of the bursting of one of the "President's" main-deck guns, which blew up the forecastle deck, killing or wounding sixteen men, including Commodore Rodgers himself, whose leg was broken; partly, and according to the British account chiefly, on account of stopping to fire at all, when Rodgers should have run alongside, and in that case could not have failed to capture his enemy. Whatever was the reason, the "Belvidera" escaped; and Rodgers and Decatur, instead of returning immediately into port as they had been ordered, turned in pursuit of the British West India convoy, and hung doggedly to the chase without catching sight of their game, until after three weeks' pursuit they found themselves within a day's sail of the British Channel and the convoy safe in British waters.

This beginning of the naval war was discouraging. The American ships should not have sailed in a squadron, and only their good luck saved them from disaster. Rodgers and Decatur showed no regard to the wishes of the Government, although had they met with misfortune, the navy would have lost its last hope. Yet if the two commodores had obeyed the secretary's commands their cruise would probably have been in the highest degree disastrous. The Government's true intentions have been a matter of much dispute; but beyond a doubt the President and a majority of his advisers inclined to keep the navy within reach at first—to use them for the protection of commerce, to drive away the British blockaders; and aware that the British naval force would soon be greatly increased, and that the American navy must be blockaded in port, the Government expected in the end to use the frigates as harbor defences rather than send them to certain destruction.

With these ideas in his mind Secretary Hamilton, in his orders of June 18, told Rodgers and Decatur that "more extensive" orders should be sent to them on their return to New York. A day or two afterward Secretary Gallatin complained to the President that these orders had not been sent.

I believe the weekly arrivals from foreign ports [said Galla-
tin] will for the coming four weeks average from one to one-
and-a-half million dollars a week. To protect these and our
coasting vessels, while the British have still an inferior force
on our coasts, appears to me of primary importance. I think
that orders to that effect, ordering them to cruise accordingly,
ought to have been sent yesterday, and that at all events not
one day longer ought to be lost.

June 22 the orders were sent according to Gallatin's wish.
They directed Rodgers with his part of the squadron to cruise
from the Chesapeake eastwardly, and Decatur with his ships
to cruise from New York southwardly, so as to cross and support each other and protect with their united force the merchantmen and coasters entering New York harbor, the Delaware, and
the Chesapeake. Rodgers and Decatur were then beginning their
private cruise across the ocean, and never received these orders
until the commerce they were to protect either reached port in
safety or fell into British hands.

Probably this miscarriage was fortunate, for not long after
Rodgers and Decatur passed the Banks the British Vice-Admiral Sawyer sent from Halifax a squadron to prevent the
American navy from doing what Secretary Hamilton had just
ordered to be done. July 5 Captain Broke, with his own frigate
the "Shannon," 38, the "Belvidera," 36, the "Africa," 64, and
Aeolus," 32, put to sea from Halifax and was joined, July 9,
off Nantucket by the "Guerriere," 38. Against such a force
Rodgers and Decatur, even if together, would have risked total
destruction, while a success would have cost more than it was
worth. The Americans had nothing to gain and everything to
lose by fighting in line-of-battle.

As Broke's squadron swept along the coast it seized whatever it met, and July 16 caught one of President Jefferson's
16-gun brigs, the "Nautilus." The next day it came on a richer
prize. The American navy seemed ready to outstrip the army
in the race for disaster. The "Constitution," the best frigate in
the United States service, sailed into the midst of Broke's five
ships. Captain Isaac Hull, in command of the "Constitution,"

had been detained at Annapolis shipping a new crew, until July 5—the day when Broke's squadron left Halifax—then the ship got under way and stood down Chesapeake Bay on her voyage to New York. The wind was ahead and very light. Not till July 10 did the ship anchor off Cape Henry lighthouse, and not till sunrise of July 12 did she stand to the eastward and northward. Light head-winds and a strong current delayed her progress till July 17, when at two o'clock in the afternoon, off Barnegat on the New Jersey coast, the lookout at the mast-head discovered four sails to the northward, and two hours later a fifth sail to the northeast. Hull took them for Rodgers's squadron. The wind was light, and Hull being to windward determined to speak the nearest vessel, the last to come in sight. The afternoon passed without bringing the ships together, and at ten in the evening, finding that the nearest ship could not answer the night signal, Hull decided to lose no time in escaping.

Then followed one of the most exciting and sustained chases recorded in naval history. At daybreak the next morning one British frigate was astern within five or six miles, two more were to the leeward, and the rest of the fleet some ten miles astern, all making chase. Hull put out his boats to tow the "Constitution"; Broke summoned the boats of his squadron to tow the "Shannon." Hull then bent all his spare rope to the cables, dropped a small anchor half a mile ahead, in twenty-six fathom water, and warped his ship along. Broke quickly imitated the device, and slowly gained on the chase. The "Guerriere" crept so near Hull's lee-beam as to open fire, but her shot fell short. Fortunately the wind, though slight, favored Hull. All night the British and American crews toiled on, and when morning came the "Belvidera," proving to be the best sailer, got in advance of her consorts, working two kedge-anchors, until at two o'clock in the afternoon she tried in her turn to reach the "Constitution" with her bow guns, but in vain. Hull expected capture, but the "Belvidera" could not approach nearer without bringing her boats under the "Con-

stitution's" stern guns; and the wearied crews toiled on, tow-
ing and kedging, the ships barely out of gunshot, till another
morning came. The breeze, though still light, then allowed Hull
to take in his boats, the "Belvidera" being two and a half miles
in his wake, the "Shannon" three and a half miles on his lee,
and the three other frigates well to leeward. The wind fresh-
ened, and the "Constitution" drew ahead, until toward seven
o'clock in the evening of July 19 a heavy rain-squall struck the
ship, and by taking skilful advantage of it Hull left the "Belvidera" and "Shannon" far astern; yet until eight o'clock the
next morning they were still in sight keeping up the chase.

Perhaps nothing during the war tested American seamanship
more thoroughly than these three days of combined skill and
endurance in the face of an irresistible enemy. The result
showed that Hull and the "Constitution" had nothing to fear
in these respects. There remained the question whether the superiority extended to his guns; and such was the contempt of
British naval officers for American ships, that with this experience before their eyes they still believed one of their 38-gun
frigates to be more than a match for an American forty-four,
although the American, besides the heavier armament, had
proved his capacity to out-sail and out-manœuvre the Englishman. Both parties became more eager than ever for the test.
For once, even the Federalists of New England felt their blood
stir; for their own President and their own votes had called
these frigates into existence, and a victory won by the "Constitution," which had been built by their hands, was in their
eyes a greater victory over their political opponents than over
the British. With no half-hearted spirit, the sea-going Bostonians showered well-weighed praises on Hull when his ship entered Boston harbor, July 26, after its narrow escape; and
when he sailed again, New England waited with keen interest
to learn his fate.

Hull could not expect to keep command of the "Constitution." Bainbridge was much his senior, and had the right to a
preference in active service. Bainbridge then held and was

ordered to retain command of the "Constellation," fitting out
at the Washington Navy Yard; but Secretary Hamilton, July
28, ordered him to take command also of the "Constitution"
on her arrival in port. Doubtless Hull expected this change,
and probably the expectation induced him to risk a dangerous
experiment; for without bringing his ship to the Charlestown
Navy Yard, but remaining in the outer harbor, after obtaining such supplies as he needed, August 2, he set sail without
orders, and stood to the eastward. Having reached Cape Race
without meeting an enemy he turned southward, until on the
night of August 18 he spoke a privateer, which told him of a
British frigate near at hand. Following the privateersman's
directions the "Constitution" on the next day, August 19, at
two o'clock in the afternoon, latitude 41° 42', longitude 55° 48',
sighted the "Guerriere."

The meeting was welcome on both sides. Only three days before, Captain Dacres had entered on the log of a merchantman a challenge to any American frigate to meet him off Sandy
Hook. Not only had the "Guerriere" for a long time been extremely offensive to every sea-faring American, but the mistake
which caused the "Little Belt" to suffer so seriously for the
misfortune of being taken for the "Guerriere" had caused a
corresponding feeling of anger in the officers of the British
frigate. The meeting of August 19 had the character of a pre-
concerted duel.

The wind was blowing fresh from the northwest, with the
sea running high. Dacres backed his main-top-sail and waited.
Hull shortened sail and ran down before the wind. For about
an hour the two ships wore and wore again, trying to get advantage of position; until at last, a few minutes before six
o'clock, they came together side by side, within pistol-shot, the
wind almost astern, and running before it they pounded each
other with all their strength. As rapidly as the guns could be
worked, the "Constitution" poured in broadside after broadside,
double-shotted with round and grape—and, without exaggeration, the echo of these guns startled the world. "In less than

thirty minutes from the time we got alongside of the enemy," reported Hull, "she was left without a spar standing, and the hull cut to pieces in such a manner as to make it difficult to keep her above water."

That Dacres should have been defeated was not surprising; that he should have expected to win was an example of British arrogance that explained and excused the war. The length of the "Constitution" was 173 feet; that of the "Guerriere" was 156 feet; the extreme breadth of the "Constitution" was 44 feet; that of the "Guerriere" was 40 feet, or within a few inches in both cases. The "Constitution" carried thirty-two long 24-pounders, the "Guerriere" thirty long 18-pounders and two long 12-pounders; the "Constitution" carried twenty 32-pound carronades, the "Guerriere" sixteen. In every respect, and in proportion of ten to seven, the "Constitution" was the better ship; her crew was more numerous in proportion of ten to six. Dacres knew this very nearly as well as it was known to Hull, yet he sought a duel. What he did not know was that in a still greater proportion the American officers and crew were better and more intelligent seamen than the British, and that their passionate wish to repay old scores gave them extraordinary energy. So much greater was the moral superiority than the physical, that while the "Guerriere's" force counted as seven against ten, her losses counted as though her force were only two against ten.

Dacres' error cost him dear, for among the "Guerriere's" crew of two hundred and seventy-two, seventy-nine were killed or wounded; and the ship was injured beyond saving before Dacres realized his mistake, although he needed only thirty minutes of close fighting for the purpose. He never fully understood the causes of his defeat, and never excused it by pleading, as he might have done, the great superiority of his enemy.

Hull took his prisoners on board the "Constitution," and after blowing up the "Guerriere" sailed for Boston, where he arrived on the morning of August 30. The Sunday silence of the

Puritan city broke into excitement as the news passed through the quiet streets that the "Constitution" was below, in the outer harbor, with Dacres and his crew prisoners on board. No experience of history ever went to the heart of New England more directly than this victory, so peculiarly its own; but the delight was not confined to New England, and extreme though it seemed it was still not extravagant, for however small the affair might appear on the general scale of the world's battles, it raised the United States in one half hour to the rank of a first-class Power in the world.

Hull's victory was not only dramatic in itself, but was also supremely fortunate in the moment it occurred. The "Boston Patriot" of September 2, which announced the capture of the "Guerriere," announced in the next column that Rodgers and Decatur, with their squadron, entered Boston harbor within four-and-twenty hours after Hull's arrival, returning empty-handed after more than two months of futile cruising; while in still another column the same newspaper announced "the melancholy intelligence of the surrender of General Hull and his whole army to the British General Brock." Isaac Hull was nephew to the unhappy General, and perhaps the shattered hulk of the "Guerriere," which the nephew left at the bottom of the Atlantic Ocean, eight hundred miles east of Boston, was worth for the moment the whole province which the uncle had lost, eight hundred miles to the westward; it was at least the only equivalent the people could find, and they made the most of it. With the shock of new life, they awoke to the consciousness that after all the peace teachings of Pennsylvania and Virginia, the sneers of Federalists and foreigners; after the disgrace of the "Chesapeake" and the surrender of Detroit— Americans could still fight. The public had been taught, and had actually learned, to doubt its own physical courage; and the reaction of delight in satisfying itself that it still possessed the commonest and most brutal of human qualities was the natural result of a system that ignored the possibility of war.

Hull's famous victory taught the pleasures of war to a new

generation, which had hitherto been sedulously educated to think only of its cost. The first taste of blood maddens; and hardly had the "Constitution" reached port and told her story than the public became eager for more. The old Jeffersonian jealousy of the navy vanished in the flash of Hull's first broadside. Nothing would satisfy the craving of the popular appetite but more battles, more British frigates, and more daring victories. Even the cautious Madison was dragged by public excitement upon the element he most heartily disliked.

The whole navy, was once more, September 1, safe in port, except only the "Essex," a frigate rated at thirty-two but carrying forty-four guns, commanded by Captain David Porter. She left New York, July 3, with orders, dated June 24, to join Rodgers, or failing this to cruise southwardly as far as St. Augustine. June 11 she met a convoy of seven transports conveying a battalion of the Frst Regiment, or Royal Scots, from the West Indies to reinforce Prevost and Brock in Canada. Porter cut out one transport. With the aid of another frigate he could have captured the whole, to the great advantage of Dearborn's military movements; but the British commander managed his convoy so well that the battalion escaped, and enabled Prevost to strengthen the force at Niagara which threatened and defeated Van Rensselaer. August 13 the British 20-gun sloop-of-war "Alert" came in sight, bore down within short pistol-shot, and opened fire on the "Essex." Absurd as the idea seemed, the British captain behaved as though he hoped to capture the American frigate, and not until Porter nearly sunk him with a broadside did the Englishman strike his colors. After taking a number of other prizes, but without further fighting, September 7 Porter brought his ship back to the Delaware River.

The return of the "Essex" to port, September 7, brought all the national vessels once more under the direct control of the Department. Nearly every ship in the service was then at Boston. The three forty-fours—the "Constitution," "United States," and "President"—were all there; two of the thirty-eights—the "Congress" and "Chesapeake"—were there, and the "Constellation" was at Washington. The "Adams," 28, was also at Washington; but the "Hornet," 18, and "Argus," 16, were with Rodgers and Decatur at Boston. The "Syren," 16, was at New Orleans; the "Essex," 32, and the "Wasp," 18, were in the Delaware.

Carried away by Hull's victory, the Government could no longer hesitate to give its naval officers the liberty of action they asked, and which in spite of orders they had shown the intention to take. A new arrangement was made. The vessels were to be divided into three squadrons, each consisting of one forty-four, one light frigate, and one sloop-of-war. Rodgers in the "President" was to command one squadron, Bainbridge in the "Constitution" was to command another, and Decatur in the "United States" was to take the third. Their sailing orders, dated October 2, simply directed the three commodores to proceed to sea: "You are to do your utmost to annoy the enemy, to afford protection to our commerce, pursuing that course which to your best judgment may under all circumstances appear the best calculated to enable you to accomplish these objects as far as may be in your power, returning into port as speedily as circumstances will permit consistently with the great object in view."

Before continuing the story of the frigates, the fate of the little "Wasp" needs to be told. Her career was brief. The "Wasp," a sloop-of-war rated at eighteen guns, was one of President Jefferson's additions to the navy to supply the loss of the "Philadelphia"; she was ship-rigged, and armed with two long 12-pounders and sixteen 32-pound carronades. She carried a crew of one hundred and thirty-seven men, commanded by Captain Jacob Jones, a native of Delaware, lieutenant in the "Philadelphia" when lost in war with Tripoli. The "Wasp" was attached to Rodgers's squadron, and received orders from the commodore to join him at sea. She sailed from the Delaware October 13, and when about six hundred miles east of Norfolk, October 17, she fell in with the British 18-gun brig "Frolic," convoying fourteen merchantmen to England. The two vessels were equal in force, but the "Frolic's" broadside threw a weight of two hundred and seventy-four pounds, while that of the "Wasp" threw some few pounds less; the "Frolic" measured, by British report, one hundred feet in length, the "Wasp" one hundred and six; their breadth on deck was the same; and although the "Wasp's" crew exceeded that of her enemy, being one hundred and thirty-five men against one hundred and ten, the British vessel had all the men she needed, and suffered little from this inferiority. The action began at half-past eleven in the morning, the two sloops running parallel, about sixty yards apart, in a very heavy sea, which caused both to pitch and roll so that marksmanship had the most decisive share in victory. The muzzles of the guns went under water, and clouds of spray dashed over the crews, while the two vessels ran side by side for the first fifteen minutes. The British fire cut the "Wasp's" rigging, while the American guns played havoc with the "Frolic's" hull and lower masts. The vessels approached each other so closely that the rammers of the guns struck the enemy's side and at last they fell foul—the "Wasp" almost squarely across the "Frolic's" bow. In the heavy sea boarding was difficult; but as soon as the "Wasp's" crew could clamber down the "Frolic's" bowsprit, they found on the deck the British captain and lieutenant, both severely wounded, and one brave sailor at the wheel. Not twenty of the British crew were left unhurt, and these had gone below to escape the American musketry. The "Wasp" had only ten men killed and wounded. The battle lasted forty-three minutes.

If the American people had acquired a taste for blood, the battle of the "Wasp" and "Frolic" gratified it, for the British sloop was desperately defended, and the battle, won by the better marksmanship of the Americans, was unusually bloody. Captain Jones lost the full satisfaction of his victory, for a few hours afterward the "Poictiers," a British seventy-four, came upon the two disabled combatants and carried both into Bermuda; but the American people would have been glad to part with their whole navy on such terms, and the fight between the "Wasp" and the "Frolic" roused popular enthusiasm to a point where no honors seemed to satisfy their gratitude to Captain Jones and his crew.

The "Wasp's" brilliant career closed within a week from the day she left the Delaware. A week afterward another of these ship-duels occurred, which made a still deeper impression. Rodgers and Decatur sailed from Boston October 8, with the "President," the "United States," "Congress," and "Argus," leaving the "Constitution," "Chesapeake," and "Hornet" in port. Rodgers in the "President," with the "Congress," cruised far and wide, but could find no enemy to fight, and after making prize of a few merchantmen returned to Boston, December 31. The "Argus" also made some valuable prizes, but was chased by a British squadron, and only by excellent management escaped capture, returning Jan. 3, 1813, to New York. Decatur in the "United States," separating from the squadron October 12, sailed eastward to the neighborhood of the Azores, until, October 25, he sighted a sail to windward. The stranger made chase. The wind was fresh from south-southeast, with a heavy sea. Decatur stood toward his enemy, who presently came about, abreast of the "United States" but beyond gun-shot, and both ships being then on the same tack approached each other until the action began at long range. The British ship was the 38-gun frigate "Macedonian" commanded by Captain Carden, and about the same force as the "Guerriere." At first the "United States" used only her long 24-pounders, of which she carried fifteen on her broadside, while the "Macedonian" worked a broadside of fourteen long 18-pounders. So unequal a contest could not continue. Not only was the American metal heavier, but the American fire was quicker and better directed than that of the Englishman; so that Carden, after a few minutes of this experience, bore down to close. His manoeuvre made matters worse. The carronades of the "United States" came into play; the "Macedonian's" mizzen-mast fell, her fore and main top-mast were shot away, and her main-yard;

almost all her rigging was cut to pieces, and most of the guns on her engaged side were dismounted. She dropped gradually to leeward, and Decatur, tacking and coming up under his enemy's stern, hailed, and received her surrender.

The British ship had no right to expect a victory, for the disparity of force was even greater than between the "Constitution" and the "Guerriere;" but in this case the British court-martial subsequently censured Captain Carden for mistakes. The battle lasted longer than that with the "Guerriere," and Decatur apologized for the extra hour because the sea was high and his enemy had the weather-gauge and kept at a distance; but the apology was not needed. Decatur proved his skill by sparing his ship and crew. His own loss was eleven men killed and wounded; the "Macedonian's" loss was nine times as great. The "United States" suffered little in her hull, and her spars and rigging suffered no greater injury than could be quickly repaired; while the "Macedonian" received a hundred shot in her hull, and aloft nothing remained standing but her fore and main masts and her fore-yard.

Decatur saved the "Macedonian," and brought her back to New London—the only British frigate ever brought as a prize into an American port. The two ships arrived December 4, and from New London the "Macedonian" was taken to New York and received in formal triumph. Captain Jones of the "Wasp" took command of her in reward for his capture of the "Frolic."

Before the year closed, the "Constitution" had time for another cruise. Hull at his own request received command of the Navy Yard at Charlestown, and also took charge of the naval defences in New York harbor, but did not again serve at sea during the war. The "Constitution" was given to Captain Bainbridge, one of the oldest officers in the service. A native of New Jersey, Bainbridge commanded the "Philadelphia" when lost in the Tripolitan war, and was held for eighteen months a prisoner in Tripoli. In 1812, when he took command of the "Constitution," though a year older than Hull and five years older than Decatur, he had not yet reached his fortieth year, while Rodgers, born in 1771, had but lately passed it. The difference in age between these four naval officers and the four chief generals—Dearborn, Wilkinson, Wade Hampton, and William Hull—was surprising; for the average age of the naval commanders amounted barely to thirty-seven years, while that of the four generals reached fifty-eight. This difference alone accounted for much of the difference in their fortune, and perhaps political influence accounted for the rest.

Bainbridge showed no inferiority to the other officers of the service, and no one grumbled at the retirement of Hull. The "Constitution" sailed from Boston, October 25, with the "Hornet." The "Essex," then in the Delaware, was ordered to join the squadron at certain specified ports in the south Atlantic, and sailed October 28, expecting a very long cruise. December 13 Bainbridge arrived at San Salvador, on the coast of Brazil, where he left the "Hornet" to blockade the "Bonne Citoyenne," a British 18-gun sloop-of-war bound to England with specie. Cruising southward, within sight of the Brazilian coast, in latitude 13° 6′ south, Bainbridge sighted the British frigate "Java," a ship of the same tonnage as the "Guerriere," throwing a slightly heavier broadside and carrying a large crew of four hundred and twenty-six men, if the American account was correct. Bainbridge tacked and made sail off shore, to draw the stranger away from a neutral coast; the British frigate followed him, until at half-past one o'clock in the afternoon Bainbridge shortened sail, tacked again, and stood for his enemy. Soon after two o'clock the action began, the two ships being on the same tack, the "Java" to windward and the better sailer, and both fighting their long-range guns. The British frigate insisted upon keeping at a distance, obliging Bainbridge after half an hour to risk the danger of being raked; and at twenty minutes before three o'clock the "Constitution" closed within pistol-shot. At ten minutes before three the ships were foul, the "Java's" jibboom in the "Constitution's" mizzen rigging; and from that point the battle became slaughter. In fifteen minutes the "Java's" bowsprit, fore-mast, and main top-mast were cut away, and a few minutes after four o'clock she ceased firing. Her captain, Lambert, was mortally wounded; the first lieutenant was wounded; forty-eight of her officers and crew were dead or dying; one hundred and two were wounded; little more than a hulk filled with wreck and with dead or wounded men floated on the water.

The "Constitution" had but twelve men killed and twenty-two wounded, and repaired damages in an hour. Owing perhaps to the death of Captain Lambert the reports of the battle were more contradictory than usual, but no one disputed that although the "Java" was to windward and outsailed the American frigate, and although her broadside counted as nearly nine against her enemy's ten—for the "Constitution" on this cruise carried two guns less than in her fight with the "Guerriere"— yet the "Java" inflicted no more damage than she ought to have done had she been only one fourth the size of the American frigate, although she was defended more desperately than either the "Guerriere" or the "Macedonian."

With this battle the year ended. Bainbridge was obliged to blow up his prize, and after landing and paroling his prisoners at San Salvador sailed for Boston, where he arrived in safety, February 27, 1813. During the six months the war had lasted the little United States navy captured three British frigates, besides the 20-gun "Alert" and the 18-gun "Frolic;" privateers by scores had ravaged British commerce, while the immense British force on the ocean had succeeded only in capturing the little "Nautilus," the 12-gun brig "Vixen," and the "Wasp." The commerce of America had indeed suffered almost total destruction; but the dispute was to be decided not so much by the loss which England could inflict upon America, as by that which America could inflict upon England.

Privateering

THE people of the Atlantic coast felt the loss of the "Chesapeake"* none too keenly. Other nations had a history to support them in moments of mortification, or had learned by centuries of experience to accept turns of fortune as the fate of war. The American of the sea-coast was not only sensitive and anxious, but he also saw with singular clearness the bearing of every disaster, and did not see with equal distinctness the general drift of success. The loss of the "Chesapeake" was a terrible disaster, not merely because it announced the quick recovery of England's pride and power from a momentary shock, but also because it threatened to take away the single object of American enthusiasm which redeemed shortcomings elsewhere. After the loss of the "Chesapeake," no American frigate was allowed the opportunity to fight with an equal enemy. The British frigates, ordered to cruise in company, gave the Americans no chance to renew their triumphs of 1812.

Indeed, the experience of 1813 tended to show that the frigate was no longer the class of vessel best suited to American wants. Excessively expensive compared with their efficiency, the "Constitution," "President," and "United States" could only with difficulty obtain crews; and when after much delay they were ready for sea, they could not easily evade a blockading squadron. The original cost of a frigate varied from two hundred thousand dollars to three hundred thousand; that of a sloop-of-war, like the "Hornet," "Wasp," or "Argus," varied between forty and fifty thousand dollars. The frigate required a crew of about four hundred men; the sloop carried about one hundred and fifty. The annual expense of a frigate in active service was about one hundred and thirty-four thousand dollars; that of the brig was sixty thousand. The frigate required much time and heavy timber in her construction; the sloop could be built quickly and of ordinary material. The loss of a frigate was a

Vol. VII, Chap. XIII.
* Captured by the British frigate *Shannon*, June 1, 1813. P.M.A.

severe national disaster; the loss of a sloop was not a serious event.

For defensive purposes neither the frigate nor the brig counted heavily against a nation which employed ships-of-the-line by dozens; but even for offensive objects the frigate was hardly so useful as the sloop-of-war. The record of the frigates for 1813 showed no results equivalent to their cost. Their cruises were soon told. The "President," leaving Boston April 30, ran across to the Azores, thence to the North Sea, and during June and July haunted the shores of Norway, Scotland, and Ireland, returning to Newport September 27, having taken thirteen prizes. The "Congress," which left Boston with the "President," cruised nearly eight months in the Atlantic, and returned to Boston December 14, having captured but four merchantmen. The "Chesapeake," which sailed from Boston Dec. 13, 1812, cruised four months in the track of British commerce, past Madeira and Cape de Verde, across the equator, and round through the West Indies, returning to Boston April 9, having taken six prizes; at the beginning of her next cruise, June 1, the "Chesapeake" was herself captured. The adventures of the "Essex" in the Pacific were such as might have been equally well performed by a sloop-of-war, and belonged rather to the comparative freedom with which the frigates moved in 1812 than to the difficult situation that followed. No other frigates succeeded in getting to sea till December 4, when the "President" sailed again. The injury inflicted by the frigates on the Atlantic was therefore the capture of twenty-three merchantmen in a year. At the close of 1813, the "President" and the "Essex" were the only frigates at sea; the "Constitution" sailed from Boston only Jan. 1, 1814; the "United States" and "Macedonian" were blockaded at New London; the "Constellation" was still at Norfolk; the "Adams" was at Washington, and the "Congress" at Boston.

When this record was compared with that of the sloops-of-war, the frigates were seen to be luxuries. The sloop-of-war was a single-decked vessel, rigged sometimes as a ship, sometimes as a brig, but never as a sloop, measuring about one hundred and ten feet in length by thirty in breadth, and carrying usually eighteen thirty-two-pound carronades and two long twelve-pounders. Of this class the American navy possessed in 1812 only four examples—the "Hornet," the "Wasp," the "Argus," and the "Syren." The "Wasp" was lost Oct. 18, 1812, after capturing the "Frolic." The "Syren" remained at New Orleans during the first year of the war, and then came to Boston, but saw no ocean service of importance during 1813. The "Hornet" made three prizes, including the sloop-of-war "Peacock," and was then blockaded with the "United States" and "Macedonian"; but the smaller vessel could do what the frigates could not, and in November the "Hornet" slipped out of New London and made her way to New York, where she waited an opportunity to escape to sea. The story will show her success. Finally, the "Argus" cruised for a month in the British Channel, and made twenty-one prizes before she was captured by the "Pelican."

The three frigates, "President," "Congress," and "Chesapeake," captured twenty-three prizes in the course of the year, and lost the "Chesapeake." The two sloops, the "Hornet" and "Argus," captured twenty-four prizes, including the sloop-of-war "Peacock," and lost the "Argus."

The government at the beginning of the war owned four smaller vessels—the "Nautilus" and "Vixen" of fourteen guns, and the "Enterprise" and "Viper" of twelve. Another brig, the "Rattlesnake," sixteen, was bought. Experience seemed to prove that these were of little use. The "Nautilus" fell into the hands of Broke's squadron July 16, 1812, within a month after the declaration of war. The "Vixen" was captured Nov. 22, 1812, by Sir James Yeo. The "Viper," Jan. 17, 1813, became prize to Captain Lumley in the British frigate "Narcissus." The "Enterprise" distinguished itself by capturing the "Boxer," and was regarded as a lucky vessel, but was never a good or fast one. The "Rattlesnake," though fast, was at last caught on a lee shore by the frigate "Leander," July 11, 1814, and carried into Halifax.

In the enthusiasm over the frigates in 1812, Congress voted that six forty-fours should be built, besides four ships-of-the-line. The Act was approved Jan. 2, 1813. Not until March 3 did Congress pass an Act for building six new sloops-of-war. The loss of two months was not the only misfortune in this legislation. Had the sloops been begun in January, they might have gone to sea by the close of the year. The six sloops were all launched within eleven months from the passage of the bill, and the first of them, the "Frolic," got to sea within that time, while none of the frigates or line-of-battle ships could get to sea within two years of the passage of the law. A more remarkable oversight was the building of only six sloops, when an equal number of forty-fours and four seventy-fours were ordered. Had Congress voted twenty-four sloops, the proportion would not have been improper; but perhaps the best policy would have been to build fifty such sloops, and to prohibit privateering. The reasons for such a course were best seen in the experiences of the privateers.

The history of the privateers was never satisfactorily written. Neither their number, their measurements, their force, their captures, nor their losses were accurately known. Little ground could be given for an opinion in regard to their economy. Only with grave doubt could any judgment be reached even in regard to their relative efficiency compared with government vessels of the same class. Yet their experience was valuable, and their services were very great.

In the summer of 1812 any craft that could keep the sea in fine weather set out as a privateer to intercept vessels approaching the coast. The typical privateer of the first few months was the pilot-boat, armed with one or two long-nine or twelve-pound guns. Of twenty-six privateers sent from New York in the first four months of war, fifteen carried crews of eighty men or less. These small vessels especially infested the West Indies, where fine weather and light breezes suited their qualities. After the seas had been cleared of such prey as these petty marauders could manage, they were found to be unprofitable—too small to fight and too light to escape. The typical privateer of 1813 was a larger vessel—a brig or schooner of two or three hundred tons, armed with one long pivot-gun, and six or eight lighter guns in broadside; carrying crews which varied in number from one hundred and twenty to one hundred and sixty men; swift enough to escape under most circumstances even a frigate, and strong enough to capture any armed merchantman.

After the war was fairly begun, the British mercantile shipping always sailed either under convoy or as armed "running ships" that did not wait for the slow and comparatively rare opportunities of convoy, but trusted to their guns for defence. The new American privateer was adapted to meet both chances. Two or three such craft hanging about a convoy could commonly cut off some merchantman, no matter how careful the convoying man-of-war might be. By night they could run directly into the fleet and cut out vessels without even giving an alarm, and by day they could pick up any craft that lagged behind or happened to stray too far away. Yet the "running ships" were the chief objects of their search, for these were the richest prizes; and the capture of a single vessel, if it reached an American port in safety, insured success to the cruise. The loss of these vessels caused peculiar annoyance to the British, for they sometimes carried considerable amounts of specie, and usually were charged with a mail which was always sunk and lost in case of capture.

As the war continued, experience taught the owners of privateers the same lesson that was taught to the government. The most efficient vessel of war corresponded in size with the "Hornet" or the new sloops-of-war building in 1813. Tonnage was so arbitrary a mode of measurement that little could be learned from the dimensions of five hundred tons commonly given for these vessels; but in a general way they might be regarded as about one hundred and fifteen or one hundred and twenty feet long on the spar-deck and thirty-one feet in extreme breadth. Unless such vessels were swift sailers, particularly handy in working to windward, they were worse than useless; and for that reason the utmost effort was made both by the public and private constructors to obtain speed. At the close of the war the most efficient vessel afloat was probably the American sloop-of-war, or privateer, of four or five hundred tons, rigged as a ship or brig, and carrying one hundred and fifty or sixty men, with a battery varying according to the ideas of the captain and owners, but in the case of privateers almost invariably including one "long Tom," or pivot-gun.

Yet for privateering purposes the smaller craft competed closely with the larger. For ordinary service no vessel could do more effective work in a more economical way than was done by Joshua Barney's "Rossie" of Baltimore, or Boyle's "Comet" of the same port, or Champlin's "General Armstrong" of New York—schooners or brigs of two or three hundred tons, uncomfortable to their officers and crews, but most dangerous enemies to merchantmen. Vessels of this class came into favor long before the war, because of their speed, quickness in handling, and economy during the experience of twenty years in blockade-running and evasion of cruisers. Such schooners could be built in any Northern sea-port in six weeks or two months at half the cost of a government cruiser.

The government sloop-of-war was not built for privateering purposes. Every government vessel was intended chiefly to fight, and required strength in every part and solidity throughout. The frame needed to be heavy to support the heavier structure; the quarters needed to be thick to protect the men at the guns from grape and musketry; the armament was as weighty as the frame would bear. So strong were the sides of American frigates that even thirty-two-pound shot fired at forty or fifty feet distance sometimes failed to penetrate, and the British complained as a grievance that the sides of an American forty-four were thicker than those of a British seventy-four. The American ship-builders spared no pains to make all their vessels in every respect—in size, strength, and speed—superior to the vessels with which they were to compete; but the government ship-carpenter had a harder task than the private ship-builder, for he was obliged to obtain greater speed at the same time that he used heavier material than the British constructors. As far as the navy carpenters succeeded in their double object, they did so by improving the model and increasing the proportions of the spars.

The privateer was built for no such object. The last purpose of a privateer was to fight at close range, and owners much preferred that their vessels, being built to make money, should not fight at all unless much money could be made. The private armed vessel was built rather to fly than to fight, and its value depended far more on its ability to escape than on its capacity to attack. If the privateer could sail close to the wind, and wear or tack in the twinkling of an eye; if she could spread an immense amount of canvas and run off as fast as a frigate before the wind; if she had sweeps to use in a calm, and one long-range gun pivoted amidships, with plenty of men in case boarding became necessary—she was perfect. To obtain these results the builders and sailors ran excessive risks. Too lightly built and too heavily sparred, the privateer was never a comfortable or a safe vessel. Beautiful beyond anything then known in naval construction, such vessels roused boundless admiration, but defied imitators. British constructors could not build them, even when they had the models; British captains could not sail them; and when British admirals, fascinated by their beauty and tempted by the marvellous qualities of their model, ordered such a prize to be taken into the service, the first act of the carpenters in the British navy-yards was to reduce to their own standard the long masts, and to strengthen the hull and sides till the vessel should be safe in a battle or a gale. Perhaps an American navy-carpenter must have done the same; but though not a line in the model might be altered, she never sailed again as she sailed before. She could not bear conventional restraints.

Americans were proud of their privateers, as they well might be; for this was the first time when in competition with the world, on an element open to all, they proved their capacity to excel, and produced a creation as beautiful as it was practical.

The British navy took a new tone in regard to these vessels. Deeply as the American frigates and sloops-of-war had wounded the pride of the British navy, they never had reduced that fine service to admitted inferiority. Under one pretext or another, every defeat was excused. Even the superiority of American gunnery was met by the proud explanation that the British navy, since Trafalgar, had enjoyed no opportunity to use their guns. Nothing could convince a British admiral that Americans were better fighters than Englishmen; but when he looked at the American schooner he frankly said that England could show no such models, and could not sail them if she had them. In truth, the schooner was a wonderful invention. Not her battles, but her escapes won for her the open-mouthed admiration of the British captains, who saw their prize double like a hare and slip through their fingers at the moment when capture was sure. Under any ordinary condition of wind and weather, with an open sea, the schooner, if only she could get to windward, laughed at a frigate.

As the sailing rather than the fighting qualities of the privateer were the chief object of her construction, those were the points best worth recording; but the newspapers of the time were so much absorbed in proving that Americans could fight, as to cause almost total neglect of the more important question whether Americans could sail better than their rivals. All great nations had fought, and at one time or another every great nation in Europe had been victorious over every other; but no people, in the course of a thousand years of rivalry on the ocean, had invented or had known how to sail a Yankee schooner. Whether ship, brig, schooner, or sloop, the American vessel was believed to outsail any other craft on the ocean, and the proof of this superiority was incumbent on the Americans to furnish. They neglected to do so. No clear evidence was ever recorded of the precise capacities of their favorite vessels. Neither the lines of the hull, the dimensions of the spars, the rates of sailing by the log in different weather, the points of sailing—nothing precise was ever set down.

Of the superiority no doubts could be entertained. The best proof of the American claim was the British admission. Hardly an English writer on marine affairs—whether in newspapers, histories, or novels—failed to make some allusion to the beauty and speed of American vessels. The naval literature of Great Britain from 1812 to 1860 was full of such material. The praise of the invention was still commonly accompanied by some expression of dislike for the inventor, but even in that respect a marked change followed the experiences of 1812–1814. Among the Englishmen living on the island of Jamaica, and familiar with the course of events in the West Indies from 1806 to 1817, was one Michael Scott, born in Glasgow in 1789, and in the prime of his youth at the time of the American war. In the year 1829, at the age of forty, he began the publication in "Blackwood's Magazine" of a series of sketches which rapidly became popular as "Tom Cringle's Log." Scott was the best narrator and probably the best informed man who wrote on the West Indies at that period; and his frequent allusions to the United States and the war threw more light on the social side of history than could be obtained from all official sources ever printed.

I don't like Americans [Scott said]; I never did and never shall like them. I have seldom met an American gentleman in the large and complete sense of the term. I have no wish to eat with them, drink with them, deal with or consort with them in any way; but let me tell the whole truth—*nor fight* with them, were it not for the laurels to be acquired by overcoming an enemy so brave, determined, and alert, and every way so worthy of one's steel as they have always proved.

The Americans did not fight the War of 1812 in order to make themselves loved. According to Scott's testimony they gained the object for which they did fight. "In gunnery and small-arm practice we were as thoroughly weathered on by the Americans during the war as we overtopped them in the bull-dog courage with which our boarders handled those genuine English weapons—the cutlass and the pike." Superiority in the intellectual branches of warfare was conceded to the Americans; but even in regard to physical qualities, the British were not inclined to boast.

In the field [said Scott] or grappling in mortal combat on the blood-slippery quarter-deck of an enemy's vessels, a British soldier or sailor is the bravest of the brave. No soldier or sailor of any other country, saving and excepting those damned Yankees, can stand against them.

Had English society known so much of Americans in 1807, war would have been unnecessary.

Yet neither equality in physical courage nor superiority in the higher branches of gunnery and small-arms was the chief success of Americans in the war. Beyond question the schooner was the most conclusive triumph. Readers of Michael Scott could not forget the best of his sketches—the escape of the little American schooner "Wave" from two British cruisers, by running to windward under the broadside of a man-of-war. With keen appreciation Scott detailed every motion of the vessels, and dwelt with peculiar emphasis on the apparent desperation of the attempt. Again and again the thirty-two-pound shot, as he described the scene, tore through the slight vessel as the two crafts raced through the heavy seas within musket-shot of one another, until at last the firing from the corvette ceased. "The breeze had taken off, and the 'Wave,' resuming her superiority in light winds, had escaped." Yet this was not the most significant part of "Tom Cringle's" experience. The "Wave," being afterward captured at anchor, was taken into the royal service and fitted as a ship-of-war. Cringle was ordered by the vice-admiral to command her, and as she came to report he took a look at her—

When I had last seen her she was a most beautiful little craft, both in hull and rigging, as ever delighted the eye of a sailor; but the dock-yard riggers and carpenters had fairly bedevilled her, at least so far as appearances went. First they had replaced the light rail on her gunwale by heavy solid bulwarks four feet high, surmounted by hammock nettings at least another foot;

so that the symmetrical little vessel that formerly floated on
the foam light as a sea-gull now looked like a clumsy, dish-
shaped Dutch dogger. Her long, slender wands of masts which
used to swing about as if there were neither shrouds nor stays
to support them were now as taut and stiff as church-steeples,
with four heavy shrouds of a side, and stays and back-stays, and
the Devil knows what all.

"If them heave-'emtaughts at the yard have not taken the
speed out of the little beauty I am a Dutchman" was the natural comment—as obvious as it was sound.

The reports of privateer captains to their owners were rarely
published, and the logs were never printed or deposited in any
public office. Occasionally, in the case of a battle or the loss of
guns or spars or cargo in a close pursuit, the privateer captain
described the causes of his loss in a letter which found its way
into print; and from such letters some idea could be drawn of
the qualities held in highest regard, both in their vessels and
in themselves. The first and commonest remark was that privateers of any merit never seemed to feel anxious for their
own safety so long as they could get to windward a couple of
gunshots from their enemy. They would risk a broadside in the
process without very great anxiety. They chiefly feared lest
they might be obliged to run before the wind in heavy weather.
The little craft which could turn on itself like a flash and dart
away under a frigate's guns into the wind's eye long before the
heavy ship could come about, had little to fear on that point
of sailing; but when she was obliged to run to leeward, the
chances were more nearly equal. Sometimes, especially in light
breezes or in a stronger wind, by throwing guns and weighty
articles overboard privateers could escape; but in heavy weather
the ship-of-war could commonly outcarry them, and more often
could drive them on a coast or into the clutches of some other
man-of-war.

Of being forced to fly to leeward almost every privateer could
tell interesting stories. A fair example of such tales was an
adventure of Captain George Coggeshall, who afterward com-

piled, chiefly from newspapers, an account of the privateers, among which he preserved a few stories that would otherwise have been lost. Coggeshall commanded a two-hundred-ton schooner, the "David Porter," in which he made the run to France with a cargo and a letter-of-marque. The schooner was at Bordeaux in March, 1814, when Wellington's army approached. Afraid of seizure by the British if he remained at Bordeaux, Coggeshall sailed from Bordeaux for La Rochelle with a light wind from the eastward, when at daylight March 15, 1814, he found a large ship about two miles to windward. Coggeshall tried to draw his enemy down to leeward, but only lost ground until the ship was not more than two gunshots away. The schooner could then not run to windward without taking the enemy's fire within pistol-shot, and dared not return to Bordeaux. Nothing remained but to run before the wind. Coggeshall got out his square-sail and studding-sails ready to set, and when everything was prepared he changed his course and bore off suddenly, gaining a mile in the six or eight minutes lost by the ship in spreading her studding-sails. He then started his water-casks, threw out ballast, and drew away from his pursuer, till in a few hours the ship became a speck on the horizon.

Apparently a similar but narrower escape was made by Captain Champlin of the "Warrior," a famous privateer-brig of four hundred and thirty tons, mounting twenty-one guns and carrying one hundred and fifty men. Standing for the harbor of Fayal, Dec. 15, 1814, he was seen by a British man-of-war lying there at anchor. The enemy slipped her cables and made sail in chase. The weather was very fresh and squally, and at eight o'clock in the evening the ship was only three miles distant. After a run of about sixty miles, the man-of-war came within grape-shot distance and opened fire from her two bow-guns. Champlin luffed a little, got his long pivot-gun to bear, and ran out his starboard guns as though to fight, which caused the ship to shorten sail for battle. Then Champlin at two o'clock in the morning threw overboard eleven guns, and escaped. The

British ship was in sight the next morning, but did not pursue farther.

Often the privateers were obliged to throw everything overboard at the risk of capsizing, or escaped capture only by means of their sweeps. In 1813 Champlin commanded the "General Armstrong," a brig of two hundred and forty-six tons and one hundred and forty men. Off Surinam, March 11, 1813, he fell in with the British sloop-of-war "Coquette," which he mistook for a letter-of-marque, and approached with the intention of boarding. Having come within pistol-shot and fired his broadsides, he discovered his error. The wind was light, the two vessels had no headway, and for three quarters of an hour, if Champlin's account could be believed, he lay within pistol-shot of the man-of-war. He was struck by a musket-ball in the left shoulder; six of his crew were killed and fourteen wounded; his rigging was cut to pieces; his foremast and bowsprit injured, and several shots entered the brig between wind and water, causing her to leak; but at last he succeeded in making sail forward, and with the aid of his sweeps crept out of range. The sloop-of-war was unable to cripple or follow him.

Sometimes the very perfection of the privateer led to dangers as great as though perfection were a fault. Captain Shaler of the "Governor Tompkins," a schooner, companion to the "General Armstrong," chased three sail Dec. 25, 1812, and on near approach found them to be two ships and a brig. The larger ship had the appearance of a government transport; she had boarding-nettings almost up to her tops, but her ports appeared to be painted, and she seemed prepared for running away as she fought. Shaler drew nearer, and came to the conclusion that the ship was too heavy for him; but while his first officer went forward with the glass to take another look, a sudden squall struck the schooner without reaching the ship, and in a moment, before the light sails could be taken in, "and almost before I could turn round, I was under the guns, not of a transport, but of a large frigate, and not more than a quarter of a mile from her." With impudence that warranted punishment,

Shaler fired his little broadside of nine or twelve pounders into
the enemy, who replied with a broadside of twenty-four pounders, killing three men, wounding five, and causing an explosion
on deck that threw confusion into the crew; but the broadside
did no serious injury to the rigging. The schooner was then just
abaft the ship's beam, a quarter of a mile away, holding the
same course and to windward. She could not tack without
exposing her stern to a raking fire, and any failure to come about
would have been certain destruction. Shaler stood on, taking
the ship's fire, on the chance of outsailing his enemy before a
shot could disable the schooner. Side by side the two vessels
raced half an hour, while twenty-four-pound shot fell in foam
about the schooner, but never struck her, and at last she drew
ahead beyond range. Even then her dangers were not at an end.
A calm followed; the ship put out boats; and only by throwing
deck-lumber and shot overboard, and putting all hands at the
sweeps, did Shaler "get clear of one of the most quarrelsome
companions that I ever met with."

The capacities of the American privateer could to some extent be inferred from its mishaps. Nothwithstanding speed,
skill, and caution, the privateer was frequently and perhaps
usually captured in the end. The modes of capture were numerous. April 3, 1813, Admiral Warren's squadron in the Chesapeake captured by boats, after a sharp action, the privateer
"Dolphin" of Baltimore, which had taken refuge in the Rappahannock River. April 27 the "Tom" of Baltimore, a schooner of
nearly three hundred tons, carrying fourteen guns, was captured by his Majesty's ships "Surveillante" and "Lyra" after
a smart chase. Captain Collier of the "Surveillante" reported:
"She is a remarkably fine vessel of her class, and from her
superior sailing has already escaped from eighteen of his Majesty's cruisers." May 11, the "Holkar" of New York was driven
ashore off Rhode Island and destroyed by the "Orpheus" frigate. May 19, Captain Gordon of the British man-of-war "Rat-
ler," in company with the schooner "Bream," drove ashore
and captured the "Alexander" of Salem, off Kennebunk, "con-

sidered the fastest sailing privateer out of the United States,"
according to Captain Gordon's report. May 21, Captain Hyde
Parker of the frigate "Tenedos," in company with the brig
"Curlew," captured the "Enterprise" of Salem, pierced for
eighteen guns. May 23, the "Paul Jones," of sixteen guns and
one hundred and twenty men, fell in with a frigate in a thick
fog off the coast of Ireland, and being crippled by her fire surrendered. July 13, Admiral Cockburn captured by boats at
Ocracoke Inlet the fine privateer-brig "Anaconda" of New York,
with a smaller letter-of-marque. July 17, at sea, three British
men-of-war, after a chase of four hours, captured the "York-
town" of twenty guns and one hundred and forty men. The
schooner "Orders in Council" of New York, carrying sixteen
guns and one hundred and twenty men, was captured during
the summer, after a long chase of five days, by three British
cutters that drove her under the guns of a frigate. The "Ma-
tilda," privateer of eleven guns and one hundred and four men,
was captured off San Salvador by attempting to board the
British letter-of-marque "Lyon" under the impression that she
was the weaker ship.

In these ten instances of large privateers captured or destroyed in 1813, the mode of capture happened to be recorded;
and in none of them was the privateer declared to have been
outsailed and caught by any single British vessel on the open
seas. Modes of disaster were many, and doubtless among the
rest a privateer might occasionally be fairly beaten in speed,
but few such cases were recorded, although British naval officers were quick to mention these unusual victories. Unless the
weather gave to the heavier British vessel-of-war the advantage
of carrying more sail in a rough sea, the privateer was rarely
outsailed.

The number of privateers at sea in 1813 was not recorded.
The list of all private armed vessels during the entire war included somewhat more than five hundred names. Most of these
were small craft, withdrawn after a single cruise. Not two hundred were so large as to carry crews of fifty men. Nearly two

hundred and fifty, or nearly half the whole number of privateers, fell into British hands. Probably at no single moment were more than fifty seagoing vessels on the ocean as privateers, and the number was usually very much less; while the large privateer-brigs or ships that rivalled sloops-of-war in size were hardly more numerous than the sloops themselves.

The total number of prizes captured from the British in 1813 exceeded four hundred, four fifths of which were probably captured by privateers, national cruisers taking only seventy-nine. If the privateers succeeded in taking three hundred and fifty prizes, the whole number of privateers could scarcely have exceeded one hundred. The government cruisers "President," "Congress," "Chesapeake," "Hornet," and "Argus" averaged nearly ten prizes apiece. Privateers averaged much less; but they were ten times as numerous as the government cruisers, and inflicted four times as much injury.

Such an addition to the naval force of the United States was very important. Doubtless the privateers contributed more than the regular navy to bring about a disposition for peace in the British classes most responsible for the war. The colonial and shipping interests, whose influence produced the Orders in Council, suffered the chief penalty. The West India colonies were kept in constant discomfort and starvation by swarms of semi-piratical craft darting in and out of every channel among their islands; but the people of England could have borne with patience the punishment of the West Indies had not the American cruisers inflicted equally severe retribution nearer home.

Great Britain was blockaded. No one could deny that manifest danger existed to any merchant-vessel that entered or left British waters. During the summer the blockade was continuous. Toward the close of 1812 an American named Preble, living in Paris, bought a small vessel, said to have belonged in turn to the British and French navy, which he fitted as a privateer-brig, carrying sixteen guns and one hundred and sixty men. The "True-Blooded Yankee," commanded by Captain Hailey, sailed from Brest March 1, 1813, and cruised thirty-seven days on the coasts of Ireland and Scotland, capturing twenty-seven valuable vessels; sinking coasters in the very bay of Dublin; landing and taking possession of an island off the coast of Ireland, and of a town in Scotland, where she burned seven vessels in the harbor. She returned safely to Brest, and soon made another cruise. At the same time the schooner "Fox" of Portsmouth burned or sunk vessel after vessel in the Irish Sea, as they plied between Liverpool and Cork. In May, the schooner "Paul Jones" of New York, carrying sixteen guns and one hundred and twenty men, took or destroyed a dozen vessels off the Irish coast, until she was herself caught in a fog by the frigate "Leonidas," and captured May 23 after a chase in which five of her crew were wounded.

While these vessels were thus engaged, the brig "Rattlesnake" of Philadelphia, carrying sixteen guns and one hundred and twenty men, and the brig "Scourge" of New York, carrying nine guns and one hundred and ten men, crossed the ocean and cruised all the year in the northern seas off the coasts of Scotland and Norway, capturing some forty British vessels, and costing the British merchants and shipowners losses to the amount of at least two million dollars. In July the "Scourge" fell in with Commodore Rodgers in the "President," and the two vessels remained several days in company off the North Cape, while the British admiralty sent three or four squadrons in search of them without success. July 19, after Rodgers had been nearly a month in British waters, one of these squadrons drove him away, and he then made a circuit around Ireland before he turned homeward. At the same time, from July 14 to August 14, the "Argus" was destroying vessels in the British Channel at the rate of nearly one a day. After the capture of the "Argus," August 14, the "Grand Turk" of Salem, a brig carrying sixteen guns and one hundred and five men, cruised for twenty days in the mouth of the British Channel without being disturbed. Besides these vessels, others dashed into British waters from time to time as they sailed forward and back across the ocean in the track of British commerce.

No one disputed that the privateers were a very important branch of the American navy; but they suffered under serious drawbacks, which left doubtful the balance of merits and defects. Perhaps their chief advantage compared with government vessels was their lightness—a quality which no government would have carried to the same extent. The long-range pivot-gun was another invention of the privateer, peculiarly successful and easily adapted for government vessels. In other respects, the same number or even half the number of sloops-of-war would have probably inflicted greater injury at less cost. The "Argus" showed how this result could have been attained. The privateer's first object was to save prizes; and in the effort to send captured vessels into port the privateer lost a large proportion by recapture. Down to the moment when Admiral Warren established his blockade of the American coast from New York southward, most of the prizes got to port. After that time the New England ports alone offered reasonable chance of safety, and privateering received a check. During the war about twenty-five hundred vessels all told were captured from the British. Many were destroyed; many released as cartels; and of the remainder not less than seven hundred and fifty, probably one half the number sent to port, were recaptured by the British navy. Most of these were the prizes of privateers, and would have been destroyed had they been taken by government vessels. They were usually the most valuable prizes, so that the injury that might have been inflicted on British commerce was diminished nearly one half by the system which encouraged private war as a money-making speculation.

Another objection was equally serious. Like all gambling ventures, privateering was not profitable. In the list of five hundred privateers furnished by the Navy Department, three hundred were recorded as having never made a prize. Of the remainder, few made their expenses. One of the most successful cruises of the war was that of Joshua Barney on the Baltimore schooner "Rossie" at the outbreak of hostilities, when every prize reached port. Barney sent in prizes supposed to be worth fifteen hundred thousand dollars; but after paying charges and duties and selling the goods, he found that the profits were not sufficient to counterbalance the discomforts, and he refused to repeat the experiment. His experience was common. As early as November, 1812, the owners of twenty-four New York privateers sent to Congress a memorial declaring that the profits of private naval war were by no means equal to the hazards, and that the spirit of privateering stood in danger of extinction unless the government would consent in some manner to grant a bounty for the capture or destruction of the enemy's property.

If private enterprise was to fail at the critical moment, and if the government must supply the deficiency, the government would have done better to undertake the whole task. In effect, the government in the end did so. The merchants asked chiefly for a reduction of duties on prize-goods. Gallatin pointed out the serious objections to such legislation, and the little probability that the measure would increase the profits of privateering or the number of privateers. The actual privateers, he said, were more than enough for the food offered by the enemy's trade, and privateering, like every other form of gambling, would always continue to attract more adventurers than it could support.

Congress for the time followed Gallatin's advice, and did nothing; but in the summer session of 1813, after Gallatin's departure for Europe, the privateer owners renewed their appeal, and the acting Secretary of the Treasury, Jones, wrote to the chairman of the Naval Committee July 21, 1813—

The fact is that . . . privateering is nearly at an end; and from the best observation I have been enabled to make, it is more from the deficiency of remuneration in the net proceeds of their prizes than from the vigilance and success of the enemy in recapturing.

In deference to Jones's opinion, Congress passed an Act, approved Aug. 2, 1813, reducing one third the duties on prize-goods. Another Act, approved August 3, granted a bounty of twenty-five dollars for every prisoner captured and delivered to a United States agent by a private armed vessel. A third Act, approved August 2, authorized the Secretary of the Navy to place on the pension list any privateersman who should be wounded or disabled in the line of his duty.

These complaints and palliations tended to show that the privateer cost the public more than the equivalent government vessel would have cost. If instead of five hundred privateers of all sizes and efficiency, the government had kept twenty sloops-of-war constantly at sea destroying the enemy's commerce, the result would have been about the same as far as concerned injury to the enemy, while in another respect the government would have escaped one of its chief difficulties. Nothing injured the navy so much as privateering. Seamen commonly preferred the harder but more profitable and shorter cruise in a privateer, where fighting was not expected or wished, to the strict discipline and murderous battles of government ships, where wages were low and prize-money scarce. Of all towns in the United States, Marblehead was probably the most devoted to the sea; but of nine hundred men from Marblehead who took part in the war, fifty-seven served as soldiers, one hundred and twenty entered the navy, while seven hundred and twenty-six went as privateersmen. Only after much delay and difficulty could the frigates obtain crews. The "Constitution" was nearly lost by this cause at the beginning of the war; and the loss of the "Chesapeake" was supposed to be chiefly due to the determination of the old crew to quit the government service for that of the privateers.

Such drawbacks raised reasonable doubts as to the balance of advantages and disadvantages offered by the privateer system. Perhaps more careful inquiry might show that, valuable as the privateers were, the government would have done better to retain all military and naval functions in its own hands, and to cover the seas with small cruisers capable of pursuing a system of thorough destruction against the shipping and colonial interests of England.

MANY humiliations were yet in store for the Americans both on sea and on land. At the River Raisin the combined British and Indian force overwhelmed the Kentucky riflemen and killed four hundred of them. The galling series of reverses on land were partly redeemed by Perry's heroic though costly victory on Lake Erie and by General Harrison's success at the Battle of the Thames, which broke the power of the Indian confederacy and secured the Northwest. The other northern campaigns bogged down ineffectually in spite of the bravery of the Americans at Chippewa and Lundy's Lane. Fort Erie fell and the initiative passed to the British. The most humiliating episode of the war occurred in August, 1814, when a British expedition arrived in Chesapeake Bay to attack Washington itself. Bladensburg was the key to the city, and the account of that battle gives a vivid picture of the inefficiency and confusion which marked so much of the conduct of the war.

Battle of Bladensburg

ARMSTRONG'S* management of the Northern campaign caused severe criticism; but his neglect of the city of Washington exhausted the public patience. For two years Washington stood unprotected; not a battery or a breastwork was to be found on the river bank except the old and untenable Fort Washington, or Warburton. A thousand determined men might reach the town in thirty-six hours, and destroy it before any general alarm could be given. Yet no city was more easily protected than Washington, at that day, from attack on its eastern side; any good engineer could have thrown up works in a week that would have made approach by a small force impossible. Armstrong neglected to fortify. After experience had proved his error, he still argued in writing to a committee of Congress that fortifications would have exhausted the Treasury; "that bayonets are known to form the most efficient barriers; and that

Vol. VIII, Chap. V.
* John Armstrong, Secretary of War. E.S.

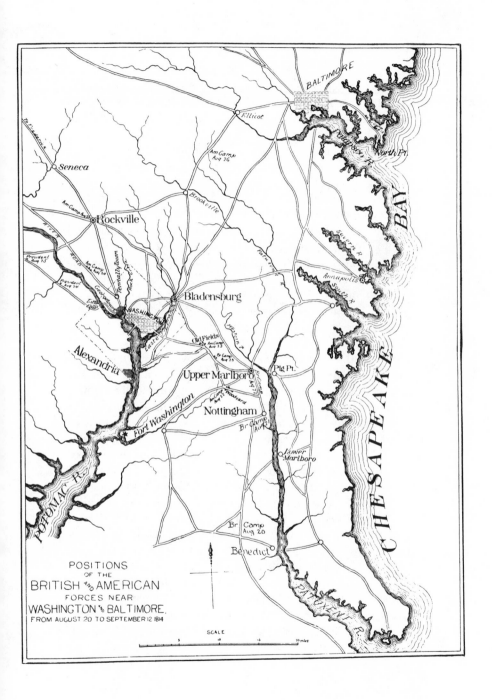

POSITIONS
OF THE
BRITISH AND AMERICAN
FORCES NEAR
WASHINGTON TO BALTIMORE,
FROM AUGUST 20 TO SEPTEMBER 12 1814

SCALE

there was no reason in this case to doubt beforehand the willingness of the country to defend itself"—as though he believed that militia were most efficient when most exposed! He did not even provide the bayonets.

In truth, Armstrong looking at the matter as a military critic decided that the British having no strategic object in capturing Washington, would not make the attempt. Being an indolent man, negligent of detail, he never took unnecessary trouble; and having no proper staff at Washington, he was without military advisers whose opinion he respected. The President and Monroe fretted at his indifference, the people of the District were impatient under it, and every one except Armstrong was in constant terror of attack; but according to their account the secretary only replied: "No, no! Baltimore is the place, sir; that is of so much more consequence." Probably he was right, and the British would have gone first to Baltimore had his negligence not invited them to Washington.

In May the President began to press Armstrong for precautionary measures. In June letters arrived from Gallatin and Bayard in London which caused the President to call a Cabinet meeting. June 23 and 24 the Cabinet met and considered the diplomatic situation. The President proposed then for the first time to abandon impressment as a *sine qua non* of negotiation, and to approve a treaty that should be silent on the subject. Armstrong and Jones alone supported the idea at that time, but three days afterward, June 27, Monroe and Campbell acceded to it. The Cabinet then took the defences of Washington in hand, and July 1 decided to organize a corps of defence from the militia of the District and the neighboring States. July 2, the first step toward efficient defence was taken by creating a new military district on the Potomac, with a military head of its own. Armstrong wished to transfer Brigadier-General Moses Porter from Norfolk, to command the new Potomac District; but the President selected Brigadier-General Winder, because his relationship to the Federalist governor of Maryland was likely to make co-operation more effective.

Political appointments were not necessarily bad; but in appointing Winder to please the governor of Maryland Madison assumed the responsibility, in Armstrong's eyes, for the defence of Washington. The Secretary of War seemed to think that Madison and Monroe were acting together to take the defence of Washington out of his hands, and to put it in hands in which they felt confidence. Armstrong placed Winder instantly in command, and promptly issued the orders arranged in Cabinet; but he left further measures to Winder, Monroe, and Madison. His conduct irritated the President; but no one charged that the secretary refused to carry out the orders, or to satisfy the requisitions of the President or of General Winder. He was merely passive.

Winder received his appointment July 5, and went to Washington for instructions. He passed the next month riding between Washington, Baltimore, and points on the lower Potomac and Patuxent, obtaining with great fatigue a personal knowledge of the country. August 1 he established his permanent headquarters at Washington, and the entire result of his labors till that time was the presence of one company of Maryland militia at Bladensburg. No line of defence was selected, no obstructions to the roads were prepared, and not so much as a ditch or a breastwork was marked out or suggested between Annapolis and Washington. Another fortnight passed, and still Winder was not further advanced. He had no more men, arms, fortifications, and no more ideas, on the 18th of August than on the 5th of July. "The call for three thousand militia under the requisition of July 4 had produced only two hundred and fifty men at the moment the enemy landed at Benedict." Winder had then been six weeks in command of the Washington defences.

Meanwhile a British expedition under command of Major-General Robert Ross, a distinguished officer of the Peninsula army, sailed from the Gironde, June 27, to Bermuda. Ross was instructed "to effect a diversion on the coasts of the United States of America in favor of the army employed in the de-

fence of Upper and Lower Canada." The point of attack was
to be decided by Vice-Admiral Cochrane, subject to the general's approval; but the force was not intended for "any extended operation at a distance from the coast," nor was Ross
to hold permanent possession of any captured district.

When the object of the descent which you may make on the
coast is to take possession of any naval or military stores, you
will not delay the destruction of them in preference to the taking
them away, if there is reasonable ground of apprehension that
the enemy is advancing with superior force to effect their recovery. If in any descent you shall be enabled to take such a position as to threaten the inhabitants with the destruction of their
property, you are hereby authorized to levy upon them contributions in return for your forbearance; but you will not by this
understand that the magazines belonging to the government,
or their harbors, or their shipping, are to be included in such an
arrangement. These, together with their contents, are in all
cases to be taken away or destroyed.

Negroes were not to be encouraged to rise upon their masters,
and no slaves were to be taken away as slaves; but any negro
who should expose himself to vengeance by joining the expedition or lending it assistance, might be enlisted in the black corps,
or carried away by the fleet.

Nothing in these orders warranted the destruction of private
or public property, except such as might be capable of military
uses. Ross was not authorized, and did not intend, to enter on
a mere marauding expedition; but Cochrane was independent
of Ross, and at about the time when Ross reached Bermuda
Cochrane received a letter from Sir George Prevost which gave
an unexpected character to the Chesapeake expedition. A small
body of American troops had crossed Lake Erie to Long Point,
May 15, and destroyed the flour-mills, distilleries, and some
private houses there. The raid was not authorized by the United
States government, and the officer commanding it was afterward court-martialed and censured; but Sir George Prevost,
without waiting for explanations, wrote to Vice-Admiral Cochrane, June 2, suggesting that he should "assist in inflicting that

measure of retaliation which shall deter the enemy from a repetition of similar outrages."

When Cochrane received this letter, he issued at Bermuda, July 18, orders to the ships under his command, from the St. Croix River to the St. Mary's, directing general retaliation. The orders were interesting as an illustration of the temper the war had taken.

You are hereby required and directed [wrote the Vice-Admiral to the British blockading squadrons] to destroy and lay waste such towns and districts upon the coast as you may find assailable. You will hold strictly in view the conduct of the American army toward his Majesty's unoffending Canadian subjects, and you will spare merely the lives of the unarmed inhabitants of the United States. For only by carrying this retributory justice into the country of our enemy can we hope to make him sensible of the impropriety as well as of the inhumanity of the system he has adopted. You will take every opportunity of explaining to the people how much I lament the necessity of following the rigorous example of the commander of the American forces. And as these commanders must obviously have acted under instructions from the Executive government of the United States, whose intimate and unnatural connection with the late government of France has led them to adopt the same system of plunder and devastation, it is therefore to their own government the unfortunate sufferers must look for indemnification for their loss of property.

This ill-advised order was to remain in force until Sir George Prevost should send information "that the United States government have come under an obligation to make full remuneration to the injured and unoffending inhabitants of the Canadas for all the outrages their troops have committed." Cochrane further wrote to Prevost that "as soon as these orders have been acted upon," a copy would be sent to Washington for the information of the Executive government.

Cochrane's retaliatory order was dated July 18, and Ross's transports arrived at Bermuda July 24. As soon as the troops were collected and stores put on board, Cochrane and Ross sailed, August 3, for Chesapeake Bay. They arrived a few days in advance of the transports, and passing up the bay to the mouth of the Potomac, landed, August 15, with Rear Admiral Cockburn, to decide on a plan for using to best effect the forces under their command.

Three objects were within reach. The first and immediate aim was a flotilla of gunboats, commanded by Captain Joshua Barney, which had taken refuge in the Patuxent River, and was there blockaded. The next natural object of desire was Baltimore, on account of its shipping and prize-money. The third was Washington and Alexandria, on account of the navy-yard and the vessels in the Potomac. Baltimore was the natural point of attack after destroying Barney's flotilla; but Cockburn, with a sailor's recklessness, urged a dash at Washington. Ross hesitated, and postponed a decision till Barney's flotilla should be disposed of.

Two days afterward, August 17, the troops arrived, and the squadron, commanded by Vice-Admiral Cochrane, moved twenty miles up the bay to the mouth of the Patuxent—a point about fifty miles distant from Annapolis on the north, and from Washington on the northwest. Having arrived there August 18, Cochrane wrote, or afterward ante-dated, an official letter to Secretary Monroe—

Having been called on by the Governor-General of the Canadas to aid him in carrying into effect measures of retaliation against the inhabitants of the United States for the wanton destruction committed by their army in Upper Canada, it has become imperiously my duty, conformably with the nature of the Governor-General's application, to issue to the naval force under my command an order to destroy and lay waste such towns and districts upon the coast as may be found assailable.

The notice was the more remarkable because Cochrane's order was issued only to the naval force. The army paid no attention to it. Ross's troops were landed at Benedict the next day, August 19; but neither there nor elsewhere did they destroy or lay waste towns or districts. They rather showed unusual respect for private property.

At Benedict, August 19, the British forces were organized in

three brigades, numbering, according to different British accounts, four thousand five hundred, or four thousand rank-and-
file. Cockburn with the boats of the fleet the next day, August
20, started up the river in search of Barney's flotilla; while
the land force began its march at four o'clock in the afternoon
abreast of the boats, and camped four miles above Benedict
without seeing an enemy, or suffering from a worse annoyance
than one of the evening thunder-storms common in hot weather.

The next day at dawn the British army started again, and
marched that day, Sunday, August 21, twelve miles to the
village of Nottingham, where it camped. The weather was hot,
and the march resembled a midsummer picnic. Through a
thickly wooded region, where a hundred militia-men with axes
and spades could have delayed their progress for days, the
British army moved in a solitude apparently untenanted by
human beings, till they reached Nottingham on the Patuxent
—a deserted town, rich in growing crops and full barns.

At Nottingham the army passed a quiet night, and the next
morning, Monday, August 22, lingered till eight o'clock, when
it again advanced. Among the officers in the Eighty-fifth regiment was a lieutenant named Gleig, who wrote afterward a
charming narrative of the campaign under the title, "A Subaltern in America." He described the road as remarkably good,
running for the most part through the heart of thick forests,
which sheltered it from the rays of the sun. During the march
the army was startled by the distant sound of several heavy
explosions. Barney had blown up his gunboats to prevent their
capture. The British naval force had thus performed its part
in the enterprise, and the army was next to take the lead. Ross
halted at Marlboro after a march of only seven miles, and there
too he camped, undisturbed by sight or sound of an armed
enemy, although the city of Washington was but sixteen miles
on his left, and Baltimore thirty miles in his front. Ross had
then marched twenty or twenty-one miles into Maryland without seeing an enemy, although an American army had been
close on his left flank, watching him all day.

At Marlboro Ross was obliged to decide what he should next

do. He was slow in forming a conclusion. Instead of marching
at daybreak of August 23, and moving rapidly on Baltimore
or Washington, the army passed nearly the whole day at Marlboro in idleness, as though it were willing to let the Americans
do their utmost for defence. "Having advanced within sixteen
miles of Washington," Ross officially reported, "and ascertained the force of the enemy to be such as might authorize
an attempt to carry his capital, I determined to make it, and
accordingly put the troops in movement on the evening of the
23d." More exactly, the troops moved at two o'clock in the
afternoon, and marched about six miles on the road to Washington, when they struck American outposts at about five o'clock,
and saw a force posted on high ground about a mile in their
front. As the British formed to attack, the American force
disappeared, and the British army camped about nine miles
from Washington by way of the navy-yard bridge over the
Eastern Branch.

Thus for five days, from August 18 to August 23, a British
army, which though small was larger than any single body of
American regulars then in the field, marched in a leisurely
manner through a long-settled country, and met no show of
resistance before coming within sight of the Capitol. Such an
adventure resembled the stories of Cortez and De Soto; and
the conduct of the United States government offered no contradiction to the resemblance.

News of the great fleet that appeared in the Patuxent August
17 reached Washington on the morning of Thursday, August
18, and set the town in commotion. In haste the President sent
fresh militia requisitions to the neighboring States, and ordered
out the militia and all the regular troops in Washington and
its neighborhood. Monroe started again as a scout, arriving in
the neighborhood of Benedict at ten o'clock on the morning of
August 20, and remaining there all day and night without
learning more than he knew before starting. Winder was excessively busy, but did, according to his own account, nothing.
"The innumerably multiplied orders, letters, consultations, and

demands which crowded upon me at the moment of such an alarm can more easily be conceived than described, and occupied me nearly day and night, from Thursday the 18th of August till Sunday the 21st, and had nearly broken down myself and assistants in preparing, dispensing, and attending to them." Armstrong, at last alive to the situation, made excellent suggestions, but could furnish neither troops, means, nor military intelligence to carry them out; and the President could only call for help. The single step taken for defence was taken by the citizens, who held a meeting Saturday evening, and offered at their own expense to erect works at Bladensburg. Winder accepted their offer. Armstrong detailed Colonel Wadsworth, the only engineer officer near the Department, to lay out the lines, and the citizens did such work as was possible in the time that remained.

After three days of confusion, a force was at last evolved. Probably by Winder's order, although no such order was preserved, a corps of observation was marched across the navy-yard bridge toward the Patuxent, or drawn from Bladensburg, to a place called the Woodyard, twelve miles beyond the Eastern Branch. The force was not to be despised. Three hundred infantry regulars of different regiments, with one hundred and twenty light dragoons, formed the nucleus; two hundred and fifty Maryland militia, and about twelve hundred District volunteers or militia, with twelve six-pound field-pieces, composed a body of near two thousand men, from whom General Brown or Andrew Jackson would have got good service. Winder came out and took command Sunday evening, and Monroe, much exhausted, joined them that night.

There the men stood Monday, August 22, while the British army marched by them, within sight of their outposts, from Nottingham to Marlboro. Winder rode forward with his cavalry and watched all day the enemy's leisurely movements close in his front, but the idea of attack did not appear to enter his mind. "A doubt at that time," he said, "was not entertained by anybody of the intention of the enemy to proceed direct to

Washington." At nine o'clock that evening Monroe sent a note to the President, saying that the enemy was in full march for Washington; that Winder proposed to retire till he could collect his troops; that preparations should be made to destroy the bridges, and that the papers in the government offices should be removed. At the same time Monroe notified Serurier, the only foreign minister then in Washington, that the single hope of saving the capital depended on the very doubtful result of an engagement, which would probably take place the next day or the day after, at Bladensburg.

At Bladensburg, of necessity, the engagement must take place, unless Winder made an attack or waited for attack on the road. One of two courses was to be taken—Washington must be either defended or evacuated. Perhaps Winder would have done better to evacuate it, and let the British take the undefended village; but no suggestion of the sort was made, nor did Winder retreat to Bladensburg as was necessary if he meant to unite his troops and make preparations for a battle. Instead of retreating to Bladensburg as soon as he was satisfied —at noon of Monday, August 22—that the British were going there, he ordered his troops to fall back, and took position at the Old Fields, about five miles in the rear of the Woodyard, and about seven miles by road from the navy-yard. Another road led from the Old Fields to Bladensburg about eight miles away. The American force might have been united at Bladensburg Monday evening, but Winder camped at the Old Fields and passed the night.

That evening the President and the members of the Cabinet rode out to the camp, and the next morning the President reviewed the army, which had been reinforced by Commodore Barney with four hundred sailors, the crews of the burned gunboats. Winder then had twenty-five hundred men, of whom near a thousand were regulars, or sailors even better fighting troops than ordinary regulars. Such a force vigorously led was sufficient to give Ross's army a sharp check, and at that moment Ross was still hesitating whether to attack Washington. The loss of a few hundred men might have turned the scale at any moment during Tuesday, August 23; but Winder neither fought nor retreated, but once more passed the day on scout. At noon he rode with a troop of cavalry toward Marlboro. Satisfied that the enemy was not in motion and would not move that day, he started at one o'clock for Bladensburg, leaving his army to itself. He wished to bring up a brigade of militia from Bladensburg.

Winder had ridden about five miles, when the British at two o'clock suddenly broke up their camp and marched directly on the Old Fields. The American army hastily formed in line, and sent off its baggage to Washington. Winder was summoned back in haste, and arrived on the field at five o'clock as the British appeared. He ordered a retreat. Every military reason required a retreat to Bladensburg. Winder directed a retreat on Washington by the navy-yard bridge.

The reasons which actuated him to prefer the navy-yard to Bladensburg, as explained by him, consisted in anxiety for the safety of that "direct and important pass," which could not without hazard be left unguarded. In order to guard a bridge a quarter of a mile long over an impassable river covered by the guns of war-vessels and the navy-yard, he left unguarded the open high-road which led through Bladensburg directly to the Capitol and the White House. After a very rapid retreat that "literally became a run of eight miles," Winder encamped in Washington near the bridge-head at the navy-yard at eight o'clock that night, and then rode three miles to the White House to report to the President. On returning to camp, he passed the night until three or four o'clock in the morning making in person arrangements to destroy the bridge "when necessary," assuring his officers that he expected the enemy to attempt a passage there that night. Toward dawn he lay down, exhausted by performing a subaltern's duty all day, and snatched an hour or two of sleep.

The British in their camp that evening were about eight miles from Bladensburg battle-field. Winder was about five miles distant from the same point. By a quick march at dawn he might still have arrived there, with six hours to spare for arranging his defence. He preferred to wait till he should know with certainty that the British were on their way there. On the morning of Wednesday, August 24, he wrote to Armstrong—

I have found it necessary to establish my headquarters here, the most advanced position convenient to the troops, and nearest information. I shall remain stationary as much as possible, that I may be the more readily found, to issue orders, and collect together the various detachments of militia, and give them as rapid a consolidation and organization as possible. . . . The news up the river is very threatening. Barney's or some other force should occupy the batteries at Greenleaf's Point and the navy-yard. I should be glad of the assistance of counsel from yourself and the Government. If more convenient, I should make an exertion to go to you the first opportunity.

This singular note was carried first to the President, who, having opened and read it, immediately rode to headquarters. Monroe, Jones, and Rush followed. Armstrong and Campbell arrived last. Before Armstrong appeared, a scout arrived at ten o'clock with information that the British army had broken up its camp at daylight, and was probably more than half way to Bladensburg.

Winder's persistence in remaining at the navy-yard was explained as due to the idea that the enemy might move toward the Potomac, seize Fort Washington or Warburton, secure the passage of his ships, and approach the city by the river. The general never explained how his presence at the navy-yard was to prevent such a movement if it was made.

The whole eastern side of Washington was covered by a broad estuary called the Eastern Branch of the Potomac, bridged only at two points, and impassable, even by pontoons, without ample warning. From the Potomac River to Bladensburg, a distance of about seven miles, the city was effectually protected. Bladensburg made the point of a right angle. There the Baltimore road entered the city as by a pass; for beyond, to the west, no general would venture to enter, leaving an enemy at

Bladensburg in his rear. Roads were wanting, and the country was difficult. Through Bladensburg the attacking army must come; to Bladensburg Winder must go, unless he meant to retreat to Georgetown, or to re-cross the Eastern Branch in the enemy's rear. Monroe notified Serurier Monday evening that the battle would be fought at Bladensburg. Secretary Jones wrote to Commodore Rodgers, Tuesday morning, that the British would probably "advance to-day toward Bladensburg." Every one looked instinctively to that spot, yet Winder to the last instant persisted in watching the navy-yard bridge, using the hours of Wednesday morning to post Barney's sailors with twenty-four-pound guns to cover an approach where no enemy could cross.

No sooner did Winder receive intelligence at ten o'clock Wednesday morning that the British were in march to Bladensburg, than in the utmost haste he started for the same point, preceded by Monroe and followed by the President and the rest of the Cabinet and the troops. Barney's sailors and their guns would have been left behind to guard the navy-yard bridge had Secretary Jones not yielded to Barney's vigorous though disrespectful remonstrances, and allowed him to follow.

In a long line the various corps, with their military and civil commanders, streamed toward Bladensburg, racing with the British, ten miles away, to arrive first on the field of battle. Monroe was earliest on the ground. Between eleven and twelve o'clock he reached the spot where hills slope gently toward the Eastern Branch a mile or more in broad incline, the little straggling town of Bladensburg opposite, beyond a shallow stream, and hills and woods in the distance. Several militia corps were already camped on the ground, which had been from the first designated as the point of concentration. A Baltimore brigade, more than two thousand strong, had arrived there thirty-six hours before. Some Maryland regiments arrived at the same time with Monroe. About three thousand men were then on the field, and their officers were endeavoring to form them in line of battle. General Stansbury of the Baltimore brigade made such an arrangement as he thought best. Monroe, who had no military rank, altered it without Stansbury's knowledge. General Winder arrived at noon, and rode about the field. At the same time the British light brigade made its appearance, and wound down the opposite road, a mile away, a long column of redcoats, six abreast, moving with the quick regularity of old soldiers, and striking directly at the American centre. They reached the village on one side of the stream as Winder's troops poured down the hill on the other; and the President with two or three of his Cabinet officers, considerably in advance of all their own troops, nearly rode across the bridge into the British line, when a volunteer warned them of their danger.

Much the larger portion of the American force arrived on the ground when the enemy was in sight, and were hastily drawn up in line wherever they could be placed. They had no cover. Colonel Wadsworth's intrenchments were not used, except in the case of one field-work which enfiladed the bridge at close range, where field-pieces were placed. Although some seven thousand men were present, nothing deserving the name of an army existed. "A few companies only," said the Subaltern, "perhaps two or at the most three battalions, wearing the blue jacket which the Americans have borrowed from the French, presented some appearance of regular troops. The rest seemed country-people, who would have been much more appropriately employed in attending to their agricultural occupations than in standing with muskets in their hands on the brow of a bare, green hill." Heterogeneous as the force was, it would have been sufficient had it enjoyed the advantage of a commander.

The British light brigade, some twelve or fifteen hundred men, under Colonel Thornton of the Eighty-fifth regiment, without waiting for the rear division, dashed across the bridge, and were met by a discharge of artillery and musketry directly in their face. Checked for an instant, they pressed on, crossed the bridge or waded the stream, and spread to the right and left, while their rockets flew into the American lines. Almost instantly a portion of the American line gave way; but the rest stood firm, and drove the British skirmishers back under a heavy fire to the cover of the bank with its trees and shrubs. Not until a fresh British regiment, moving well to the right, forded the stream and threatened to turn the American left, did the rout begin. Even then several strong corps stood steady, and in good order retired by the road that led to the Capitol; but the mass, struck by panic, streamed westward toward Georgetown and Rockville.

Meanwhile Barney's sailors, though on the run, could not reach the field in time for the attack, and halted on the hillside, about a mile from Bladensburg, at a spot just outside the District line. The rout had then begun, but Barney put his five pieces in position and waited for the enemy. The American infantry and cavalry that had not fled westward moved confusedly past the field where the sailors stood at their guns. Winder sent Barney no orders, and Barney, who was not acting under Winder, but was commander-in-chief of his own forces under authority of the Navy Department, had no idea of running away. Four hundred men against four thousand were odds too great even for sailors, but a battle was not wholly disgraceful that produced such a commander and such men. Barney's account of the combat was as excellent as his courage—

At length the enemy made his appearance on the main road in force and in front of my battery, and on seeing us made a halt. I reserved our fire. In a few minutes the enemy again advanced, when I ordered an eighteen-pounder to be fired, which completely cleared the road; shortly after, a second and a third attempt was made by the enemy to come forward, but all were destroyed. They then crossed over into an open field, and attempted to flank our right. He was met there by three twelve-pounders, the marines under Captain Miller, and my men acting as infantry, and again was totally cut up. By this time not a vestige of the American army remained, except a body of five or six hundred posted on a height on my right, from which I expected much support from their fine situation.

Such a battle could not long continue. The British turned Barney's right; the corps on the height broke and fled, and the British, getting into the rear, fired down upon the sailors. The

British themselves were most outspoken in praise of Barney's men. "Not only did they serve their guns with a quickness and precision that astonished their assailants," said the Subaltern, "but they stood till some of them were actually bayoneted with fuses in their hands; nor was it till their leader was wounded and taken, and they saw themselves deserted on all sides by the soldiers, that they left the field." Barney held his position nearly half an hour, and then, being severely wounded, ordered his officers to leave him where he lay. There he was taken by the British advance, and carried to their hospital at Bladensburg. The British officers, admiring his gallantry, treated him, he said, "with the most marked attention, respect, and politeness as if I was a brother"—as though to show their opinion that Barney instead of Winder should have led the American army.

After the sailors retired, at about four o'clock, the British stopped two hours to rest. Their victory, easy as it seemed, was not cheaply bought. General Ross officially reported sixty-four killed and one hundred and eighty-five wounded. A loss of two hundred and fifty men among fifteen hundred said to be engaged was not small; but Gleig, an officer of the light brigade, himself wounded, made twice, at long intervals, an assertion which he must have intended as a contradiction of the official report. "The loss on the part of the English was severe," he said, "since out of two thirds of the army which were engaged upward of five hundred men were killed and wounded." According to this assertion, Ross lost five hundred men among three thousand engaged, or one in six. Had Winder inflicted that loss while the British were still on the Patuxent, Ross would have thought long before risking more, especially as Colonel Thornton was among the severely injured. The Americans reported only twenty-six killed and fifty-one wounded.

At six o'clock, after a rest of two hours, the British troops resumed their march; but night fell before they reached the first houses of the town. As Ross and Cockburn, with a few officers, advanced before the troops, some men, supposed to have been Barney's sailors, fired on the party from the house formerly occupied by Gallatin, at the northeast corner of Capitol Square. Ross's horse was killed, and the general ordered the house to be burned, which was done. The army did not enter the town, but camped at eight o'clock a quarter of a mile east of the Capitol. Troops were then detailed to burn the Capitol, and as the great building burst into flames, Ross and Cockburn, with about two hundred men, marched silently in the darkness to the White House, and set fire to it. At the same time Commodore Tingey, by order of Secretary Jones, set fire to the navy-yard and the vessels in the Eastern Branch. Before midnight the flames of three great conflagrations made the whole country light, and from the distant hills of Maryland and Virginia the flying President and Cabinet caught glimpses of the ruin their incompetence had caused.

Serurier lived then in the house built by John Tayloe in 1800, called the Octagon, a few hundred yards from the War and Navy Departments and the White House. He was almost the only civil official left in Washington, and hastened to report the event to Talleyrand—

I never saw a scene at once more terrible and more magnificent. Your Highness, knowing the picturesque nature and the grandeur of the surroundings, can form an idea of it. A profound darkness reigned in the part of the city that I occupy, and we were left to conjectures and to the lying reports of negroes as to what was passing in the quarter illuminated by these frightful flames. At eleven o'clock a colonel, preceded by torches, was seen to take the direction of the White House, which is situated quite near mine; the negroes reported that it was to be burned, as well as all those pertaining to government offices. I thought best, on the moment, to send one of my people to the general with a letter, in which I begged him to send a guard to the house of the Ambassador of France to protect it. . . . My messenger found General Ross in the White House, where he was collecting in the drawing-room all the furniture to be found, and was preparing to set fire to it. The general made answer that the King's Hotel should be respected as much as though his Majesty were there in person; that he would give orders to that effect; and that if he was still in Washington the next day, he would have the pleasure to call on me.

Ross and Cockburn alone among military officers, during more than twenty years of war, considered their duty to involve personal incendiarism. At the time and subsequently various motives were attributed to them—such as the duty of retaliation—none of which was alleged by either of them as their warranty. They burned the Capitol, the White House, and the Department buildings because they thought it proper, as they would have burned a negro kraal or a den of pirates. Apparently they assumed as a matter of course that the American government stood beyond the pale of civilization; and in truth a government which showed so little capacity to defend its capital, could hardly wonder at whatever treatment it received.

A violent thunder-storm checked the flames; but the next morning, Thursday, August 25, fresh detachments of troops were sent to complete the destruction of public property. Without orders from his Government, Ross converted his campaign, which till then had been creditable to himself and flattering to British pride, into a marauding raid of which no sensible Englishman spoke without mortification. Cockburn amused himself by revenging his personal grievances on the press which had abused him. Mounted on a brood mare, white, uncurried, with a black foal trotting by her side, the Admiral attacked the office of the "National Intelligencer," and superintended the destruction of the types. "Be sure that all the C's are destroyed," he ordered, "so that the rascals cannot any longer abuse my name." Ross was anxious to complete the destruction of the public buildings with the least possible delay, that the army might retire without loss of time; and the work was pressed with extreme haste. A few private buildings were burned, but as a rule private property was respected, and no troops except small detachments were allowed to leave the camp.

Soon after noon, while the work was still incomplete, a tornado burst on the city and put an end to the effort. An accidental explosion at the navy-yard helped to check destruction. Ross could do no more, and was in haste to get away. No sooner had the hurricane, which lasted nearly two hours and seemed especially violent at the camp, passed over, than Ross began preparations to retire. With precautions wholly unnecessary, leaving its camp-fires burning, the British column in extreme silence, after nine o'clock at night, began its march. Passing Bladensburg, where the dead were still unburied, Ross left his wounded in the hospital to American care, and marched all night till seven o'clock Friday morning, when the troops, exhausted with fatigue, were allowed a rest. At noon they were again in motion, and at night-fall, after marching twenty-five miles within twenty-four hours, they arrived at Marlboro. Had the advance from Benedict been equally rapid, Ross would have entered Washington without a skirmish.

By *late September, 1814, the war was approaching a stalemate. After an ineffectual bombardment of the Baltimore forts the British commander decided against storming the heights and prudently withdrew his fleet. Almost at the same time Sir George Prevost employed similar prudence at Plattsburg, the bloody repulse of General Drummond at Fort Erie having shown the high price of such ventures. Although military disaster was staved off, time was running out for Madison's expedients. The system of voluntary enlistments yielded fewer and fewer effectives, and except in Massachusetts, where separatist sentiment ran strong, the militia was an actual liability to Washington. Thanks also to the British blockade the drain upon specie led to suspension of payments, thus throwing the currency into the chaos of state bank issues. With Congress unwilling to finance an increase of the regular army, the war had to be conducted by hand-to-mouth measures and by continued reliance on the unpredictable militia. Fears were widespread that no successful resistance could be made at New Orleans. At this juncture word came of the terms offered by England to the American peace commissioners at Ghent. The New England Federalists, eager to end the indecisive war on almost any terms and determined to alter the Union in whatever way needed to give New England freedom of action and remission of its portion of the national taxes, marched off to the Hartford Convention and possible disunion. The movement evaporated, however, at the news of the signing of the peace treaty. Jackson's brilliant victory at New Orleans over Pakenham, though it came two weeks after the peace, showed the Massachusetts partisans of England that theirs was a lost cause.*

While the Federalists debated at Hartford, the five American peace commissioners—John Quincy Adams, Albert Gallatin, J. A. Bayard, Jonathan Russell, and Henry Clay—who had been at Ghent since June, 1814, reached an impasse with their British counterparts, the instructions of neither side being acceptable to the other.

In the following pages Adams recounts how the deadlock was broken.

The Treaty of Ghent

THE British note of August 19 and the American rejoinder of August 24, brought about a situation where Lord Castlereagh's influence could make itself felt. Castlereagh had signed the British instructions of July 28 and August 14 and himself brought the latter to Ghent, where he passed August 19, before going to Paris on his way to the Congress at Vienna. He was at Ghent when Goulburn and his colleagues held their conference and wrote their note of August 19; and he could not be supposed ignorant of their language or acts. Yet when he received at Paris letters from Goulburn, dated August 24 and 26, he expressed annoyance that the American commissioners should have been allowed to place England in the attitude of continuing the war for purposes of conquest, and still more that the British commissioners should be willing to accept that issue and break off negotiations upon it. In a letter to Lord Bathurst, who took charge of the negotiation in his absence, Castlereagh suggested ideas altogether different from those till then advanced in England.

The substance of the question is [said Castlereagh], Are we prepared to continue the war for territorial arrangements? And if not, is this the best time to make our peace, saving all our rights, and claiming the fisheries, which they do not appear to question? In which case the territorial questions might be reserved for ulterior discussion. Or is it desirable to take the chance of the campaign, and then to be governed by circumstances? . . . If we thought an immediate peace desirable, as they are ready to waive all the abstract questions, perhaps they might be prepared to sign a provisional article of Indian peace as distinct from limits, and relinquish their pretensions to the islands in Passamaquoddy Bay, and possibly to admit minor adjustments of frontier, including a right of communication from Quebec to Halifax across their territory. But while I state this, I feel the difficulty of so much letting down the question under present circumstances.

Vol. IX, Chap. II.

At the same time Castlereagh wrote to Goulburn, directing him to wait at Ghent for new instructions from London. Lord Liverpool shared his disapproval of the manner in which the British commissioners had managed the case, and replied to Castlereagh, September 2, that the Cabinet had already acted in the sense he wished—

Our commissioners had certainly taken a very erroneous view of our policy. If the negotiations had been allowed to break off upon the two notes already presented, or upon such an answer as they were disposed to return, I am satisfied that the war would have become quite popular in America.

The idea that the war might become popular in America was founded chiefly on the impossibility of an Englishman's conceiving the contrary; but in truth the Ministry most feared that the war might become unpopular in England.

It is very material to throw the rupture of the negotiation, if it is to take place, upon the Americans [wrote Liverpool, the same day, to the Duke of Wellington]; and not to allow them to say that we have brought forward points as ultimata which were only brought forward for discussion, and at the desire of the American commissioners themselves. The American note is a most impudent one, and, as to all its reasoning, capable of an irresistible answer.

New instructions were accordingly approved in Cabinet. Drawn by Bathurst, and dated September 1, they contained what Liverpool considered an "irresistible answer" to the American note of August 24; but their force of logic was weakened by the admission that the previous British demands, though certainly stated as a *sine qua non*, were in reality not to be regarded as such. In private this retreat was covered by the pretext that it was intended only to keep the negotiation alive until better terms could be exacted.

We cannot expect that the negotiation will proceed at present [continued Liverpool's letter to Castlereagh]; but I think it not unlikely, after our note has been delivered in, that the American commissioners will propose to refer the subject to their Government. In that case the negotiation may be adjourned till the answer is received, and we shall know the result of the campaign before it can be resumed. If our commander does his duty, I am persuaded we shall have acquired by our arms every point on the Canadian frontier which we ought to insist on keeping.

Lord Gambier and his colleagues communicated their new instructions to the American negotiators in a long note dated September 4, and were answered by a still longer note dated September 9, which was also sent to London, and considered by the Cabinet. Bathurst felt no anxiety about the negotiation in its actual stage. Goulburn wrote to him that "as long as we answer their notes, I believe that they will be ready to give us replies," and urged only that Sir George Prevost should hasten his reluctant movements in Canada. Bathurst wrote more instructions, dated September 16, directing his commissioners to abandon the demands for Indian territory and exclusive control of the Lakes, and to ask only that the Indians should be included in the peace. The British commissioners sent their note with these concessions to the Americans September 19; and then for the first time the Americans began to suspect the possibility of serious negotiation. For six weeks they had dealt only with the question whether they should negotiate at all.

The demand that the Indians should be included in the treaty was one that under favorable circumstances the Americans would have rejected; but none of them seriously thought of rejecting it as their affairs then stood. When the American commissioners discussed the subject among themselves, September 20, Adams proposed to break off the negotiation on that issue; but Gallatin good-naturedly overruled him, and Adams would not himself, on cool reflection, have ventured to take such responsibility. Indeed, he suggested an article for an Indian amnesty, practically accepting the British demand. He also yielded to Gallatin the ungrateful task of drafting the answers to the British notes; and thus Gallatin became in effect the head of the commission.

All Gallatin's abilities were needed to fill the place. In his

entire public life he had never been required to manage so un-
ruly a set of men. The British commissioners were trying, and
especially Goulburn was aggressive in temper and domineering
in tone; but with them Gallatin had little trouble. Adams and
Clay were persons of a different type, as far removed from
British heaviness as they were from the Virginian ease of
temper which marked the Cabinet of Jefferson, or the incompetence which characterized that of Madison. Gallatin was obliged
to exert all his faculties to control his colleagues; but whenever
he succeeded, he enjoyed the satisfaction of feeling that he had
colleagues worth controlling. They were bent on combat, if
not with the British, at all events with each other; and Gallatin
was partly amused and partly annoyed by the unnecessary energy of their attitude.

The first divergence occurred in framing the reply to the
British note of September 19, which while yielding essentials
made a series of complaints against the United States—and
among the rest reproached them for their attempt to conquer
Canada, and their actual seizure of Florida. Adams, who knew
little about the secrets of Jefferson's and Madison's Administrations, insisted on resenting the British charges, and especially
on justifying the United States government in its attacks upon
Florida. Bayard protested that he could not support such a
view, because he had himself publicly in Congress denounced
the Government on the subject of Florida; and Gallatin was
almost equally committed, for, as he frankly said, he had opposed in Cabinet for a whole year what had been done in
Florida before he could succeed in stopping it. Clay said nothing, but he had strong reasons for wishing that the British
negotiators should not be challenged to quote his notorious
speeches on the conquest of Canada. Adams produced Monroe's instructions, and in the end compelled his colleagues to
yield. His mistake in pressing such an issue was obvious to
every one but himself, and would have been evident to him had
he not been blinded by irritation at the British note. His colleagues retaliated by summarily rejecting as cant his argument

that moral and religious duty required the Americans to take and settle the land of the Indians.

After much discussion their note was completed and sent, September 26, to the British commissioners, who forwarded it as usual to London, with a letter from Goulburn of the same date, written in the worst possible temper, and charging the American commissioners with making a variety of false and fraudulent statements. While the British Cabinet detained it longer than usual for consideration, the Americans at Ghent felt their position grow weaker day by day.

Nothing warranted a serious hope of peace. Goulburn and his colleagues showed no thought of yielding acceptable conditions. The London "Courier" of September 29 announced what might be taken for a semi-official expression of the Ministry—

Peace they [the Americans] may make, but it must be on condition that America has not a foot of land on the waters of the St. Lawrence, . . . no settlement on the Lakes, . . . no renewal of the treaties of 1783 and 1794; . . . and they must explicitly abandon their new-fangled principles of the law of nations.

Liverpool, writing to Castlereagh September 23, said that in his opinion the Cabinet had "now gone to the utmost justifiable point in concession, and if they [the Americans] are so unreasonable as to reject our proposals, we have nothing to do but to fight it out. The military accounts from America are on the whole satisfactory." The news of the cruel humiliation at Bladensburg and the burning of Washington arrived at Ghent October 1, and caused British and Americans alike to expect a long series of British triumphs, especially on Lake Champlain, where they knew the British force to be overwhelming.

Goulburn exerted himself to produce a rupture. His letter of September 26 to Bathurst treated the American offer of an Indian amnesty as a rejection of the British ultimatum. Again Lord Bathurst set him right by sending him, October 5, the draft of a reciprocal article replacing the Indians in their situation before the war; and the British commissioners in a note dated October 8, 1814, communicated this article once more as an ultimatum. Harrison's treaty of July 22 with the Wyandots, Delawares, Shawnees, and other tribes, binding them to take up arms against the British, had then arrived, and this news lessened the interest of both parties in the Indian question. None of the American negotiators were prepared to break off negotiations on that point at such a time, and Clay was so earnest to settle the matter that he took from Gallatin and Adams the task of writing the necessary acceptance of the British ultimatum. Gallatin and Clay decided to receive the British article as according entirely with the American offer of amnesty, and the note was so written.

With this cordial admission of the British ultimatum the Americans coupled an intimation that the time had come when an exchange of general projects for the proposed treaty should be made. More than two months of discussion had then resulted only in eliminating the Indians from the dispute, and in agreeing to maintain silence in regard to the Lakes. Another great difficulty which had been insuperable was voluntarily removed by President Madison and his Cabinet, who after long and obstinate resistance at last authorized the commissioners, by instructions dated June 27, to omit impressment from the treaty. Considering the frequent positive declarations of the United States government, besides the rejection of Monroe's treaty in 1807 and of Admiral Warren's and Sir George Prevost's armistice of 1812 for want of an explicit concession on that point, Monroe's letter of June 27 was only to be excused as an act of common-sense or of necessity. The President preferred to represent it as an act of common-sense, warranted by the peace in Europe, which promised to offer no further occasion for the claim or the denial of the British right. On the same principle the subject of blockades was withdrawn from discussion; and these concessions, balanced by the British withdrawal from the Indian ultimatum and the Lake armaments, relieved the American commissioners of all their insuperable difficulties.

The British commissioners were not so easily rescued from their untenable positions. The American note of October 13, sent as usual to London, was answered by Bathurst October 18 and 20, in instructions revealing the true British terms more completely than had yet been ventured. Bathurst at length came to the cardinal point of the negotiation. As the American commissioners had said in their note of August 24, the British government must choose between the two ordinary bases of treaties of peace—the state before the war, or *status ante bellum;* and the state of possession, or *uti possidetis.* Until the middle of October, 1814, the *uti possidetis,* as a basis of negotiation, included whatever country might have been occupied by Sir George Prevost in his September campaign. Bathurst from the first intended to insist on the state of possession, but had not thought proper to avow it. His instructions of October 18 and 20 directed the British commissioners to come to the point, and to claim the basis of *uti possidetis* from the American negotiators.

On their admitting this to be the basis on which they are ready to negotiate, but not before they have admitted it, you will proceed to state the mutual accommodations which may be entered into in conformity with this basis. The British occupy Fort Michillimackinaw, Fort Niagara, and all the country east of the Penobscot. On the other hand the forces of the United States occupy Fort Erie and Fort Amherstburg [Malden]. On the government of the United States consenting to restore these two forts, Great Britain is ready to restore the forts of Castine and Machias, retaining Fort Niagara and Fort Michillimackinaw.

Thus the British demand, which had till then been intended to include half of Maine and the whole south bank of the St. Lawrence River from Plattsburg to Sackett's Harbor, suddenly fell to a demand for Moose Island, a right of way across the northern angle of Maine, Fort Niagara with five miles circuit, and the Island of Mackinaw. The reason for the new spirit of moderation was not far to seek. On the afternoon of October 17, while the British Cabinet was still deliberating on the basis of *uti possidetis,* news reached London that the British invasion of northern New York, from which so much had been expected, had totally failed, and that Prevost's large army had precipitately retreated into Canada. The London "Times" of October 19 was frank in its expressions of disappointment—

This is a lamentable event to the civilized world. . . . The subversion of that system of fraud and malignity which constitutes the whole policy of the Jeffersonian school . . . was an event to which we should have bent and yet must bend all our energies. The present American government must be displaced, or it will sooner or later plant its poisoned dagger in the heart of the parent State.

The failure of the attempt on Baltimore and Drummond's bloody repulse at Fort Erie became known at the same time, and coming together at a critical moment threw confusion into the Ministry and their agents in the press and the diplomatic service throughout Europe. The "Courier" of October 25 declared that "peace with America is neither practicable nor desirable till we have wiped away this late disaster;" but the "Morning Chronicle" of October 21–24 openly intimated that the game of war was at an end. October 31, the Paris correspondent of the London "Times" told of the cheers that rose from the crowds in the Palais Royal gardens at each recital of the Plattsburg defeat; and October 21 Goulburn wrote from Ghent to Bathurst—

The news from America is very far from satisfactory. Even our brilliant success at Baltimore, as it did not terminate in the capture of the town, will be considered by the Americans as a victory and not as an escape. . . . If it were not for the want of fuel in Boston, I should be quite in despair.

In truth the blockade was the single advantage held by England; and even in that advantage the Americans had a share as long as their cruisers surrounded the British Islands.

Liverpool wrote to Castlereagh, October 21, commenting severely on Prevost's failure, and finding consolation only in the thought that the Americans showed themselves even less patriotic than he had supposed them to be—

The capture and destruction of Washington has not united the Americans: quite the contrary. We have gained more credit with them by saving private property than we have lost by the destruction of their public works and buildings. Madison clings to office, and I am strongly inclined to think that the best thing for us is that he should remain there.

Castlereagh at Vienna found himself unable to make the full influence of England felt, so long as such mortifying disasters by land and sea proved her inability to deal with an enemy she persisted in calling contemptible.

On the American commissioners the news came, October 21, with the effect of a reprieve from execution. Gallatin was deeply moved; Adams could not believe the magnitude of the success; but as far as regarded their joint action, the overthrow of England's scheme produced no change. Their tone had always been high, and they saw no advantage to be gained by altering it. The British commissioners sent to them, October 21, the substance of the new instructions, offering the basis of *uti possidetis*, subject to modifications for mutual convenience. The Americans by common consent, October 23, declined to treat on that basis, or on any other than the mutual restoration of territory. They thought that the British government was still playing with them, when in truth Lord Bathurst had yielded the chief part of the original British demand, and had come to what the whole British empire regarded as essentials—the right of way to Quebec, and the exclusion of American fishermen from British shores and waters.

The American note of October 24, bluntly rejecting the basis of *uti possidetis*, created a feeling akin to consternation in the British Cabinet. At first, ministers assumed that the war must go on, and deliberated only on the point to be preferred for a rupture. "We still think it desirable to gain a little more time before the negotiation is brought to a close," wrote Liverpool to the Duke of Wellington, October 28; and on the same day he wrote to Castlereagh at Vienna to warn him that the American war "will probably now be of some duration," and treating

of its embarrassments without disguise. The Czar's conduct at
Vienna had annoyed and alarmed all the great Powers, and the
American war gave him a decisive advantage over England;
but even without the Russian complication, the prospect for
ministers was not cheering.

Looking to a continuance of the American war, our financial
state is far from satisfactory [wrote Lord Liverpool]; . . . the
American war will not cost us less than £10,000,000, in addition to our peace establishment and other expenses. We must
expect, therefore, to hear it said that the property tax is continued for the purpose of securing a better frontier for Canada.

A week passed without bringing encouragement to the British
Cabinet. On the contrary the Ministry learned that a vigorous
prosecution of hostilities would cost much more than ten million pounds, and when Liverpool next wrote to Castlereagh,
November 2, although he could still see "little prospect for our
negotiations at Ghent ending in peace," he added that "the
continuance of the American war will entail upon us a pro-
digious expense, much more than we had any idea of." A
Cabinet meeting was to be held the next day, November 3, to
review the whole course of policy as to America.

Throughout the American difficulties, from first to last, the
most striking quality shown by the British government was the
want of intelligence which caused the war, and marked the
conduct of both the war and the negotiations. If the foreign
relations of every government were marked by the same character, politics could be no more than rivalry in the race to
blunder; but in October, 1814, another quality almost equally
striking became evident. The weakness of British councils was
as remarkable as their want of intelligence. The government
of England had exasperated the Americans to an animosity
that could not forget or forgive, and every dictate of self-interest required that it should carry out its policy to the end.
Even domestic politics in Parliament might have been more
easily managed by drawing public criticism to America, while
in no event could taxes be reduced to satisfy the public demand.

Another year of war was the consistent and natural course for ministers to prefer.

So the Cabinet evidently thought; but instead of making a decision, the Cabinet council of November 3 resorted to the expedient of shifting responsibility upon the Duke of Wellington. The Duke was then Ambassador at Paris. His life had been threatened by angry officers of Napoleon, who could not forgive his victories at Vittoria and Toulouse. For his own security he might be sent to Canada, and if he went, he should go with full powers to close the war as he pleased.

The next day, November 4, Liverpool wrote to Wellington, explaining the wishes of the Cabinet, and inviting him to take the entire command in Canada, in order to bring the war to an honorable conclusion. Wellington replied November 9—and his words were the more interesting because, after inviting and receiving so decided an opinion from so high an authority, the Government could not easily reject it. Wellington began by reviewing the military situation, and closed by expressing his opinion on the diplomatic contest—

I have already told you and Lord Bathurst that I feel no objection to going to America, though I don't promise to myself much success there. I believe there are troops enough there for the defence of Canada forever, and even for the accomplishment of any reasonable offensive plan that could be formed from the Canadian frontier. I am quite sure that all the American armies of which I have ever read would not beat out of a field of battle the troops that went from Bordeaux last summer, if common precautions and care were taken of them. That which appears to me to be wanting in America is not a general, or a general officer and troops, but a naval superiority on the Lakes.

These views did not altogether accord with those of Americans, who could not see that the British generals made use of the Lakes even when controlling them, but who saw the troops of Wellington retire from one field of battle after another—at Plattsburg, Baltimore, and New Orleans—while taking more than common precautions. Wellington's military comments showed little interest in American affairs, and evidently he saw

nothing to be gained by going to Canada. His diplomatic ideas
betrayed the same bias—

In regard to your present negotiations, I confess that I think
you have no right, from the state of the war, to demand any
concession of territory from America. . . . You have not been
able to carry it into the enemy's territory, notwithstanding your
military success and now undoubted military superiority, and
have not even cleared your own territory on the point of attack.
You cannot on any principle of equality in negotiation claim
a cession of territory excepting in exchange for other advantages which you have in your power. . . . Then if this reasoning
be true, why stipulate for the *uti possidetis?* You can get no
territory; indeed, the state of your military operations, however creditable, does not entitle you to demand any.

After such an opinion from the first military authority of
England, the British Ministry had no choice but to abandon
its claim for territory. Wellington's letter reached London about
November 13, and was duly considered in the Cabinet. Liverpool wrote to Castlereagh, November 18, that the Ministry had
made its decision; the claim for territory was to be abandoned.
For this retreat he alleged various excuses—such as the unsatisfactory state of the negotiations at Vienna, and the alarming
condition of France; the finances, the depression of rents, and
the temper of Parliament. Such reasoning would have counted
for nothing in the previous month of May, but six months
wrought a change in public feeling. The war had lost public
favor. Even the colonial and shipping interests and the navy
were weary of it, while the army had little to expect from it
but hard service and no increase of credit. Every Englishman
who came in contact with Americans seemed to suffer. Broke,
the only victor by sea, was a lifelong invalid; and Brock and
Ross, the only victors on land, had paid for their success with
their lives. Incessant disappointment made the war an unpleasant thought with Englishmen. The burning of Washington was an exploit of which they could not boast. The rate of
marine insurance was a daily and intolerable annoyance. So
rapidly did the war decline in favor, that in the first half of

December it was declared to be decidedly unpopular by one of the most judicious English liberals, Francis Horner; although Horner held that the Americans, as the dispute then stood, were the aggressors. The tone of the press showed the same popular tendency, for while the "Times" grumbled loudly over the Canada campaign, the "Morning Chronicle" no longer concealed its hostility to the war, and ventured to sneer at it, talking of "the entire defeat and destruction of the last British fleet but one; for it has become necessary to particularize them now."

While the Cabinet still waited, the first instalment of Ghent correspondence to August 20, published in America October 10, returned to England November 18, and received no flattering attention. "We cannot compliment our negotiators," remarked the "Morning Chronicle"; and the "Times" was still less pleased. "The British government has been tricked into bringing forward demands which it had not the power to enforce. . . . Why treat at all with Mr. Madison?" In Parliament, November 19, the liberal opposition attacked the Government for setting up novel pretensions. Ministers needed no more urging, and Bathurst thenceforward could not be charged with waste of time.

During this interval of more than three weeks the negotiators at Ghent were left to follow their own devices. In order to provide the Americans with occupation, the British commissioners sent them a note dated October 31 calling for a counter-project, since the basis of *uti possidetis* was refused. This note, with all the others since August 20, was sent by the Americans to Washington on the same day, October 31; and then Gallatin and Adams began the task of drafting the formal project of a treaty. Immediately the internal discords of the commission broke into earnest dispute. A struggle began between the East and the West over the fisheries and the Mississippi.

The treaty of 1783 coupled the American right of fishing in British waters and curing fish on British shores with the British right of navigating the Mississippi River. For that arrangement the elder Adams was responsible. The fisheries were a Massachusetts interest. At Paris in 1783 John Adams, in season and out of season, with his colleagues and with the British negotiators, insisted, with the intensity of conviction, that the fishing rights which the New England people held while subjects of the British crown were theirs by no grant or treaty, but as a natural right, which could not be extinguished by war; and that where British subjects had a right to fish, whether on coasts or shores, in bays, inlets, creeks, or harbors, Americans had the same right, to be exercised wherever and whenever they pleased. John Adams's persistence secured the article of the definitive treaty, which, without expressly admitting a natural right, coupled the in-shore fisheries and the navigation of the Mississippi with the recognition of independence. In 1814 as in 1783 John Adams clung to his trophies, and his son would have waged indefinite war rather than break his father's heart by sacrificing what he had won; but at Ghent the son stood in isolation which the father in the worst times had never known. Massachusetts left him to struggle alone for a principle that needed not only argument but force to make it victorious. Governor Strong did not even write to him as he did to Pickering, that Massachusetts would give an equivalent in territory for the fisheries. As far as the State could influence the result, the fisheries were to be lost by default.

Had Adams encountered only British opposition he might have overborne it as his father had done; but since 1783 the West had become a political power, and Louisiana had been brought into the Union. If the fisheries were recognized as an indefeasible right by the treaty of 1783, the British liberty of navigating the Mississippi was another indefeasible right, which must revive with peace. The Western people naturally objected to such a proposition. Neither they nor the Canadians could be blamed for unwillingness to impose a mischievous servitude forever upon their shores, and Clay believed his popularity to depend on preventing an express recognition of the British right to navigate the Mississippi. Either Clay or Adams was sure to refuse signing any treaty which expressly sacrificed the local interests of either.

In this delicate situation only the authority and skill of Gallatin saved the treaty. At the outset of the discussion, October 30, Gallatin quietly took the lead from Adams's hands, and assumed the championship of the fisheries by proposing to renew both privileges, making the one an equivalent for the other. Clay resisted obstinately, while Gallatin gently and patiently overbore him. When Gallatin's proposal was put to the vote November 5, Clay and Russell alone opposed it—and the support then given by Russell to Clay was never forgotten by Adams. Clay still refusing to sign the offer, Gallatin continued his pressure, until at last, November 10, Clay consented to insert, not in the project of treaty, but in the note which accompanied it, a paragraph declaring that the commissioners were not authorized to bring into discussion any of the rights hitherto enjoyed in the fisheries: "From their nature, and from the peculiar character of the treaty of 1783 by which they were recognized, no further stipulation has been deemed necessary by the Government of the United States to entitle them to the full enjoyment of all of them."

Clay signed the note, though unwillingly; and it was sent, November 10, with the treaty project, to the British commissioners, who forwarded it to London, where it arrived at the time when the British Cabinet had at last decided on peace. Bathurst sent his reply in due course; and Goulburn's disgust was great to find that instead of breaking negotiation on the point of the fisheries as he wished, he was required once more to give way. "You know that I was never much inclined to give way to the Americans," he wrote, November 25. "I am still less inclined to do so after the statement of our demands with which the negotiation opened, and which has in every point of view proved most unfortunate."

The British reply, dated November 26, took no notice of the American reservation as to the fisheries, but inserted in the project the old right of navigating the Mississippi. Both

Bathurst and Goulburn thought that their silence, after the
American declaration, practically conceded the American right
to the fisheries, though Gambier and Dr. Adams thought differently. In either case the British note of November 26, though
satisfactory to Adams, was far from agreeable to Clay, who
was obliged to endanger the peace in order to save the Mississippi. Adams strongly inclined to take the British project precisely as it was offered, but Gallatin overruled him, and Clay
would certainly have refused to sign. In discussing the subject,
November 28, Gallatin proposed to accept the article on the
navigation of the Mississippi if the British would add a provision recognizing the fishing rights. Clay lost his temper, and
intimated something more than willingness to let Massachusetts
pay for the pleasure of peace; but during the whole day of
November 28, and with the same patience November 29, Gallatin continued urging Clay and restraining Adams, until at last
on the third day he brought the matter to the point he wished.

The result of this long struggle saved not indeed the fisheries,
but the peace. Clay made no further protest when, in conference with the British commissioners December 1, the Americans
offered to renew both the disputed rights. Their proposal was
sent to London, and was answered by Bathurst December 6,
in a letter offering to set aside for future negotiation the terms
under which the old fishing liberty and the navigation of the
Mississippi should be continued for fair equivalents. The British commissioners communicated this suggestion in conference
December 10, and threw new dissension among the Americans.

The British offer to reserve both disputed rights for future
negotiation implied that both rights were forfeited, or subject
to forfeit, by war—an admission which Adams could not make,
but which the other commissioners could not reject. At that
point Adams found himself alone. Even Gallatin admitted that
the claim to the natural right of catching and curing fish on
British shores was untenable, and could never be supported.
Adams's difficulties were the greater because the question of
peace and war was reduced to two points—the fisheries and

Moose Island—both interesting to Massachusetts alone. Yet the Americans were unwilling to yield without another struggle, and decided still to resist the British claim as inconsistent with the admitted basis of the *status ante bellum*.

The struggle with the British commissioners then became warm. A long conference, December 12, brought no conclusion. The treaty of 1783 could neither be followed nor ignored, and perplexed the Englishmen as much as the Americans. During December 13 and December 14, Adams continued to press his colleagues to assert the natural right to the fisheries, and to insist on the permanent character of the treaty of 1783; but Gallatin would not consent to make that point an ultimatum. All the commissioners except Adams resigned themselves to the sacrifice of the fisheries; but Gallatin decided to make one more effort before abandoning the struggle, and with that object drew up a note rejecting the British stipulation because it implied the abandonment of a right, but offering either to be silent as to both the fisheries and the Mississippi, or to admit a general reference to further negotiation of all subjects in dispute, so expressed as to imply no abandonment of right.

The note was signed and sent December 14, and the Americans waited another week for the answer. Successful as they had been in driving their British antagonists from one position after another, they were not satisfied. Adams still feared that he might not be able to sign, and Clay was little better pleased. "He said we should make a damned bad treaty, and he did not know whether he would sign it or not." Whatever Adams thought of the treaty, his respect for at least two of his colleagues was expressed in terms of praise rarely used by him. Writing to his wife, September 27, Adams said: "Mr. Gallatin keeps and increases his influence over us all. It would have been an irreparable loss if our country had been deprived of the benefit of his talents in this negotiation." At the moment of final suspense he wrote again, December 16—

Of the five members of the American mission, the Chevalier [Bayard] has the most perfect control of his temper, the most deliberate coolness; and it is the more meritorious because it is real self-command. His feelings are as quick and his spirits as high as those of any one among us, but he certainly has them more under government. I can scarcely express to you how much both he and Mr. Gallatin have risen in my esteem since we have been here living together. Gallatin has not quite so constant a supremacy over his own emotions; yet he seldom yields to an ebullition of temper, and recovers from it immediately. He has a faculty, when discussion grows too warm, of turning off its edge by a joke, which I envy him more than all his other talents; and he has in his character one of the most extraordinary combinations of stubbornness and of flexibility that I ever met with in man. His greatest fault I think to be an ingenuity sometimes trenching upon ingenuousness.

Gallatin's opinion of Adams was not so enthusiastic as Adams's admiration for him. He thought Adams's chief fault to be that he lacked judgment "to a deplorable degree." Of Clay, whether in his merits or his faults, only one opinion was possible. Clay's character belonged to the simple Southern or Virginia type, somewhat affected, but not rendered more complex, by Western influence—and transparent beyond need of description or criticism.

The extraordinary patience and judgment of Gallatin, aided by the steady support of Bayard, carried all the American points without sacrificing either Adams or Clay, and with no quarrel of serious importance on any side. When Lord Bathurst received the American note of December 14, he replied December 19, yielding the last advantage he possessed: "The Prince Regent regrets to find that there does not appear any prospect of being able to arrive at such an arrangement with regard to the fisheries as would have the effect of coming to a full and satisfactory explanation on that subject"; but since this was the case, the disputed article might be altogether omitted.

Thus the treaty became simply a cessation of hostilities, leaving every claim on either side open for future settlement. The formality of signature was completed December 24, and closed an era of American history. In substance, the treaty sacrificed much on both sides for peace. The Americans lost their claims

for British spoliations, and were obliged to admit question of
their right to Eastport and their fisheries in British waters; the
British failed to establish their principles of impressment and
blockade, and admitted question of their right to navigate the
Mississippi and trade with the Indians. Perhaps at the moment
the Americans were the chief losers; but they gained their greatest triumph in referring all their disputes to be settled by time,
the final negotiator, whose decision they could safely trust.

PERHAPS *the most dramatic consequence of the treaty was its effect upon the position of Massachusetts in the Union. The Hartford Convention would become a byword of the futility of separatist tendencies in the face of nationalizing pressures, just as fifty years later the Civil War would show the futility of armed insurrection. The war and the peace that followed made it clear that doctrinaire politics could not alter the social and economic movement of the nation. For Henry Adams, a Massachusetts man whose ancestors had so vigorously fought the Federalist intrigues of the time, the fate of Massachusetts had a special poignancy. The narrative does not relax its tone of scientific detachment, but it leaves no doubt that State Street and Massachusetts had earned their fate.*

Decline of Massachusetts

THE long, exciting, and splendid panorama of revolution and war, which for twenty-five years absorbed the world's attention and dwarfed all other interests, vanished more quickly in America than in Europe, and left fewer elements of disturbance. The transformation scene of a pantomime was hardly more sudden or complete than the change that came over the United States at the announcement of peace. In a single day, almost in a single instant, the public turned from interests and passions that had supplied its thought for a generation, and took up a class of ideas that had been unknown or but vaguely defined before.

At Washington the effect of the news was so extraordinary as to shake faith in the seriousness of party politics. Although the peace affected in no way party doctrine or social distinctions, a new epoch for the Union began from the evening of February 13, when the messenger from Ghent arrived with the treaty. No one stopped to ask why a government, which was discredited and falling to pieces at one moment, should appear as a successful and even a glorious national representative a moment afterward. Politicians dismissed the war from their thoughts, as they dismissed the treaty, with the single phrase: "Not an inch ceded or lost!" The commissioners from Massachusetts and Connecticut who appeared at Washington with the recommendations of the Hartford Convention, returned home as quietly as possible, pursued by the gibes of the press. The war was no more popular then than it had been before, as the subsequent elections proved; but the danger was passed, and passion instantly subsided.

Only by slow degrees the country learned to appreciate the extraordinary feat which had been performed, not so much by the people as by a relatively small number of individuals. Had a village rustic, with one hand tied behind his back, challenged the champion of the prize-ring, and in three or four rounds obliged him to draw the stakes, the result would have been little more surprising than the result of the American campaign of 1814. The most intelligent and best educated part of society both in the United States and in Great Britain could not believe it, and the true causes of British defeat remained a subject of conjecture and angry dispute. The enemies of the war admitted only that peace had saved Madison; but this single concession, which included many far-reaching consequences, was granted instantly, and from that moment the national government triumphed over all its immediate dangers.

While the Senate unanimously ratified the treaty February 16, the House set to work with much more alacrity than was its habit to dispose of the business before it. Haste was necessary. Barely fourteen days remained before the Thirteenth Congress should expire, and in that interval some system of peace legislation must be adopted. The struggle over the proposed Bank charter was still raging, for the Senate had passed another bill of incorporation February 11, over which the House was occupied the whole day of February 13 in a sharp and close contest. The first effect of the peace was to stop this struggle. By a majority of one vote, seventy-four to seventy-three, February 17, the House laid the subject aside.

Three days afterward, February 20, the President sent to Congress a Message transmitting the treaty with its ratifications, and congratulating the country on the close of a war "waged with the success which is the natural result of the wisdom of the legislative councils, of the patriotism of the people, of the public spirit of the militia, and of the valor of the military and naval forces of the country." After recommending to Congress the interests of the soldiers and sailors, the Message passed to the reduction of expenditures, which required immediate attention:

There are, however [continued Madison], important considerations which forbid a sudden and general revocation of the measures that have been produced by the war. Experience has taught us that neither the pacific dispositions of the American people, nor the pacific character of their political institutions, can altogether exempt them from that strife which appears, beyond the ordinary lot of nations, to be incident to the actual period of the world; and the same faithful monitor demonstrates that a certain degree of preparation for war is not only indispensable to avert disasters in the onset, but affords also the best security for the continuance of peace.

The avowal that experience had shown the error of the principle adopted by the nation in 1801 was not confined to President Madison. Monroe spoke even more plainly. In a letter to the military committee, February 24, Monroe urged that an army of twenty thousand men should be retained on the peace establishment. Each soldier of the rank-and-file was supposed to cost in peace about two hundred dollars a year, and Monroe's proposal involved an annual expense of more than five million dollars.

As far as concerned Madison and Monroe the repudiation of old Republican principles seemed complete; but the people had moved less rapidly than their leaders. Had Congress, while debating the subject February 25, known that Napoleon was then quitting Elba to seize once more the control of France, and to rouse another European convulsion with all its possible perils to neutrals, the President's views might have been adopted without serious dispute; but in the absence of evident danger, an army of twenty thousand men seemed unnecessary. The finances warranted no such extravagance. Dallas wrote to Eppes, the chairman of the Ways and Means Committee, a letter dated February 20, sketching a temporary financial scheme for the coming year. He proposed to fund at seven per cent the outstanding Treasury notes, amounting to $18,637,000; and even after thus sweeping the field clear of pressing claims, he still required the extravagant war-taxes in order to meet expenses, and depended on a further issue of Treasury notes, or a loan, to support the peace establishments of the army and navy. The state of the currency was desperate, and the revenue for the year 1815 was estimated at $18,200,000 in the notes of State banks—a sum little in excess of the estimated civil necessities.

The military committee of the House showed no sympathy with the new principles urged upon Congress by the Executive. Troup of Georgia reported a bill, February 22, fixing the peace establishment at ten thousand men, with two major-generals and four brigadiers. In submitting this proposal, Troup urged the House, February 25, to accept the reduction to ten thousand as the lowest possible standard, requiring only the expense of two and a half millions; but no sooner did he take his seat than Desha of Kentucky moved to substitute "six" for "ten," and a vigorous debate followed, ending in the adoption of Desha's amendment in committee by a majority of nineteen votes. The war leaders were greatly annoyed by this new triumph of the peace party. As a matter of principle, the vote on Desha's amendment affirmed Jefferson's pacific system and condemned the Federalist heresies of Madison and Monroe. The war leaders could not acquiesce in such a decision, and rallying for another effort, February 27, they remonstrated hotly. Forsyth of Georgia was particularly emphatic in defining the issue—

He had hoped that the spirit of calculation falsely styled economy, whose contracted view was fixed upon present expense, and was incapable of enlarging it to permanent and eventual advantage, had been laid forever by the powerful exorcisms of reason and experience. It would seem however that it had been only lulled by the presence of a more powerful demon. Since the potent spell of necessity had been broken, the troubled spirit of petty calculation was again awakened to vex the counsels and destroy the best hopes of the country.

For three years the friends of strong government, under the pressure of war, had been able to drive Congress more or less in their own direction; but at the announcement of peace their power was greatly lessened, and their unwilling associates were no longer disposed to follow their lead or to tolerate their assumptions of superiority. Desha retaliated in the tone of 1798—

Do they suppose that the House do not understand the subject; or do they suppose that by this great flow of eloquence they can make the substantial part of the House change their opinions in so short a time? When I speak of the substantial part of the House, I mean those who think much and speak but little; who make common-sense their guide, and not theoretical or visionary projects. . . . Some gentlemen advocate ten thousand and others twenty thousand of a standing army. The policy is easy to be seen through. The advocates of a perpetual system of taxation discover that if they cannot retain a considerable standing army, they will have no good plea for riveting the present taxes on the people.

In the process of national growth, public opinion had advanced since 1801 several stages in its development; but the speeches of Forsyth, Calhoun, and Lowndes on one side, like that of Desha on the other, left still in doubt the amount of change. While Forsyth admitted that he had under-estimated the strength of the economical spirit, Desha certainly over-estimated the force of the men "who think much and speak but little." With Federalist assistance, Desha's friends passed the bill for an army of six thousand men by a vote of seventy-five to sixty-five; but the Senate, by a more decided vote of eighteen to ten, substituted "fifteen" for "six." With this amendment the bill was returned to the House March 2, which by an almost unanimous vote refused to concur. The bill was sent to a conference committee, which reported the original plan of ten thousand men; and in the last hours of the session, March 3, the House yielded. By a vote of seventy to thirty-eight the peace establishment was fixed at ten thousand men.

The movement of public opinion was more evident in regard to the navy. Instead of repeating the experiments of 1801, Congress maintained the whole war establishment, and appropriated four million dollars chiefly for the support of frigates and ships-of-the-line. The vessels on the Lakes were dismantled and laid up; the gunboats, by an Act approved February 27, were ordered to be sold; but the sum of two hundred thousand dollars was appropriated for the annual purchase of ship-timber during the next three years, and the whole navy thenceforward consisted of cruisers, which were to be kept as far as possible in active service. As the first task of the new ships, an Act, approved March 3, authorized hostilities against the Dey of Algiers, who had indulged in the plunder of American commerce.

These hasty arrangements for the two services, coupled with an equally hasty financial makeshift, completed the career of the Thirteenth Congress, which expired March 4, as little admired or regretted as the least popular of its predecessors. Not upon Congress but upon the Executive Departments fell the burden of peace as of war, and on the Executive the new situation brought many embarrassments.

The first and most delicate task of the Government was the reduction of the army. No one could greatly blame Monroe for shrinking from the invidious duty of dismissing two thirds of the small force which had sustained so well and with so little support the character of the country; but the haste which he showed in leaving the War Department suggested also how keenly he must have suffered under its burdens. His name was sent to the Senate, February 27, as Secretary of State; no Secretary of War was nominated, but Dallas, with the courage that marked his character, undertook to manage the War Department as well as the Treasury until the necessary arrangements for the new army should be made.

April 8 Dallas wrote to six generals—Brown, Jackson, Scott, Gaines, Macomb, and Ripley—requesting their attendance at Washington to report a plan for the new army. Jackson and Gaines were unable to attend. The rest of the board reported a scheme dividing the country into two military districts, north and south; and into nine departments, five in the northern, four in the southern division—allotting to each the troops needed for its service. May 17 the new arrangements were announced. Brown was ordered to command the northern district, with Ripley and Macomb as brigadiers. Jackson took the southern district, with Scott and Gaines as brigadiers. Eight regiments of infantry, one of riflemen, and one of light artillery were retained, together with the corps of artillery and engineers. As far as possible, all the officers whose names became famous for a generation received rank and reward.

No such operation was necessary for the navy, where no reduction was required. In the civil service, Madison enjoyed the satisfaction of rewarding the friends who had stood by him in his trials. February 27 he sent to the Senate, with the nomination of Monroe as Secretary of State, the name of J. Q. Adams as Minister to England. At the same time Bayard was appointed to St. Petersburg, and Gallatin to Paris. The nomination of Bayard proved to be an empty compliment, for he arrived, August 1, in the Delaware River, in the last stages of illness, and was carried ashore the next day only to die.

These appointments were well received and readily confirmed by the Senate; but Madison carried favoritism too far for the Senate's approval when, March 1, he nominated Major-General Dearborn to be Secretary of War. Dearborn had few or no enemies, but the distinction thus shown him roused such strong remonstrance that Madison hastened to recall the nomination, and substituted Crawford in Dearborn's place. The Senate had already rejected Dearborn, but consented to erase the record from their journal, and Crawford became Secretary of War.

Thus the government in all its branches glided into the new conditions, hampered only by the confusion of the currency, which could not be overcome. The people were even more quick than the government to adapt themselves to peace. In New Orleans alone a few weeks of alarm were caused by extraordinary acts of arbitrary power on the part of General Jackson during the interval before the peace became officially known; but public order was not seriously disturbed, and the civil authority was restored March 13. Elsewhere the country scarcely stopped to notice the cost or the consequences of the war.

In truth the cost was moderate. Measured by loss of life in battle, it was less than that reported in many single battles fought by Napoleon. An army which never exceeded thirty thousand effectives, or placed more than four thousand regular rank-and-file in a single action, could not sacrifice many lives. According to the received estimates the number of men killed in battle on land did not much exceed fifteen hundred, including militia, while the total of killed and wounded little exceeded five thousand. Sickness was more fatal than wounds, but a population of eight millions felt camp-diseases hardly more than its periodical malarial fevers.

The precise financial cost of the war, measured only by increase of debt, was equally moderate. During three years—from February, 1812, until February, 1815—the government sold six per cent bonds at various rates of discount, to the amount of fifty million dollars, and this sum was the limit of its loans, except for a few bank discounts of Treasury notes not exceeding a million in all. By forcing Treasury notes on its creditors the Treasury obtained the use of twenty millions more. After the peace it issued bonds and new Treasury notes, which raised the aggregate amount of war debt, as far as could be ascertained, to about eighty million five hundred thousand dollars, which was the war-addition to the old nominal capital of debt, and increased the total indebtedness to one hundred and twenty-seven millions at the close of the year 1815.

The debt had exceeded eighty millions twenty years before, and in the interval the country had greatly increased its resources. The war debt was a trifling load, and would not have been felt except for the confusion of the currency and the unnecessary taxation imposed at the last moments of the war. That the currency and the war taxes were severe trials was not be to be denied, but of other trials the people had little to complain.

Considering the dangers to which the United States were exposed, they escaped with surprising impunity. The shores of Chesapeake Bay and of Georgia were plundered; but the British government paid for the slaves carried away, and no town of importance except Washington was occupied by an enemy. Contrary to the usual experience of war, the richest parts of the country suffered least. Only the Niagara frontier was systematically ravaged. When the blockade of the coast was raised, every seaboard city was able instantly to resume its commercial habits without having greatly suffered from the interruption. The harvests of two seasons were ready for immediate export, and the markets of Europe were waiting to receive them. Every man found occupation, and capital instantly returned to its old channels. From the moment of peace the exports of domestic produce began to exceed five million dollars a month, while four millions was the highest average for any previous twelvemonth, and the average for the seven years of embargo and blockade since 1807 fell much short of two and a half millions. The returns of commerce and navigation showed that during the seven months from March 1 to October 1, 1815, domestic produce valued at forty-six million dollars was exported, and American shipping to the amount of eight hundred and fifty-four thousand tons was employed in the business of export.

The ease and rapidity of this revolution not only caused the war to be quickly forgotten, but also silenced political passions. For the first time in their history as a nation, the people of the United States ceased to disturb themselves about politics or patronage. Every political principle was still open to dispute, and was disputed; but prosperity put an end to faction. No evidence could be given to prove that the number or weight of persons who held the opinions commonly known as Federalist, diminished either then or afterward. Massachusetts showed no regret for the attitude she had taken. At the April election, six weeks after the proclamation of peace, although Samuel Dexter was the Republican candidate, the State still gave to Governor Strong a majority of about seven thousand in a total vote of ninety-five thousand. The Federalists reasonably regarded this vote as an express approval of the Hartford Convention and its proposed measures, and asked what would have been their majority had peace not intervened to save the Government from odium. They believed not only that their popular support would have been greater, but that it would also have shown a temper beyond control; yet the Federalist majority in April was no longer hostile to the Government.

The other elections bore the same general character. Even in New York the popular reaction seemed rather against the war than in its favor. New York city in April returned Federalist members to the State legislature, causing a tie in the Assembly, each party controlling sixty-three votes. In Virginia the peace produced no change so decided as to warrant a belief that the war had become popular. In April John Randolph defeated Eppes and recovered control of his district. The State which had chosen sixteen Republicans and seven opposition congressmen in 1813, elected in 1815 seventeen Republicans and six opposition members. The stability of parties was the more remarkable in New York and Virginia, because those States were first to feel the effects of renewed prosperity.

After the excitement of peace was past, as the summer drew toward a close, economical interests dwarfed the old political distinctions and gave a new character to parties. A flood of wealth poured into the Union at a steady rate of six or seven million dollars a month, and the distribution of so large a sum could not fail to show interesting results. The returns soon

proved that the larger portion belonged to the Southern States.
Cotton, at a valuation of twenty cents a pound, brought seventeen and a half millions to the planters; tobacco brought eight
and a quarter millions; rice produced nearly two million eight
hundred thousand dollars. Of fifty millions received from
abroad in payment for domestic produce within seven or eight
months after the peace, the slave States probably took nearly
two thirds, though the white population of the States south of
the Potomac was less than half the white population of the
Union. The stimulus thus given to the slave system was violent, and was most plainly shown in the cotton States, where
at least twenty million dollars were distributed in the year
1815 among a white population hardly exceeding half a million in all, while the larger portion fell to the share of a few
slave-owners.

Had the Northern States shared equally in the effects of this
stimulus, the situation would have remained relatively as before; but the prosperity of the North was only moderate. The
chief export of the Northern States was wheat and Indian corn.
Even of these staples, Maryland and Virginia furnished a share;
yet the total value of the wheat and corn exported from the
Union was but eight million three hundred and fifty thousand
dollars, while that of tobacco alone was eight and a quarter
millions. While flour sold at nine or ten dollars a barrel, and
Napoleon's armies were vying with the Russians and Austrians
in creating an artificial demand, the Middle States made a fair
profit from their crops, although much less than was made by
the tobacco and cotton planters; but New England produced
little for export, and there the peace brought only ruin.

Ordinarily shipping was the source of New England's profits.
For twenty-five years the wars in Europe had given to New
England shipping advantages which ceased with the return
of peace. At first the change of condition was not felt, for every
ship was promptly employed; but the reappearance of foreign
vessels in American harbors showed that competition must
soon begin, and that the old rates of profit were at an end.

Had this been all, Massachusetts could have borne it; but the shipping on the whole suffered least among New England interests. The new manufactures, in which large amounts of capital had been invested, were ruined by the peace. If the United States poured domestic produce valued at fifty million dollars into the markets of Great Britain, Great Britain and her dependencies poured in return not less than forty million dollars' worth of imports into the United States, and inundated the Union with manufactured goods which were sold at any sacrifice to relieve the British markets. Although the imported manufactures paid duties of twenty-five per cent or more, they were sold at rates that made American competition impossible.

The cotton manufacturers of Rhode Island, in a memorial to Congress, dated October 20, 1815, declared that their one hundred and forty manufactories, operating one hundred and thirty thousand spindles, could no longer be worked with profit, and were threatened with speedy destruction. New England could foresee with some degree of certainty the ultimate loss of the great amount of capital invested in these undertakings; but whether such fears for the future were just or not, the loss of present profits was not a matter of speculation, but of instant and evident notoriety. Before the close of the year 1815 little profit was left to the new industries. The cotton manufacture, chiefly a New England interest, was supposed to employ a capital of forty million dollars, and to expend about fifteen millions a year in wages. The woollen manufacture, largely in Connecticut, was believed to employ a capital of twelve million dollars. Most of the large factories for these staples were altogether stopped.

From every quarter the peace brought distress upon New England. During the war most of the richer prizes had been sent to New England ports, and the sale of their cargoes brought money and buyers into the country; but this monopoly ceased at the same moment with the monopoly of manufactures. The lumber trade was almost the last surviving interest of considerable value, but in November Parliament imposed duties on American lumber which nearly destroyed the New England trade. The fisheries alone seemed to remain as a permanent resource.

The effect of these changes from prosperity to adversity was shown in the usual forms. Emigration became active. Thousands of native New Englanders transferred themselves to the valley of the Mohawk and Western New York. All the cities of the coast had suffered a check from the war; but while New York and Philadelphia began to recover their lost ground, Boston was slow to feel the impulse. The financial reason could be partly seen in the bank returns of Massachusetts. In January, 1814, the Massachusetts banks held about $7,300,000 in specie. In January and February, 1815, when peace was declared, the same banks probably held still more specie, as the causes which led to the influx were not removed. In June, about three months later, they held only $3,464,000 in specie, and the drain steadily continued, until in June, 1816, the specie in their vaults was reduced to $1,260,000, while their discounts were not increased and their circulation was diminished.

The state of the currency and the policy pursued by the Treasury added to the burden carried by New England. There alone the banks maintained specie payments. In the autumn of 1815, while the notes of the Boston banks were equivalent to gold, Treasury notes were at eleven per cent discount in Boston; New York bank-notes were at eleven and a half per cent discount; Philadelphia at sixteen; Baltimore at seventeen and eighteen; and United States six-per-cent bonds sold at eighty-six. In New England the Government exacted payments either in Treasury notes or in the notes of local banks equivalent to specie. Elsewhere it accepted the notes of local banks at a rate of depreciation much greater than that of Treasury notes. This injustice in exacting taxes was doubled by an equivalent injustice in paying debts. In New England the Treasury compelled creditors to take payment in whatever medium it had at hand, or to go unpaid. Elsewhere the Treasury paid its debts in the currency it received for its taxes.

Dallas admitted the wrong, but made no serious attempt to correct it. So complicated was the currency that the Treasury was obliged to keep four accounts with each of its ninety-four banks of deposit—(1) in the currency of the bank itself; (2) in special deposits of other bank currency; (3) in special deposits of Treasury notes bearing interest; (4) in small Treasury notes not bearing interest. In New England, and also in the cities of New York and Philadelphia, for some months after the peace the taxes were paid in Treasury notes. So little local currency was collected at these chief centres of business that the Treasury did not attempt to discharge its warrants there in currency. As the Treasury notes gradually appreciated in value above the local bank-notes of the Middle States, tax-payers ceased to make payments in them, and paid in their local bank-notes. Little by little the accumulation of local currency in the Treasury deposits at Philadelphia and New York increased, until the Treasury was able to draw on them in payment of its warrants; but even at those points this degree of credit was not attained in 1815, and in New England the Treasury still made no payments except in Treasury notes, or the notes of distant banks at a discount still greater than that of Treasury notes. This exceptional severity toward New England was admitted by Dallas, and excused only for the reason that if he were just to New England he must be severe to the rest of the country. Every holder of a Treasury warrant would have demanded payment at the place where the local medium was of the highest value, which was Boston; and as the Treasury could not pay specie at Boston without exacting specie elsewhere, Dallas paid no attention to Constitutional scruples or legal objections, but arbitrarily excluded Boston from the number of points where warrants were paid in local currency.

The people of Boston criticised, with much severity and with apparent justice, Dallas's management of the finances, which seemed to require some explanation not furnished in his reports. By an Act approved March 3, Congress authorized a loan of $18,452,800 to absorb the outstanding Treasury notes. At that time, under the momentary reaction of peace excitement, Treasury notes were supposed to be worth about ninety-four cents in the dollar, and Dallas expected to convert them nearly dollar for dollar into six-per-cent bonds. His proposals were issued March 10, inviting bids for twelve millions, and requiring only "that the terms of the proposals should bear some relation to the actual fair price of stock in the market of Philadelphia or New York." When the bids were received, Dallas rejected them all, because in his opinion they were below the market rates. "In point of fact," he afterward said, "no direct offer was made to subscribe at a higher rate than eighty-nine per cent, while some of the offers were made at a rate even lower than seventy-five per cent." Although the old six-per-cents were then selling at eighty-nine, eighty-eight, and eighty-seven in Boston and New York, Dallas held that "the real condition of the public credit" required him to insist upon ninety-five as the value of the new stock.

After failing to obtain ninety-five or even ninety as the price of his bonds, Dallas resorted to expedients best described in his own words. As he could not fund the Treasury notes at the rate he wished, he abandoned the attempt, and used the loan only to supply the local wants of the Treasury—

The objects of the loan being to absorb a portion of the Treasury-note debt, and to acquire a sufficiency of local currency for local purposes, the price of the stock at the Treasury was of course independent of the daily up-and-down prices of the various stock markets in the Union, and could only be affected by the progress toward the attainment of those objects. Thus while the wants of the Treasury were insufficiently supplied, offers to subscribe were freely accepted, and the parties were sometimes authorized and invited to increase the amount of their offers; but where the local funds had so accumulated as to approach the probable amount of the local demands, the price of the stock was raised at the Treasury, and when the accumulation was deemed adequate to the whole amount of the local demands the loan was closed.

Governments which insisted upon borrowing at rates higher than the money market allowed, could do so only by helping to debase the currency. Dallas's course offered encouragement to the suspended banks alone. The schedule of his loans proved that he paid a premium to insolvency. Of all places where he most needed "a sufficiency of local currency for local purposes," Boston stood first; but he borrowed in Boston less than one hundred thousand dollars, and this only in Treasury notes. Next to Boston stood New York; but in New York Dallas borrowed only $658,000, also in Treasury notes. In Philadelphia he obtained more than three millions, and took $1,845,000 in the depreciated local currency. In Baltimore he took nearly two millions in local currency; and in the bank paper of the District of Columbia, which was the most depreciated of all, he accepted $2,282,000 in local currency. Thus the loan which he had asked Congress to authorize for the purpose of absorbing the excess of Treasury notes, brought into the Treasury only about three millions in these securities, while it relieved the banks of Philadelphia, Baltimore, and Washington of six millions of their depreciated paper, worth about eighty cents in the dollar, and provided nothing to redeem the government's overdue bills at Boston and New York.

Had Dallas pursued a different course and funded all the overdue Treasury notes at the market rate, he might not have relieved New England, but he would have placed the government in a position to deal effectually with the suspended banks elsewhere. The immediate result of his refusal to redeem the dishonored Treasury notes was to depress their market value, and to discredit the government. Treasury notes fell to eighty-eight and eighty-seven, while the six-per-cents fell as low as eighty-one. In Washington, Baltimore, and Philadelphia Dallas obtained enough local currency to meet local obligations, and

doubtless saved to the government a small percentage by thus
trafficking in its own discredit; but in gaining this advantage
he offered encouragement to the over-issues of the suspended
banks, and he helped to embarrass the solvent banks in the
chief commercial centres as well as those in New England.

At the close of the year 1815 the general effect of the peace
was already well defined. The Southern States were in the full
enjoyment of extraordinary prosperity. The Middle States
were also prosperous and actively engaged in opening new
sources of wealth. Only the Eastern States suffered under depression; but there it was so severe as to warrant a doubt
whether New England could recover from the shock. The new
epoch of American history began by the sudden decline of
Massachusetts to the lowest point of relative prosperity and
influence she had ever known, and by an equally sudden stimulus to the South and West. So discredited was Massachusetts
that she scarcely ventured to complain, for every complaint
uttered by her press was answered by the ironical advice that
she should call another Hartford Convention.

Epilogue: The United States in 1817

WITH the retirement of Madison in March, 1817, the long and complicated drama that exhibited the transformation of the Union into a modern state came to a close. But it was not a drama with a well-made plot; too many lines of development were still unresolved and uncertain in direction. All possibilities had not been exhausted. Nonetheless, great changes had taken place—in effect a revolution in governmental theory and practice. The introductory cross-section of six chapters provided a datum line, beneath the rising tide of change, against which to measure its height and configuration. If Adams's thesis was sound and his demonstration adequate, he should be able once again to cut across the lines of history, measure progress and take his soundings, and establish a new level of national existence. This Adams proceeds to do in the final four chapters, the Epilogue, as he referred to it. In most respects they parallel the Prologue. Especially notable in these concluding chapters is Adams's way of looking at society and history dynamically, moving along lines of force beyond the power of mere individuals to deflect or alter. As he once remarked to the historian Francis Parkman, "Should history ever become a true science, it must expect to establish its laws, not from the complicated story of rival nationalities, but from the economical evolution of a great democracy."

Economical Results

THE Union, which contained 5,300,000 inhabitants in 1800, numbered 7,240,000 in 1810, and 9,634,000 in 1820. At the close of Madison's Administration, in 1817, the population probably numbered not less than 8,750,000 persons. The average rate of annual increase was about three and five-tenths per cent, causing the population to double within twenty-three years.

The rate of increase was not uniform throughout the country, but the drift of population was well defined. In 1800 the five New England States contained about 1,240,000 persons. Virginia and North Carolina, united, then contained nearly 1,360,000, or ten per cent more than New England. In 1820 the two groups were still nearer equality. New England numbered about 1,665,000; the two Southern States numbered 1,700,000, or about two per cent more than New England. While these two groups, containing nearly half the population of the Union, increased only as one hundred to one hundred and twenty-nine, the middle group, comprising New York, New Jersey, and Pennsylvania, increased in the relation of one hundred to one hundred and ninety-two—from 1,402,000 in 1800, to 2,696,000 in 1820. Their rate was about the average ratio for the Union; and the three Western States—Ohio, Kentucky, and Tennessee—grew proportionally faster. Their population of 370,000 in 1800 became 1,567,000 in 1820, in the ratio of one hundred to four hundred and twenty-three.

Careful study revealed a situation alarming to New England and Virginia. If only Connecticut, Rhode Island, and Massachusetts, without its district of Maine, were considered, a total population numbering 742,000 in 1800 increased only to 881,000 in 1820, or in the ratio of one hundred to one hundred and eighteen in twenty years. If only the white population of Virginia and North Carolina were taken into the estimate, omitting the negroes, 852,000 persons in 1800 increased to 1,022,000 in 1820, or in the ratio of one hundred to one hundred and twenty. Maryland showed much the same result, while Delaware, which rose from 64,270 in 1800 to 72,674 in 1810, remained stationary, numbering only 72,749 in 1820—a gain of seventy-five persons in ten years. The white population showed a positive decrease, from 55,361 in 1810 to 55,282 in 1820.

Probably a census taken in 1817 would have given results still less favorable to the sea-coast. The war affected population more seriously than could have been reasonably expected, and stopped the growth of the large cities. New York in 1800 contained 60,000 persons; in 1810 it contained 96,400, but a corporation census of 1816 reported a population of only one hundred thousand, although two of the six years were years of peace and prosperity. From that time New York grew rapidly, numbering 124,000 in 1820—a gain of about twenty-five per cent in four years. Even the interior town of Albany, which should have been stimulated by the war, and which increased four thousand in population between 1800 and 1810, increased only three thousand between 1810 and 1820. Philadelphia fared worse, for its population of 96,000 in 1810 grew only to 108,000 in 1820, and fell rapidly behind New York. Baltimore grew from 26,000 in 1800 to 46,000 in 1810, and numbered less than 63,000 in 1820. Boston suffered more than Baltimore; for its population, which numbered 24,000 in 1800, grew only to 32,000 in 1810, and numbered but 43,000 in 1820. Charleston was still more unfortunate. In 1800 its population numbered about eighteen thousand; in 1810, 24,700; in 1817 a local census reported a decrease to 23,950 inhabitants, and the national census of 1820 reported 24,780 or eighty persons more than in 1810. The town of Charleston and the State of Delaware increased together by the same numbers.

Although the war lasted less than three years, its effect was so great in checking the growth of the cities that during the period from 1810 to 1820 the urban population made no relative increase. During every other decennial period in the national history the city population grew more rapidly than that of the rural districts; but between 1810 and 1820 it remained stationary, at four and nine-tenths per cent of the entire population. While Boston, Philadelphia, and Charleston advanced slowly, and New York only doubled its population in twenty years, Western towns like Pittsburg, Cincinnati, and Louisville grew rapidly and steadily, and even New Orleans, though exposed to capture, more than trebled in size; but the Western towns were still too small to rank as important. Even in 1820 the only cities which contained a white population of more than twenty thousand were New York, Philadelphia, Baltimore, and Boston.

The severest sufferers from this situation were the three southern States of New England—Connecticut, Rhode Island,

and Massachusetts, excluding the district of Maine, which was about to become a separate State. Fortunately the northern part of New England, notwithstanding the war, increased much more rapidly than the southern portion; but this increase was chiefly at the cost of Massachusetts, and returned little in comparison with the loss. The situation of Massachusetts and Connecticut was dark. Had not wealth increased more rapidly than population, Massachusetts would have stood on the verge of ruin; yet even from the economical point of view, the outlook was not wholly cheerful.

Judged by the reports of Massachusetts banks, the increase of wealth was surprising. The official returns of 1803, the first year when such returns were made, reported seven banks in the State, with a capital of $2,225,000 and deposits of $1,500,000. In June, 1816, twenty-five banks returned capital stock amounting nearly to $11,500,000 and deposits of $2,133,000. The deposits were then small, owing to the decline of industry and drain of specie that followed the peace, but the capital invested in banks had more than quintupled in thirteen years.

This multiplication was not a correct measure of the general increase in wealth. Indeed, the banks were in excess of the public wants after the peace, and their capital quickly shrunk from $11,500,000 in June, 1816, to $9,300,000 in June, 1817, a decline of nearly twenty per cent in a year. From that time it began to increase again, and held its improvement even in the disastrous year 1819. Assuming 1803 and 1817 as the true terms of the equation, the banking capital of Massachusetts increased in fourteen years from $2,225,000 to $9,300,000, or more than quadrupled.

Gauged by bank discounts the increase of wealth was not so great. In 1803 the debts due to the banks were returned at $3,850,000; in June, 1817, they were $12,650,000. If the discounts showed the true growth of industry, the business of the State somewhat more than trebled in fourteen years. Probably the chief industries that used the increased banking capital were the new manufactures, for the older sources of Massachusetts wealth showed no equivalent gain. Tested by the imports, the improvement was moderate. In 1800 the gross amount of duties collected in Massachusetts was less than $3,200,000; in 1816 it somewhat exceeded $6,100,000, but had not permanently doubled in sixteen years. Tested by exports of domestic produce, Massachusetts showed no gain. In 1803 the value of such produce amounted to $5,400,000; in 1816, to $5,008,000.

Other methods of calculating the increase of wealth gave equally contradictory results. The registered tonnage of Massachusetts engaged in foreign trade exceeded two hundred and ten thousand tons in 1800; in 1816 it was two hundred and seventy-four thousand tons. In the coasting-trade Massachusetts employed seventy-five thousand tons in 1800, and one hundred and twenty-nine thousand in 1816. The tonnage employed in the fisheries showed no growth. The shipping of Massachusetts seemed to indicate an increase of about forty per cent in sixteen years.

The system of direct taxation furnished another standard of comparison. In 1798 a valuation was made in certain States of houses and lands for direct taxes; another was made in 1813; a third in 1815. That of 1798 amounted to eighty-four million dollars for Massachusetts; that of 1813, to one hundred and forty-nine millions; that of 1815, to one hundred and forty-three millions—a gain of seventy per cent in sixteen years; but such a valuation in 1817 would probably have shown a considerable loss on that of 1815.

Evidently the chief increase in wealth consisted in the growth of manufactures, but after the prostration of the manufacturing interest in 1816 no plausible estimate of their true value could be made, unless the bank discounts measured their progress. The result of the whole inquiry, though vague, suggested that wealth had increased in Massachusetts more rapidly than population, and had possibly gained seventy or eighty per cent in sixteen years; but in spite of this increase the State was in a pitiable situation. Neither steamboats, canals, nor roads could help it. Thousands of its citizens migrated to New York and Ohio, beyond the possibility of future advantage to the land they left. Manufactures were prostrate. Shipping was driven from the carrying trade. Taxation weighed far more heavily than ever before. A load of obloquy rested on the State on account of its war policy and the Hartford Convention. The national government treated it with severity, and refused to pay for the Massachusetts militia called into service by the President during the war, because the governor had refused to place them under national officers.

The condition of Massachusetts and Maine was a picture of New England. Democratic Rhode Island suffered equally with Federalist Connecticut. Maine, New Hampshire, and Vermont showed growth, but the chief possibility of replacing lost strength lay in immigration. During the European wars, no considerable number of immigrants were able to reach the United States; but immediately after the return of peace, emigration from Europe to America began on a scale as alarming to European governments as the movement to Western New York and Ohio was alarming to the seaboard States of the Union. During the year 1817 twenty-two thousand immigrants were reported as entering the United States. Twelve or fourteen thousand were probably Irish; four thousand were German. More than two thousand arrived in Boston, while about seven thousand landed in New York and the same number in Philadelphia. The greater part probably remained near where they landed, and in some degree supplied the loss of natives who went west. The rapid growth of the northern cities of the seacoast began again only with the flood of immigration.

Although the three southern States of New England were the severest sufferers, the Virginia group—comprising Delaware, Maryland, Virginia, and North Carolina—escaped little better. In twenty years their white population increased nineteen and five tenths per cent, while that of Massachusetts, Connecticut, and Rhode Island increased eighteen per cent. The wealth of Southern States consisted largely in slaves; and the negro population of the Virginia group increased about twenty-five per cent in numbers during the sixteen years from 1800 to 1816. The exports of domestic produce increased about forty per cent in value, comparing the average of 1801–1805 with that of 1815–1816. The net revenue collected in Virginia increased nearly seventy per cent, comparing the year 1815 with the average of the five years 1800–1804; while that collected in North Carolina more than doubled.

Measured by these standards, the growth of wealth in the Virginia group of States was not less rapid than in Massachusetts, and the same conclusion was established by other methods. In 1816 Virginia contained two State banks, with branches, which returned for January 1 a capital stock of $4,590,000, with a note circulation of $6,000,000, and deposits approaching $2,500,000. Their discounts amounted to $7,768,-000 in January, 1816, and were contracted to $6,128,000 in the following month of November. Although Virginia used only half the banking capital and credits required by Massachusetts, the rate of increase was equally rapid, and the tendency toward banking was decided. In 1817 the legislature created two new banks, one for the valley of Virginia, the other for western Virginia, with a capital stock of $600,000, and branches with capital stock of $100,000 for each. Between 1800 and 1817, banking capital exceeding five million dollars was created in Virginia, where none had existed before.

If the estimates made by Timothy Pitkin, the best statistician of the time, were correct, the returns for direct taxes showed a greater increase of wealth in Virginia than in Massachusetts. The valuation of Virginia for 1799 was $71,000,000; that of 1815 was $165,000,000. The valuation of North Carolina in 1799 was $30,000,000; that of 1815 was $51,000,000. Maryland was estimated at $32,000,000 in 1799, at $106,000,-000 in 1815. The average increase for the three States was in the ratio of one hundred to two hundred and forty, while that for Massachusetts, Rhode Island, and Connecticut was nearer one hundred to one hundred and seventy-five. The normal increase for the Union was in the ratio of one hundred to two hundred and sixty-three.

The result obtained from the estimates for direct taxes was

affected by a doubt in regard to the correctness of the valuation of 1799, which was believed to have been too low in the Southern States; but the general conclusion could not be doubted that the Virginia group of States increased steadily in wealth. The rapidity of increase was concealed by an equally rapid impoverishment of the old tobacco-planting aristocracy, whose complaints drowned argument. As the lands of the ancient families became exhausted, the families themselves fell into poverty, or emigrated to the richer Ohio valley. Their decline or departure gave rise to many regrets and alarms. With the impressions thus created, the people associated the want of economical machinery as a cause of their backwardness, and became clamorous for roads, canals, and banks. The revolution in their ideas between 1800 and 1816 was complete.

The North Carolinians were first to denounce their old habits of indifference, and to declare their State in danger of ruin on that account. A committee of the State legislature reported Nov. 30, 1815, that vigorous measures for self-protection could no longer be postponed—

With an extent of territory sufficient to maintain more than ten millions of inhabitants, . . . we can only boast of a population something less than six hundred thousand, and it is but too obvious that this population under the present state of things already approaches its maximum. Within twenty-five years past more than two hundred thousand of our inhabitants have removed to the waters of the Ohio, Tennessee, and Mobile; and it is mortifying to witness the fact that thousands of our wealthy and respectable citizens are annually moving to the West, . . . and that thousands of our poorer citizens follow them, being literally driven away by the prospect of poverty. In this state of things our agriculture is at a stand.

The Virginians showed an equally strong sense of their perils. Twelve months after the North Carolina legislature took the matter in hand, a committee of the Virginia legislature in December, 1816, discussed the same topic and reached the same conclusion. Although something had been done by corporations to open canals on the Potomac, the James River, and to the

Dismal Swamp, the State of Virginia had in sixteen years made little advance in material welfare. While New England had built turnpikes wherever a profit could be expected, in Virginia, said the committee, "the turnpike-roads of the Commonwealth, except a few short passes of particular mountains and a road recently begun from Fredericksburg to the Blue Ridge, are confined principally to the county of Loudon, the adjacent counties of Fairfax, Fauquier, and Frederick, and to the vicinity of the seat of government." In other respects the situation was worse.

While many other States [said the committee] have been advancing in wealth and numbers with a rapidity which has astonished themselves, the ancient Dominion and elder sister of the Union has remained stationary. A very large proportion of her western territory is yet unimproved, while a considerable part of her eastern has receded from its former opulence. How many sad spectacles do her low-lands present of wasted and deserted fields, of dwellings abandoned by their proprietors, of churches in ruins! The genius of her ancient hospitality, benumbed by the cold touch of penury, spreads his scanty hoard in naked halls, or seeks a coarser but more plenteous repast in the lonely cabins of the West. The fathers of the land are gone where another outlet to the ocean turns their thoughts from the place of their nativity, and their affections from the haunts of their youth.

Another committee reported to the House of Delegates Jan. 5, 1816, in favor of extending the banking system of the State. The report used language new as an expression of Virginia opinions.

Your committee believe that a prejudice has gone abroad, which they confidently trust experience will prove to be unfounded even to the satisfaction of those by whom it is entertained, that the policy of Virginia is essentially hostile to commerce and to the rights of commercial men. Upon the removal of this prejudice must depend the future contributions of this Commonwealth toward the prosperity and glory if not the happiness and safety of the United States. Without the confidence of foreigners there can exist no foreign commerce. Without foreign commerce there can exist neither ships, seamen, nor a navy; and a tremendous lesson has taught Virginia that without a navy she can have no security for her repose.

Notwithstanding the gloom of these recitals, the evidence tended to show that while the white population of Virginia increased only about nineteen per cent in sixteen years, its wealth nearly doubled. Comparison with the quicker growth of the Middle States—New York, New Jersey, and Pennsylvania—caused much of the uneasiness felt by New England and Virginia. The banking capital of New York, which probably did not much exceed three million dollars in 1800, amounted in 1816 to nearly $19,000,000; that of Pennsylvania exceeded $16,000,000. The valuation of houses and lands for the direct tax rose in New York from $100,000,000 in 1799 to nearly $270,000,000 in 1815; and in Pennsylvania, from $102,-000,000 in 1799 to $346,000,000 in 1815. The net revenue collected in New York was $2,700,000 in 1800, and $14,500,000 in 1815; that collected in Pennsylvania was $1,350,000 in 1800, and $7,140,000 in 1815. This rate of increase did not extend to exports. The value of the domestic exports from New York in 1803 was about $7,500,000; in 1816 it exceeded $14,000,000; while the value of Pennsylvanian exports increased little— being $4,021,000 in 1803 and $4,486,000 in 1816. The population of New York doubled while that of Massachusetts and Virginia hardly increased one third. Pennsylvania grew less rapidly in numbers, but still about twice as fast as New England.

Although this rate of progress seemed to leave New England and Virginia far behind the Middle States, it was less striking than the other economical changes already accomplished or foreseen. The movement of population or of wealth was not so important as the methods by which the movement was effected. The invention of the steamboat gave a decisive advantage to New York over every rival. Already in 1816 the system had united New York city so closely with distant places that a traveller could go from New York to Philadelphia by steamboat and stage in thirteen hours; or to Albany in twenty-four hours; and taking stage to Whitehall in twelve hours could reach Montreal in thirty hours, and go on to Quebec in twenty-four hours—thus consuming about five and a half successive days in the long journey from Philadelphia to Quebec, sleeping comfortably on his way, and all at an expense of fifty dollars. This economy of time and money was a miracle; but New York could already foresee that it led to other advantages of immeasurable value. The steamboat gave impetus to travel, and was a blessing to travellers; but its solid gain for the prosperity of the United States lay not in passenger traffic so much as in freight, and New York was the natural centre of both.

While Pennsylvania, Virginia, and the Carolinas were building roads and canals across a hundred miles of mountains, only to reach at last an interior region which enjoyed an easier outlet for freight, New York had but to people a level and fertile district, nowhere fifty miles from navigable water, in order to reach the great Lake system, which had no natural outlet within the Union except through the city of New York. So obvious was the idea of a canal from the Lakes to the Hudson that it was never out of men's minds, even before the war; and no sooner did peace return than the scheme took large proportions. Active leaders of both political parties pressed the plan —De Witt Clinton, Gouverneur Morris, and Peter B. Porter were all concerned in it; but the legislature and people then supposed that so vast an undertaking as a canal to connect Lake Erie with the ocean, national in character and military in its probable utility, required national aid. Supposing the Administration to be pledged to the policy outlined by Gallatin and approved by Jefferson in the Annual Message of 1806, the New York commissioners applied to Congress for assistance, and uniting with other local interests procured the passage of Calhoun's bill for internal improvements.

They were met by Madison's veto. This act, although at first it seemed to affect most the interests of New York, was in reality injurious only to the Southern States. Had the government lent its aid to the Erie Canal, it must have assisted similar

schemes elsewhere, and in the end could hardly have refused
to carry out Gallatin's plan of constructing canals from the
Chesapeake to the Ohio, and from the Santee to the Tennessee River. The veto disappointed New York only for the
moment, but was fatal to Southern hopes. After the first shock
of discouragement, the New York legislature determined to
persevere, and began the work without assistance. The legislature of Pennsylvania at the same time appropriated half a million dollars for roads and canals, and for improvements of
river navigation, devoting nearly one hundred and fifty thousand dollars to aid the turnpike-road to Pittsburg. The fund
established by the State of Ohio, as a condition of its admission
to the Union, had in 1816 produced means to construct the
National or Cumberland Road to the hundred and thirteenth
mile. The indifference to internal improvements which had
been so marked a popular trait in 1800, gave place to universal
interest and activity in 1816; but the Middle States were far
in advance of the Eastern and Southern in opening communications with the West; and New York, owing in no small degree
to the veto, could already foresee the time when it would wrest
from Pennsylvania the supply of the valley of the Ohio, while
expanding new tributary territory to an indefinite extent along
the Lakes.

When Madison retired from the Presidency, the limits of
civilization, though rapidly advancing, were still marked by
the Indian boundary, which extended from the western end of
Lake Erie across Indiana, Kentucky, Tennessee, and the Southwestern territory. Only weak and helpless tribes remained east
of the Mississippi, waiting until the whites should require the
surrender of their lands; but the whites, already occupying
land far in advance of their needs, could not yet take the whole.
Not until 1826 were the Indian titles generally extinguished
throughout Indiana. The military work was done, and the short
space of sixteen years had practically accomplished the settlement of the whole country as far as the Mississippi; but an-

other generation was needed in order to take what these sixteen years had won.

As population spread, the postal service struggled after it. Except on the Hudson River, steamboats were still irregular in their trips; and for this reason the mails continued to be carried on horseback through the interior. In 1801 the number of post-offices was 957; in 1817 it was 3,459. In 1801 the length of post-roads was less than 25,000 miles; in 1817 it was 52,689. In 1800 the gross receipts from postage were $280,000; in 1817 they slightly exceeded $1,000,000. In each case the increase much surpassed the ratio for population, and offered another means for forming some estimate of the increase of wealth. The Fourteenth Congress pressed the extension of post-routes in western New York, Ohio, and Indiana; they were already established beyond the Mississippi. Rapidity of motion was also increased on the main routes. From New York to Buffalo, four hundred and seventy-five miles, the traveller went at an average rate of five miles an hour, and, sleeping every night, he arrived in about four days. Between Philadelphia and Pittsburg, where no watercourse shortened the distance, the stagecoach consumed five and a half days, allowing for stoppage at night. These rates of travel were equal to those common on routes of similar length in Europe; but long after 1817 the mail from Washington to New Orleans, by a route 1,380 miles in length, required twenty-four days of travel.

Had the steamboat system been at once perfected, the mail could have been carried with much more rapidity; but the progress of the new invention was slow. After the trial trip of the "Clermont," Aug. 17, 1807, five years elapsed before the declaration of war; yet in 1812 New York possessed no other steamline than the Albany packets. Steam-ferries plied to Hoboken, Amboy, and other places in the immediate neighborhood; but neither Newport, New London, or New Haven enjoyed steam communication with New York until after the war. In the spring of 1813 eight or nine steamboats belonged to the city of New York, but only three, which ran to Albany, were more than ferries. At the same time Philadelphia possessed six such ferry-boats. From Baltimore a steamer ran to the head of Chesapeake Bay; but the southern coast and the town of Charleston saw no steamboat until a year after the war was ended.

The West was more favored. In 1811 a boat of four hundred tons was built at Pittsburg and sent down the river to New Orleans, where it plied between New Orleans and Natchez. Two more were built at the same place in 1813–1814; and one of them, the "Vesuvius," went down the river in the spring of 1814, rousing general interest in the midst of war by making the trip in nine days and a half, or two hundred and twenty-seven hours. The "Vesuvius" remained on the Mississippi for the next two years, but was burned with her cargo in the summer of 1816. By that time the world was thinking much of steamboats, and their use was rapidly extending, though regular trips were still uncommon except in the east.

The result of the sixteen years, considered only in the economical development of the Union, was decisive. Although population increased more rapidly than was usual in human experience, wealth accumulated still faster. From such statistics as the times afforded, a strong probability has been shown that while population doubled within twenty-three years, wealth doubled within twenty. Statistics covering the later period of national growth, warrant the belief that a valuation of $1,742,000,000 in 1800 corresponded to a valuation of $3,-734,000,000 in 1820; and that if a valuation of $328 per capita is assumed for 1800, a valuation of $386 per capita may be estimated for 1820.

These sixteen years set at rest the natural doubts that had attended the nation's birth. The rate of increase both in population and wealth was established and permanent, unless indeed it should become even more rapid. Every serious difficulty which seemed alarming to the people of the Union in 1800 had been removed or had sunk from notice in 1816. With the disappearance of every immediate peril, foreign or domestic, society could devote all its energies, intellectual and physical, to its favorite objects. This result was not the only or even the chief proof that economical progress was to be at least as rapid in the future as at the time when the nation had to struggle with political difficulties. Not only had the people during these sixteen years escaped from dangers, they had also found the means of supplying their chief needs. Besides clearing away every obstacle to the occupation and development of their continent as far as the Mississippi River, they created the steamboat, the most efficient instrument yet conceived for developing such a country. The continent lay before them, like an uncovered ore-bed. They could see, and they could even calculate with reasonable accuracy, the wealth it could be made to yield. With almost the certainty of a mathematical formula, knowing the rate of increase of population and of wealth, they could read in advance their economical history for at least a hundred years.

Religious and Political Thought

THE movement of thought, more interesting than the movement of population or of wealth, was equally well defined. In the midst of political dissension and economical struggles, religion still took precedence; and the religious movement claimed notice not merely for its depth or for its universality, but also and especially for its direction. Religious interest and even excitement were seen almost everywhere, both in the older and in the newer parts of the country; and every such movement offered some means of studying or illustrating the development of national character. For the most part the tendency seemed emotional rather than intellectual; but in New England the old intellectual pre-eminence, which once marked the Congregational clergy, developed a quality both new and distinctive.

The Congregational clergy, battling with the innate vices of human nature, thought themselves obliged to press on their hearers the consequences of God's infinite wrath rather than those of his infinite love. They admitted that in a worldly sense they erred, and they did not deny that their preaching sometimes leaned to severity; but they would have been false to their charge and undeserving of their high character had they lost sight of their radical doctrine that every man was by nature personally depraved, and unless born again could not hope to see the kingdom of God. Many intellectual efforts had been made by many ages of men to escape the logic of this doctrine, but without success. The dogma and its consequences could not be abandoned without abandoning the Church.

From this painful dilemma a group of young Boston clergymen made a new attempt to find a path of escape. Their movement drew its inspiration from Harvard College, and was simultaneous with the sway of Jefferson's political ideas; but the relationship which existed between religious and political innovation was remote and wholly intellectual. Harvard College seemed to entertain no feeling toward Jefferson but antipathy,

Vol. IX, Chap. VIII.

when in 1805 the corporation appointed Henry Ware, whose Unitarian tendencies were well known, to be Hollis Professor of Theology. The Unitarianism of Henry Ware and his supporters implied at that time no well-defined idea beyond a qualified rejection of the Trinity, and a suggestion of what they thought a more comprehensible view of Christ's divine character; but it still subverted an essential dogma of the Church, and opened the way to heresy. The Calvinists could no longer regard Harvard College as a school proper for the training of clergy; and they were obliged to establish a new theological seminary, which they attached to a previously existing Academy at Andover, in Essex County, Massachusetts. The two branches of the New England Calvinists—known then as old Calvinism and Hopkinsianism—united in framing for the instructors of the Andover school a creed on the general foundation of the Westminster Assembly's Shorter Catechism, and thus provided for the future education of their clergy in express opposition to Unitarians and Universalists.

Thenceforward the theological school of Harvard College became more and more Unitarian. The Massachusetts parishes, divided between the two schools of theology, selected, as pleased a majority of their church-members, either Orthodox or Unitarian pastors; and while the larger number remained Calvinistic, though commonly preferring ministers who avoided controversy, the Boston parishes followed the Unitarian movement, and gradually filled their pulpits with young men. The Unitarian clergy soon won for themselves and for their city a name beyond proportion with their numbers.

Joseph Stevens Buckminster, the first, and while he lived the most influential, of these preachers, began his career in 1805 by accepting a call from one of the old Boston churches. He died in 1812 at the close of his twenty-eighth year. His influence was rather social and literary than theological or controversial. During his lifetime the Unitarian movement took no definite shape, except as a centre of revived interest in all that was then supposed to be best and purest in religious, literary,

and artistic feeling. After his death, Unitarians learned to regard William Ellery Channing as their most promising leader.
Channing had accepted the charge of a Boston church as early
as 1803, and was about four years older than Buckminster.
A third active member of the Boston clergy was Samuel Cooper
Thacher, who took charge of a Boston parish in 1811, and was
five years younger than Channing. In all, some seven or eight
churches were then called Unitarian; but they professed no
uniform creed, and probably no two clergymen or parishes
agreed in their understanding of the precise difference between
them and the Orthodox church. Shades of difference distinguished each Unitarian parish from every other, and the degree
of their divergence from the old creed was a subject of constant
interest and private discussion, although the whole body of
churches, Congregational as well as Unitarian, remained in external repose.

The calm was not broken until the close of the war relieved
New England from a political anxiety which for fifteen years
had restrained internal dissensions. No sooner did peace restore to New England the natural course of its intellectual
movement than the inevitable schism broke out. In June, 1815,
the "Panoplist," the mouthpiece of the Congregational clergy,
published an article charging the Unitarians with pursuing an
unavowed propaganda, and calling upon the Church to refuse
them communion. Channing and his friends thought the attack
to require reply, and, after consultation, Channing published
a "Letter to the Rev. Samuel C. Thacher," which began a discussion and a theological movement of no slight interest to
American history.

Channing's theology at that time claimed no merit for originality. His letter to Thacher betrayed more temper than he
would afterward have shown; but in no particular was he more
earnest than in repelling the idea that he or his brethren were
innovators. In whatever points they disagreed, they were most
nearly unanimous in repudiating connection with the English
Unitarians who denied the divinity of Christ. Channing de-

clared "that a majority of our brethren believe that Jesus
Christ is more than man; that he existed before the world; that
he literally came from heaven to save our race; that he sus-
tains other offices than those of a teacher and witness to the
truth; and that he still acts for our benefit, and is our inter-
cessor with the Father." So far was Channing from wishing to
preach a new theology that he would gladly have accepted the
old had he thought it intelligible:

> It is from deep conviction that I have stated once and again
> that the differences between Unitarians and Trinitarians lie
> more in sounds than in ideas; that a barbarous phraseology is
> the chief wall of partition between these classes of Christians;
> and that could Trinitarians tell us what they mean, their system
> would generally be found little else than a mystical form of the
> Unitarian doctrine.

Calvinists could not be blamed for thinking that their vener-
able creed, the painful outcome of the closest and most strenuous reasoning known in the Christian world, was entitled to
more respect than to be called "little else than a mystical form
of the Unitarian doctrine." The Unitarians themselves scarcely
attempted to make the infinite more intelligible to the finite
by any new phraseology. They avowed a dislike for dogma as
their merit. During these early years they systematically
avoided controversy; in the pulpit they never assailed and seldom mentioned other forms of Christian faith, or even the
scheme of Trinity which caused their schism.

> So deeply are we convinced [said Channing's letter] that
> the great end of preaching is to promote a spirit of love, a sober,
> righteous, and godly life, and that every doctrine is to be urged
> simply and exclusively for this end, that we have sacrificed our
> ease, and have chosen to be less striking preachers rather than
> to enter the lists of controversy.

Yet the popular dislike of Calvinistic severity could not
wholly make good the want of doctrinal theology. The Unitarian clergy, however unwilling to widen the breach between
themselves and the old Church, were ill at ease under the chal-

lenges of Orthodox critics, and could not escape the necessity
of defining their belief.

According to your own concession [rejoined Dr. Samuel
Worcester to Channing's letter], the party in whose behalf you
plead generally deny the essential divinity of the Saviour, and
hold him to be a being entirely "distinct from God," entirely
"dependent"—in other words, a mere creature. . . . You doubtless do not suppose that by any mere creature atonement could
be made for the sins of an apostate world of sufficient merit for
the pardon, sanctification, and eternal salvation of all who
should trust in him; therefore if you hold to atonement in any
sense, yet unquestionably not in the sense of a proper propi-
tiatory sacrifice. Upon this denial of atonement must follow
of course the denial of pardon procured by the blood of Christ,
of justification through faith in him, of redemption from eternal
death unto everlasting life by him. Connected, and generally if
not invariably concomitant, with the denial of these doctrines
is a denial of the Holy Spirit in his personal character and
offices, and of the renewal of mankind unto holiness by his
sovereign agency, as held by Orthodox Christians. Now, sir, are
these small and trivial points of difference between you and us?

Channing protested against these inferences; but he did not
deny—indeed, he affirmed—that Unitarians regarded dogma
as unnecessary to salvation. "In our judgment of professed
Christians," he replied, "we are guided more by their temper
and lives than by any peculiarities of opinion. We lay it down
as a great and indisputable opinion, clear as the sun at noon-
day, that the great end for which Christian truth is revealed
is the sanctification of the soul, the formation of the Christian
character; and wherever we see the marks of this character displayed in a professed disciple of Jesus, we hope, and rejoice
to hope, that he has received all the truth which is necessary
to his salvation." The hope might help to soothe anxiety and
distress, but it defied conclusions reached by the most anxious
and often renewed labors of churchmen for eighteen hundred
years. Something more than a hope was necessary as the foundation of a faith.

Not until the year 1819, did Channing quit the cautious attitude he at first assumed. Then, in his "Sermon on the Ordination of Jared Sparks" at Baltimore, he accepted the obligation to define his relation to Christian doctrine, and with the support of Andrews Norton, Henry Ware, and other Unitarian clergymen gave a doctrinal character to the movement. With this phase of his influence the present story has nothing to do. In the intellectual development of the country, the earlier stage of Unitarianism was more interesting than the later, for it marked a general tendency of national thought. At a time when Boston grew little in population and but moderately in wealth, and when it was regarded with antipathy, both political and religious, by a vast majority of the American people, its society had never been so agreeable or so fecund. No such display of fresh and winning genius had yet been seen in America as was offered by the genial outburst of intellectual activity in the early days of the Unitarian schism. No more was heard of the Westminster doctrine that man had lost all ability of will to any spiritual good accompanying salvation, but was dead in sin. So strong was the reaction against old dogmas that for thirty years society seemed less likely to resume the ancient faith in the Christian Trinity than to establish a new Trinity, in which a deified humanity should have place. Under the influence of Channing and his friends, human nature was adorned with virtues hardly suspected before, and with hopes of perfection on earth altogether strange to theology. The Church then charmed. The worth of man became under Channing's teachings a source of pride and joy, with such insistence as to cause his hearers at last to recall, almost with a sense of relief, that the Saviour himself had been content to regard them only as of more value than many sparrows.

The most remarkable quality of Unitarianism was its high social and intellectual character. The other more popular religious movements followed for the most part a less ambitious path, but were marked by the same humanitarian tendency. In contrast with old stringency of thought, the religious activity of the epoch showed warmth of emotion. The elder Buckminster, a consistent Calvinist clergyman, settled at Portsmouth in New Hampshire, while greatly distressed by his son's leanings toward loose theology, was at the same time obliged to witness the success of other opinions, which he thought monstrous, preached by Hosea Ballou, an active minister in the same town. This new doctrine, which took the name of Universalism, held as an article of faith "that there is one God, whose nature is love, revealed in one Lord Jesus Christ, by one Holy Spirit of grace, who will finally restore the whole family of mankind to holiness and happiness." In former times any one who had publicly professed belief in universal salvation would not have been regarded as a Christian. With equal propriety he might have preached the divinity of Ammon or Diana. To the old theology one god was as strange as the other; and so deeply impressed was Dr. Buckminster with this conviction, that he felt himself constrained in the year 1809 to warn Hosea Ballou of his error, in a letter pathetic for its conscientious self-restraint. Yet the Universalists steadily grew in numbers and respectability, spreading from State to State under Ballou's guidance, until they became as well-established and as respectable a church as that to which Buckminster belonged.

A phenomenon still more curious was seen in the same year, 1809, in western Pennsylvania. Near the banks of the Monongahela, in Washington County, a divergent branch of Scotch Presbyterianism established a small church, and under the guidance of Thomas Campbell, a recent emigrant from Scotland, issued, Sept. 7, 1809, a Declaration:

Being well aware from sad experience of the heinous nature and pernicious tendency of religious controversy among Christians, tired and sick of the bitter jarrings and janglings of a party spirit, we would desire to be at rest; and were it possible, would also desire to adopt and recommend such measures as would give rest to our brethren throughout all the churches, as would restore unity, peace, and purity to the whole Church of God. This desirable rest, however, we utterly despair either to find for ourselves, or to be able to recommend to our brethren, by continuing amid the diversity and rancor of party contentions the varying uncertainty and clashings of human opinions; nor indeed can we reasonably expect to find it anywhere but in Christ and his simple word, which is the same yesterday, to-day, and forever. Our desire, therefore, for ourselves and our brethren would be that rejecting human opinions and the inventions of men as of any authority, or as having any place in the Church of God, we might forever cease from further contentions about such things, returning to and holding fast by the original standard.

Campbell's Declaration expressed so wide a popular want that his church, in a few years, became one of the largest branches of the great Baptist persuasion. Perhaps in these instances of rapid popular grouping, love of peace was to some extent supplemented by jealousy of learning, and showed as much spirit of social independence as of religious instinct. The growth of vast popular sects in a democratic community might testify to intellectual stagnation as well as to religious or social earnestness; but whatever was the amount of thought involved in such movements, one character was common to them all, as well as to the Unitarians—they agreed in relaxing the strictness of theological reasoning. Channing united with Campbell in suggesting that the Church should ignore what it could not comprehend. In a popular and voluntary form they proposed self-restraints which should have the same effect as the formal restraints of the hierarchies. "Rejecting," like Campbell, "human opinions and the inventions of men"—preaching, like Channing and Ballou, "that there is one God, whose nature is love," and that doctrine was useless except to promote a spirit of love—they founded new churches on what seemed to resemble an argument that the intellectual difficulties in their path must be unessential because they were insuperable.

Wide as the impulse was to escape the rigor of bonds and relax the severity of thought, organizations so deeply founded as the old churches were not capable of destruction. They had seen many similar human efforts, and felt certain that sooner or later such experiments must end in a return to the old standards. Even the Congregational Church of New England, though reduced in Boston to a shadow of its old authority, maintained itself at large against its swarm of enemies—Unitarian, Universalist, Baptist, Methodist—resisting, with force of character and reasoning, the looseness of doctrine and vagueness of thought which marked the time. Yale College remained true to it. Most of the parishes maintained their old relations. If the congregations in some instances crumbled away or failed to increase, the Church could still stand erect, and might reflect with astonishment on its own strength, which survived so long a series of shocks apparently fatal. For half a century the Congregational clergy had struggled to prevent innovation, while the people emigrated by hundreds of thousands in order to innovate. Obliged to insist on the infinite justice rather than on the infinite mercy of God, they shocked the instincts of the new generation, which wanted to enjoy worldly blessings without fear of future reckoning. Driven to bay by the deistic and utilitarian principles of Jefferson's democracy, they fell into the worldly error of defying the national instinct, pressing their resistance to the war until it amounted to treasonable conspiracy. The sudden peace swept away much that was respectable in the old society of America, but perhaps its noblest victim was the unity of the New England Church.

The Church, whether Catholic or Protestant, Lutheran or Calvinistic, always rested in the conviction that every divergence from the great highways of religious thought must be temporary, and that no permanent church was possible except on foundations already established; but the State stood in a position less self-confident. The old principles of government were less carefully developed, and Democrats in politics were more certain than Unitarians or Universalists in theology that their intellectual conclusions made a stride in the progress of thought. Yet the sixteen years with which the century opened were singularly barren of new political ideas. Apparently the extreme activity which marked the political speculations of the period between 1775 and 1800, both in America and in Europe, had exhausted the energy of society, for Americans showed interest only in the practical working of their experiments, and added nothing to the ideas that underlay them. With such political thought as society produced, these pages have been chiefly filled; the result has been told. The same tendency which in religion led to reaction against dogma, was shown in politics by general acquiescence in practices which left unsettled the disputed principles of government. No one could say with confidence what theory of the Constitution had prevailed. Neither party was satisfied, although both acquiesced. While the Legislative and Executive branches of the government acted on no fixed principle, but established precedents at variance with any consistent theory, the Judiciary rendered so few decisions that Constitutional law stood nearly still. Only at a later time did Chief-Justice Marshall begin his great series of judicial opinions —McCulloch against the State of Maryland in 1819; Dartmouth College in the same year; Cohens against the State of Virginia in 1821. No sooner were these decisive rulings announced, than they roused the last combative energies of Jefferson against his old enemy the Judiciary: "That body, like gravity, ever acting, with noiseless foot and unalarming advance, gaining ground step by step, and holding what it gains, is engulfing insidiously the special governments."

Marshall had few occasions to decide Constitutional points during the Administrations of Jefferson and Madison, but the opinions he gave were emphatic. When Pennsylvania in 1809 resisted, in the case of Gideon Olmstead, a process of the Supreme Court, the chief-justice, without unnecessary words, declared that "if the legislature of the several States may at will annul the judgments of the courts of the United States, and destroy the rights acquired under those judgments, the Constitution itself becomes a solemn mockery, and the nation is deprived of the means of enforcing its laws by the instrumentality of its own tribunals." Pennsylvania yielded; and Marshall, in the following year, carried a step further the authority of his court. He overthrew the favorite dogma of John Randolph and the party of States rights, so long and vehemently maintained in the Yazoo dispute.

The Yazoo claims came before the court in the case of

Fletcher against Peck, argued first in 1809 by Luther Martin, J. Q. Adams, and Robert G. Harper; and again in 1810 by Martin, Harper, and Joseph Story. March 16, 1810, the chief-justice delivered the opinion. Declining, as "indecent in the extreme," to enter into an inquiry as to the corruption of "the sovereign power of a State," he dealt with the issue whether a legislature could annul rights vested in an individual by a law in its nature a contract.

It may well be doubted [he argued], whether the nature of society and government does not prescribe some limits to the legislative power; and if any are to be prescribed, where are they to be found if the property of an individual, fairly and honestly acquired, may be seized without compensation? To the legislature all legislative power is granted; but the question whether the act of transferring the property of an individual to the public be in the nature of the legislative power, is well worthy of serious reflection. It is the peculiar province of the legislature to prescribe general rules for the government of society: the application of those rules to individuals in society would seem to be the duty of other departments. How far the power of giving the law may involve every other power, in cases where the Constitution is silent, never has been and perhaps never can be definitely stated.

In the case under consideration, Marshall held that the Constitution was not silent. The provision that no State could pass any law impairing the obligation of contracts, as well as "the general principles which are common to our free institutions," restrained the State of Georgia from passing a law whereby the previous contract could be rendered void. His decision settled, as far as concerned the Judiciary, a point regarded as vital by the States-rights school. Four years afterward Congress gave the required compensation for the contract broken by Georgia.

The chief-justice rendered no more leading Constitutional decisions during Madison's term of office; but his influence was seen in a celebrated opinion delivered by Justice Story in 1816, in the case of Martin against Hunter's Lessee. There the court came in conflict with the State of Virginia. The Court of Appeals of that State refused to obey a mandate of the Supreme Court, alleging that the proceedings of the Supreme Court were *coram non judice,* or beyond its jurisdiction, being founded on section 25 of the Judiciary Act of 1789, which was unconstitutional in extending the appellate jurisdiction of the Supreme Court over the State courts.

The Court of Appeals was unfortunate in the moment of its resistance to the authority of the national courts. While the case was passing through its last stage peace was declared, and the national authority sprang into vigor unknown before. The chief-justice would not with his own hand humiliate the pride of the Court of Appeals, for which as a Virginian and a lawyer he could feel only deep respect. He devolved the unpleasant duty on young Justice Story, whose own State of Massachusetts was then far from being an object of jealousy to Virginia, and who, a Republican in politics, could not be prejudiced by party feeling against the Virginia doctrine. Much of the opinion bore the stamp of Marshall's mind; much showed the turn of Story's intelligence; yet the same principle lay beneath the whole, and no one could detect a divergence between the Federalism of the Virginia chief-justice and the Democracy of the Massachusetts lawyer.

It has been argued [said the court] that such an appellate jurisdiction over State courts is inconsistent with the genius of our governments and the spirit of the Constitution; that the latter was never designed to act upon State sovereignties, but only upon the people; and that if the power exists, it will materially impair the sovereignty of the States and the independence of their courts. We cannot yield to the force of this reasoning; it assumes principles which we cannot admit, and draws conclusions to which we do not yield our assent. It is a mistake that the Constitution was not designed to operate upon States in their corporate capacity. It is crowded with provisions which restrain or annul the sovereignty of the States in some of the highest branches of their prerogatives. . . . When, therefore, the States are stripped of some of the highest attributes of sovereignty, and the same are given to the United States; when the legislatures of the States are in some respects under the control of Congress, and in every case are, under the Constitution, bound by the paramount authority of the United States—it is certainly difficult to support the argument that the appellate power over the decisions of State courts is contrary to the genius of our institutions.

So far were the political principles of the people from having united in a common understanding, that while the Supreme Court of the United States thus differed from the Virginia Court of Appeals in regard to the genius of the government and the spirit of the Constitution, Jefferson still publicly maintained that the national and state governments were "as independent, in fact, as different nations," and that the function of one was foreign, while that of the other was domestic. Madison still declared that Congress could not build a road or clear a watercourse; while Congress believed itself authorized to do both, and in that belief passed a law which Madison vetoed. In politics as in theology, the practical system which resulted from sixteen years of experience seemed to rest on the agreement not to press principles to a conclusion.

No new idea was brought forward, and the old ideas, though apparently incapable of existing together, continued to exist in rivalry like that of the dogmas which perplexed the theological world; but between the political and religious movement a distinct difference could be seen. The Church showed no tendency to unite in any creed or dogma—indeed, religious society rather tended to more divisions; but in politics public opinion slowly moved in a fixed direction. The movement could not easily be measured, and was subject to reaction; but its reality was shown by the protests of Jefferson, the veto of Madison, and the decisions of the Supreme Court. No one doubted that a change had occurred since 1798. The favorite States-rights dogma of that time had suffered irreparable injury. For sixteen years the national government in all its branches had acted, without listening to remonstrance, on the rule that it was the rightful interpreter of its own powers. In this assumption the Executive, the Legislature, and the Judiciary had agreed.

Massachusetts and Pennsylvania, as well as Virginia and Georgia, yielded. Louisiana had been bought and admitted into the Union; the Embargo had been enforced; one National Bank had been destroyed and another established; every essential function of a sovereignty had been performed, without an instance of failure, though not without question. However unwilling the minority might be to admit in theory the overthrow of their principles, every citizen assented in daily practice to the rule that the national government alone interpreted its own powers in the last resort. From the moment the whole people learned to accept the practice, the dispute over theory lost importance, and the Virginia Resolutions of 1798 marked only a stage in the development of a sovereignty.

The nature of the sovereignty that was to be the result of American political experiment, the amount of originality which could be infused into an idea so old, was a matter for future history to settle. Many years were likely to elapse before the admitted practice of the government and people could be fully adopted into the substance of their law, but the process thus far had been rapid. In the brief space of thirty years, between 1787 and 1817—a short generation—the Union had passed through astonishing stages. Probably no great people ever grew more rapidly and became more mature in so short a time. The ideas of 1787 were antiquated in 1815, and lingered only in districts remote from active movement. The subsidence of interest in political theories was a measure of the change, marking the general drift of society toward practical devices for popular use, within popular intelligence. The only work that could be said to represent a school of thought in politics was written by John Taylor of Caroline, and was probably never read—or if read, certainly never understood—north of Baltimore by any but curious and somewhat deep students, although to them it had value.

John Taylor of Caroline might without irreverence be described as a *vox clamantis*—the voice of one crying in the wilderness. Regarded as a political thinker of the first rank by

Jefferson, Monroe, John Randolph, and the Virginia school, he admitted, with the geniality of the class to which he belonged, that his disciples invariably deserted in practice the rules they praised in his teaching; but he continued to teach, and the further his scholars drifted from him the more publicly and profusely he wrote. His first large volume, "An Inquiry into the Principles and Policy of the Government of the United States," published in 1814, during the war, was in form an answer to John Adams's "Defence of the Constitutions" published in London twenty-five years before. In 1787 John Adams, like Jefferson, Hamilton, Madison, Jay, and other constitution-makers, might, without losing the interest of readers, indulge in speculations more or less visionary in regard to the future character of a nation yet in its cradle; but in 1814 the character of people and government was formed; the lines of their activity were fixed. A people which had in 1787 been indifferent or hostile to roads, banks, funded debt, and nationality, had become in 1815 habituated to ideas and machinery of the sort on a great scale. Monarchy or aristocracy no longer entered into the public mind as factors in future development. Yet Taylor resumed the discussions of 1787 as though the interval were a blank; and his only conclusion from the experience of thirty years was that both political parties were equally moving in a wrong direction.

The two parties, called Republican and Federal [he concluded], have hitherto undergone but one revolution. Yet each when in power preached Filmer's old doctrine of passive obedience in a new form, with considerable success; and each, out of power, strenuously controverted it. The party in power asserted that however absurd or slavish this doctrine was under other forms of the numerical analysis, the people under ours were *identified* (the new term to cog this old doctrine upon the United States) with the government; and that therefore an opposition to the government was an opposition to the nation itself. . . . This identifying doctrine . . . puts an end to the idea of a responsibility of the government to the nation; . . . it renders useless the freedom of speech and of the press; it converts the representative into the principal; it destroys the division of power between the people and the government, as being themselves indivisible; and in short it is inconsistent with every principle by which politicians and philosophers have hitherto defined a free government.

The principle to which Taylor so strenuously objected was nevertheless the chief political result of national experience. Somewhere or another a point was always reached where opposition became treasonable—as Virginia, like Massachusetts, had learned both when in power and when out. Taylor's speculations ended only in an admission of their own practical sterility, and his suggestions for restraining the growth of authority assumed the possibility of returning to the conditions of 1787. Banks were his horror. Stocks and bonds, or paper evidences of indebtedness in any form, he thought destructive to sound principles of government. The Virginia and Kentucky Resolutions of 1798 were his best resource for the preservation of civil liberty. However well-founded his fears might be, his correctives could no longer be applied. Political philosophers of all ages were fond of devising systems for imaginary Republics, Utopias, and Oceanas, where practical difficulties could not stand in their way. Taylor was a political philosopher of the same school, and his Oceana on the banks of the Rappahannock was a reflection of his own virtues.

Literature and Art

SOCIETY showed great interest in the statesmen or preachers who won its favor, and earnestly discussed the value of political or religious dogmas, without betraying a wish to subject itself ever again to the rigor of a strict creed in politics or religion. In a similar spirit it touched here and there, with a light hand, the wide circuit of what was called *belles lettres*, without showing severity either in taste or temper.

For the first four or five years of the century, Dennie's "Portfolio" contained almost everything that was produced in the United States under the form of light literature. The volumes of the "Portfolio" for that period had the merit of representing the literary efforts of the time, for Philadelphia insisted on no standard of taste so exacting as to exclude merit, or even dulness, in any literary form. Jacobins, as Dennie called Democrats, were not admitted into the circle of the "Portfolio"; but Jacobins rarely troubled themselves with *belles lettres*.

The "Portfolio" reflected a small literary class scattered throughout the country, remarkable chiefly for close adhesion to established English ideas. The English standard was then extravagantly Tory, and the American standard was the same. At first sight the impression was strange. A few years later, no ordinary reader could remember that ideas so illiberal had seriously prevailed among educated Americans. By an effort, elderly men could, in the next generation, recall a time when they had been taught that Oliver Cromwell was a monster of wickedness and hypocrisy; but they could hardly believe that at any period an American critic coldly qualified "Paradise Lost," and "Avenge, O Lord, thy slaughtered saints," as good poetry, though written by a Republican and an enemy of established order. This was the tone of Dennie's criticism, and so little was it confined to him that even young Buckminster, in his Phi Beta Kappa Oration of 1809, which was regarded as making almost an epoch in American literature, spoke of Milton's eyes as "quenched in the service of a vulgar and usurping faction," and of Milton's life as "a memorable instance of the temporary degradation of learning." Buckminster was then remonstrating against the influence of politics upon letters rather than expressing a political sentiment, but his illustration was colored by the general prejudices of British Toryism. Half a century before, Dr. Johnson had taken the tone of Tory patronage toward Milton's genius, and Johnson and Burke were still received in America as final authorities for correct opinion in morals, literature, and politics. The "Portfolio" regarded Johnson not only as a "superlative" moralist and politician, but also as a "sublime" critic and a "transcendent" poet. Burke and Cicero stood on the same level, as masters before whose authority criticism must silently bow.

Yet side by side with these conventional standards, the "Portfolio" showed tendencies which seemed inconsistent with conservatism—a readiness to welcome literary innovations contradicting every established canon. No one would have supposed that the critic who accepted Johnson and Pope as transcendent poets, should also delight in Burns and Wordsworth; yet Dennie was unstinted in praise of poetry which, as literature, was hardly less revolutionary than the writings of Godwin in politics. Dennie lost no opportunity of praising Coleridge, and reprinted with enthusiasm the simplest ballads of Wordsworth. Moore was his personal friend, and Moore's verses his models. Wherever his political prejudices were untouched, he loved novelty. He seemed to respect classical authority only because it was established, but his literary instincts were broader than those of Jefferson.

The original matter of the "Portfolio" was naturally unequal, and for the most part hardly better than that of a college magazine. Dennie was apt to be commonplace, trivial, and dull. His humor was heavy and commonly coarse; he allowed himself entire freedom, and no little grossness of taste. Of scholarship, or scholarly criticism, his paper showed great want. He tried to instruct as well as to amuse, but society soon passed the stage to which his writing belonged. The circulation of the "Port-folio" probably never exceeded fifteen hundred copies, and Dennie constantly complained that the paper barely supported itself. When the Bostonians, in the year 1805, began to feel the spirit of literary ambition, they took at once a stride beyond Dennie's power, and established a monthly magazine called the "Anthology and Boston Review," which in 1806 numbered four hundred and forty subscribers. The undertaking was doubly remarkable; for the Anthology Society which supported the Review combined with it the collection of a library, limited at first to periodical publications, which expanded slowly into the large and useful library known as the Boston Athenaeum. The Review and Library quickly became the centre of literary taste in Boston, and, in the words of Josiah Quincy many years after-ward, might be considered as a revival of polite learning in America. The claim was not unreasonable, for the Review far surpassed any literary standards then existing in the United States, and was not much inferior to any in England; for the Edinburgh was established only in 1802, and the Quarterly not till 1809.

The Anthology Society, which accomplished the feat of giv-ing to Boston for the first time the lead of American literary effort, consisted largely of clergymen, and represented, perhaps unintentionally, the coming Unitarian movement. Its president and controlling spirit had no sympathy with either division of the Congregational Church, but was a clergyman of the Church of England. John Sylvester John Gardiner, the rector of Trinity, occupied a peculiar position in Boston. Of American descent, but English birth and education, he was not prevented by the isolation of his clerical character from taking an active part in affairs, and his activity was sometimes greater than his discretion. His political sermons rivalled those of the Congre-gational ministers Osgood and Parish, in their violence against Jefferson and the national government; his Federalism was that of the Essex Junto, with a more decided leaning to disunion;

but he was also an active and useful citizen, ready to take his share in every good work. When he became president of the Anthology Society, he was associated with a clergyman of Unitarian opinions as vice-president—the Rev. William Emerson, a man of high reputation in his day, but better known in after years as the father of Ralph Waldo Emerson. The first editor was Samuel Cooper Thacher, to whom, ten years afterward, Channing addressed his earliest controversial letter. Young Buckminster and William Tudor, a Boston man, who for the next twenty years was active in the literary life of Massachusetts, were also original members. The staff of the "Anthology" was greatly superior to ordinary editorial resources; and in a short time the Review acquired a reputation for ability and sharpness of temper never wholly forgiven. Its unpopularity was the greater because its aggressiveness took the form of assaults on Calvinism, which earned the ill-will of the Congregational clergy.

Buckminster and Channing were the editor's closest friends, and their liberality of thought was remarkable for the time and place; yet the point from which the liberality of Boston started would have been regarded in most parts of the Union as conservative. Channing's fear of France and attachment to England were superstitious.

I will not say [began his Fast Day Sermon in 1810] that the present age is as strongly marked or distinguished from all other ages as that in which Jesus Christ appeared; but with that single exception, perhaps the present age is the most eventful the world has ever known. We live in times which have no parallel in past ages; in times when the human character has almost assumed a new form; in time of peculiar calamity, of thick darkness, and almost of despair. . . . The danger is so vast, so awful, and so obvious, that the blindness, the indifference, which prevail argue infatuation, and give room for apprehension that nothing can rouse us to those efforts by which alone the danger can be averted. Am I asked what there is so peculiar and so tremendous in the times in which we live? . . . I answer: In the very heart of Europe, in the centre of the

civilized world, a new power has suddenly arisen on the ruins
of old institutions, peculiar in its character, and most ruinous
in its influence.

While Channing felt for France the full horror of his Federalist principles, he regarded England with equivalent affection.

I feel a peculiar interest in England [he explained in a note
appended to the Fast Day Sermon]; for I believe that there
Christianity is exerting its best influences on the human character; that there the perfections of human nature, wisdom,
virtue, and piety are fostered by excellent institutions, and are
producing the delightful fruits of domestic happiness, social
order, and general prosperity.

The majority of Americans took a different view of the subject; but even those who most strongly agreed with Channing
would have been first to avow that their prejudice was invet-
erate, and its consequences sweeping. Such a conviction admitted little room for liberalism where politics were, directly
or remotely, involved. Literature bordered closely on politics,
and the liberalism of Unitarian Boston was bounded even in
literature by the limits of British sympathies. Buckminster's
Phi Beta Kappa Oration of 1809 was as emphatic on this point
as Channing's Fast Day Sermon of 1810 was outspoken in its
political antipathies.

It is our lot [said Buckminster] to have been born in an age
of tremendous revolution, and the world is yet covered with
the wrecks of its ancient glory, especially of its literary renown.
The fury of that storm which rose in France is passed and spent,
but its effects have been felt through the whole system of liberal
education. The foul spirit of innovation and sophistry has been
seen wandering in the very groves of the Lyceum, and is not
yet completely exorcised, though the spell is broken.

The liberalism of Boston began in a protest against "the foul
spirit of innovation," and could hardly begin at any point
more advanced. "Infidelity has had one triumph in our days,
and we have seen learning as well as virtue trampled under the
hoofs of its infuriated steeds, let loose by the hand of impiety."

From this attitude of antipathy to innovation, the Unitarian movement began its attempts to innovate, and with astonishing rapidity passed through phases which might well have required ages of growth. In five years Channing began open attack upon the foundation, or what had hitherto been believed the foundation, of the Church; and from that moment innovation could no longer be regarded as foul.

Of the intellectual movement in all its new directions, Harvard College was the centre. Between 1805 and 1817 the college inspired the worn-out Federalism of Boston with life till then unimagined. Not only did it fill the pulpits with Buckminsters, Channings, and Thachers, whose sermons were an unfailing interest, and whose society was a constant stimulus, but it also maintained a rivalry between the pulpit and the lecture-room. The choice of a new professor was as important and as much discussed as the choice of a new minister. No ordinary political event caused more social interest than the appointment of Henry Ware as Professor of Theology in 1805. In the following year J. Q. Adams was made Professor of Rhetoric, and delivered a course of lectures, which created the school of oratory to which Edward Everett's generation adhered. Four younger men, whose influence was greatly felt in their branches of instruction, received professorships in the next few years—Jacob Bigelow, who was appointed Professor of Medicine in 1813; Edward Everett, Greek Professor in 1815; John Collins Warren, Professor of Anatomy in the same year; and George Ticknor, Professor of *Belles Lettres* in 1816. In the small society of Boston, a city numbering hardly forty thousand persons, this activity of college and church produced a new era. Where thirty-nine students a year had entered the college before 1800, an average number of sixty-six entered it during the war, and took degrees during the four or five subsequent years. Among them were names familiar to the literature and politics of the next half century. Besides Ticknor and Everett, in 1807 and 1811, Henry Ware graduated in 1812, and his brother William, the author of "Zenobia," in 1816; William Hickling Prescott, in 1814; J. G.

Palfrey, in 1815; in 1817, George Bancroft and Caleb Cushing graduated, and Ralph Waldo Emerson entered the college. Boston also drew resources from other quarters, and perhaps showed no stronger proof of its vigor than when, in 1816, it attracted Daniel Webster from New Hampshire to identify himself with the intellect and interests of Massachusetts. Even by reaction the Unitarians stimulated Boston—as when, a few years afterward, Lyman Beecher accepted the charge of a Boston church in order to resist their encroachments.

The "Anthology," which marked the birth of the new literary school, came in a few years to a natural end, but was revived in 1815 under the name of the "North American Review," by the exertions of William Tudor. The life of the new Review belonged to a later period, and was shaped by other influences than those that surrounded the "Anthology." With the beginning of the next epoch, the provincial stage of the Boston school was closed. More and more its influence tended to become national, and even to affect other countries. Perhaps by a natural consequence rather than by coincidence, the close of the old period was marked by the appearance of a short original poem in the "North American Review" for September, 1817—

> . . . The hills,
> Rock-ribbed and ancient as the sun; the vales
> Stretching in pensive quietness between;
> The venerable woods; the floods that move
> In majesty, and the complaining brooks
> That wind among the meads and make them green—
> Are but the solemn declarations all,
> Of the great tomb of man. The golden sun,
> The planets, all the infinite host of heaven
> Are glowing on the sad abodes of death
> Through the still lapse of ages. All that tread
> The globe are but a handful to the tribes
> That slumber in its bosom. Take the wings
> Of morning, and the Borean desert pierce;
> Or lose thyself in the continuous woods
> That veil Oregan, where he hears no sound
> Save his own dashings—yet the dead are there;

And millions in these solitudes, since first
The flight of years began, have laid them down
In their last sleep: the dead reign there alone.
So shalt thou rest: and what if thou shalt fall
Unnoticed by the living, and no friend
Take note of thy departure?   Thousands more
Will share thy destiny.   The tittering world
Dance to the grave.   The busy brood of care
Plod on, and each one chases as before
His favorite phantom.   Yet all these shall leave
Their mirth and their employments, and shall come
And make their bed with thee.

The appearance of "Thanatopsis" and "Lines to a Water-
fowl" in the early numbers of the "North American Review,"
while leaving no doubt that a new national literature was close
at hand, proved also that it was not to be the product of a
single source; for Bryant, though greatly tempted to join the
Emersons, Channing, Dana, Allston, and Tudor in Boston,
turned finally to New York, where influences of a different kind
surrounded him. The Unitarian school could not but take a
sober cast, and even its humor was sure to be tinged with sad-
ness, sarcasm, or irony, or some serious purpose or passion; but
New York contained no atmosphere in which such a society
could thrive. Busy with the charge of practical work—the development of industries continually exceeding their power of
control—the people of New York wanted amusement, and
shunned what in Boston was considered as intellectual. Their
tastes were gratified by the appearance of a writer whose first
book created a school of literature as distinctly marked as the
Unitarian school of Boston, and more decidedly original. "The
History of New York, by Diedrich Knickerbocker," appeared
in 1809, and stood alone. Other books of the time seemed to
recognize some literary parentage. Channing and Buckminster
were links in a chain of theologians and preachers. "Thanatopsis" evidently drew inspiration from Wordsworth. Diedrich
Knickerbocker owed nothing to any living original.

The "History of New York" was worth more than passing

notice. In the development of a national character, as well as
of the literature that reflected it, humor was a trait of the
utmost interest; and Washington Irving was immediately recognized as a humorist whose name, if he fulfilled the promise
of his first attempt, would have a chance of passing into the
society of Rabelais, Cervantes, Butler, and Sterne. Few literary
tasks were more difficult than to burlesque without vulgarizing,
and to satirize without malignity; yet Irving in his first effort
succeeded in doing both. The old families, and serious students
of colonial history, never quite forgave Irving for throwing an
atmosphere of ridicule over the subject of their interest; but
Diedrich Knickerbocker's History was so much more entertaining than ordinary histories, that even historians could be excused for regretting that it should not be true.

Yet the book reflected the political passions which marked
the period of the Embargo. Besides the burlesque, the "History"
contained satire; and perhaps its most marked trait was the
good-nature which, at a time when bitterness was universal in
politics, saved Irving's political satire from malignity. Irving
meant that no one should mistake the character of the universal genius, Governor Wilhelmus Kieft, surnamed the Testy,
who as a youth had made many curious investigations into the
nature and operations of windmills, and who came well-nigh
being smothered in a slough of unintelligible learning—"a fearful peril, from the effects of which he never perfectly recovered."

No sooner had this bustling little man been blown by a whiff
of fortune into the seat of government, than he called together
his council and delivered a very animated speech on the affairs
of the government; . . . and here he soon worked himself into
a fearful rage against the Yankees, whom he compared to the
Gauls who desolated Rome, and to the Goths and Vandals who
overran the fairest plains of Europe. . . . Having thus artfully
wrought up his tale of terror to a climax, he assumed a self-
satisfied look, and declared with a nod of knowing import that
he had taken measures to put a final stop to these encroachments—that he had been obliged to have recourse to a dreadful
engine of warfare, lately invented, awful in its effects but author-

ized by direful necessity; in a word, he was resolved to conquer
the Yankees—by Proclamation.

Washington Irving's political relations were those commonly
known as Burrite, through his brother Peter, who edited in
Burr's interest the "Morning Chronicle." Antipathy to Jefferson
was a natural result, and Irving's satire on the President was
the more interesting because the subject offered temptations
for ill-tempered sarcasm such as spoiled Federalist humor. The
Knickerbocker sketch of Jefferson was worth comparing with
Federalist modes of expressing the same ideas—

The great defect of Wilhelmus Kieft's policy was that though
no man could be more ready to stand forth in an hour of emergency, yet he was so intent upon guarding the national pocket
that he suffered the enemy to break its head. . . . All this was
a remote consequence of his education at the Hague; where,
having acquired a smattering of knowledge, he was ever a great
conner of indexes, continually dipping into books without ever
studying to the bottom of any subject, so that he had the scum
of all kinds of authors fermenting in his pericranium. In some
of these titlepage researches he unluckily stumbled over a grand
political *cabalistic word*, which with his customary facility he
immediately incorporated into his great scheme of government,
to the irretrievable injury and delusion of the honest province
of Nieuw Nederlands, and the eternal misleading of all experi-
mental rulers.

Little was wanting to make such a sketch bitter; but Irving
seemed to have the power of deadening venom by a mere trick
of hand. Readers of the "History," after a few years had passed,
rarely remembered the satire, or supposed that the story contained it. The humor and the style remained to characterize a
school.

The originality of the Knickerbocker humor was the more
remarkable because it was allowed to stand alone. Irving published nothing else of consequence until 1819, and then, abandoning his early style, inclined to imitate Addison and Steele,
although his work was hardly the less original. Irving preceded
Walter Scott, whose "Waverley" appeared in 1814, and "Guy

Mannering" in 1815; and if either author could be said to influence the other, the influence of Diedrich Knickerbocker on Scott was more evident than that of "Waverley" on Irving.

In the face of the spontaneous burst of genius which at that moment gave to English literature and art a character distinct even in its own experience, Americans might have been excused for making no figure at all. Other periods produced one poet at a time, and measured originality by single poems; or satisfied their ambition by prose or painting of occasional merit. The nineteenth century began in England with genius as plenty as it was usually rare. To Beattie, Cowper, and Burns, succeeded Wordsworth, Coleridge, Scott, Byron, Crabbe, Campbell, Charles Lamb, Moore, Shelley, and Keats. The splendor of this combination threw American and even French talent into the shade, and defied hope of rivalry; but the American mind, as far as it went, showed both freshness and originality. The divergence of American from English standards seemed insignificant to critics who required, as they commonly did, a national literature founded on some new conception—such as the Shawanee or Aztecs could be supposed to suggest; but to those who expected only a slow variation from European types, the difference was well marked. Channing and Irving were American in literature, as Calhoun and Webster were American in politics. They were the product of influences as peculiar to the country as those which produced Fulton and his steamboat.

While Bryant published "Thanatopsis" and Irving made his studies for the "Sketch-Book," another American of genius perhaps superior to theirs—Washington Allston—was painting in London, before returning to pass the remainder of his life in the neighborhood of Boston and Harvard College. Between thirty and forty years of age, Allston was then in the prime of his powers; and even in a circle of artists which included Turner, Wilkie, Mulready, Constable, Callcott, Crome, Cotman, and a swarm of others equally famous, Allston was distinguished. Other Americans took rank in the same society. Leslie and Stuart Newton were adopted into it, and Copley died only in

1815, while Trumbull painted in London till 1816; but remarkable though they were for the quality of their art, they belonged to a British school, and could be claimed as American only by blood. Allston stood in a relation somewhat different. In part, his apparent Americanism was due to his later return, and to his identification with American society; but the return itself was probably caused by a peculiar bent of character. His mind was not wholly English.

Allston's art and his originality were not such as might have been expected from an American, or such as Americans were likely to admire; and the same might be said of Leslie and Stuart Newton. Perhaps the strongest instance of all was Edward Malbone, whose grace of execution was not more remarkable than his talent for elevating the subject of his exquisite work. So far from sharing the imagination of Shawanee Indians or even of Democrats, these men instinctively reverted to the most refined and elevated schools of art. Not only did Allston show from the beginning of his career a passion for the nobler standards of his profession, but also for technical quality—a taste less usual. Washington Irving met him in Rome in 1805, when both were unknown; and they became warm friends.

I do not think I have ever been more captivated on a first acquaintance [wrote Irving long afterward]. He was of a light and graceful form, with large blue eyes and black silken hair. Everything about him bespoke the man of intellect and refinement. . . . He was exquisitely sensitive to the graceful and the beautiful, and took great delight in paintings which excelled in color; yet he was strongly moved and aroused by objects of grandeur. I well recollect the admiration with which he contemplated the sublime statue of Moses, by Michael Angelo.

The same tastes characterized his life, and gave to his work a distinction that might be Italian, but was certainly not English or usual.

"It was Allston," said Leslie, "who first awakened what little sensibility I may possess to the beauties of color. For a long time I took the merit of the Venetians on trust, and if left to myself should have preferred works which I now feel to be comparatively worthless. I remember when the picture of 'The Ages' by Titian was first pointed out to me by Allston as an exquisite work, I thought he was laughing at me." Leslie, if not a great colorist, was seldom incorrect; Stuart Newton had a fine eye for color, and Malbone was emphatically a colorist; but Allston's sensibility to color was rare among artists, and the refinement of his mind was as unusual as the delicacy of his eye.

Allston was also singular in the liberality of his sympathies. "I am by nature, as it respects the arts, a wide liker," he said. In Rome he became acquainted with Coleridge; and the remark of Coleridge which seemed to make most impression on him in their walks "under the pines of the Villa Borghese" was evidently agreeable because it expressed his own feelings. "It was there he taught me this golden rule: never to judge of any work of art by its defects." His admiration for the classics did not prevent him from admiring his contemporaries; his journey through Switzerland not only showed him a new world of Nature, but also "the truth of Turner's Swiss scenes—the poetic truth—which none before or since have given." For a young American art-student in 1804, such sympathies were remarkable; not so much because they were correct, as because they were neither American nor English. Neither in America nor in Europe at that day could art-schools give to every young man, at the age of twenty-five, eyes to see the color of Titian, or imagination to feel the "poetic truth" of Turner.

Other painters, besides those whose names have been mentioned, were American or worked in America, as other writers beside Bryant and Irving, and other preachers besides Buckminster and Channing, were active in their professions; but for national comparisons, types alone serve. In the course of sixteen years certain Americans became distinguished. Among these, suitable for types, were Calhoun and Clay in Congress, Pinkney and Webster at the bar, Buckminster and Channing in the pulpit, Bryant and Irving in literature, Allston and Malbone in painting. These men varied greatly in character and qualities. Some possessed strength, and some showed more delicacy than vigor; some were humorists, and some were incapable of a thought that was not serious; but all were marked by a keen sense of form and style. So little was this quality expected, that the world inclined to regard them as un-American because of their refinement. Frenchmen and Italians, and even Englishmen who knew nothing of America but its wildness, were disappointed that American oratory should be only a variation from Fox and Burke; that American literature should reproduce Steele and Wordsworth; and that American art should, at its first bound, go back to the ideals of Raphael and Titian. The incongruity was evident. The Americans themselves called persistently for a statesmanship, religion, literature, and art which should be American; and they made a number of experiments to produce what they thought their ideals. In substance they continued to approve nothing which was not marked by style as its chief merit. The oratory of Webster and Calhoun, and even of John Randolph, bore the same general and common character of style. The poetry of Bryant, the humor of Irving, the sermons of Channing, and the painting of Allston were the objects of permanent approval to the national mind. Style remained its admiration, even when every newspaper protested against the imitation of outworn forms. Dennie and Jefferson, agreeing in nothing else, agreed in this; the South Carolinian Allston saw color as naturally as the New Englander Bryant heard rhythm; and a people which seemed devoid of sense or standards of beauty, showed more ambition than older societies to acquire both.

Nothing seemed more certain than that the Americans were not artistic, that they had as a people little instinct of beauty; but their intelligence in its higher as in its lower forms was both quick and refined. Such literature and art as they produced, showed qualities akin to those which produced the swift-sailing schooner, the triumph of naval architecture. If the artistic instinct weakened, the quickness of intelligence increased.

American Character

UNTIL 1815 nothing in the future of the American Union was regarded as settled. As late as January, 1815, division into several nationalities was still thought to be possible. Such a destiny, repeating the usual experience of history, was not necessarily more unfortunate than the career of a single nationality wholly American; for if the effects of divided nationality were certain to be unhappy, those of a single society with equal certainty defied experience or sound speculation. One uniform and harmonious system appealed to the imagination as a triumph of human progress, offering prospects of peace and ease, contentment and philanthropy, such as the world had not seen; but it invited dangers, formidable because unusual or altogether unknown. The corruption of such a system might prove to be proportionate with its dimensions, and uniformity might lead to evils as serious as were commonly ascribed to diversity.

The laws of human progress were matter not for dogmatic faith, but for study; and although society instinctively regarded small States, with their clashing interests and incessant wars, as the chief obstacle to improvement, such progress as the world knew had been coupled with those drawbacks. The few examples offered by history of great political societies, relieved from external competition or rivalry, were not commonly thought encouraging. War had been the severest test of political and social character, laying bare whatever was feeble, and calling out whatever was strong; and the effect of removing such a test was an untried problem.

In 1815 for the first time Americans ceased to doubt the path they were to follow. Not only was the unity of their nation established, but its probable divergence from older societies was also well defined. Already in 1817 the difference between Europe and America was decided. In politics the distinction was more evident than in social, religious, literary, or scientific

Vol. IX, Chap. X.

directions; and the result was singular. For a time the aggressions of England and France forced the United States into a path that seemed to lead toward European methods of government; but the popular resistance, or inertia, was so great that the most popular party leaders failed to overcome it, and no sooner did foreign dangers disappear than the system began to revert to American practices; the national government tried to lay aside its assumed powers. When Madison vetoed the bill for internal improvements he could have had no other motive than that of restoring to the government, as far as possible, its original American character.

The result was not easy to understand in theory or to make efficient in practice; but while the drift of public opinion, and still more of practical necessity, drew the government slowly toward the European standard of true political sovereignty, nothing showed that the compromise, which must probably serve the public purpose, was to be European in form or feeling. As far as politics supplied a test, the national character had already diverged from any foreign type. Opinions might differ whether the political movement was progressive or retrograde, but in any case the American, in his political character, was a new variety of man.

The social movement was also decided. The war gave a severe shock to the Anglican sympathies of society, and peace seemed to widen the breach between European and American tastes. Interest in Europe languished after Napoleon's overthrow. France ceased to affect American opinion. England became an object of less alarm. Peace produced in the United States a social and economical revolution which greatly curtailed the influence of New England, and with it the social authority of Great Britain. The invention of the steamboat counterbalanced ocean commerce. The South and West gave to society a character more aggressively American than had been known before. That Europe, within certain limits, might tend toward American ideas was possible, but that America should under any circumstances follow the experiences of European development might thenceforward be reckoned as improbable. American character was formed, if not fixed.

The scientific interest of American history centred in national character, and in the workings of a society destined to become vast, in which individuals were important chiefly as types. Although this kind of interest was different from that of European history, it was at least as important to the world. Should history ever become a true science, it must expect to establish its laws, not from the complicated story of rival European nationalities, but from the economical evolution of a great democracy. North America was the most favorable field on the globe for the spread of a society so large, uniform, and isolated as to answer the purposes of science. There a single homogeneous society could easily attain proportions of three or four hundred million persons, under conditions of undisturbed growth.

In Europe or Asia, except perhaps in China, undisturbed social evolution had been unknown. Without disturbance, evolution seemed to cease. Wherever disturbance occurred, permanence was impossible. Every people in turn adapted itself to the law of necessity. Such a system as that of the United States could hardly have existed for half a century in Europe except under the protection of another power. In the fierce struggle characteristic of European society, systems were permanent in nothing except in the general law, that, whatever other character they might possess they must always be chiefly military.

The want of permanence was not the only or the most confusing obstacle to the treatment of European history as a science. The intensity of the struggle gave prominence to the individual, until the hero seemed all, society nothing; and what was worse for science, the men were far more interesting than the societies. In the dramatic view of history, the hero deserved more to be studied than the community to which he belonged; in truth, he was the society, which existed only to produce him and to perish with him. Against such a view historians were among the last to protest, and protested but faintly when they did so at all. They felt as strongly as their audiences that the highest achievements were alone worth remembering either in history or in art, and that a reiteration of commonplaces was commonplace. With all the advantages of European movement and color, few historians succeeded in enlivening or dignifying the lack of motive, intelligence, and morality, the helplessness characteristic of many long periods in the face of crushing problems, and the futility of human efforts to escape from difficulties religious, political, and social. In a period extending over four or five thousand years, more or less capable of historical treatment, historians were content to illustrate here and there the most dramatic moments of the most striking communities. The hero was their favorite. War was the chief field of heroic action, and even the history of England was chiefly the story of war.

The history of the United States promised to be free from such disturbances. War counted for little, the hero for less; on the people alone the eye could permanently rest. The steady growth of a vast population without the social distinctions that confused other histories—without kings, nobles, or armies; without church, traditions, and prejudices—seemed a subject for the man of science rather than for dramatists or poets. To scientific treatment only one great obstacle existed. Americans, like Europeans, were not disposed to make of their history a mechanical evolution. They felt that they even more than other nations needed the heroic element, because they breathed an atmosphere of peace and industry where heroism could seldom be displayed; and in unconscious protest against their own social conditions they adorned with imaginary qualities scores of supposed leaders, whose only merit was their faculty of reflecting a popular trait. Instinctively they clung to ancient history as though conscious that of all misfortunes that could befall the national character, the greatest would be the loss of the established ideals which alone ennobled human weakness.

Without heroes, the national character of the United States had few charms of imagination even to Americans.

Historians and readers maintained Old-World standards. No historian cared to hasten the coming of an epoch when man should study his own history in the same spirit and by the same methods with which he studied the formation of a crystal. Yet history had its scientific as well as its human side, and in American history the scientific interest was greater than the human. Elsewhere the student could study under better conditions the evolution of the individual, but nowhere could he study so well the evolution of a race. The interest of such a subject exceeded that of any other branch of science, for it brought mankind within sight of its own end.

Travellers in Switzerland who stepped across the Rhine where it flowed from its glacier could follow its course among mediaeval towns and feudal ruins, until it became a highway for modern industry, and at last arrived at a permanent equilibrium in the ocean. American history followed the same course. With prehistoric glaciers and mediaeval feudalism the story had little to do; but from the moment it came within sight of the ocean it acquired interest almost painful. A child could find his way in a river-valley, and a hoy could float on the waters of Holland; but science alone could sound the depths of the ocean, measure its currents, foretell its storms, or fix its relations to the system of Nature. In a democratic ocean science could see something ultimate. Man could go no further. The atom might move, but the general equilibrium could not change.

Whether the scientific or the heroic view were taken, in either case the starting-point was the same, and the chief object of interest was to define national character. Whether the figures of history were treated as heroes or as types, they must be taken to represent the people. American types were especially worth study if they were to represent the greatest democratic evolution the world could know. Readers might judge for themselves what share the individual possessed in creating or shaping the nation; but whether it was small or great, the nation could be understood only by studying the individual. For that reason, in the story of Jefferson and Madison individuals retained their old interest as types of character, if not sources of power.

In the American character antipathy to war ranked first among political traits. The majority of Americans regarded war in a peculiar light, the consequence of comparative security. No European nation could have conducted a war, as the people of America conducted the War of 1812. The possibility of doing so without destruction explained the existence of the national trait, and assured its continuance. In politics, the divergence of America from Europe perpetuated itself in the popular instinct for peaceable methods. The Union took shape originally on the general lines that divided the civil from the military elements of the British constitution. The party of Jefferson and Gallatin was founded on dislike of every function of government necessary in a military system. Although Jefferson carried his pacific theories to an extreme, and brought about military reaction, the reactionary movement was neither universal, violent, nor lasting; and society showed no sign of changing its convictions. With greater strength the country might acquire greater familiarity with warlike methods, but in the same degree was less likely to suffer any general change of habits. Nothing but prolonged intestine contests could convert the population of an entire continent into a race of warriors.

A people whose chief trait was antipathy to war, and to any system organized with military energy, could scarcely develop great results in national administration; yet the Americans prided themselves chiefly on their political capacity. Even the war did not undeceive them, although the incapacity brought into evidence by the war was undisputed, and was most remarkable among the communities which believed themselves to be most gifted with political sagacity. Virginia and Massachusetts by turns admitted failure in dealing with issues so simple that the newest societies, like Tennessee and Ohio, understood them by instinct. That incapacity in national politics should appear as a leading trait in American character was unexpected by Americans, but might naturally result from their conditions. The better test of American character was not political but social, and was to be found not in the government but in the people.

The sixteen years of Jefferson's and Madison's rule furnished international tests of popular intelligence upon which Americans could depend. The ocean was the only open field for competition among nations. Americans enjoyed there no natural or artificial advantages over Englishmen, Frenchmen, or Spaniards; indeed, all these countries possessed navies, resources, and experience greater than were to be found in the United States. Yet the Americans developed, in the course of twenty years, a surprising degree of skill in naval affairs. The evidence of their success was to be found nowhere so complete as in the avowals of Englishmen who knew best the history of naval progress. The American invention of the fast-sailing schooner or clipper was the more remarkable because, of all American inventions, this alone sprang from direct competition with Europe. During ten centuries of struggle the nations of Europe had labored to obtain superiority over each other in ship-construction, yet Americans instantly made improvements which gave them superiority, and which Europeans were unable immediately to imitate even after seeing them. Not only were American vessels better in model, faster in sailing, easier and quicker in handling, and more economical in working than the European, but they were also better equipped. The English complained as a grievance that the Americans adopted new and unwarranted devices in naval warfare; that their vessels were heavier and better constructed, and their missiles of unusual shape and improper use. The Americans resorted to expedients that had not been tried before, and excited a mixture of irritation and respect in the English service, until Yankee smartness became a national misdemeanor.

The English admitted themselves to be slow to change their habits, but the French were both quick and scientific; yet Americans did on the ocean what the French, under stronger inducements, failed to do. The French privateer preyed upon

British commerce for twenty years without seriously injuring it; but no sooner did the American privateer sail from French ports, than the rates of insurance doubled in London, and an outcry for protection arose among English shippers which the Admiralty could not calm. The British newspapers were filled with assertions that the American cruiser was the superior of any vessel of its class, and threatened to overthrow England's supremacy on the ocean.

Another test of relative intelligence was furnished by the battles at sea. Instantly after the loss of the "Guerriere" the English discovered and complained that American gunnery was superior to their own. They explained their inferiority by the length of time that had elapsed since their navy had found on the ocean an enemy to fight. Every vestige of hostile fleets had been swept away, until, after the battle of Trafalgar, British frigates ceased practice with their guns. Doubtless the British navy had become somewhat careless in the absence of a dangerous enemy, but Englishmen were themselves aware that some other cause must have affected their losses. Nothing showed that Nelson's line-of-battle ships, frigates, or sloops were as a rule better fought than the "Macedonian" and "Java," the "Avon" and "Reindeer." Sir Howard Douglas, the chief authority on the subject, attempted in vain to explain British reverses by the deterioration of British gunnery. His analysis showed only that American gunnery was extraordinarily good. Of all vessels, the sloop-of-war—on account of its smallness, its quick motion, and its more accurate armament of thirty-two-pound carronades—offered the best test of relative gunnery, and Sir Howard Douglas in commenting upon the destruction of the "Peacock" and "Avon" could only say—

In these two actions it is clear that the fire of the British vessels was thrown too high, and that the ordnance of their opponents were expressly and carefully aimed at and took effect chiefly in the hull.

The battle of the "Hornet" and "Penguin" as well as those of the "Reindeer" and "Avon," showed that the excellence of American gunnery continued till the close of the war. Whether at point-blank range or at long-distance practice, the Americans used guns as they had never been used at sea before.

None of the reports of former British victories showed that the British fire had been more destructive at any previous time than in 1812, and no report of any commander since the British navy existed showed so much damage inflicted on an opponent in so short a time as was proved to have been inflicted on themselves by the reports of British commanders in the American war. The strongest proof of American superiority was given by the best British officers, like Broke, who strained every nerve to maintain an equality with American gunnery. So instantaneous and energetic was the effort that, according to the British historian of the war, "a British forty-six-gun frigate of 1813 was half as effective again as a British forty-six-gun frigate of 1812"; and, as he justly said, "the slaughtered crews and the shattered hulks" of the captured British ships proved that no want of their old fighting qualities accounted for their repeated and almost habitual mortifications.

Unwilling as the English were to admit the superior skill of Americans on the ocean, they did not hesitate to admit it, in certain respects, on land. The American rifle in American hands was affirmed to have no equal in the world. This admission could scarcely be withheld after the lists of killed and wounded which followed almost every battle; but the admission served to check a wider inquiry. In truth, the rifle played but a small part in the war. Winchester's men at the river Raisin may have owed their over-confidence, as the British Forty-first owed its losses, to that weapon, and at New Orleans five or six hundred of Coffee's men, who were out of range, were armed with the rifle; but the surprising losses of the British were commonly due to artillery and musketry fire. At New Orleans the artillery was chiefly engaged. The artillery battle of January 1, according to British accounts, amply proved the superiority of American gunnery on that occasion, which was probably the fairest test during the war. The battle of January 8 was also chiefly an artillery battle; the main British column never arrived within fair musket range; Pakenham was killed by a grape-shot, and the main column of his troops halted more than one hundred yards from the parapet.

The best test of British and American military qualities, both for men and weapons, was Scott's battle of Chippawa. Nothing intervened to throw a doubt over the fairness of the trial. Two parallel lines of regular soldiers, practically equal in numbers, armed with similar weapons, moved in close order toward each other, across a wide open plain, without cover or advantage of position, stopping at intervals to load and fire, until one line broke and retired. At the same time two three-gun batteries, the British being the heavier, maintained a steady fire from positions opposite each other. According to the reports, the two infantry lines in the centre never came nearer than eighty yards. Major-General Riall reported that then, owing to severe losses, his troops broke and could not be rallied. Comparison of the official reports showed that the British lost in killed and wounded four hundred and sixty-nine men; the Americans, two hundred and ninety-six. Some doubts always affect the returns of wounded, because the severity of the wound cannot be known; but dead men tell their own tale. Riall reported one hundred and forty-eight killed; Scott reported sixty-one. The severity of the losses showed that the battle was sharply contested, and proved the personal bravery of both armies. Marksmanship decided the result, and the returns proved that the American fire was superior to that of the British in the proportion of more than fifty per cent if estimated by the entire loss, and of two hundred and forty-two to one hundred if estimated by the deaths alone.

The conclusion seemed incredible, but it was supported by the results of the naval battles. The Americans showed superiority amounting in some cases to twice the efficiency of their enemies in the use of weapons. The best French critic of the naval war, Jurien de la Gravière said: "An enormous superiority in the rapidity and precision of their fire can alone explain the difference in the losses sustained by the combatants." So

far from denying this conclusion the British press constantly
alleged it, and the British officers complained of it. The discovery caused great surprise, and in both British services much
attention was at once directed to improvement in artillery and
musketry. Nothing could exceed the frankness with which Englishmen avowed their inferiority. According to Sir Francis
Head, "gunnery was in naval warfare in the extraordinary state
of ignorance we have just described, when our lean children,
the American people, taught us, rod in hand, our first lesson
in the art." The English textbook on Naval Gunnery, written
by Major-General Sir Howard Douglas immediately after the
peace, devoted more attention to the short American war than
to all the battles of Napoleon, and began by admitting that
Great Britain had "entered with too great confidence on war
with a marine much more expert than that of any of our European enemies." The admission appeared "objectionable" even
to the author; but he did not add, what was equally true, that
it applied as well to the land as to the sea service.

No one questioned the bravery of the British forces, or the
ease with which they often routed larger bodies of militia; but
the losses they inflicted were rarely as great as those they suffered. Even at Bladensburg, where they met little resistance,
their loss was several times greater than that of the Americans.
At Plattsburg, where the intelligence and quickness of Macdon-
ough and his men alone won the victory, his ships were in effect
stationary batteries, and enjoyed the same superiority in gunnery. "The 'Saratoga,'" said his official report, "had fifty-five
round-shot in her hull; the 'Confiance,' one hundred and five.
The enemy's shot passed principally just over our heads, as
there were not twenty whole hammocks in the nettings at the
close of the action."

The greater skill of the Americans was not due to special
training, for the British service was better trained in gunnery,
as in everything else, than the motley armies and fleets that
fought at New Orleans and on the Lakes. Critics constantly
said that every American had learned from his childhood the

use of the rifle; but he certainly had not learned to use cannon in shooting birds or hunting deer, and he knew less than the Englishman about the handling of artillery and muskets. As if to add unnecessary evidence, the battle of Chrystler's Farm proved only too well that this American efficiency was not confined to citizens of the United States.

Another significant result of the war was the sudden development of scientific engineering in the United States. This branch of the military service owed its efficiency and almost its existence to the military school at West Point, established in 1802. The school was at first much neglected by government. The number of graduates before the year 1812 was very small; but at the outbreak of the war the corps of engineers was already efficient. Its chief was Colonel Joseph Gardner Swift, of Massachusetts, the first graduate of the academy: Colonel Swift planned the defences of New York harbor. The lieutenant-colonel in 1812 was Walker Keith Armistead, of Virginia—the third graduate, who planned the defences of Norfolk. Major William McRee, of North Carolina, became chief engineer to General Brown, and constructed the fortifications at Fort Erie, which cost the British General Gordon Drummond the loss of half his army, besides the mortification of defeat. Captain Eleazer Derby Wood, of New York, constructed Fort Meigs, which enabled Harrison to defeat the attack of Proctor in May, 1813. Captain Joseph Gilbert Totten, of New York, was chief engineer to General Izard at Plattsburg, where he directed the fortifications that stopped the advance of Prevost's great army. None of the works constructed by a graduate of West Point was captured by the enemy; and had an engineer been employed at Washington by Armstrong and Winder, the city would have been easily saved.

Perhaps without exaggeration the West Point Academy might be said to have decided, next to the navy, the result of the war. The works at New Orleans were simple in character, and as far as they were due to engineering skill were directed by Major Latour, a Frenchman; but the war was already ended when the battle of New Orleans was fought. During the critical campaign of 1814, the West Point engineers doubled the capacity of the little American army for resistance, and introduced a new and scientific character into American life.

In the application of science the steamboat was the most striking success; but Fulton's invention, however useful, was neither the most original nor the most ingenious of American efforts, nor did it offer the best example of popular characteristics. Perhaps Fulton's torpedo and Stevens's screw-propeller showed more originality than was proved by the "Clermont." The fast-sailing schooner with its pivot-gun—an invention that grew out of the common stock of nautical intelligence—best illustrated the character of the people.

That the individual should rise to a higher order either of intelligence or morality than had existed in former ages was not to be expected, for the United States offered less field for the development of individuality than had been offered by older and smaller societies. The chief function of the American Union was to raise the average standard of popular intelligence and well-being, and at the close of the War of 1812 the superior average intelligence of Americans was so far admitted that Yankee acuteness, or smartness, became a national reproach; but much doubt remained whether the intelligence belonged to a high order, or proved a high morality. From the earliest ages, shrewdness was associated with unscrupulousness; and Americans were freely charged with wanting honesty. The charge could neither be proved nor disproved. American morality was such as suited a people so endowed, and was high when compared with the morality of many older societies; but, like American intelligence, it discouraged excess. Probably the political morality shown by the government and by public men during the first sixteen years of the century offered a fair gauge of social morality. Like the character of the popular inventions, the character of the morals corresponded to the wants of a growing democratic society; but time alone could decide whether it would result in a high or a low national ideal.

Finer analysis showed other signs of divergence from ordinary standards. If Englishmen took pride in one trait more than in another, it was in the steady uniformity of their progress. The innovating and revolutionary quality of the French mind irritated them. America showed an un-English rapidity in movement. In politics, the American people between 1787 and 1817 accepted greater changes than had been known in England since 1688. In religion, the Unitarian movement of Boston and Harvard College would never have been possible in England, where the defection of Oxford or Cambridge, and the best educated society in the United Kingdom, would have shaken Church and State to their foundations. In literature the American school was chiefly remarkable for the rapidity with which it matured. The first book of Irving was a successful burlesque of his own ancestral history; the first poem of Bryant sang of the earth only as a universal tomb; the first preaching of Channing assumed to overthrow the Trinity; and the first paintings of Allston aspired to recover the ideal perfection of Raphael and Titian. In all these directions the American mind showed tendencies that surprised Englishmen more than they struck Americans. Allston defended himself from the criticism of friends who made complaint of his return to America. He found there, as he maintained, not only a growing taste for art, but "a quicker appreciation" of artistic effort than in any European land. If the highest intelligence of American society were to move with such rapidity, the time could not be far distant when it would pass into regions which England never liked to contemplate.

Another intellectual trait, as has been already noticed, was the disposition to relax severity. Between the theology of Jonathan Edwards and that of William Ellery Channing was an enormous gap, not only in doctrines but also in methods. Whatever might be thought of the conclusions reached by Edwards and Hopkins, the force of their reasoning commanded respect. Not often had a more strenuous effort than theirs been made to ascertain God's will, and to follow it without regard to weaknesses of the flesh. The idea that the nature of God's attributes was to be preached only as subordinate to the improvement of man, agreed little with the spirit of their religion. The Unitarian and Universalist movements marked the beginning of an epoch when ethical and humanitarian ideas took the place of metaphysics, and even New England turned from contemplating the omnipotence of the Deity in order to praise the perfections of his creatures.

The spread of great popular sects like the Universalists and Campbellites, founded on assumptions such as no Orthodox theology could tolerate, showed a growing tendency to relaxation of thought in that direction. The struggle for existence was already mitigated, and the first effect of the change was seen in the increasing cheerfulness of religion. Only when men found their actual world almost a heaven, could they lose overpowering anxiety about the world to come. Life had taken a softer aspect, and as a consequence God was no longer terrible. Even the wicked became less mischievous in an atmosphere where virtue was easier than vice. Punishments seemed mild in a society where every offender could cast off his past, and create a new career. For the first time in history, great bodies of men turned away from their old religion, giving no better reason than that it required them to believe in a cruel Deity, and rejected necessary conclusions of theology because they were inconsistent with human self-esteem.

The same optimism marked the political movement. Society was weary of strife, and settled gladly into a political system which left every disputed point undetermined. The public seemed obstinate only in believing that all was for the best, as far as the United States were concerned, in the affairs of mankind. The contrast was great between this temper of mind and that in which the Constitution had been framed; but it was no greater than the contrast in the religious opinions of the two periods, while the same reaction against severity marked the new literature. The rapid accumulation of wealth and increase in physical comfort told the same story from the standpoint of economy. On every side society showed that ease was for a time to take the place of severity, and enjoyment was to have its full share in the future national existence.

The traits of intelligence, rapidity, and mildness seemed fixed in the national character as early as 1817, and were likely to become more marked as time should pass. A vast amount of conservatism still lingered among the people; but the future spirit of society could hardly fail to be intelligent, rapid in movement, and mild in method. Only in the distant future could serious change occur, and even then no return to European characteristics seemed likely. The American continent was happier in its conditions and easier in its resources than the regions of Europe and Asia, where Nature revelled in diversity and conflict. If at any time American character should change, it might as probably become sluggish as revert to the violence and extravagances of Old-World development. The inertia of several hundred million people, all formed in a similar social mould, was as likely to stifle energy as to stimulate evolution.

With the establishment of these conclusions, a new episode in American history began in 1815. New subjects demanded new treatment, no longer dramatic but steadily tending to become scientific. The traits of American character were fixed; the rate of physical and economical growth was established; and history, certain that at a given distance of time the Union would contain so many millions of people, with wealth valued at so many millions of dollars, became thenceforward chiefly concerned to know what kind of people these millions were to be. They were intelligent, but what paths would their intelligence select? They were quick, but what solution of insoluble problems would quickness hurry? They were scientific, and what control would their science exercise over their destiny? They were mild, but what corruptions would their relaxations bring? They were peaceful, but by what machinery were their corruptions to be purged? What interests were to vivify a society so vast and uniform? What ideals were to ennoble it? What object, besides physical content, must a democratic continent aspire to attain? For the treatment of such questions, history required another century of experience.

Bibliographical Note

History of the United States of America during the First Administration of Thomas Jefferson, 1801–1805. Cambridge, Mass.: John Wilson & Son, 1884. Six copies were privately printed. No copies have ever been located.

History of the United States of America during the Second Administration of Thomas Jefferson, 1805–1809. Cambridge, Mass.: John Wilson & Son, 1885. Six copies were privately printed. The Massachusetts Historical Society has one.

History of the United States of America during the First Administration of James Madison, 1809–1813. Cambridge, Mass.: John Wilson & Son, 1888. Six copies were privately printed. The Massachusetts Historical Society has one.

History of the United States of America during the First Administration of Thomas Jefferson. 2 vols. New York: Charles Scribner's Sons, 1889. Corrected and revised from the private printing.

History of the United States of America during the Second Administration of Thomas Jefferson. 2 vols. New York: Charles Scribner's Sons, 1890. Corrected and revised from the private printing.

History of the United States of America during the First Administration of James Madison. 2 vols. New York: Charles Scribner's Sons, 1890. Corrected and revised from the private printing.

History of the United States of America during the Second Administration of James Madison. 3 vols. New York: Charles Scribner's Sons, 1891. Set from the manuscript.

History of the United States of America during the Administrations of Jefferson and Madison. 9 vols. New York: Charles Scribner's Sons, 1921. New edition with an introduction by Henry Cabot Lodge. This work incorporates the corrections and additions made by Henry Adams.

History of the United States of America during the Administrations of Thomas Jefferson and James Madison. 4 vols. New York: Boni, 1930. Introduction by Henry S. Commager.

Index